English Electric Canberra
and Martin B-57

English Electric
CANBERRA
AND MARTIN B-57

Barry Jones

The Crowood Press

First published in 1999 by
The Crowood Press Ltd
Ramsbury, Marlborough
Wiltshire SN8 2HR

British Library Cataloguing-in-Publication Data
A catalogue record for this book is available from
the British Library.

ISBN 1 86126 255 8

Photograph previous page: No.231 Operational
Conversion Unit's display team of T.4s, led by
Sqn Ldr F.P. Walker, AFC, rehearsing for its
demonstration at the Coventry Air Pageant
on 21 July 1956. Author's collection.

Typefaces used: Goudy (*text*),
Cheltenham (*headings*).

Typeset and designed by
D & N Publishing
Membury Business Park, Lambourn Woodlands
Hungerford, Berkshire.

Printed and bound by Bookcraft, Bath.

Dedication

To Ian Mactaggert, remembering many pleasant years of aeronautical friendship shared with focal-plane shutters.

Acknowledgements

During the writing of this book, the great affection engendered by the Canberra has become very apparent. I have been most fortunate in receiving information, as well as photographs, generously supplied by many individuals and companies. I would like to state my appreciation to Gordon G. Bartley of BAe; R.P. Beamont CBE, DSO*, DFC*, DL, FRAeS; Brenzett Aeronautical Museum Trust; Bob Bolton of BAe; Winston Brent; Dennis Brown; Phil Cripps of DERA, Boscombe Down; Ray Deacon; Bill Gunston; Del Holyland of Martin-Baker Aircraft; Philip Jarrett; Alec McRitchie of Short Bros; Ian Mactaggart; Newark Air Museum; Michael Oakey of *Aeroplane*; George Pennick; Steve Pickup; William S. Sleigh; Sue and Richard Ward; R.A. Walker; Brandon J. White; Yorkshire Air Museum; and to my family, who have no aeronautical leanings whatsoever, but have come to appreciate that the Canberra was something special.

Contents

Introduction   6

1 FOUNDATIONS OF AN AIRCRAFT COMPANY   7

2 ANTIPODEAN DAWN   13

3 THE PROTOTYPE QUARTET   21

4 BOMBER COMMAND GOES PROPLESS   29

5 A MATTER OF RECORD   41

6 MORE SQUADRONS AND MORE VARIANTS   51

7 CANBERRA GETS THE LOW-DOWN   58

8 CANBERRA 'GETS ITS KNEES BROWN'   63

9 ALTITUDE AND LONGEVITY   73

10 CANBERRA GOES ORIENTAL   79

11 TARGETS, DRONES AND NOSE JOBS   88

12 UNCLE SAM'S CANBERRAS   99

13 A NICE LITTLE EARNER   119

14 SPECIALIZED CANBERRAS   147

15 CANBERRA CONCLUSIONS   181

Appendix   I   Canberra Production and Serial Blocks   183
Appendix II   Canberra Squadrons   185
Appendix III   Canberra Conservation   187
Index   190

Introduction

We sat on rickety, wooden-slatted seats, which teetered on the uneven grass in front of Farnborough's flight sheds. It was Monday 6 September 1949 and Bill Pegg had brought acres of well-intentioned but underpowered aluminium lumbering up from Filton. The prototype of the world's first production pure-jet airliner was displayed by John Cunningham, and 'Mutt' Summers showed off the first four-propjet commercial aircraft that would go into service. A plethora of fighters, with single engines, twin engines, swept wings and twin tailbooms, together with engine flying test beds, all demonstrated that Britain's status in turbojet technology was looking very healthy.

The final item on the programme, held over from its earlier scheduled slot, was a bomber making its debut under the rather uninspiring company appellation of A.1, although the suggested name Canberra was firm enough for it to be painted in script on the nose. Furthermore, this aircraft was not produced by one of the established aircraft manufacturers, but came from a firm born of an amalgamation of various electrical and mechanical engineering companies. Avro, de Havilland, Handley Page, Hawker and Short were family names that we had lived with for decades. But English Electric? Had they not just churned out masses of Hampdens and Halifaxes under licence during the recent world conflict and, in fact, were they not still similarly engaged, producing

Vampires for de Havilland? Furthermore, although the pilot, Wg Cdr Roland Beamont, was known to have had a distinguished war record and to have undertaken extensive test flying for Hawkers, he was not exactly well known as a display pilot.

The aircraft certainly looked good as it taxied on to operational runway 25, glistening in an overall coat of Cerulean Blue. The two Rolls-Royce AJ.65s were opened up and the next ten minutes gave us the introduction to a combination of new aeroplane and demonstration test pilot, which possibly has never been equalled. A steep climb from lift-off; a 500mph (800km/h) ultra low-level pass; an under-100mph (160km/h) return with full flaps, bomb-bay doors open and undercarriage down with the pilot making fierce rocking manoeuvres; high-G turns; slow rolls; rolls off the top of loops; all were executed with the agility of the preceding fighters, within the tight confines of the RAE's airfield, so that not a single moment was wasted or lost. Could it be true that this was a bomber designed to carry a 10,000lb (4,550kg) bomb load at high altitude? We certainly had seen nothing like it before and the aeronautical press from around the world, putting down their gin and tonics, eulogized in an abundance of column inches about the demonstration. The precarious seating was forgotten. The title A.1 was certainly applicable – to the aircraft, to the pilot and to the display.

In the fifty years since that demonstration, the Canberra, the English Electric Aircraft Company and 'Bee' Beamont have all etched themselves into the record books, as well as aviation history, in equal proportions. After the Canberra, the company designed, and Beamont evaluated, the RAF's first operational supersonic fighter, the Lightning, and both, in association with Vickers Armstrong, were responsible for producing and testing that technically superb, but short-lived, political football, the TSR.2.

Sixty-five Royal Air Force squadrons, the air forces of sixteen overseas countries, just about every British research establishment and nearly the whole aircraft engine industry have all operated the Canberra over the years. Furthermore, a few flying examples of the beautiful aircraft are still with us – No.39 Squadron, the RAF's photographic survey unit, is scheduled to keep its PR.9s until around 2005.

The following chapters are an attempt to qualify, in words and pictures, the achievements of the Canberra and the great ubiquity of William Edward Willoughby Petter's durable design.

Barry Jones
Hatton Green
Warwickshire
April 1999

CHAPTER ONE

Foundations of an Aircraft Company

The genealogy of the English Electric Company Limited, as such, commences on 14 December 1918, when it was registered as a private company at 3 Abchurch Yard, London EC, with a working capital of £5 million. Over the years, it grew with the absorption of the Phoenix Dynamo Manufacturing Company, the Coventry Ordnance Works, Dick, Kerr and Co. Ltd, the United Electric Car Company, and Willans and Robinson.

Phoenix Dynamo Co.

Between them, the individual firms had deviated from their established manufacturing into aviation, in various forms and at various times. At the Phoenix Dynamo Co.'s works at Bradford in Yorkshire, low-power, rotating electrical machinery was produced for the coal and textile industries. During the First World War, orders received to manufacture shells for the Army and Navy were followed by a request to prepare for large-scale aircraft production. Short Type 184 patrol seaplanes were succeeded by the Short Bomber; Maurice Farman Longhorn training biplanes were also produced, as were over one hundred Felixstowe F.3 and F.5 flying boats. The arrival of Lt W.O. Manning in the company became the catalyst for the setting up of a design team; the Phoenix Type No.1 helicopter observation platform was its first project, although it did not progress beyond the design stage. After the end of hostilities, in 1919, the licensed manufacture of aircraft ended. Manning continued drawing up designs, including a flying boat with an all-up weight of 100,000lb (45,350kg), but they remained on the drawing board.

Coventry Ordnance Works Ltd

Coventry Ordnance originated in Birmingham during 1866 as a coach manufacturer. Expansion, via the acquisition of a tract of Warwickshire at Coventry, led to the formation of the Coventry Ordnance Works Ltd, on 2 June 1905. The main shareholders in the £1 million capital were the steel manufacturers John Brown & Co. Ltd and Cammell, Laird & Co. Ltd. In July 1909, Rear-Admiral Reginald Bacon joined the board, becoming Managing Director shortly afterwards. His interest in aviation, in respect of its use in military operations, led to COW taking over the business of Howard Wright, who had constructed aeroplanes in association with W.O. Manning and T.O.M. Sopwith. 1915 saw the enlargement of COW's aviation department and over the next three years it handled the building of R.E.7s, as well as R.E.8s, in large numbers. One hundred and fifty Sopwith Snipes were built in 1918, but a follow-up order for a similar number was cancelled when the war ended and, like Phoenix Dynamo, COW's aircraft division closed in 1919.

However, Coventry Ordnance Works' core business of ordnance continued in aviation with the design of a 37mm, 1.5-pounder cannon for aircraft armament. Known by its natural acronym, the 'COW gun' was first flown in an F.E.3, and a D.H.4 gave the gun its first live operation. Both Westland and Vickers Armstrong designed an aircraft around the cannon to Specification F.29/27, each company producing a prototype with the 'COW gun' inclined upwards at an angle of 55 degrees. The Westland was first flown in December 1930 with the serial J9565, while the Vickers aircraft, numbered J9566, followed on 21 January 1931. The RAF expressed no interest in either aircraft, nor in the idea of upwards-firing guns, and no production order was sanctioned. During the Second World War, the *Luftwaffe* resurrected the principle, fitting two fixed 20mm cannons firing obliquely upwards on some Messerschmitt Me110G and Junkers Ju88C/ Ju88G nightfighters. Known as *Schräge Musik* ('Jazz Music'), the installation achieved considerable success against the RAF night-bomber offensive in 1943/44.

English Electric

Dick, Kerr & Co. Ltd

With a prime business of manufacturing electrical equipment for railway companies and tramcars, Dick, Kerr & Co. Ltd was formed in 1875. Fifteen years later, on 31 May 1890, it was re-formed as a public company with a capital of £160,000. Within seven years, the company had taken over factory premises owned by the English Electric Manufacturing Co. Ltd at Preston in Lancashire. The supplying of complete tramway systems brought about by this expansion led to Dick, Kerr joining forces with English Electric. In June 1905, this amalgamation produced a splitting of the Dick, Kerr manufacturing divisions, with mechanical engineering being centred in Scotland and all electrical work being handled by the newly named United Electric Car Co. Ltd.

Further diversification on the part of Dick, Kerr was a liaison, again involving Warwickshire, with the Rugby-based electrical engineering company of Willans & Robinson Ltd, which had been founded as a registered company in March 1894 at Kingston-upon-Thames in Surrey. With the declaration of war in 1914, both companies became involved in armaments, Willans & Robinson taking on Salmson aircraft engine work, while Dick, Kerr undertook heavy gun production. The United Electric Car Co. started the assembly of Felixstowe F.3 flying boats in 1917 and continued the operation until the armistice.

Flying Boats

During the early 1920s, the interests of English Electric gravitated towards things aeronautical and a small design team was set up, under William Oke Manning, who had worked for Phoenix Dynamo during the First World War. A series of designs for single-engined flying boats, with the lower wing set at a high dihedral angle to form a lateral extension of the hull's forward

The S.1 Wren at the Light Aircraft Competition in 1923, with Flt Lt Walter Loughton in the cockpit and the required can of petrol featuring in both photographs. Author's collection

planing surface, culminated in the M.3 Ayr. One of these was completed in February 1925, with the serial N148. Despite various refinements and modifications, the aircraft refused to get airborne and the project was cancelled, with a second prototype being halted early in its construction.

Better results were attained with the twin-engined Kingston range of flying boats designed to Specification 23/23, for a coastal patrol and anti-submarine aircraft, which employed a more conventional hull. The first prototype, N168, was damaged when striking Lytham St Annes pier on the Lancashire coast. However, production was put in hand and three examples, with serials N9709, N9712 and N9713, flew before the aviation side of English Electric was closed, in April 1926.

The Wren

Before the closure of English Electric, W.O. Manning started designing, in 1922, the only indigenous landplane to be built prior to the Canberra. The S.1 Wren was

a result of his belief that a cantilever-winged, small-engined aircraft would provide economical flying.

In essence, the Wren was a powered glider, with a 37ft (11.25m) wingspan, powered by a 398cc ABC flat-twin motorcycle engine, which developed 3h.p. The Air Ministry saw merit in the idea as a training aircraft for the RAF, and £600 was allocated for English Electric to build a prototype at Preston the following year. Given the service serial J6973, the Wren had its maiden flight on 8 April 1923, taking off from Lytham Sands with Air Ministry pilot Sqn Ldr Maurice Wright at the controls. Subsequent flight testing was sufficiently successful for a decision to be made to put the aircraft into production, at a unit cost of £350. Two aircraft, with

British Empire Exhibition at Wembley, before going to the Science Museum at South Kensington in London. The Lytham-stored Wren was privately purchased in 1926, when English Electric closed its Aircraft Department, and placed on the civil register as G-EBNV. Three years later it was back in store, this time in Scotland.

In 1954, Mr R.H. Grant, who had held the aircraft in his Dumfries storage, offered the aircraft to the Shuttleworth Trust, but it was too deteriorated for a 'flying condition' restoration to be possible. However, the Science Museum had, for several years, considered rejuvenating its Wren and the aircraft was sent to Preston on 4 February 1946. On completion, this fourth Wren was stored until Shuttleworth's offer to completely rebuild the aircraft to flying

and an overhaul was made during the winter of 1980/81. Although it does make the odd venture out at Shuttleworth Trust Open Days, the Wren's average flying time per year is about seventeen minutes and it is believed that the airframe has amassed less than ten hours in the air since 1956, when records began.

Schemes F *and* L

When the aviation side of English Electric closed during the first half of April 1926, the small design team was split up. W.O. Manning continued to be involved in various design projects, as well as supplying copy for the aeronautical literature. In the early 1930s, the gradual expansion in the manufacturing of military equipment insti-

Still going strong. The Wren had an outing at the Shuttleworth Trust's Old Warden airfield on 30 September 1979. Philip Jarrett

the wing dihedral reduced from the original four degrees to two degrees, were entered for the *Daily Mail* Light Aircraft Competition of 1923, held at Lympne airfield in Kent. Flown by Flt Lt Walter Loughton, the third aircraft to be built tied for first place in the fuel-consumption trials with an ANEC 1, both aircraft recording exactly 87½ miles (140.81km) on 1 gallon (4.5 litres) of petrol.

No more Wrens were produced and further flying was on a limited scale, before the third aircraft was stored, suspended from the roof of a Lytham flight shed. The fourth aircraft was put on display as the centrepiece to English Electric's stand at the 1924

condition was taken up. Following unsuccessful flight attempts in 1955, improvements to the engine eventually provided enough power for a post-war maiden flight to be made by Peter Hillwood, on 25 September 1956. The next year, on 15 September 1957, the aircraft was officially handed over to the Shuttleworth Trust, at the Royal Aeronautical Society's Garden Party at Wisley in Surrey. The ceremony was made all the more poignant by the presence of the Wren's designer W.O. Manning, just six months before he died.

Not too many flying hours have been logged over the years. 'Bee' Beamont had a ten-minute flight on 10 September 1968

gated the enlargement of the Royal Air Force and, in February 1936, *Scheme F* was announced. This required the building of 8,000 modern aircraft, to be introduced into RAF service within three years. However, events on the mainland of Europe brought about a major revision of official thought and *Scheme L* was introduced in April 1938. The RAF's aircraft requirements were increased to 12,000, and the time-scale was reduced to two years. It was recognized that the industry's existing capacity could not cope with production of this magnitude and, as had been the case during the 1914–18 war, sub-contracting was introduced. A series of 'shadow' aircraft

Don Crowe, who went to English Electric as Handley Page's representative and finished as Chief Engineer on the Canberra design team after the departure of W.E.W. Petter. Via R.P. Beamont

factories were established solely to produce aircraft, without any design input. With its existing Preston factory in Strand Road, which had good potential for extension, English Electric was back into aviation.

In June 1938, the Air Ministry selected the company for Hampden production and in July, George (later Sir George) Nelson, the English Electric chairman, led a team to Handley Page's factories in the north London suburb of Cricklewood to see the bombers being built. A good relationship was established with the parent company and a small team of Handley Page specialists was transferred to Preston, with F.D. Crowe being appointed as the company's representative. (This assignment was to lead to Crowe joining the post-war English Electric design team and becoming chief draughtsman responsible for the Canberra's structural design.) The first contract, for seventy-five Hampdens, received on 3 August 1938, was the foundation upon which the enormous output of aircraft from this part of Lancashire over the years was built.

A New Aerodrome

Due to English Electric's expressed desire to be responsible for complete assembly and flight testing, the company urgently required one particular asset that it did not possess in 1938 – an aerodrome. As final assembly would be undertaken there, it had to be close to the Preston works, so that the large Hampden airframe sections did not have to be transported too far by road. A satisfactory site was found in open country near the village of Samlesbury, 3 miles east of Preston, on the Blackburn road. As it was roughly equidistant between the two towns, plans had been drawn up before the war for the site to be developed as a jointly operated municipal airport. However, English Electric's requirements were far more pressing and the government made arrangements for the site's acquisition, which was completed in time for the construction of hangars to commence on 10 April 1939. By October the first hangar was ready and the laying of two tarmac runways was well in hand.

At the same time, at Preston, further large-scale extensions of the factory were stimulated by Air Ministry instructions received in February, to prepare for production of Handley Page's successor to the Hampden, the four-engined Halifax. Although the prototype's maiden flight on 25 October at Bicester in Oxfordshire was eight months away, Preston was notified that the first contract would involve one hundred aircraft. When the contract arrived in April 1940, the number had increased to 200.

Final assembly of the Hampden was scheduled to be made in the first completed hangar at Samlesbury and, on 22 February 1940, the first sub-contracted aircraft, P2026, made its maiden flight, just fourteen months from receipt of contract. Delivery of the aircraft to RAF squadron service was made a month later, on 30 March. In July 1940, a further expansion of business for the company came with the contractual agreement that Hampden salvage and repair would be handled. One month later, approval was given for the erection of two further hangars at Samlesbury to allow for this additional work and RAF presence increased as the airfield became a base for No.9 Group's Communications Flight, which occupied a small area away from the main buildings.

An English Electric-built Handley Page HP.52 Hampden Mk.1 starts tucking its undercarriage up after taking off from Samlesbury, circa 1940. The windsock alongside the fence and the direction of the smoke indicate a fairly calm day.
Philip Jarrett

Brand-new Handley Page HP.61 Halifax Mk.III on the tarmac at Samlesbury. The Halifax in the background shows signs of having been given squadron code letters and is possibly in for modification. Philip Jarrett

Production

By April 1941, Hampden production had reached fifty aircraft a month and Halifax sub-assemblies were starting to take shape. A necessary runway extension was completed as elements of the first of the four-engined bombers went to Samlesbury early in June. Two months later, on 15 August 1941, English Electric's first production Halifax, V9976, made its maiden flight. Early in 1942, by which time 1,520 aircraft were on the order books, Halifax production was already averaging one aircraft per day and March saw the last Hampden fly out from Samlesbury. The production rate rose during 1943 to sixty aircraft per month, with the eighty Halifaxes produced in February 1944 being the peak of output.

Total wartime bomber production amounted to 2,903 aircraft, 770 being Hampdens and Halifax assembly totalling 2,133, which was 571 more than Handley Page themselves produced.

The Sabre

Two days before Christmas 1942, English Electric secured all the ordinary shares of the aero-engineering company D. Napier & Son Ltd, whose roots went back to 1808. By 1939, they were starting production of the most powerful piston engine to enter RAF service, the Sabre. This was a 24-cylinder 'H'-section engine, which was to have more than its fair share of problems

during production and even more once it was in service with the Hawker Typhoon. The engine company was really in over its head in building such an advanced engine and English Electric's Chairman and Managing Director, George Nelson, was requested by Ministry of Aircraft Production (MAP) to oversee a complete re-organization of Sabre production. This involvement with the Sabre led to the initial contact between English Electric and the Hawker Aircraft test pilot on secondment from RAF service, Roland Beamont. Beamont was closely involved in Sabre-engined aircraft development before returning to RAF operations as Wing Leader of No.150 Wing, flying the Tempest Mk.V.

Enlarging the Design Department

A small design department had been set up in 1944 by English Electric to handle Halifax modifications. Bearing this in mind, MAP began discussions with the company with a view to their producing the Folland Fo.117A, a Bristol Centaurus-powered, single-seat, cannon-armed fighter proposed to Specification F.19/43. However, the advent of turbojet-powered aircraft led to the Folland fighter being abandoned and, in the same year, it was decided that sub-contracted production of de Havilland's first jet fighter designed to Specification E.6/41, the Vampire, would be placed with English Electric. A contract

for 120 Mk.I variants, placed on 13 May 1944, was later increased to 300. TG274 (originally serialled TG274/G), the first production aircraft, made its maiden flight from Samlesbury on 20 April 1945.

With experience in Hampden and Halifax production firmly rooted in the company, coupled with the founding of a design department, English Electric now 'had a taste' for aeroplanes. It was resolved in the spring of 1944 that the company would continue in aviation after the end of the current conflict and, as large-scale sub-contract work was bound to dry up then, it was recognized that the design department would become a major factor. The company sought premises suitable for an enlarged design department, with on-site capacity for mock-up and prototype construction. Corporation Street, in the heart of Preston, provided the answer. In April 1944, English Electric took over the former home of Barton Motors, a building that had been requisitioned during the early days of the Second World War for the setting-up of a tradesman's training centre. Its use during the war gained it the nickname 'TC' within the company. A month later, on 24 May, TC was sufficiently staffed for work on Vampire production planning to commence, without impeding the Halifax programme.

Possibly one of the most important months in the history of the English Electric Aircraft Division was July 1944, when George Nelson invited W.E.W. Petter to join the company and take the post of Chief

The Canberra's birthplace. The premises of the former Barton Motors in Corporation Street, Preston, into which the embryonic design team moved in April 1944. Via R.P. Beamont

Engineer. His prime responsibilities were to initiate future aircraft designs and establish a design office that could convert them into viable production drawings. 'Teddy' Petter came to Preston from Westland Aircraft at Yeovil in Somerset, where within six years he had become the company's Technical Director. The Welkin high-altitude interceptor had been his last design to fly.

A High-Altitude Fighter-Bomber

The potential of the turbojet engine in respect of nearly all future operational aircraft was at last being recognized by the Air Staff and, in 1943, conferences were held with the MAP on the practicalities of producing a jet-propelled 'Mosquito-type' fighter-bomber. Such a concept greatly interested Petter, who, at only 35 years of age, was not constrained by the conventional approach prevalent in some parts of

Britain's aircraft industry. His ideas moved with him from Somerset to Lancashire, but they had to be put on hold when he arrived at TC and found out how much work he needed to do if he were to get an embryonic design team organized. Young specialists in all aspects of high-performance aerodynamics were sought and, within nine months, Petter had a team that he knew he could trust to meet the high demands that would be made.

Once the design team was settled to Petter's liking, the turbojet fighter-bomber concept was back on the agenda – just in time to coincide with the Air Staff's change of direction. The revised requirement was for a high-altitude, turbojet-powered bomber. Petter and his new team turned their attention to this, fully aware that they would be breaking new ground in nearly all spheres, and that there was very little in the way of research support in Britain at that time.

The end of the Second World War in 1945 brought about inevitable cutbacks in military equipment of every category, and four-engined bombers featured high on the list of cancellations. English Electric was fortunate in having the Vampire assembly contract, as well as contracts received in

January 1946 to undertake the complete modification of existing Avro Lincoln electronics. This involved the installation of Gee, Loran and Rebecca navigation systems, together with an updated H_2S radar. Existing rear gun-turret modifications were also introduced, with the installation of an automatic gun-laying system, incorporating a rearward-looking scanner codenamed *Boozer*.

The three years occupied by the Lincoln programmes – the last of over 200 aircraft departed from Samlesbury just before Christmas 1948 – enabled a continuity of aircraft production experience to be maintained on the shop floor and gave the design team the necessary breathing space to formulate the high-altitude bomber concept. The result would prove to have a longevity and adaptability far greater than the team could ever have envisaged as the 1945 diaries were being started. Furthermore, it would give sub-contract employment to three other aircraft companies. Ironically, one of these would be Handley Page, for whom Hampden and Halifax sub-contracting by English Electric had provided the very bedrock upon which the Preston company now stood.

CHAPTER TWO

Antipodean Dawn

A High-Altitude Bomber

From the beginning of 1946, when all Vampire work from airframe number fifty-one was centred at the Strand Road works, plans for a high-altitude bomber fully occupied everyone at English Electric's TC premises. The company title A.1 was to be applied to the design. The main elements were sufficiently confirmed for a brochure to be tendered in September 1945 to the Ministry of Supply (MoS, which had replaced the wartime MAP), in response to the Specification B.3/45 (originally drawn up as E.3/45) that had been issued a few months earlier.

Many variations on the theme of a Mosquito-type, jet-propelled fighter-bomber passed through Chief Engineer Teddy Petter's fertile mind. While he was still in the depths of Somerset, in March 1944, plans for a twin-engined aircraft featuring a large bifurcated intake in the nose, with a four-cannon armament sited underneath and large blown canopy above, was drawn up in Westland's project office. Power was to be supplied by a pair of Metropolitan-Vickers engines, developed from their axial-flow range, which had culminated in production form as the F.2/4 Beryl M.V.B.1. A pair of these was fitted in each of the three Saunders Roe SR.A/1 prototype flying-boat fighters, although the engine was progressing further into the F.9 design. When Metrovick evacuated the world of turbojet aircraft engines, the F.9 was passed over to Armstrong Siddeley Engines at Coventry, which developed and produced it as the Sapphire.

Engines

When the Air Ministry modified its thinking into a high-speed, high-altitude bomber, Petter considered that the existing range of engines would not meet the operational requirements. Consideration was given to Rolls-Royce designing a large 12,000lb- (5,440kg) thrust centrifugal-flow engine specifically for the

bomber. In the variant that was hardened in May 1945, narrow slit-type intakes were positioned in the wing-root leading edge, on either side of a circular-sectioned fuselage. Certain aspects of this design, such as the fin/rudder shape and dihedral tailplane, were carried over to the eventual A.1. The project with the large single engine only lasted about three months, as Rolls-Royce's AJ.65 axial-flow turbojet was progressing well, with thrusts of over 6,000lb (2,725kg) being predicted. Furthermore, with an overall diameter of 42.4in (106cm), there was every prospect of being able to bury the engines in the wing roots, without paying the penalty of greatly increasing the thickness/chord ratio of the wing-root section. (Burying turbojet engines in the wings was something of an obsession within the British aircraft industry during the late 1940s and 1950s.)

Swept or Straight Wings?

In July 1945, a 30-degree swept-wing design was drawn up, with a pair of AJ.65s buried in the wing roots. This provided increased space within the fuselage, allowing a much larger bomb-bay and further fuel tanks to be incorporated. When the AJ.65's specific fuel-consumption figures were examined, a 10 per cent improvement was found, compared with the figures relating to the centrifugal-flow engine that had previously been proposed. As a result, fuselage tankage could be slightly reduced, so that the bomb-bay could be even further enlarged. The original proposal had been for an internal load of six 1,000lb (455kg) bombs. Now, a single 8,000lb (3,628kg) bomb could be carried with the aircraft operating at a service ceiling above 50,000ft (15,200m) and a cruising speed of nearly 550mph (885km/h).

Although swept wings would permit the speed to be increased to around 585mph (940km/h), the fact that swept-wing development for an aircraft of this size would impose an unacceptable timescale, coupled

with the increase in structural weight, quickly convinced Petter and his team that such a configuration should be discarded. The die was cast. The high-altitude bomber would be straight-winged, with the engines repositioned outboard, in slim, circular-sectioned nacelles. With a diameter of 42.4in (106cm) and a length of 119in (300cm), the AJ.65's dimensions meant that the engines could be mounted forward of the wing main spar, which in turn enabled a more conventional wing structure to be employed, the jet-pipe diameter dictating the size of cutout in the spar. The repositioned engines gave the undercarriage main wheels a good wide track and an inward-retracting action made good use of the deepest section of the wing at its roots. This layout was proposed by Petter's right-hand man, F.W. 'Freddy' Page, who had been recruited from Hawker Aircraft at Kingston, in March 1945. He, together with Harry Harrison and Don Crowe from the Halifax production programme, formed the leadership of the TC-based design team.

B.3/45 and E.A1

Requirements

Specification B.3/45 was raised by the Ministry of Supply (MoS) to meet an Air Ministry Staff requirement for a high-speed, high-altitude, unarmed bomber. Minimal operational requirements were to be a cruising speed of 518mph (830km/h) at 40,000ft (12,200m), and a service ceiling of 50,000ft (15,200m). A crew of two was required – one pilot and one navigator/radar operator – and the bomb-aiming system to be non-visual. In September 1945, Petter submitted a brochure for an English Electric project to meet B.3/45, and a front-fuselage mock-up was constructed at TC, to show the proposed seating for the crew, together with a layout for the bomb-aiming system, scanner and instrumentation.

In 1945, the Society of British Aircraft Constructors (SBAC) instigated a new

W.E.W. Petter CBE, BA, FRAeS – The Innovative Aircraft Designer

On 8 August 1908, William Edward Willoughby Petter's arrival was welcomed by his parents, but they could not have known that they would present the British aircraft industry with an engineer whose designs would testify to his aeronautical abilities for well over sixty years.

Educated at Marlborough School and Caius College, Cambridge, Petter joined the Yeovil-based Westland Aircraft Works as an engineering apprentice in 1929 at the age of 21. In 1931, he became a member of the design office, where elements of the Wessex, the P.V.6 and one-off Goshawk-engined F.7/30 were on the drawing boards.

'Teddy' Petter became Westland's Technical Director in July 1935, when the Westland Aircraft Works became Westland Aircraft Limited. The first aircraft for which he was wholly responsible was a high-wing monoplane designed to the army-cooperation specification A.39/34 – the Lysander. Construction was completed in time for the prototype, K6127, to be exhibited at the 1936 Society of British Aircraft Constructors (SBAC) display at Hatfield in Hertfordshire, where it was flown by Westland's Chief Test Pilot, Harald Penrose. The 'aircraft-spotter's dream',

the Lysander went into RAF service in 1938 and production totalled 1,425, with a further 325 being built in Canada.

Specification F.37/35, for a single-seat, twin-engined, high-performance, long-range fighter, was met by Petter with the aerodynamically smooth P.9 Whirlwind, which packed the unprecedented (for its day) punch of four 20mm Hispano cannon in the nose. (Interestingly, the Whirlwind featured in German aircraft recognition manuals early in the Second World War, complete with a three-view silhouette and all technical data, at least a year before its existence was even admitted in Britain!)

Unfortunately for Petter and Westland, proper development of the chosen Rolls-Royce Peregrine engines was delayed by the need for uninterrupted Merlin production, so it earned a reputation for unreliability. Engine delays caused the aircraft's originally specified fighter requirements to be amended and, with an underwing armament of two 500lb (225kg) bombs, the Whirlwind was confined to RAF service only with Nos.137 and 263 Squadrons as a fighter-bomber. Production ended at Yeovil after 112 aircraft had been completed.

During the three years that it served with No.263 Squadron, the Whirlwind earned a reputation with them for being a good ground-attack aircraft. Three Messerschmitt Bf109s had been destroyed in combat, two being shot down in a single engagement between four Whirlwinds and twenty Bf109s. No.137 Squadron operated the Whirlwind for over two years. With its clean aerodynamics and four-cannon armament, it might well have seen a much more successful operational service had it had a pair of Merlins driving it.

Petter followed the Whirlwind with the P.14 Welkin, a single-seat, twin-engined interceptor. Designed to Specification F.4/40, it was required to have a six-cannon armament, radar and the capability of operating up to 45,000ft (13,700m). The first prototype, DG558/G, had its maiden flight on 1 November 1942, but a number of accidents involving engine fires delayed prototype development and fewer than one hundred Welkin Mk.Is were built, with none being issued for service. A Mk.II night-fighter variant was developed to meet Specification F.9/43. Its prototype, PF370, was constructed by the conversion of a production Mk.I airframe, and it was first flown on 23 October 1944, with Harald Penrose at the controls. However, the aircraft was not well received either by the A&AEE or RAF trials units and PF370 was destined to remain the only Welkin Mk.II.

In July 1944, before the Welkin Mk.II's first flight, Teddy Petter left Westland to join English Electric's Aviation Division as Chief Engineer. His Assistant Designer at Yeovil, Dennis Edkins, took over the company's W.34 submission to Specification N.11/44, which, via three different engines, eventually went into Fleet Air Arm service as the Wyvern.

At Preston, after his original high-altitude, jet-powered bomber concept was converted into the A.1 Canberra, Petter became involved in two experimental research specifications with the RAE to investigate the aerodynamic properties of highly swept wings. The first, ER.100, went to Short Brothers and Harland, which built the S.B.5 to examine the handling properties at low speeds. Specification ER.103 was written around Petter's high-speed proposals and, in May 1947, English Electric began to investigate the shape for a supersonic research aircraft, capable of speeds up to Mach 1.5 at 36,000ft (11,000m), with all the tests involving wind-tunnel models. The RAE disagreed with Petter in considering that the all-moving tailplane should be set on top of the fin/rudder in a 'T-tail' configuration, while English Electric's Chief Engineer was adamant that a location at the base of the rear fuselage was far superior.

Petter maintained courage in his convictions and continued on a design which, on 3 August 1948, resulted in a formal contract being received by English Electric. On 1 November, the company proffered its P.1 proposal to the MoS. The company received the go-ahead on 12 May 1949, to design a prototype P.1A research aircraft, which would undertake the flight development of a supersonic fighter to meet Specification F.23/49, followed in early 1952 by the P.1B design, eventually christened Lightning.

By February 1950, the ever-increasing costs of military aircraft, matched by the Treasury's ever-decreasing allocation of funds for research, convinced Teddy Petter that he should give serious consideration to an investigation

The Canberra's creator, W.E.W. Petter, in his office at 'TC' in 1947. Via R.P. Beamont

WG760, the prototype P.1, Petter's final design before leaving English Electric. Philip Jarrett

into lightweight fighter designs. He resigned his position with English Electric, and joined Folland Aircraft Limited at Hamble in Hampshire as Managing Director and Chief Engineer. Over the following twelve months he followed many different courses in his quest for a successful, cost-effective, jet-powered fighter. A design drawn around Bristol Engines' BE.22 Saturn engine, producing 3,750lb (1,700kg) static thrust, looked very promising. Although Bristol discontinued Saturn development, Petter was convinced that the design was sound and could demonstrate the legitimacy of his lightweight-fighter concept. Folland Aircraft elected to produce a prototype on a Private Venture (PV) basis, giving it the type number Fo.139. The far less powerful Armstrong Siddeley ASV.5 Viper axial-flow turbojet, giving 1,640lb (745kg) thrust, was selected and one Fo.139 prototype, named the Midge, was built. It made its first flight on 11 August 1954, from Boscombe Down, with Sqn Ldr Edward Tennant at the controls. Resplendent with the Class 'B' registration G-39-1, it was ready in time to appear at the 1954 SBAC Display at Farnborough.

Although underpowered in relation to Petter's original design, the Midge proved to be fully capable of attaining 600mph (960km/h) at sea level. A service ceiling of 38,000ft (11,600m) was demonstrated and G-39-1 was dived at supersonic speed during A&AEE evaluations. Several overseas air force pilots flew the Midge until, unfortunately, a Swiss pilot destroyed the aircraft in a fatal crash at Chilbolton, on 26 September 1955. As was to be expected, although the aircraft fully proved Petter's concept, the Air Ministry was unmoved.

On 17 December 1954, Bristol Engines first ran their PV Orpheus axial-flow engine at 3,285lb (1,490kg) thrust and Teddy Petter refined his original Midge design into the Fo.141 Gnat, still on a PV basis. A prototype, registered G-39-2, was first flown at Boscombe Down on 18 July 1955, again with Sqn Ldr Tennant at the controls. A 4,000lb (1,820kg) Orpheus BOr.1 powered the aircraft when it appeared at the 1955 SBAC Display and the A&AEE's good reports on it led the MoS to order six development examples.

Petter's basic concept of the Gnat as an operational fighter with the Royal Air Force never gained favour, although the Finnish Air Force received thirteen aircraft and the Indian Air Force took delivery of twenty-five complete aircraft, as well as fifteen in kit form. These became the basis of licence production by Hindustan Aeronautics Limited at Bangalore, where 174 Gnats were built. RAF use of the Gnat was confined to a two-seat transonic variant, for its all-through jet training scheme. Folland received an order for fourteen pre-production aircraft, which was followed by orders, at twelve-month intervals, for thirty, twenty and forty-one production aircraft Gnat T.1s. They served with No.4 Flying Training School (FTS) at Valley, on the island of Anglesey and an official RAF aerobatic display team was formed, named the Yellowjacks.

The Central Flying School (CFS) at Little Rissington in Gloucestershire started taking delivery of Gnats in February 1962 and, three years later, they took over the mantle of the RAF display team when they formed the Red Arrows. Between them, the two units showed Petter's 'small is beautiful' concept in many hundreds of well-executed aerobatic displays all over the world until 1979.

Gnat T.1 XS102, a former 4FTS aircraft, which passed to No.1 School of Technical Training (SofTT) at Halton, Buckinghamshire, as Instructional Airframe 8624M and was later registered G-MOUR, was lovingly restored at Leavesden in Hertfordshire. Today, it is operated from North Weald, the former Battle of Britain airfield in Essex, by the Intrepid Aviation Company. It appears at various international air displays, in a Yellowjack colour scheme, and carrying the XR991 serial of an original team aircraft. During 1998, it was joined at Intrepid Aviation by another airworthy example, XR538, civil-registered G-RORI. With at least two further airworthy Gnats, XS104/G-FRCE and XS101/G-GNAT, together with a dozen static-display standard examples, a couple of Lysanders, and the various Canberras held all over the UK, there is little chance of Teddy Petter's design abilities being forgotten.

The Folland Gnat T.1 in its Red Arrows days during the mid-1970s. Author's collection

numbering system for prototype aircraft. Each aircraft manufacturer was allocated an individual identification letter. English Electric's was 'E'. The manufacturer appended a suffix letter, starting with 'A', followed by numbers from '1'. When, on 7 January 1946, English Electric received a contract for the detail design of their B.3/45 submission and the construction of four prototype aircraft, the designation E.A1 was applied; it remained until the design was officially named.

The TC design team became fully occupied throughout 1946 with perfecting the basic design. Variants to meet other provisional military applications were the logical progression, but the mooting of a sixteen- or thirty-four-seat civil airliner, with a range of 930 or 1,600 miles (1,500 or 2,575km), seems to have been a misguided way of using the limited design resources. History has proved that the discarding of any civil application was probably a wise move.

Warton Airfield

In October 1941, an airfield was constructed at Warton in Lancashire, on the northern side of the River Ribble estuary. Earmarked as a satellite for Squires Gate (now Blackpool Airport), a United States commission recognized that it would be an ideal site for a depot, being close to the port of Liverpool and in an area that was safer from enemy air attention than southern or eastern counties. Consequently, Base Air Depot No.2 was established. Although it made a slow start, by 1944 it employed over 10,000 military personnel on around-the-clock maintenance, modification and repairs for the US Eighth Army Air Force, which, from 17 July 1943, operated the unit as Station 582. Aeroengine overhaul became a speciality, with over 6,000 being handled, as well as close on 10,000 airframes.

The end of hostilities in May 1945 initiated the inevitable run-down of activities and, on 19 November, Warton was handed back to the RAF, which installed No.90 Maintenance Unit (MU) there as a storage facility, until early in 1951. English Electric's Samlesbury complex, together with the airfield, was committed to Vampire licensed production and test flying, as well as fulfilling the Lincoln electronics modification contracts. The acceptance of the A.1 design to meet B.3/45, which was quite rightly viewed as only the start of a

concentrated new programme, meant that English Electric required additional facilities. Warton, with its extensive hangars, buildings and three tarmac runways – one of which was 6,000ft (1,829m) in length – was considered by the company to be ideal for it's A.1 programme. By early in 1947, research facilities, together with a low-speed wind tunnel, were being established in Warton's first hangar as RAF presence was gradually reduced.

Test Pilots

The need to confirm the post of Chief Experimental Test Pilot was considered a priority by Teddy Petter, who had short-listed two suitable candidates by December 1946. At the Royal Aircraft Establishment (RAE), Farnborough, Sqn Ldr Tony Martindale had registered his credentials as an experienced test pilot, as well as being a certified engineer. He had successfully undertaken an intensive programme to establish the absolute limits of control in compressibility. In the course of the trials, he had, in 1946, the distinction of landing Spitfire PR.XI EN409 after the tearing away of its whole propeller and reduction gear during a high-speed vertical dive from 40,000ft (12,200m). During this dive, he is reported to have achieved over Mach 0.9. The safe landing of EN409 was made at Farnborough after a 20-mile (35-km) glide,

the wheels having to be lowered by emergency control, as the hydraulics had been rendered unserviceable.

Martindale's short-list competitor was Wg Cdr R.P. Beamont. Teddy Petter and Freddy Page were in full agreement that whoever took the post would be required to integrate fully with the design team during the whole project development. Petter favoured Martindale, with his engineering qualifications. Freddy Page took the view that there would be an abundance of engineers. The operationally experienced Beamont, who had flight-test involvement in two postings with Hawker Aircraft, as well as Meteor development testing at Gloster Aircraft and demonstration flying at de Havillands, got Page's vote. Petter conceded to Page's view and, in May 1947, Roland Beamont joined the English Electric Aircraft Division as Chief Test Pilot.

The Design of the A.1

Cockpit Layout

Although Warton slowly came into use, the wood and cardboard mock-up remained at TC and Petter's design team did not move until the end of 1948. As soon as he joined the team, Beamont's input was required, to determine the cockpit layout. As with

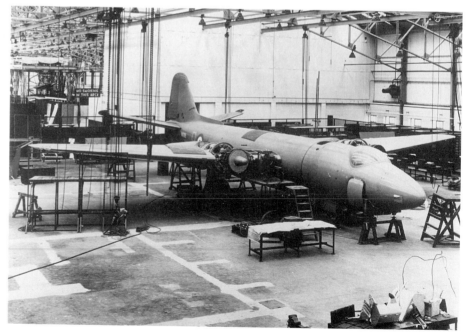

VN799 stands in No.25 Hangar at Warton, being prepared for the roll-out.
Via R.P Beamont

Wg Cdr R.P. Beamont CBE, DSO*, DFC*, DL, FRAeS – The 'Train-Busting' Test Pilot

Born on 10 August 1920 at Enfield in Middlesex, Roland Prosper Beamont moved to Chichester in Sussex with his parents in 1930. He describes the catalyst for his life in aviation as follows: 'Tangmere was half an hour away by bike and I spent most of my holidays sitting in the grass on the west boundary of the aerodrome, watching Nos.1 and 43 Squadrons fly their glorious Hawker Fury biplanes – no more inspiration needed!'

Beamont was educated at Eastbourne College and, at 18 years of age, took a short service commission in the RAF. His flying began on Tiger Moths with No.13 Reserve Flying School (EFTS) at White Waltham in 1939 and, when the Second World War started, he was completing his training with No.13 Advanced Flying School (AFTS), based at the Scottish grass airfield of Drem, flying Hawker Harts and Audaxes. He received his 'wings' a week later, on 10 September 1939 at Drem, and was posted as a fully qualified pilot to No.11 Group Fighter Pool, at St Athan in South Wales. His conversion to the Hawker Hurricane was completed at St Athan before he joined No.87 Squadron, which formed a part of the Advanced Air Striking Force on the European mainland, operating from Le Touquet, Lille/Seclin, Amiens and Merville in France and Belgium. Fighting through the Allied collapse in May 1940, he returned to the UK, landing at RAF Hendon.

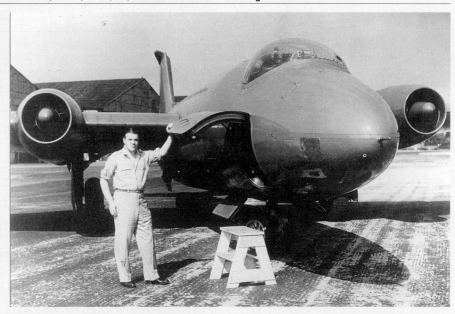

'Bee' poses beside VN799, a few weeks after the first flight (above), before settling into the Martin-Baker ejector seat in the 'greenhouse'. Via R.P. Beamont

(Continued overleaf)

Wg Cdr R.P. Beamont CBE, DSO*, DFC*, DL, FRAeS – The 'Train-Busting' Test Pilot *(continued)*

No.87 Squadron re-formed at Church Fenton in Yorkshire on 24 May 1940. Flt Lt Beamont joined them there and then moved with the whole squadron to Exeter, to fight throughout the Battle of Britain; he was Mentioned in Despatches in August. Posted as a flight commander to No.79 Squadron, which was equipped with the Hurricane Mk.IIB at its Fairwood Common base, 'Bee' flew in the first exploratory offensive sweeps over the enemy-occupied European mainland in the early spring of 1941, under the codename *Night Intruder*. He was awarded the DFC for his actions. At the end of the year, the squadron moved to Baginton in Warwickshire and then embarked for three years' service in the Far East, arriving at Kanchrapara in India on 27 June 1942. They were without 'Bee'. Towards the end of 1941, he was due a rest period, which he spent at Hawker Aircraft's Langley complex in Buckinghamshire on a Special Duties List posting, flight testing production Hurricanes, and, later, becoming involved in experimental development flying.

Arriving at Langley in December 1941, having flown Hurricanes for two years, Beamont felt that he knew the aircraft inside out. He quickly learned that operational and test flying were two different worlds. During his spell with Hawkers, besides production Hurricane testing, 'Bee' undertook ferry flights in their Tornado predecessor to the mighty Typhoon, as well as conducting some early vibration tests in R8220, the fourth production Typhoon Mk.IA built at Langley. Another eleven Typhoons were manufactured there, before the balance of the grand total of 3,330 to be built was transferred to a new factory on Gloster Aircrafts' site at Hucclecote.

No.56 Squadron, based at Duxford in September 1941, had been the first unit to be equipped with the Typhoon IA and Beamont joined the squadron the following year for a short period. He was then posted to Duxford's other Typhoon operator, No.609 Squadron, first as a Flight Commander, then as Commanding Officer. The winter of 1942/43 saw the squadron, under 'Bee', developing the Typhoon ground-attack role, including 'train-busting', with the CO's personal score standing at twenty-five trains. He received a bar to his DFC for these successful operations. On 7 May 1943, having been awarded the DSO, Beamont handed over command of No.609 Squadron to Sqn Ldr Alec Ingle at Manston and returned to Langley for a second spell of test flying.

On 2 June, 'Bee' made his first flight in HM599, the prototype Tempest Mk.I, at the beginning of over six months' concentrated testing of the Typhoon's successor on Hawker's production lines. At the completion of this period, at the beginning of 1944, the aircraft had been developed into the ultimate Sabre-engined production Mk.V and was ready for allocation to the RAF. His extensive experience with the type made Beamont an ideal candidate to take it into squadron service. Once again, he was posted from Hawker Aircraft at Langley and, in February 1944, No.150 Tempest Wing was formed under the command of Wg Cdr Beamont, at the Kentish fighter station of Newchurch, with Nos.3, 486 (New Zealand) and 56 Squadrons.

There followed eight months in which the pilots of the Wing, with their new aircraft, proved themselves in combat with enemy aircraft, as well as against the Fiesler FZG76 flying bomb – colloquially referred to as the V-1, derived from the German *Vergeltungswaffe* (reprisal weapon). They brought down six hundred and thirty-two of them; the CO's contribution was thirty. The Wing moved on to the European mainland after land-forces had captured the Dutch airfield at Volkel. On 12 October 1944, it lost its Wing Commander, when the Sabre of 'Bee's Tempest was terminated by groundfire during a low-level operation against targets near Bocholt. He was destined not to add to his tally of ten enemy aircraft destroyed.

Seven months as a prisoner of war in *Stalag Luft III* ended with the cessation of hostilities on 8 May 1945. Having been awarded a bar to his DSO, Beamont was posted to the Air Fighting Development (AFD) squadron at the Central Fighter Establishment (CFE), as Commanding Officer. Leaving the RAF in January 1946, he joined Gloster Aircraft and tested the special Meteor IVs, in preparation for the RAF's successful attack on the world speed record later in the year. He then fulfilled a period as a demonstration pilot with the de Havilland Aircraft Company, flying Vampires, the Dove prototype G-AGPJ and the first Chipmunk received from Canada.

Having declined the offer of a permanent commission in the RAF, 'Bee' became Chief Test Pilot at English Electric in May 1947, with the brief to lead the test programme and development of the A.1 jet bomber. During a visit to the British Joint Services Mission in Washington, USA, the following year, he was able to gain flight experience with the P-80 and the P-84 at Wright Field, as well as with the second XP-86 at Muroc. He flew the latter at Mach 1+, becoming the first British pilot to achieve this.

The maiden flight of VN799, the first A.1 prototype on 13 May 1949, was the start of many years managing all the prototype tests of each mark of the type, which on 19 January 1951 was officially christened 'Canberra'. He was the pilot when the aircraft established two Atlantic speed records, on 31 August 1951 and 26 August 1952; the latter was the first two-way Atlantic crossing in one day. Flown by VX185, the only B.5, the Aldergrove to Gander leg was accomplished in 4 hours 18 minutes, at an average speed of 411.99mph (663.01km/h). The return flight, Gander to Aldergrove, took 3 hours 25 minutes 18.13 seconds, the average speed of 605.52mph (974.46km/h) being helped by the 'gulf stream'.

Dovetailed in with Canberra development testing was the design and building of English Electric's supersonic submission to Specification ER.103, the P.1. The company's policy of having the Chief Test Pilot deeply involved in a project more or less from inception meant that 'Bee's time was split between the two programmes. The prototype P.1A, WG760, had its maiden flight from Boscombe Down on 4 August 1954, with Beamont at the controls. Contracts had already been signed for the aircraft to become the aerodynamic

research vehicle for the aircraft English Electric was designing to meet Specification F.23/49, which culminated in the RAF's first supersonic fighter, the P.1B Lightning. 'Bee' undertook the first flight of the fighter prototype, XA847, on 4 April 1957 and, in the course of the P.1A/P.1B test programme, he became the first pilot to fly a British aircraft at Mach 1 in level flight. On 25 November 1958, flying XA847, he became the first pilot to take a British aircraft beyond Mach 2, in a test that was to lead to the Lightning being cleared for operational service at this speed.

The acme of Wg Cdr Beamont's test-flying career must be the TSR.2 supersonic bomber/reconnaissance aircraft designed to meet Operational Requirement (OR) 339 and considered as the Canberra's replacement. The aircraft was developed in association with Vickers Armstrong (Aircraft) Limited and, as its Chief Test Pilot, Beamont was involved throughout, from initial design to the maiden flight, which was made from Boscombe Down on 27 September 1964. Although contracts had been received for the building of nine prototype development aircraft, with serials XR219 to XR227, a further eleven pre-production aircraft plus thirty production aircraft, only two prototypes, XR219 and XR222, were completed, with only XR219 flying.

Beamont had flown a total of 5 hours 15 minutes in nine flights plus 2 hours 20 minutes taxiing in the aircraft, when the Chancellor of the Exchequer delivered his Budget Day speech, on 6 April 1965. The whole programme – finished aircraft, under-construction airframes, ancillary components, jigs, the lot – was cancelled, and even the logical suggestion to use XR219 for research flying was abandoned. Politics had annihilated the TSR.2 faster than any potential enemy could ever have dreamed.

In 1965, 'Bee' Beamont became a director of the Warton Division of Britain's condensed aircraft industry, first named the British Aircraft Corporation (BAC) and, later, British Aerospace (BAe). As Director Flight Operations, he was a founder member of the Al Yamama export programme, which set up the Saudi Arabian defence system, Britain's longest-ever export programme, and still on-going. His Director Flight Operations status also placed him, from 1970 to 1979, in charge of international Tornado flight testing, for both BAe and Panavia.

After a glittering aeronautical career spanning four decades, 'Bee' retired to the Wiltshire countryside, to involve himself ardently in a new career as an aviation author. He also supplies the answers to the many hundreds of queries that annually touch down on his doormat. A Fellow of the Royal Aeronautical Society and Honorary Fellow of the Society of Experimental Test Pilots (USA), 'Bee' was awarded the Britannia Trophy in 1953; OBE, 1954; GAPAN Derry and Richards Medal, 1955; RAeS R.P. Alston Medal, 1960; RAeS British Silver Medal for Aeronautics, 1965; CBE, 1965; and the Wings Club of New York Distinguished Achievement Award, 1992.

Those hours spent in the grass outside Tangmere certainly started something!

all military aircraft, this had to be a compromise between what the crew wanted and what service requirements decreed. The involvement from an early stage of 'Bee', an ex-operational pilot, probably gave the aircraft a more environmentally friendly 'office' than many aircrew received when a new type arrived at the squadrons. Inevitably, later equipment developments would impinge on the original crew area – boffins rarely seem to appreciate that a pressurized cockpit area does not have expandable sides – but at least the designers of this prototype were being guided by an experimental test and former squadron pilot. As things turned out, when a third crew member had to be accommodated, it was just as well that a good cockpit layout had been established at the design stage.

The Structure

All hydraulic, electrical and control layouts were determined on the mock-up during 1947 so that, once metal was cut the following year, and construction of the first prototype, VN799, commenced at Strand Road, the actual assembly was comparatively trouble-free. A large number of new aircraft up to the 1970s were virtually 'hand-knitted'. But English Electric's wartime experience with the Hampden and Halifax made extensive use of Frederick Handley-Page's split-production technology, which was totally dependent on intensified jig and tool limits being of dimensional accuracy, which, while common practice today, was not at all prevalent in the 1930s. In designing his jet-powered bomber, Petter perfected an airframe to be manufactured as a set of five independent primary structures, which could be mixed and matched to meet any role type. The prototypes made extensive use of the jigs laid down for full production, with very few sections being hand made. The five manufactured elements were:

- the front fuselage, from frames 1 to 12A;
- the centre fuselage, from frames 12B to 31A;
- the rear fuselage, from frame 31B to the tail;
- mainplanes with non-anti-icing Avon Mk.1 engines; and
- mainplanes with anti-icing Avon Mk.109 engines and integral fuel tanks.

The philosophy behind this primary structure was to prove invaluable over the years, not only where new-role marks were introduced but, particularly, in relation to airframes used by research establishments.

The design incorporated a centre-section spar of strong webbed forging, sandwiched between two aluminium diaphragms, to which the mainplanes were attached. Rolls-Royce's Research Laboratory at Derby had perfected a very strong aluminium alloy early in the Second World War, for use in forgings. Derby registered this as Alloy R.R.77; when it was taken up by the Government, it became DTD683. It had a tensile strength of 32 tons per sq in (156 tonnes per sq m), compared with 10 tons per sq in for similar-application aluminium alloys. Petter selected DTD683 for all the strong load-bearing components, such as the centre-section main spar, undercarriage structure members and engine-bearing attachment points, as well as all fuselage interface attachments. (The choice of DTD683 features later in this history.)

Controls

Flying controls, apart from the horn-balanced rudder and ailerons, were to be fitted with a spring-tab system, in order to give light stick forces, while a variable incidence tailplane was to make for powerful longitudinal trimming. In view of a small amount of uncertainty existing in relation to the aerodynamic coefficient between the hinge moment and incidence, it was detailed that the rudder horn balance should be fashioned from wood.

This decision certainly paid off once the prototype took to the air.

Power Source

Once Petter's ideas had crystallized into a twin-engined design, the Rolls-Royce AJ.65 axial-flow turbojet, initially producing 6,500lb (2,950kg) static thrust, was the selected power source. In fact, the AJ.65 was the power source for nearly every project and design spilling out from aircraft-industry project offices. The whole future of the RAF's fighter and attack potentials were tied in to the engine, which, at the time, represented Britain's largest single aviation investment. Inevitably, problems arose during the engine's development and a slippage in the projected delivery time-scale led to the re-engineering of the second A.1 prototype, VN813, to accept a pair of 5,000-lb (2,270kg)-thrust Rolls-Royce Nene engines as an insurance. The Nene was a centrifugal-flow engine; the bulk of the nine individual combustion chambers ranged around its compressor housing gave the engine an overall diameter of 49.5in (123.75cm), compared with the AJ.65's 42.4in (106cm). VN813's nacelles had to be re-contoured; although this might have contributed to a drag penalty, the possible risk was preferable to a delay in the proposed A.1 prototype test-flying programme.

Experiments and Variations

In the course of preparing both the pilot and the aircraft for a maiden flight early in 1949, several subsidiary programmes were

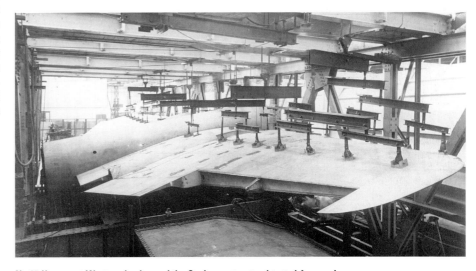

No.25 Hangar at Warton also housed the Canberra structural test airframe, shown undergoing tests in 1949. Via R.P. Beamont

initiated. Gloster Meteor Mk.IV EE545 was loaned to English Electric, so that Beamont could investigate the effects on the aircraft's handling and performance of high Mach numbers at high altitude. The programme was conducted from Warton in the three months of September to November 1947, at altitudes above 40,000ft (12,200m). While it was a reasonably valuable exercise, the main conclusion drawn was that the Meteor was useless as a true interceptor at altitudes above 40,000ft. The Ministry was presented with the fact that the A.1 would be far superior as an aeroplane, let alone as an attacking bomber, above this altitude.

Consideration was given to employing Servodyne-powered elevators on the A.1 and a Samlesbury-built Halifax B.VI, ST808, was modified in 1948 to flight test the system. The results were not satisfactory and no further consideration was given to their association with the English Electric bomber. Another Samlesbury-produced aircraft, Vampire F.3 VT861, was borrowed in the same year, in order for 'Bee' to conduct further experimental flights above 40,000ft, as well as a series of landing and take-off trials at Warton.

With the original rounded top to the rudder, VN799 is rolled out – a far cry from the modern laser-show production that a prototype receives.
Author's collection

The First A.1

By early 1949, VN799 had been completed at Strand Road and system checks were carried out before the aircraft was dismantled for transportation to Warton. There, English Electric had a low-speed wind-tunnel at one end of No.25 hangar, while the other end was earmarked for the A.1 prototype's reassembly and future flight testing. The month of March saw the first prototype once more as a complete airframe.

At Rolls-Royce, the AJ.65 engine had acquired the name 'Avon' and flight testing had been carried out in two Lancastrians. The first of the two, VM732, gave the engine its maiden flight on 15 August 1948 and two Avon RA.2s first flew in Lancastrian VL970 on 16 June 1949. A small pre-production batch of Avon RA.2s was built, two of them, engine numbers A13/A617963 and A14/A617964, were received at Warton during the month to power VN799 on its maiden flight.

With installation completed, on 29 April 1948 the first A.1 was towed by tractor from No.25 hangar, nacelle panels being omitted for the first engine runs made later in the day.

Three days later, on 2 May, VN799 glistened on the tarmac, resplendent in an overall Cerulean Blue colour scheme, with national roundels on the rear fuselage, alongside the obligatory yellow prototype markings and white serial. The wing

undersurfaces carried large white repeats of the serial but the mainplanes had no roundels on either surface. Small national fin-bar markings were painted ahead of the rudder hinge line but, although both crew members were equipped with Martin-Baker Type 1C ejection seats, there were no external triangular warning signs.

Trials

Beamont started the first of two taxiing trials on 8 May and, apart from a minor nose-wheel vibration, or 'shimmy', very few snags were encountered. The following day, fast runs were begun down Warton's main runway. With a test take-off weight established at under 30,000lb (13,630kg), a wing loading of approximately 27lb/sq ft, and 6,500lb (2,950kg) thrust from each engine, it was easy for a series of short hops to be made down a 6,000ft (1,830m) stretch of tarmac. Control response and stability on each axis were checked during the hops and a height around 15ft (4.5m) was attained at 100mph (160km/h), with no hint of brake overheating. On 11 May, a final hop of over 500 yards (475m) was achieved but, in the eyes of the pilot and all observers, this did not constitute a first flight. This took place on the 13th.

Later in the year, the A.1 was named 'Canberra'; the name was destined to have far more impact than just a dot on a map.

CHAPTER THREE

The Prototype Quartet

Contracts and Orders

The first official notification made to English Electric in relation to the A.1 was Contract No.6/ACFT/5841/CB6(b), received on 7 January 1946. It covered four prototypes, serialled VN799, VN813, VN828 and VN850, which would all become Canberra B.1s, built to Specification B.3/45. While the original problems with the AJ.65 Avon, which prompted the re-engineering of VN813 to take two Nenes, did not materialize, a potentially much more serious situation arose. The radar bombing system, the catalyst for the original conception of a design to meet Specification E.3/45, was nowhere near ready for installation in any of the prototypes. In fact, the lack of non-visual bomb aiming could kill off the A.1 programme as it stood. (A similar situation

arose forty years later, when the aircraft, the Nimrod AEW3, *was* killed off.)

Since the RAF's current Bomber Command centred around piston-engined updates of the wartime Lancaster, the Avro Lincoln, second-hand Boeing B-29s on loan from the United States – called the Washington, but still second-hand B-29s! – and later marks of the Mosquito, there really was no alternative other than to modify the A.1. Specification B.5/47 was drawn up to cover the modifications. These made provision for a third crew member bomb-aimer to operate in a prone position, a Perspex nose-cone with a 'clear view' window built in, off-set to starboard, and the installation of a visual bombing system based on the T2 bombsight.

Even before the first aircraft had flown, the design's potential was appreciated and

the Ministry took the rare step of ordering an untried military aeroplane. On 1 March 1949, a production order was placed in Contract No.6/ACFT/3520/CB6(b) for 132 aircraft, so that English Electric could lay down production lines. Four separate variants were ordered; an extension of the modifications in Specification B.5/47 covered a tactical bomber; Specification PR.31/46 allowed for a long-range photographic reconnaissance aircraft; B.22/48 for a target-marker bomber; and T.11/47 for a trainer. Contract No.6/ACFT/2000/CB6(b) was received for the building of four B.2 prototypes with serials VX165, VX169, VX173 and VX177 (although initially only two were built), as well as one PR.Mk.3 prototype, VX181, to PR.31/46.

Contract No.6/ACFT/6265/CB6(b) was issued for one T.Mk.4 prototype, WN467,

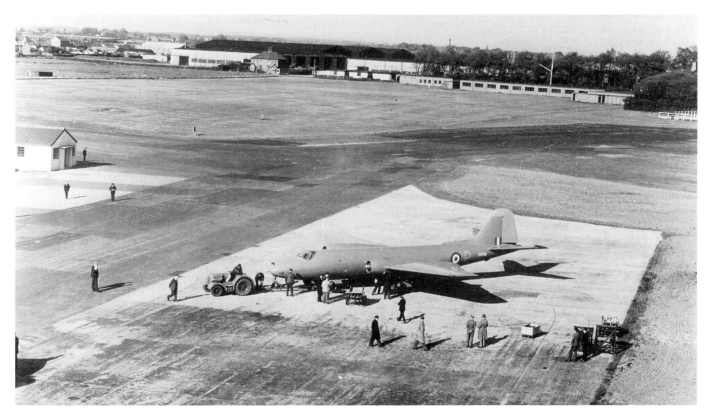

VN799 is prepared at Warton for the day's taxiing trials, on 12 May 1949. Author's collection

originally to meet Specification T.11/47, which was later amended to T.2/49. The 1 March 1949 contract comprised ninety B.2 aircraft, thirty-four PR.3s and eight T.4s. Therefore, by the time VN799 was hopping down Warton's main runway, the die had been cast for the A.1 to become an operational aircraft in the RAF.

The First Prototype

On Friday 13 May 1949, the weather was tranquil and the usual start-of-day conference endorsed the decision that this would be *the* day. Petter's young design team,

services checked. Flying control confirmed that Squier was airborne in the Vampire and, with chocks removed, the A.1 commenced taxiing towards the main runway, with brake checks being implemented at intervals and nose-wheel castoring tested. Holding on the threshold, 'Bee' opened up the Avons to full power against the brakes then, after checking pressures and temperatures again, informed the tower that he was rolling. The time was just after 1140 hours.

The 825 gallons (3,750litres) carried for the test flight constituted a load of 6,650lb (3,020kg) weight and the flight, which was curtailed to twenty-seven minutes, did not greatly reduce this weight for touch-

Problems and Solutions

The second flight was made on 18 May, when handling up to 420kt (494mph/ 795km/h) was tested at various altitudes below 15,000ft (4,600m) and found to be every bit as good as any aircraft Beamont had previously flown. However, at speeds above 400kt (470.5mph/757km/h), vibration occurred, reported by the pilot as mostly heavy tramping. Arrangements were made to conduct the next series of tests up to this speed in order to investigate the flight envelope in general, before attending to a particular phenomenon and, on 19 May, VN799 was taken up to 20,000ft (6,100m).

The day before VN799's maiden flight, 'Bee' makes one of several hops down the runway to get the feel of the controls. Author's collection

English Electric's Preston plant and Wg Cdr Roland Beamont were all deeply conscious that this was Britain's first jet bomber, built around a new engine, upon which so much depended. 'Bee' was most likely the least apprehensive of all and he certainly firmly denounced Petter's voiced observation that the date held certain superstitious associations. The aircraft was ready and he was ready – nothing else was relevant. Company Production Test Pilot J.W. 'Johnny' Squier was briefed to be prepared to fly a Vampire FB.5 from Samlesbury, as a chase aircraft, any time after 1045 hours.

The Form 700 was completed by AID Inspector 'Wilky' Wilkins, and Beamont climbed aboard VN799 shortly after 1100 hours. The Avons were started and all

down, which was made at 1213 hours. When called upon to observe any unusual visible rudder movement during the flight, Johnny Squier gave a negative reply, and commented on the aesthetic beauty of the A.1. At a later debrief in Teddy Petter's office, 'Bee' made known his opinion that the rudder hinge moment felt like overbalance which, although vocally dismissed by one member of the design team, was considered by the Chief Engineer to require investigation before another flight was made. This is where the original decision to construct the rudder horn balance in wood paid off and it was decided to reduce the horn balance progressively, with each change being test flown until the optimum was achieved.

At Mach 0.77, slight 'snaking' was encountered at various altitudes *en route*.

During the next flight, on 26 May, when a decision was made to increase speed above the previously set 400kt (470.5mph/ 757km/h) maximum, oscillations occurred at 420kt (494mph/795km/h) around 10,000ft (3,050m). The problem was considered serious enough for vibrograph sensors to be installed for the following day's flight. These pointed to incipient elevator flutter and, on 31 May, the Chief Aerodynamicist D.L. Ellis, flying in the navigator's station, was given first-hand experience of the effect. His opinion was that the phenomenon should be explored on the ground.

During the first week of July, the aircraft was grounded, in which time the rudder

First flight – B.3/45, 13 May 1949
All services were checked before flight and found to be satisfactory.

Engine figures: 7,800   600   40   45
            7,800   620   38   40
Brakes: main pressure – 440lb
Tailplane: 1.5 divisions from nose-down
Isolating switches on
Power to take-off: 7,500/7,500
Flaps down
Time 1154 – zero

The aircraft was flown off normally at approx. 90kt and, as the speed exceeded 120kt IAS, full nose-down trim was insufficient to trim out the subsequent nose-up trim change. At 200ft power was reduced and the undercarriage retracted satisfactorily. During this operation a slight yaw to port occurred, a correction for which was made by application of right rudder.

After approx. 2in of travel involving a low control force and a very small rudder reaction, the rudder control lost effectiveness in a manner which suggested over-balance in that control forces were suddenly reduced to zero, and no further rudder reaction was noticeable. This condition was corrected rapidly by left rudder pressure and the aircraft climbed straight ahead to approx. 5,000ft. Flaps were retracted satisfactorily at 170kt after holding the aircraft in trim by a 20–30lb push force together with full nose-down trim. This resulted in a mild nose-down trim change and the aircraft was trimmed hands off at 245kt IAS, tailplane 2 graduations up from 'nose-down'.

Right rudder was again applied, this time at 200kt, with the same results as before, plus the additional impression that, following on the sudden reduction of starboard rudder force to zero, a sharp minus force occurred until held and reversed with port rudder.

During this test it was confirmed that during the over-balance condition a slight tremor could be felt through the rudder system though not through the airframe.

At this condition of flight (245kt, 5–6,000ft, time: zero plus 3), the tailplane actuator was found to operate satisfactorily, though with some lag, and the aircraft was satisfactorily in trim at a tailplane setting 2 graduations up from full nose-down.

At zero plus 8.5 an ASI check was made with a standard Mk.V Vampire with the following results:

B.3/45 – 245kt
Vampire – 245kt

The Vampire reported all doors and fairings closed.

THE ENGLISH ELECTRIC CO. LTD.
AIRCRAFT DIVISION, WARTON AERODROME,
PRESTON

FLIGHT No. :   1.
SHEET No. :
DATE : 13:5:49.

EXPERIMENTAL FLIGHT REPORT

AIRCRAFT TYPE   B3/45   CREW:- PILOT W/Cdr. Beamont.
AIRCRAFT SERIAL No.   VN.799.   OBSERVER   –
OBJECT OF TEST :—

First Test Flight.

TAKE-OFF LOADING :—

TARE WEIGHT	20,337	LB.
FUEL 825 Galls.	6,650	LB.
FUEL EXTERNAL TANKS	–	LB.
OIL	–	LB.
CREW	200	LB.
BALLAST	590	LB.
TOTAL	27,877	LB.

TYRE PRESSURES:—

MAIN	72	LB. SQ. IN.
NOSE	60	LB. SQ. IN.

C.G. POSITION AT TAKE OFF 1.469 ft. aft of datum – 19.615% M/C

TIME OF FLIGHT 10.46 hrs. – 11.13 hrs.

AIRCRAFT CONDITION (MODIFICATIONS etc.):—
Aircraft in Experimental Condition with 108 lb additional ballast on ballast box.

Fuel distribution:-
No.1 Tank 500 Galls.
No.2 Tank 300   "
No.3 Tank 25

DISTRIBUTION:-
Chief Engineer   Mr.Page.
Mr.Ellis.   Mr.Harrison)
R.T.O.   Mr.Crowe)
Flight Observer. Mr.Smith.

PILOT R.P.Beamont.   DATE 13:5:49.

CERTIFICATE OF SAFETY FOR FLIGHT.

From :—   To :—
Inspector in Charge, A.I.D.,   The English Electric Co. Ltd.,
The English Electric Co. Ltd.,   Warton Aerodrome,
East Works, Preston, Lancs.   Nr. Preston, Lancs.

I HEREBY CERTIFY that the aircraft defined hereunder :—
Type.   Engine(s).   Serial No. or Registration Mark.
B3/45 Prototype   RR.Avon R.A.2. A13/A617963 A14/A617964   VN.799.

has this day been inspected including the engine(s), the engine installation(s) and instruments and is in every way safe for the undermentioned flight(s) :—

Purpose of flight(s). Initial Taxying & Flight Trials in accordance with schedule of Flight Tests & Design Certificate dated 5/5/49.
Authority* Contract 5841/CB6(b).   To take place
from   WARTON   Aerodrome with   Mr. R.P. Beamont.   as Pilot.

NOTE.—Any alterations, repairs or adjustments made to this aircraft subsequent to the issue of this certificate renders it invalid, and no further flight may be made until the certificate is renewed.

Signed.   Date.

1. INITIAL TAXYING (LESS SEAT CHARGES)   [signature]   7th MAY 1949
2. INITIAL TAXYING (LESS SEAT CHARGES)   [signature]   8th MAY 1949
3. TAXYING & HOPS. LESS SEAT GUIDARD   [signature]   9th MAY 1949
4. HOPS   [signature]   11th May 1949
5. Flights & Taxying   [signature]   12th May 1949
6. 1st Flight   [signature]   13th May 1949

(*13706—7831) WL/60659—3381 5M Pads 1/44 I.S. 700   *Contract, A.N.D., etc.

The Flight Certificate (*left*) and
Experimental Flight Report sheets for 13
May 1949. Author's collection

Report Reproduced from *Testing Years* by Roland Beamont (Ian Allen Ltd, 1980), with Permission *(continued)*

At zero plus 12 further investigation of the rudder condition was carried out at 210kt, 6,000/6,000rpm, 6–8,000ft, and the condition was confirmed without variation from the previous test, the general impression being that the rudder was effective through the very small angles either side of neutral and over-balanced outside those angles. This condition naturally restricted the scope of the test, but before descending the other controls were checked at this flight condition as follows:

Ailerons firm and positive in action with heavy wheel forces for large angles. Elevator well in harmony with ailerons; positive and firm in action and response. Possibly slightly less positive than ailerons. A slight tremor was noticeable with jerky application which was probably spring tab effect. The tailplane actuator was checked at this point and this, though smooth and effective, suffered from an initial lag of between 2–3 seconds between operation of the switch and a noticeable response. This is undesirable but need not interfere with the early flying.

At zero plus 14 it was decided that the test should be discontinued owing to the rudder condition which did not promise an adequate measure of control for the single engine case, and the descent was begun. During this it was noted that the aircraft lost speed very slowly at idling rpm and in fact would not do so at any appreciable rate of descent. The flap speed of 140kt was not reached until zero plus 15.5 after a descent from approx. 5,000ft to approx. 2,500ft, and when flaps were applied the resulting nose-up trim change could not once again be completely trimmed out with tailplane. A normal half circuit was made, the undercarriage being lowered at 129kt satisfactorily with the warning lights operating within a period of approx. 15 seconds. This did not produce a noticeable trim change.

During the crosswind leg and the first part of the final approach at 115–110kt the aircraft handled easily apart from the rudder condition, control being maintained without the use of the rudder; but during the last 1,000yd of the approach at 110kt IAS, rough air was encountered which set up a series of yaws which could be felt in phase on the

rudder but which could not be corrected or controlled by its use; an attempt to do this resulted in recurrence of the over-balance condition.

The hold-off and landing was normal apart from an excess safety speed, and after cutting the engines 500yd short of the runway at 100kt/20ft, the ASI was still reading 100kt at the moment of touchdown 7–800yd further on. The brakes were used quite severely and retarded the aircraft adequately without undue temperature rise.

General Impression

Apart from the rudder conditions described, the aircraft handled smoothly and easily. All services operated satisfactorily although in the case of tailplane actuation some alterations may be necessary. Engine behaviour was satisfactory, and no engine handling was carried out owing to the circumstances of the test. Both engines and airframe were remarkably quiet in flight and the noise level in the cockpit allows excellent radio reception.

As was to be expected from the loading conditions, the aircraft was stable longitudinally and appeared to be so directionally in smooth air conditions. Rudder and aileron trimmers were set at neutral for take-off and were not required throughout the flight.

During the approach it was noted that up to its maximum range the tailplane actuator keeps pace with the nose-up trim change caused by flap operation, so that provided the airspeed is kept below 130kt stick-free trim can be retained during the full operation.

Work before Next Flight
1. Inspect brake assemblies and check Thermo-couples;
2. Remove flap system stop for full travel;
3. Mark tailplane dial graduations 0–9 (to suit), top to bottom;
4. Investigate rudder control.

R.P. BEAMONT
Chief Test Pilot

The top of VN799's rudder had been reduced when this shot was taken during an early flight, but the additional balance at the top rear had yet to be added. Author's collection

'Bee' follows the Blackpool coastline, on a test flight before the 1949 Farnborough display. Author's collection

horn was further reduced, to what was to prove to be the production shape. Elevator horns and mass balances were also modified, so that, when flying was resumed on 6 July, a start was made on getting clearance over a large part of the whole flight envelope. This was achieved during the thirty-six test flights conducted up to 31 August. A simple 'collar' fairing behind the canopy cured the 'snaking' encountered earlier, while the revisions to the rudder and elevators greatly reduced the flutter tendencies. Flown at heights above 40,000ft (12,200m) and up to Mach 0.8, the whole intensive programme proved successful and the proposed initial service speed limit of 450kt (529.4mph/ 852km/h) was exceeded by the 20kt (23.5mph/ 37.8km/h) margin stipulated by the Ministry.

Farnborough 1949

For a flying slot at the 1949 SBAC Display at Farnborough in the first week of September, a six-minute routine was worked out by Beamont and the flight-test team.

The aim was to demonstrate the aircraft's great manoeuvrability and confound the long-established belief that bombers were just to be displayed flying down the operational runway, in a straight line. VN799's overall blue paint finish was refurbished and polished, while the proposed name 'Canberra' was scripted on the aircraft's nose. English Electric may not have displayed an aeroplane at an SBAC show before, but the company was firm in its belief that it had something special to present, and that the aircraft was going to look as good as it flew. Beamont and VN799 arrived at Farnborough on Sunday 5 September, maintaining great secrecy about how they were going to demonstrate.

The A.1's initial appearance at its appointed time on Monday was slightly marred by a fuel-tank transfer 'glitch', which left the aircraft stranded on the runway threshold with a dead engine. 'Bee' had taxied out on a near-empty rear tank, intending to switch over to the full tanks prior to take-off, so that the display could be flown with an optimum c.g. condition. The rear tank emptied before he had switched

over and the port engine expired. Teddy Petter was none too pleased and made his displeasure known to the whole team, although the SBAC organizers agreed to the aircraft flying its display at the end of the day's programme. What ensued on 6 May 1949 was a classic event that was to remain in the memory for perpetuity, and became a talking point among all those who were fortunate enough to witness it.

'Bee' brought the A.1 Canberra on to the runway and, without stopping, thundered towards Laffan's Plain to lift off in just over 600 yards (550m) and hold down before making a climbing turn, first to port, then starboard. Turning over the Plain and returning down the runway at less than 100ft, the two Avons on full power propelled it at over 470mph (755km/h) before the pilot made a sharp vertical climb adjacent to the control tower. This was followed by a roll and diving turn back to the runway threshold and a beautiful 360-degree roll at between 100 and 300ft along the flight line. The return was made with the engines throttled back to give a speed of about 175mph (280km/h), with undercarriage down and bomb-bay doors open, while the wings were rocked from side to side.

The undercarriage was retracted and bomb doors closed for the finale, scheduled to be a half loop with the bomb doors opening again and the undercarriage lowered for the landing. Dave Walker, flying in the navigator's station, suddenly reported his instruments dropping to zero, at the same time as 'Bee' saw his starboard engine instruments doing likewise. Over the R/T, flying control reported that VN799 'was dropping to pieces', but Beamont found both engines were responding to throttles satisfactorily, so continued the landing approach with the tower keeping up an R/T commentary about the 'wires and things' trailing under the fuselage.

Having landed and taxied behind the crowd line, Walker climbed out and 'got under' to discover what he and 'Bee' had been thinking while touching down. The instrumentation box had departed to somewhere in the Farnborough vicinity and, as a new pack would require time to construct, it was decided to do the rest of the week without one.

Some members of the SBAC Flight Committee made their feelings known the following day: they wanted Beamont to tone down the demonstration for the rest of the week. 'Mutt' Summers, Vickers Armstrong's Chief Test Pilot and the senior test pilot on the committee, was required to have a conversation with 'Bee' – such a display by an aircraft of that size had never been seen before. Summers talked the same language as 'Bee', however, and was convinced that the previous day's demonstration had been flown well within the aircraft's limits. He gave 'Bee' the green light. Spectators for the rest of the week saw the same routine, but even those who witnessed it every day could not become blasé about it. It was something special.

The world's press eulogized. Initially unimpressed by the straight-wing conventional design, American reporters, who saw virtually everything on the other side of the Atlantic with swept wings, very quickly changed their opinions once VN799 was airborne. A new aircraft had never made its debut in such a spectacular fashion. Bombers designed to deliver 10,000lb (4,550kg) bomb loads from high altitudes, were just not meant to perform that way, especially at low level! There was no way of getting around it; this aircraft, its pilot and its constructors had made their mark in the biggest possible way.

Acceptance Trials

After the lavish praise of Farnborough, it was back to Warton to get down to the serious work of developing the aircraft for delivery to the Aircraft and Armament Experimental Establishment (A&AEE) at Boscombe Down. This was the first real hurdle, as it was the Establishment that conducted the trials that assessed an aircraft for operational service in the RAF. On 27 October 1949, VN799 was delivered to Boscombe by Beamont, where it was handed over to 'B' Squadron, whose Wg Cdr Davies, Sqn Ldr Saxelby and Flt Lt Callard were the RAF test pilots detailed to give the aircraft its provisional acceptance trials.

The following day was spent discussing general servicing with the Establishment's technical staff, with 'Bee' giving his frank opinions of various aspects of behaviour for which the new pilots should be prepared, and weighing-in preparation for the first flight, scheduled to be made by Wg Cdr Davies on 29 October. Between this date and 14 November, the three service test pilots passed the aircraft as 'a first-class flying machine'; any criticisms, such as a certain amount of discomfort in the cockpit due to the navigator's seat being too low, were of a minor nature.

As professional test pilots, the Establishment's team came to VN799 with an open mind, but there was certainly an initial scepticism about English Electric's claims for the aircraft. However, once the pilots had flown it, they lavished unstinting praise for its handling and performance upon Petter's young team's first design.

The Second Prototype

Five days before VN799's return to Warton, the Nene-powered second prototype, VN813, made its maiden flight from Warton on 9 November, with Beamont at the controls. It was the first Canberra to be finished in the new Bomber Command Black/Light Sea Grey finish. It had been suspected that the more bulbous nacelles required to house the centrifugal-flow engines would reduce the limiting Mach number and this was ratified by 'Bee', with a 0.05 reduction being noted. This prototype was retained by Warton for general development flying, during which time it was operated by RAE Farnborough. On 30 November 1950, it was handed over to Rolls-Royce at Hucknall to partake in their Nene flying programme and start seven years of test flying.

The aircraft was subsequently flown by the Royal Radar Establishment (RRE) at Defford for nearly a year. After this, it was modified by Folland Aircraft, in June 1953, to become a flying testbed for de Havilland's first rocket motor, the Spectre, which was housed in a bulged fairing under the rear of the bomb-bay. These trials started on 9 July 1954 and VN813 remained at Hatfield until being sold for scrap in December 1959.

The Third Prototype

The early winter of 1949 was a busy and productive time. Thirteen days after VN813 was first flown, Beamont took the third prototype, VN828, for its maiden flight on 22 November; it was the first Canberra flight made from Samlesbury.

This prototype, which was the first to have the dorsal fin fillet deleted, was built to the same B.1 standard of VN799, powered by axial-flow Avon engines but, like VN813, it was finished in Bomber Command colours. The landing was made at Warton and there followed over ten years of development flying from the company's base, interspersed with periods spent at RRE Defford, on *Green Satin* doppler trials, as well as trials of AI.Mk.18 radar. On 16 January 1950, it became the first Canberra to reach 50,000ft (15,200m).

Three years later, on 10 June 1953, it suffered damage while making an asymmetric landing following an engine failure. Repairs were entrusted to Boulton Paul, who grafted on a B(I).8 front fuselage (a mark and role not thought of when VN828 first flew), with a modified nose to take AI.Mk.18 radar. It returned to the RRE to resume test flying on 17 January 1956, which it continued until undergoing another conversion. This entailed the aircraft having a B.2 front fuselage installed, with a modified nose-cone, to become the test vehicle for the T.Mk.11 radar trainer, eight of which were later operated by No.228 Operational Conversion Unit (OCU), Leuchars, for the Night-Fighter School for Javelin conversion.

VN828's last flight is recorded as having taken place on 14 December 1961, after which the front fuselage was transferred to WJ643, the long-serving B.2 operated by the Ferranti Flying Unit (FFU) at Turnhouse.

The Fourth Prototype

The last of the four B.1-standard prototypes, VN850, was also first flown in 1949, Beamont taking it up from Samlesbury on 20 December. This was the last to retain the dorsal fin fillet and the first in which fuel lines were incorporated for the carrying of tip tanks. A full trials programme was started on 11 May 1950 to investigate the aircraft's handling with a 250 gallon (1,135 litre) drop tank fitted under each wing-tip. This culminated in the successful jettisoning of both tanks on 31 July. A spot of light-heartedness was introduced into this operation – both tanks, jettisoned over Warton, landed spot on the triangle of grass within the three tarmac runways.

The tip-tank trials were interrupted on 11 June 1950. Beamont was required to introduce the aircraft, together with his style of display flying, to the gathered thousands at the Paris Air Show, at Orly. The flight from Warton to Orly took only 54 minutes, pointing towards the succession of official records that the type would achieve over the next eight years. Two weeks later, on 24 and 25 June, the Belgian Air Display at Antwerp was treated to a similar exhibition of flying, which was unanimously acclaimed as outstanding for any aircraft, and extraordinary for a bomber. Beamont flew VN850 back from Antwerp to Warton in 48 minutes on 26 June and, four days later, on 30 June, the aircraft flew 1,600 miles (2,560km), at

between 42,000 and 47,000 ft (12,800 and 14,300m), in three hours.

During 1950, the fourth prototype took over the mantle as Canberra display aircraft. It appeared at the RAF Display at Farnborough between 4 and 10 July, did a demonstration before an American mission at Boscombe Down and, finally, contributed to the year's SBAC Display at Farnborough. 'Bee' had a busy Farnborough, not only piloting VN850, but also VX165, the prototype B.2 built to Specification B.5/47, which had first flown on 21 April that year. This was the first three-seater, the first with a glazed nose and the first fitted with tip tanks from day one.

VN850 went to Rolls-Royce at Hucknall for Avon development flying on 6 October

The Quartet, photographed early in 1950. VN799 is at the back, with VN828, the third prototype, alongside. VN813, the second prototype, shows the bulged nacelles required for the Nene engines, while VN850, the fourth prototype, stands in the foreground. VN828 was the first to have the dorsal fin fillet removed, yet VN850, which had its maiden flight a month later, retained its fillet. Author's collection

Showing off its new name, WD929 stands on the tarmac at Biggin Hill on 19 January 1951. It finished as a U.10 drone which crashed at Woomera on 15 October 1959. Author's collection

1950, but the test programme was short-lived. With R-R test pilot R.B. Leach at the controls, the aircraft suffered an engine fire while approaching Hucknall for a landing on 13 June 1951. It crashed at Bulwell Common, outside Hucknall's perimeter, killing Leach. It was the first Canberra to be lost.

Continuing Trials

Meanwhile, the first prototype VN799 was being kept busy. From the A&AEE trials, the aircraft resumed English Electric's flight-test programme at Warton. Later, at RAE Farnborough, trials were conducted with the Mk.IX autopilot, after which the Type 'D' autopilot was evaluated with the aircraft operating at the Armament and Instrument Experimental Unit (AIEU), Martlesham Heath, Suffolk. In 1953, VN799 was at the Blind Landing Experimental Unit (BLEU), based at Martlesham Heath, and operating from Woodbridge. On 18 August, it suffered complete engine failure, while flying at 300ft (90m) on the approach to Woodbridge and crashed near Sutton Heath, just short of the base.

While the prototype trials programmes were progressing and, with contracts received for the aircraft to go into production, the question of a name for the A.1 had loomed large. The British practice of naming bombers after cities, begun in 1939 with the Short Stirling, was to be followed, but the name 'Canberra' rather flies

in the face of convention. Its choice has been the subject of various theories, ranging from English Electric's desire for the Royal Australian Air Force to adopt the aircraft, to the company's Chairman and Managing Director, Sir George Nelson, selecting the name. He had a fervent belief in the British Commonwealth, and apparently wanted Australia to feel associated with the United Kingdom, despite being geographically separated by over 11,000 miles. Whatever the true reason, 'Canberra' was chosen and, on 19 January 1951, the Prime Minister of Australia, Mr R.G. Menzies, attended an official naming ceremony at Biggin Hill in Kent, performed with WD929, the first production B.2.

At about the same time, there was a political upheaval within English Electric, which fortunately did not affect the Canberra programme, despite original misgivings. Relations between the engineering base at Strand Road, Preston, and the design organization at Warton had deteriorated during 1949. By the beginning of the following year, Teddy Petter had let it be known that he wanted Warton, complete with his experimental engineering department, to be an entirely separate administration, under his control, without any managerial links with Preston. He felt that the Strand Road works, although more experienced in production, did not comprehend the designer's philosophy. As far as he was concerned, the A.1's success, together with the design team's on-going P.1 plans, was

enough proof of his team's ability. Feeling sure of his case, Petter put himself on the line by laying down the condition that, if his demands were not met, he would depart.

Sir George Nelson tried hard to pacify his Chief Engineer, knowing that Petter's ambitions were anathema to Strand Road, but he did not want to lose one of the country's leading aircraft designers. Due to the retrenched attitudes on both sides, the well-established principle of compromise could not be introduced. Petter had virtually divorced himself from Warton's activities by the end of 1949, so that F.W. 'Freddy' Page had been entrusted with the routine management of the department. By March 1950, Nelson knew there was an impasse and reluctantly accepted Petter's resignation. Freddy Page was elevated to the vacant Chief Engineer post, but the MoS was rather alarmed at the situation. This was enhanced by the fact that Petter's team had been closely interrelated, and that their ex-chief's move to the new position of supremo at Folland Aircraft in Hamble was accompanied by his declaration that members of the Warton team who wished to join him would be most welcome.

A few did follow Petter to Hamble, but Page was a strong character and he had one of the leading design teams in the country under his management. It handled the Canberra's development and the P.1/Lightning from evolution to production with consummate professionalism, and thrived for well over a decade.

CHAPTER FOUR

Bomber Command Goes Propless

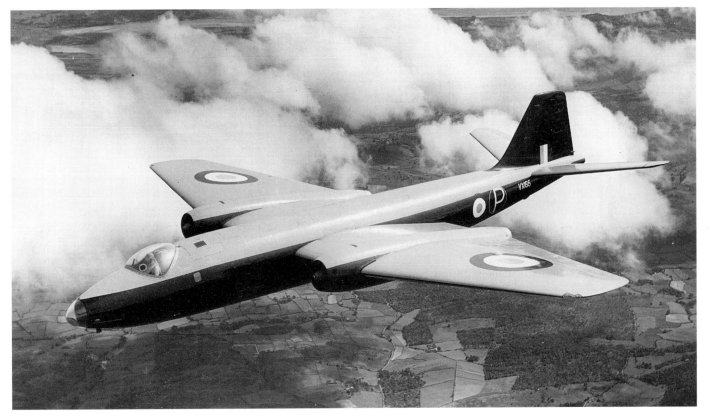

VX165, the first production Canberra B.2, had a photocall soon after its first flight on 21 April 1950, before the production rudder had been fitted. Author's collection

English Electric had received contracts for the production of the Canberra, with the B.2 scheduled as Bomber Command's first turbojet-powered bomber. Shortly afterwards, the fact that the post-Second World War run-down of the RAF had reduced it to a parlous state was brought sharply into focus when North Korea invaded South Korea on 25 June 1950. The world was forced to face the prospect of another conflict.

Specification B.5/47

The original order for the five prototypes to cover the production bomber and photographic reconnaissance variants, placed in 1948, had been reduced to three. Two bomber prototypes, VX165 and VX169, were built to Specification B.5/47, the first making its maiden flight on 23 April 1950. Cockpit accommodation had been modified to cater for the bomb-aimer third crew member, sited beside the navigator and all equipped with ejection seats. The glazed nose contained a T2 optical bombsight, which the bomb-aimer operated from a prone position after vacating his Martin-Baker ejector seat.

The second prototype, VX169, first flown on 2 August 1950, was identical to VX165. Both aircraft were powered by the first production variant of the Rolls-Royce Avon, the RA.3 (Series 101), producing 6,500lb (2,950kg) static thrust.

A concentrated series of trials programmes for both prototypes followed, conducted by Warton and the A&AEE at Boscombe Down. General engineering integrity was evaluated, and handling trials throughout the whole operational flight envelope were carried out. This culminated in the Canberra B.2 being cleared for service in time for No.101 Squadron to accept its first aircraft on 25 May 1951 and begin the replacement of the Lincoln B.2s that they had flown since August 1946. This was WD936, the eighth production aircraft, in which Beamont performed one of his usual exemplary displays before landing at the squadron's Binbrook base in Lincolnshire. The squadron also received an earlier aircraft, WD934, the sixth off

(Top) The first B.2 prototype went to the A&AEE for handling trials in November 1950; by the time the snows came down, English Electric had fitted the final rudder shape and the black had been extended ahead of the canopy. Crown Copyright, DERA Boscombe Down

(Above) No.101 Squadron lines up its B.2s for a press visit. The fifth aircraft from the front is an out-of-sequence aircraft, WP514, built as a replacement for WD929, which had been diverted off contract and flown to Australia as A84-307. Author's collection

the line, among its allocation of aircraft during the year. All were up to full B.2 production standard, with canopy rear 'collar' fairings and the small increased area visible at the rear of the rudder tip.

Avro, Handley Page and Short Brothers

The increase in international tension, coupled with the near-obsolescence of Bomber Command's aircraft, which had suddenly become apparent, concentrated Ministry minds. It was recognized that English Electric on its own could not produce enough Canberras to re-equip squadrons quickly enough. Consequently contracts were issued to Avro, Handley Page and Short Brothers to produce airframes. A.V. Roe & Co. Ltd at Woodford received Contract No.6/ACFT/5990/CB6(b) on 10 November 1950, covering the production of a hundred B.2s, which was later reduced to seventy-five. The serial numbers allocated to these aircraft were WJ971 to WJ995,

WK102 to WK146 and WK161 to WK165 inclusive.

Handley Page Ltd at Radlett had received a similar order – Contract No.6/ACFT/5943/CB6(b) – a month earlier, which also called for a hundred B.2s; like Avro's, this contract was also reduced to seventy-five. Serial numbers for this order were WJ564 to WJ582, WJ603 to WJ649 and WJ674 to WJ682 inclusive. These were the only Canberra contracts finalized by the two companies. Each received a contract for fifty B.2s in March 1951, but both were cancelled before construction started.

Short Brothers & Harland Ltd at Belfast became much more involved with the Canberra over the years. Their first order, for sixty B.2s, was a part-order within Contract No.6/ACFT/5790/CB6(b), dated 20

Bomber Command, 25 May 1951

When Roland Beamont landed WD936 at Binbrook, and No.101 Squadron became the premier jet-propelled bomber unit, it was a monumental leap in terms of performance, compared with Bomber Command's existing aircraft.

Avro 694 Lincoln B.2
Sixteen squadrons, Nos 7, 9, 12, 49, 50 (in the process of being disbanded), 58, 61, 83, 97, 100, 101, 138, 148, 199, 214 and 617 were all equipped with Lincoln B.2s. This was in reality just an improved Lancaster, designed to Specification B.14/43 for operations in the Pacific theatre, of which a total of 366 were produced for the RAF. While giving a 1,200-mile (1,920-km) improvement in maximum range over the Lancaster, it still trundled along at less than 300mph (480km/h) and could not operate above 22,000ft (6,700m).

Dimensions:	Span 120ft 0in (36.57m); length 79ft 3.5in (24.15m); wing area 1,421sq ft (132sq m)
Powerplants:	Four 1,750hp Packard Merlin 68, 68A or 300 inline engines
Weights:	Empty 44,148lb (20,021kg); loaded 82,000lb (37,187kg)
Performance:	Maximum speed 295mph (474.74km/h) Cruising speed 238mph (383km/h) Service ceiling 22,000ft (6,705.6m) Maximum range 3,750 miles (6,000km) Maximum bomb load 14,000lb (6,349kg) for 2,640 miles (4,225km)

Avro 694 Lincoln B.2, RF385, of No.57 Squadron at East Kirkby, in the black/white finish of Tiger Force aircraft destined for the war against Japan. The surrender came before the aircraft began operations. Philip Jarrett

Boeing Model 345 B-29 Washington
In order to boost the Command's abilities, via the auspices of the United States Military Aid Programme, the first of seventy second-hand B-29 Superfortresses arrived in the UK on 22 March 1950. Known in RAF service as the Washington B.1, by 25 May 1951 B-29s equipped Nos 15, 35 (the Washington Conversion Unit), 44, 57, 90, 115, 149 and 192 Squadrons. Being fully pressurized, it offered considerable improvements in creature comforts for the aircrew, compared to the Lincoln, but was still a 1940-designed aeroplane.

Dimensions:	Span 141ft 3in (43m); length 99ft 0in (30.17m); wing area 1,736sq ft (161.27sq m)
Powerplants:	Four Wright Cyclone R-3350-23 radial engines
Weights:	Empty 74,500lb (33,559kg); loaded 120,000lb (54,420kg)
Performance:	Maximum speed 357mph (574.5km/h) Cruising speed 342mph (550.3km/h) Service ceiling 33,600ft (10,241m) Maximum range 3,250 miles (5,230.22km) Maximum bomb load 20,000lb (9,072kg) for 1,000 miles (1,609km)

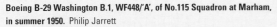

Boeing B-29 Washington B.1, WF448/'A', of No.115 Squadron at Marham, in summer 1950. Philip Jarrett

Bomber Command, 25 May 1951 (continued)

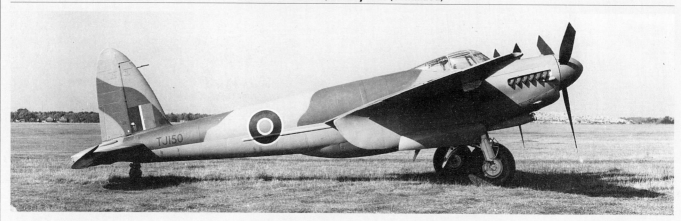

De Havilland DH.98 Mosquito B.35, TJ150, photographed on 15 October 1945, awaiting collection for squadron allocation. Philip Jarrett

De Havilland DH98 Mosquito B.35
Closer to the Canberra in terms of performance, but also an updated World War II design, the Mosquito B.35 was in service with Nos 109 and 139 Squadrons at RAF Hemswell in Lincolnshire. The two squadrons had operated various variants of the Mosquito for the past nine years.

Dimensions: Span 54ft 2in (16.50m); length 40ft 6in (12.34m); wing area 435sq ft (40.41sq m)

Powerplants: Two 1,690hp Rolls-Royce Merlin 113 and 114 inline engines

Weights: Empty 14,635lb (6,636.9kg); loaded 23,000lb (10,430.5kg)

Performance: Maximum speed 415mph (667.85km/h)
                Cruising speed 276mph (444.16km/h)
                Service ceiling 42,000ft (12,801.6m)
                Maximum range 1,955 miles (3,146.18km)
                Maximum bomb load 5,000lb (2,267kg) for 1,485 miles (2,389km)

English Electric A.1 Canberra B.2
The specification for the first production mark of Canberra, as delivered to No.101 Squadron at Binbrook, which initially did not carry wing-tip tanks, was as follows.

Dimensions: Span 64ft 0in (19.50m); length 65ft 6in (19.96m); wing area 960sq ft (89.18sq m)

Powerplants: Two Rolls-Royce RA.3 (Series 101) turbojets each producing 6,500lb (2,950kg) thrust

Weights: Empty 22,200lb (10,067.7kg); loaded 46,000lb (20,090kg)

Performance: Maximum speed 570mph (917.30km/h) at high altitude, 518mph (833.61km/h) at sea level
                Service ceiling 48,000ft (14,630.4m)
                Maximum range 2,660 miles (4,280.73km)
                Maximum bomb load 6,000lb (2,725kg) for 1,105 miles (1,778km)

Final assembly of Canberras at Belfast was shared with Sunderland production. Author's collection

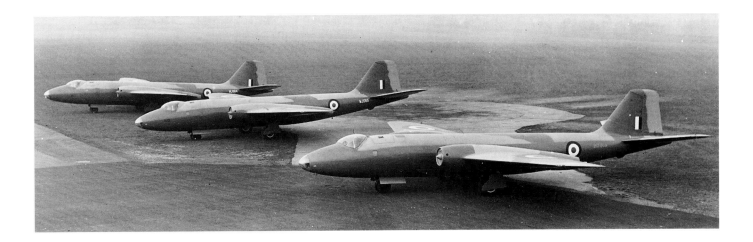

September 1950. The aircraft in this order received serials WH853 to WH887, WH902 to WH925 and WH944. (For details on orders for later Canberra variants placed with the company, *see* chapters covering the respective marks.)

Canberra Bases

Binbrook Jet Conversion Flight (JCF)

Prior to No.101 Squadron receiving its first Canberra, Binbrook set up a special unit, the Jet Conversion Flight (JCF), to wean pilots from the Lincoln on to the jet-propelled aircraft. The Canberra T.4 trainer had been contracted, but it was a couple of

Handley Page's first three B.2s, WJ564, WJ565 and, in the foreground and not yet painted, WJ566, in March 1953. WJ565 was later converted to T.17 standard, while WJ566 became a T.4, after serving with No.44 Squadron. Author's collection

years away from entering service. The B.2 was a single-pilot aircraft, so a pair of Meteor F.4s, VT142 and VT179, arrived in January 1951 for initial jet-handling training. In July, two Meteor T.7s joined the JCF and, with Canberra B.2 WD951 also in the Flight, conversion to jet flying was found to be less arduous than had been anticipated. The only real Canberra mishap at Binbrook during the whole year was a wheels-

up landing in July by WD938, after running out of fuel.

The JCF, a semi-autonomous unit supervised by No.101 Squadron, remained at the base when, in January 1952, the neighbouring Lincoln-operating No.617 Squadron took over the Flight's administration to coincide with the arrival of its first Canberra, WD961.

By August 1952, Binbrook, on top of the Lincolnshire Wolds, had become the first all-Canberra base. This fact generated

Binbrook's Jet Conversion Flight drawn up for inspection on a windy day in January 1951. Author's collection

a significant amount of attention from the media, assorted Government departments and visiting military parties. No doubt the abundance of bovine excreta these visits usually generate did not go down too well with the lower ranks! After Nos 101 and 617, the other three units sharing the base started replacing their Lincolns – No.12 Squadron in March, No.9 Squadron in May and No.50 Squadron in August.

When No.101 Squadron entered the Command's annual *Bullseye* exercise, the ineffectiveness of the Meteor as an interceptor in the new jet-bomber era had to be pandered to. An order was issued for Canberra formations to fly on a straight course limited to 42,000ft (12,800m), in order to give the fighter pilots some interception practice.

Coningsby

About twenty-five miles south of Binbrook, Washington B.1s had been operated at Coningsby by Nos 15, 44, 57 and 149 Squadrons for the past two years. In March 1953, Canberra B.2s began to be accepted by three of the squadrons, while No.57 Squadron had to wait two months before receiving its first, in May. On 28 October of the same year, No.40 Squadron, a former Avro York operator with Transport Command before disbanding in March 1950, was re-formed at Coningsby as the base's fifth jet-bomber squadron. Its first Canberra arrived the same day.

Scampton

During Coningsby's re-equipping, another Lincolnshire station steeped in Bomber Command history was going through the same procedure. This was RAF Scampton, which had hosted No.230 OCU, training Lincoln crews, since February 1949, together with the US 3930th Air Base Squadron, plus a small US Navy detachment operating a handful of WV-2 Constellations and PB-1 Fortresses. No.10 Squadron had been disbanded at Oakington on 20 February 1950, after flying Dakotas for two years. During the Second World War it had been a bomber squadron and it resumed the role on 15 January 1953 when it re-formed at Scampton to take delivery of its first Canberra B.2.

During the same year, three other squadrons were re-formed at the base. No.27 Squadron on 15 June and No.18 Squadron were re-formed on 1 August; both had been flying Dakotas when disbanded in 1950. No.21 Squadron, which had been a Mosquito B.VI operator when disbanded at Gütersloh in November 1947, became Scampton's fourth Canberra B.2 unit on 21 September.

Marham

Marham in Norfolk had been synonymous with the B-29 since the USAF 97th Bomb Group first arrived in June 1947 with the type, together with its successor, the Boeing B-50. The Group's departure, early in 1950, was followed by the landing of the first B-29 Washington B.1 in April, which heralded the establishment of the Washington Conversion Unit (WCU). In the course of the next three and a half years, seven Washington squadrons operated from Marham for varying periods. In November 1953, No.90 Squadron accepted its first Canberra B.2 and, by March 1954, the last Washington had returned to the United States.

With the base scheduled to operate a total of four Canberra units, February 1954 saw No.115 Squadron start re-equipping and, in March, No.207 Squadron followed suit. In April, No.35 Squadron was born of the old WCU.

The Radio Warfare Establishment (RWE) at Watton in Norfolk hosted No.192 Squadron, which retained a few Washingtons, flying alongside Canberra B.2s, which started to arrive in January 1953, until February 1958.

By spring 1954, just three years after WD936 had first landed at Binbrook, Bomber Command had no less than sixteen Canberra B.2 squadrons established, plus the mixed squadron at the RWE.

When No.10 Squadron rehearsed for the Coronation Review in 1953, the interim Medium Sea Grey/Light Sea Grey finish, with PRU Blue side and underside, was being introduced. *Aeroplane*

Operational Conversion Unit (OCU)

Bassingbourn

The production of Canberras coming from Preston, Belfast, Radlett and Woodford ensured that, as each squadron was formed, it was not long in receiving its full complement of aircraft. The conversion of crews had to match this rate of production and, on 1 December 1951, No.231 Operational Conversion Unit (OCU) was formed at Bassingbourn in Cambridgeshire. The original miscellany of Mosquito T.3s and PR.34s was augmented by Meteor T.7s, plus a few PR.10s, until February 1952, when the first Canberra B.2 arrived.

No.1 course, consisting of five crews, began on 27 May and passed out three months later, on 26 August. Marham had been synonymous with the B-29 in the early 1950s, and Bassingbourn was to become equally closely associated with the Canberra. However, whereas the story of Marham and the B-29 lasted only five and a half years, No.231's association with English Electric's bomber lasted seventeen years. It became an entirely self-supporting Canberra unit, with its own engineering facilities. It was divided into three squadrons; 'A' and 'B' handled light-bomber crew conversions, while 'C' Squadron was orientated towards the photographic-reconnaissance role, for which it had four Canberra PR.3s.

Preston had received Contract No.6/ACFT/2000/CB6(b) in 1948 for a PR prototype, VX181, which first flew on 19 March 1951. The subsequent order for twenty-seven production aircraft was covered by a part of Contract No.6/ACFT/3520/CB6(b) with the first production example of the variant flying on 31 July 1952.

All three crew members – pilot, radar-navigator and plotter-navigator – were trained at Bassingbourn and, on average, a new course started every four weeks. Whereas the Mosquitoes were gradually phased out, the Meteors continued to provide dual training until the first Canberra T.4 joined the unit, in August 1953. English Electric had received Contract No.6/ACFT/5786/CB6(b) on 20 September 1950, covering various numbers of different marks, including twelve Canberra T.4s. The one prototype, to Specification T.2/49, was the subject of Contract No.6/ACFT/6265/CB6(b) issued on 2 February 1951 and 'Bee' took it, WN467, for a

first flight on 12 June 1952, from Samlesbury. Beamont flew the aircraft at the 1952 SBAC Display, giving one of his characteristic routines, which certainly belied its designed operating theatre – high altitude! Following trials at the A&AEE, the aircraft went to Bassingbourn in June 1953, before joining the Station Flights of various other Canberra units, to give them experience of the dual-control variant.

The first production T.4, WE188, had its maiden flight on 30 October 1952 and, of the eight trainers in the first order, six served with No.231 OCU at various times. There was an obvious benefit in the T.4 being dual-controlled, but by no stretch of the imagination could the aircraft be described as a roomy trainer. The specification had insisted on as few cockpit instrument and control changes as possible from the standard B.2; the pupil pilot occupied the bomber pilot's station on the port side, while the instructor was seated in the additional starboard-side seat. The navigator's position was retained

A goodwill mission and training flight was made by No.12 Squadron to Central and South America during 1952. They went to Venezuela *(left)*, with their Hastings carrying the ground crews, before landing at St Eval in Cornwall on their return *(below)*. Author's collection

Handley Page-built WH856 served with No.44 Squadron and Honington's Station Flight as a bomber, before being converted to TT.18 standard. Author's collection

VX181, the prototype PR.3, undergoes handling trials with the A&AEE, in autumn 1951.
Crown Copyright, DERA Boscombe Down

so, with entry to the aircraft being via the lift-up door on the starboard side, the instructor's seat was mounted on a sliding swivel. The seat was pushed forward to allow access into the navigator's station, then the pupil pilot would take up his position, and the movable seat would be slid back and locked as the instructor installed himself. In view of the complicated entry, it was fortunate that all three occupants sat in ejection seats, ensuring that an emergency exit was a simpler operation.

In the mid-1950s, No.231 OCU formed its own display team, flying a four-aircraft formation routine that would not disgrace a fighter-equipped unit, especially with its 'bomb-burst' finale. At the Coventry Air Pageant at Baginton on 21 July 1956, T.4s WH584, WH843, WH844 and WT485 were the participating aircraft.

Losses in Training

A number of B.2s had been lost in training due to a runaway tailplane; at one time, the service had advocated the grounding of all Canberras because of this. The problem was traced to the mechanical sticking-on of the single-pole switch in the trimming circuit. All Canberras were fitted with a new dipole trim

WN467, the prototype T.4, first flew on 12 June 1952, after which it had Boscombe Down handling trials and went to No.231 OCU. Author's collection

(Above) T.4, WE193, of No.231 OCU, stands at No.5 MU Kemble, in a new light grey colour scheme, with red day-glo strips on the fin, awaiting an air test after overhaul. The aircraft was sold to India, as Q1791, in 1975. Ray Deacon

Coventry's Air Pageant, on 21 July 1956, witnessed No.231 OCU's 'bomb-burst' finale to its routine. Author's collection

switch, improved wiring and the revision of the actuator stops, to reduce the overall arc of movement; this cured the problem completely.

Ironically, the introduction of the dual-control Canberra brought about an increase in the number of fatal accidents. With the T.4, accidents were increasingly occurring soon after take-off or 'circuit-and-bumps', at night or in adverse visibility. An extensive examination of the problem came down in favour of pupil-pilot error. Pupils were experiencing a rate of horizontal acceleration that was much greater than that with which they were familiar. The artificial horizon was being misread in terms of the nose-up angle so that, thinking he was exceeding the recommended angle of climb after take-off, the pupil would correct by increasing the nose-down attitude and would fly into the ground, often shortly after clearing the airfield perimeter.

English Electric issued a recommendation that all instructors should be made aware of this situation. It was exacerbated by the fact that type conversion had been easier than expected, which meant that pupils were often undertaking their first night flights with little daytime flying experience. The situation was remedied by a change in the training curriculum, whereby the pupil pilot was made aware of the possibility of instrument misreading and the procedures required to rectify any consequential flying error that had been made. The effect was a dramatic reduction in the accident rate.

Continued Training

The Bassingbourn-based Conversion Unit continued to supply operational Canberra crews for eighteen years and the courses were not affected when it moved to Cottesmore in May 1969. Another move came in February 1976, as Cottesmore was placed on Care and Maintenance, and No.231 OCU took its Canberras to Marham, staying there until July 1982, when its penultimate relocation involved a move to RAF Wyton in Cambridgeshire. Eleven years later, in December 1993, following the Ministry's policy of centralizing Canberra operations, Marham once again became associated with the type and the OCU now operates with No.39 (1PRU) Squadron, the RAF's most recent Canberra unit.

As well as training most RAF Canberra crews in the many various roles in which the aircraft was operated, the unit trained crews for all the overseas customers purchasing the type. It also trained Commonwealth and USAF crews, who became instructors on their return to their respective air forces. Other operators in the UK that passed through the OCU included the Royal Navy, its Fleet Requirements and Air Direction Unit (FRADU), and many of the trials establishments that employed Canberras for over forty-five years. Almost every Canberra-operating squadron kept at least one T.4 on strength for continuation training and pilot check flights. Specialized radar-target trainers were produced by the conversion of bomber and PR airframes (see Chapter 11).

More Squadrons Convert

Four Mosquito squadrons moved into the jet era between August 1952 and December 1953. Nos 109 and 139 Squadrons

Serving Canberra T.4s

Many RAF bases operated a Canberra T.4 as the Station Flight aircraft. These were often interchanged between units on an unrecorded or friendly basis, but the following aircraft are confirmed as having served with the base shown.

Unit	Aircraft
Akrotiri	WJ872
Binbrook	WJ860
Brüggen	WH842
Coningsby	WH849
Cottesmore	WJ863
Gaydon	WJ864
Geilenkirchen	WH843
Gütersloh	WJ868
Hemswell	WJ877
Honington	WH850
Laarbruch	WH840
Marham	WH848
Scampton	WJ859
Upwood	WJ862
Waddington	WJ876
Weston Zoyland	WJ861
Wildenrath	WH841
Wittering	WJ857
Wyton	WE194

Other RAF and Royal Navy units confirmed as having a Canberra T.4 on charge at some time.

CFE (Target Facility Squadron)	WJ617
(Type Flight)	WT480
MEAF (Instrument Training Flight)	WJ872
Hurn (FRADU)	WJ866
Yeovilton (FRADTU)	WK142

Taxiing at Khormaksar, T.4, WJ872/'A', flew as an Akrotiri Station Flight aircraft, before joining the unit's Instrument Training Flight. Ray Deacon

Little Rissington's Central Flying School held three T.4s for pilot flight-type approval rating, one of which, WT480/'CC', taxies in on a dull autumnal day in 1960. Ray Deacon

At Honington, No.10 Squadron's B.2, WH646, displays its red 'speedbird' as it tucks its undercarriage away.
Author's collection

arrived at Hemswell in Lincolnshire on 31 March 1950, together with their Mosquito B.35s. In August 1952, Canberra B.2s started re-equipping No.109 Squadron; in November, No.139 Squadron followed suit. Production Canberra PR.3s had been coming off English Electric's lines since July 1952 and, in December, No.540 Squadron at Benson added PR.3s to their complement of Mosquito PR.34As. The last de Havilland aircraft left in September 1953, after the squadron had moved to Wyton six months earlier, on 26 March. A small number of Canberra B.2s also joined the unit in June 1953 and the squadron remained all-Canberra until disbanding at Wyton on 31 March 1956.

No.58 Squadron had been at Wyton with Mosquito PR.34As and PR.35s since 31 March 1953. Canberra PR.3s started arriving in December 1953 and this, too, became an exclusively Canberra squadron for the sixteen years up to its disbanding on 30 September 1970. Wyton was also host to No.82 Squadron, which had operated really vintage aeroplanes. Formed at Benson on 1 October 1946 with Lancaster PR.1s, it spent the next six years carrying out a photographic survey of East and West Africa, before returning to Benson on 30 October 1952. Five months later, the squadron moved to Wyton and, in November, started receiving Canberra PR.3s. What a culture shock that must have been!

Squadrons that had been disbanded in the mid-1940s started to be re-formed and to become Canberra units. On 9 December 1953, No.76 Squadron, which had flown Halifaxes during the war, re-formed at Wittering and received Canberra B.2s. Five more B.2 operators were formed during 1954, the first being No.199 Squadron at Hemswell, which received the jet-bomber in July and used it alongside Lincoln B.2s until September 1957. No.61 Squadron had operated Lincoln B.2s at Waddington for seven years before moving to Wittering on 6 August 1953. Exactly twelve months later, the squadron gave up its Avros for Canberra B.2s. No.100 Squadron had a very similar history, having taken its Lincolns from Waddington to Wittering four days earlier, but it took delivery of its first Canberra in April 1954.

During the last three months of the year, both No.102 Squadron (in October) and No.103 Squadron (in November), were re-formed at Gütersloh in Germany; the fact that there was a shortage of suitable airfields to handle the increasing number of

Three B.2s of No.9 Squadron fly a low-level formation, with the nearest aircraft slightly overshooting and having to deploy its airbrakes. *Aeroplane*

Canberras coming into service in the UK was becoming very evident. In December, No.527 Squadron added Canberra B.2s to its mixed collection of Meteor NF.11s and NF.14s, together with several Vickers Varsity T.1s that had been used at Watton. The squadron had been formed out of 'R' Calibration Squadron of Watton's Central Signals Establishment (CSE), on 1 August 1952. Its purpose – to calibrate Control and Reporting (C&R) stations throughout the service – was performed by the unit's aircraft operating along established tracks while ground navigation and radar equipment

were checked against the aircraft's course; any necessary frequency changes were incorporated. These operations entailed much use of the squadron's aircraft, which notched up quite high airframe hours. The unit was disbanded as No.527 Squadron on 21 August 1958 and renumbered No.245 Squadron, although it did stay at Watton. By this time it was an all-Canberra B.2 unit and remained as such until it was disbanded again, on 19 April 1963, to be redesignated as No.98 Squadron, still holding its B.2s. In this form, the squadron reappears later in the Canberra story.

CHAPTER FIVE

A Matter of Record

By the end of 1954, the Canberra had 'troubled the scorer' – in this case, the *Fédération Aéronautique Internationale* (FAI) – no less than fifteen times, attaining fifteen officially recognized records. (Two earlier records had also been established but, since FAI observers had not been present, they remain unofficial.) The quantum leap in speed and general performance represented by the Canberra, compared with current long-distance aircraft, convinced the makers and the RAF that there was good publicity to be had.

Unofficial Records

United States Air Force interest in the aircraft was started in 1950, when an evaluation team came to the UK in August. (For the full story of the results of this visit, *see* Chapter 12.) A production Canberra was flown to the USA in February 1951, to open the aircraft's account in terms of record-breaking; this particular record was unofficial, with no FAI observers present. WD932, the fourth production B.2, was placed on a six-month loan to the USAF, with effect from 20 February, so that they might fully evaluate the aircraft for its envisaged roles. The following day, an RAF crew, comprising pilot Sqn Ldr A.E. Callard, navigators Flt Lt Haskett and Flt Lt Robson, took off from RAF Aldergrove, adjacent to Lough Neagh in Northern Ireland. Landing at Gander in Newfoundland 4 hours 37 minutes later, they had made the first non-stop, non-refuelled crossing of the Atlantic Ocean by a jet aircraft. Furthermore, their average speed of just under 450mph (720km/h) was, at the time, the fastest-ever Atlantic crossing by a good margin but had to remain unofficial.

Also unofficial was the record set on the first Canberra flight to Australia. The Royal Australian Air Force (RAAF) purchased WD939, to become the 'pattern' aircraft to form the basis of Canberra production in Australia. It was given the

RAAF serial A84-307 and took off on 1 August 1951 from Lyneham in Wiltshire for Darwin, in the hands of an RAAF crew comprising pilot Wg Cdr Cumming and navigator Flt Lt Harvey. The total of 10,235 miles (16,487km) was covered in a flying time of 21 hours 41 minutes, giving an average speed for the flight of 477.62mph (768.63km/h). Stops were made at Tobruk, Habbaniya, Karachi,

Ceylon and Singapore, with the longest leg, from Singapore to Darwin, a distance of 1,810 miles (2,912.8km), being flown in 4 hours 29 minutes at an average speed of 402.22mph (647.26km/h). The fastest leg was the 1,090 miles (1,754km) from Tobruk to Habbaniya, which was covered in 2 hours 13 minutes, at an average speed of 486mph (782km/h). Again, no FAI observers were present.

The fourth production B.2, WD932, is presented to the USA, Beamont style.
Author's collection

Martin's Senior Vice President, Chet Pearson, greets Chief Test Pilot 'Bee' Beamont, after the display. Via R.P. Beamont

Official Recognition

These early flights indicated exactly what the Canberra could achieve, but still nothing was recorded. On 23 March 1951, a contract between English Electric and the Glenn L. Martin Company in Baltimore, USA, was ratified. The American company would manufacture Canberras under licence, a 'pattern' aircraft would be delivered, and this time FAI observers would be in attendance! The aircraft selected was WD940, the twelfth production B.2, which would be flown by the English Electric crew of 'Bee' Beamont, pilot, plus navigator D.A. Watson and radio operator R.H.T. Rylands. On 31 August 1951, WD940 was flagged off from Aldergrove by representatives of the Royal Aero Club, and, 4 hours 18 minutes later, 'Bee' touched down at Gander. The 2,072 miles (1,293.5km) had been covered at an average speed of 481.12mph (744.26km/h). This time, the flight, which sliced over two hours off the former east–west

Canberra B.2, WD940, having crossed the Atlantic in record time, is taken over by the Glenn L. Martin Company as the second 'pattern' aircraft and becomes B-57, 51-17352. The grey overspraying on the top wing surface still shows where the RAF roundels were positioned. Author's collection

VX185, having started as the second PR.3, becomes the prototype Canberra B.5 for its official photocall, in July 1951. Author's collection

(Below) **From left to right: navigator Dennis Watson, 'Bee' Beamont and the return-leg pilot, Peter Hillwood, stand ready for the Double Atlantic crossing.** Via R.P. Beamont

Atlantic crossing, was recognized in elegant script on a FAI *Diplôme de Record*.

WD940's flight from Gander to the Martin complex at Middle River in Baltimore was not without incident. While flying in the vicinity of the US radar and air-traffic reporting centre at Bangor, Maine, Beamont received an R/T message, requiring him to state his altitude. He replied that this was 'classified information', adding that he was 'well above any airways traffic'. The military ATC was adamant that this was a demand. At this stage, 'Bee' spotted vapour trails well below him, in the Cape Cod area, and realized that USAF exercises may have been in progress. Having verified the state of his fuel and the distance from Middle River with navigator Watson, Beamont climbed to 50,000ft (15,200m) over New York and the rest of the flight passed without further ATC requests.

At a meeting with the USAF Senior Officers Board the next day, English Electric's Chief Test Pilot regaled the assembly with descriptions of the Canberra's potential. He was then quizzed about his previous day's retorts to their ATC, and was directly asked at what altitude he was operating when over-flying New York. When he replied '50,000ft', they showed some surprise. When he explained about British radio security, he was politely informed that ATC had required height information 'for safety separation'. Beamont replied that he fully understood, but that 'there weren't going to be any other aircraft up there, were there?'!

In 1952, four Canberra records were officially recognized. The first was flown on 18 February. Production B.2 WD962 had been loaned to the Royal Aircraft Establishment (RAE), in order to conduct a series of ejector-seat trials. The chosen venue for the trials was Castel Benito/Idris, a dozen miles south of Tripoli, and the record attempt from London to Tripoli was flown by Sqn Ldr L.C.E. Devigne and Flt Lt P.A. Hunt. The 1,459.83 miles (2,349.3km), covered in 2 hours 41 minutes 49.5 seconds, was flown at an average speed of 538.12mph (865.99km/h).

Double Atlantic Crossing

On 26 August 1952, the Canberra achieved its best-known record – the first double crossing of the Atlantic Ocean in a single day. On 6 July, VX185 had had its maiden flight at Samlesbury in the hands of Johnny Squier. This aircraft started on English Electric's lines as the second prototype PR.3, but, prior to completion, it had been designated as the prototype for a radar-operated target-marker when the B.3/45 specification was still active. With the instigation of the three-crew visual-aiming requirements, VX185 was completed in this configuration and given the variant title B.5. The aircraft differed from the B.2 in that it had integral leading-edge tanks, supplying an additional 900 gallons (4,095 litres) of fuel and, for the first flight, had been fitted with 6,500lb (2,950kg) static thrust Avon Mk.101 (RA.3) engines. These were replaced by two Avon Mk.109 (RA.7) engines, each giving 7,500lb (3,410kg) thrust and a Dunlop 'Maxaret' anti-skid wheel-braking system. The nose was also recontoured to give a symmetrical bomb-aiming window.

In this new configuration, VX185 made its first flight on 15 July, beginning a very intensive series of long-range proving flights. These were intended to determine the aircraft's range capabilities, together with oil consumption and systems reliability, during ultra-high altitude flights lasting up to five hours. During early tests, problems occurred when flying on the integral wing tanks alone. Fuel waxing was causing engine flame-outs, but a change of fuel drill, where these tanks were used first during the climb, prevented any prolonging of the test programme and the ball was put back in the fuel company's court, with the request that they come up with a solution.

It was tedious for the crews to have to follow the UK coastline for hour after hour; at the M0.72 to M0.80 speeds that they were flying, they sometimes had to 'go round again', in order to achieve the required flight duration. The test team felt that a more realistic evaluation could be made if long-distance straight-line courses could be flown; Gibraltar, Labrador and Newfoundland were all viewed as likely destinations. From these thoughts evolved a serious plan to make the 1,800 miles (2,896.74km) distance to Gander in Newfoundland the target, as it gave adequate fuel reserves for a diversion, if necessary. The east–west crossing made the previous year, together with the westerly nature of the average prevailing winds, gave a crossing time of approximately 4 hours 30 minutes. With the winds behind, the return would take about 3 hours 30 minutes.

Clearly, both legs could be flown during the same twelve-hour period.

As might be expected, there were those who considered this would be an 'unnecessary risk to a valuable prototype', but the more positive won the day and it was soon 'all systems go'. The prospect of a double crossing of the Atlantic within twelve hours got the Royal Aero Club (RAeC) interested in recording such an event. The rules stated that the flight would have to be between capital cities; with tongue firmly in cheek, English Electric suggested that Preston was the capital of the northwest of England, but one more likely route was Belfast to St John's in Newfoundland. However, the runway at St John's was too short for the Canberra, so a compromise had to be worked out. The result was an agreement that the record attempt would take off from Aldergrove, with an over-fly at Gander and continuation to Gander Lake; this route was calculated as being similar in distance to Belfast–St John's. An RAeC observer would be stationed in a boat on Gander Lake, in order to record the arrival, then a smart turn would be made and VX185 would touch down at Gander. There, an English Electric ground-support team would prepare the aircraft for the return leg.

From the company's point of view, the flight was simply a part of the on-going long distance test programme. However, at the news that the attempt would be officially observed, the world's press pricked up its ears and the typewriters began to pound. Even the British Broadcasting Corporation made plans to give an up-to-date information service on the aircraft's progress.

On 21 August, the final proving flight, entailing a 1,200 mile (1,920 km) round trip from Warton via an Atlantic weather ship, Manston airfield in Kent, the Orkney Islands and back to Warton, was made in 3.05 hours. The prospects looked good and the record attempt was given the green light. Captain Beamont would have Peter Hillwood as second pilot, who would fly the return leg, and Dennis Watson, who had been with 'Bee' on WD940's delivery flight to Baltimore, as navigator once more. VX185 was flown to Aldergrove on 25 August and the large press contingent received a briefing from Beamont. Take-off was scheduled for 0630 the next day, 26 August, but frontal systems became active overnight and headwinds in the order of 60–70kt were anticipated at 40,000ft (12,200m).

'Bee' taxied out, made final systems checks and got clearance from the tower. At 0634, VX185 started down Aldergrove's main runway with an all-up-weight of 47,355lb (21,475.49kg), of which a fuel load of 23,672lb (10,735.25kg) included an auxiliary tank in the bomb-bay. During a tight turn over the airfield, the speed was built up to 470.5mph (757.17km/h) and the RAeC timing point was crossed at 0640 hours as Beamont climbed, on course, to 34,000ft (10,400m). He levelled

off before making a further ascent towards the 46,000ft (14,000m) altitude set for the flight. Plans had to be readjusted due to the malfunction of the Loran navigation system and lack of VHF contact with two Atlantic weather ships. Dennis Watson was kept fully occupied until the St John's beacon was picked up on course, on time, enabling Beamont to make his descent to cross the RAeC observer on Gander Lake, at 300ft; 4.34 hours after take-off, VX185 touched down at Gander.

The hospitality planned for the crew was lavish but Beamont remained at the briefing office, clearing the return flight plan. Inevitably, when he was finished and ready for his own breakfast, the aircraft was ready, so he had to climb back on board. Peter Hillwood took the left-hand seat and, at 1319 hours, VX185 took off, heading for Gander Lake. The RAeC timekeeper in his boat was crossed at 588mph (946.26km/h) and the climb was made to 42,000ft (12,800m). This was held until a VHF bearing from

Its record of 26 August 1952 duly acknowledged *(top),* **VX185 was photographed before going back into Warton's shops to be converted to the prototype B(I).8.** Author's collection

The Christchurch Centenary Air Race contestant Canberras, lined up at an under-construction Heathrow. From left to right: A84-201/'5', A84-202/'4', WE139/'3', WE142/'2' and WH773/'1'. Author's collection

Heralded as the Great London to New Zealand Air Race, the event held in October 1953 had originally drawn various RAF entries. These included the Canberra, Valiant and an Avro 698 or Handley Page HP80 (later respectively named Vulcan and Victor) in the speed section, plus a Hastings, a Douglas DC6 and a Vickers Viscount in the handicap section. Plans drawn up by the end of 1952 had hardened to the RAF entry being a Valiant and three Canberra PR.7s, the service seeing the event as providing operational benefits, as well as good publicity. The basic objective was to fly from London to

Christchurch in the shortest possible time, with the onus on the individual entrants to arrange their own routes and refuelling points.

Inevitably, there were various changes of mind and withdrawals, so that, by the cut-off date, RAF participation in the speed section had become one Canberra PR.7, WH773, given the Race No.1 and two Canberra PR.3s, WE142 (No.2) and WE139 (No.3). WH773 was the first production PR.7, which had its maiden flight on 16 August. WE139 was the fifth production PR.3, first flown on 30 January, while WE142 had its maiden flight on 27 March. The RAAF entered two Canberra Mk.20s, the B.2s produced under licence at Fisherman's Bend, Melbourne. These were the first two off the line – A84-201 (Race No.5) and A84-202 (No.4) – the former first flying on 29 May, while A84-202 had its maiden flight on 25 August. Neither had seen squadron service with the RAAF prior to the race.

The RAF entries were formed into a special section of No.540 Squadron based at Wyton. Known as the Air Race Flight, it was commanded by Wg Cdr L.M. Hodges and comprised PR.3s, plus several B.2s, which were employed as crew work-up aircraft. Modifications had to be incorporated in the standard navigation system, to ensure adequate coverage for the whole route. These included a periscope sextant for astro navigation, plus Marconi radio compasses to augment the standard Rebecca ARI5610 and Gee-H ARI5829 systems. Standard PR.3 camera equipment was discarded, additional fuel tanks being installed in the resultant spaces and both wing-tip tanks were made permanent fixtures, without any jettisoning facility. With these modifications, the take-off weight was increased, which, in turn, required the Avon RA.3s to receive attention to extract some additional thrust.

WE139/'3', the fifth production PR.3, with its winning achievement recorded on the nose. Author's collection

Training routines established by Air Race Flight included radio compass flights, as well as numerous astronavigation sorties employing the periscope sextant, in UK airspace. These were followed by flights to the Mediterranean area and proving flights over the entire route, in which the proposed staging posts were established. The final selected route, totalling 12,270 miles (19,746km), was London to Basrah/Shaibah (Iraq) – 2,875 miles (4,625km); Basrah/Shaibah to Colombo (Ceylon, now Sri Lanka) – 2,634 miles (4,215km); Colombo to Cocos Islands – 1,771 miles (2,835km); Cocos Islands to Perth (Australia) – 1,840 miles (2,945km); and Perth to Christchurch – 3,150 miles (5,040km). Service groups were despatched to all the above locations, to prepare to facilitate rapid refuelling. Originally, plans were considered for a quick 'service' for the crews, but the Canberra was not the easiest of aircraft to enter in a hurry – especially the navigator's 'black hole' – so it was agreed that crew members would stay strapped in their Martin-Bakers.

The race was scheduled to be held on 8/9 October; the selected crew captains were Flt Lt R.L.E. Burton (WE139), Flt Lt Furze (WE142) and Wg Cdr L.M. Hodges (WH773), while the two RAAF captains were Wg Cdr Cummings (A84-202) and Sqn Ldr Raw (A84-201). All five crews had trained on long-distance practice flights – some of which were up to thirty hours in duration – so there was no requirement for relief crews.

The outright winner was PR.3 WE139 (No.3), which covered the distance in a total time of 23 hours 51 minutes, averaging 514mph (827km/h) and being airborne for 22 hours 25 minutes. In the course of winning the race over the whole distance, the aircraft also broke the point-to-point record for London to Basrah, covering this distance in 5 hours 11 minutes 5.6 seconds at an average speed of 544.3mph (875.94km/h).

The second aircraft home was RAAF Canberra A84-201, in a total time of 24 hours 31 minutes (flying time 22 hours 27.5 minutes) and WE142 came third in 24 hours 33 minutes (22 hours 31 minutes), after being delayed at Basrah. PR.7 WH773, with the Flight's CO piloting, came fourth, although, having a longer range than the other aircraft, it had been expected to win. Murphy's Law struck and the aircraft was delayed for over twelve hours by generator problems at Perth. However, its superior range enabled it to cut out the Cocos Islands stop and, in so doing, break the point-to-point record for London to Colombo. The 5,509 miles (8,860km) were covered in 10 hours 25 minutes 21.5 seconds at an average speed of 519.5mph (836km/h). Its flying time for the whole race was 22 hours 22 minutes. The second RAAF aircraft, A84-202, was delayed for two days at the Cocos Islands staging post but its flying time was only 22 hours 23.5 minutes.

With three different marks involved, it is interesting that all five Canberras covered the whole course within nine minutes' flying time of each other. All had performed very reliably, as had the Avon engines, and both the RAF and RAAF viewed the whole event as having been a worthwhile exercise.

WE139 went on to serve with No.39 Squadron and, when seen on the Khormaksar Station flight pan in 1962, it had been repainted overall silver, but its 1953 accomplishment was still recorded. The aircraft is currently exhibited at the RAF Museum at Hendon. Ray Deacon

The first production Canberra Mk.20, A84-201, flying in the Christchurch Centenary Air Race as No.5, was the first Australian aircraft to cross the line and was second overall. Author's collection

Aldergrove was obtained, 150 miles (240km) off the Irish coast. Heavy rain at Aldergrove was reported and Hillwood broke through the cloud-base over Lough Neagh 5 miles from touchdown, which was made at 1639 hours, exactly 3 hours 25 minutes 18.13 seconds after crossing Gander Lake.

The round flight had taken 10 hours 3 minutes 29.28 seconds and the FAI ratified this as the record first double crossing of the Atlantic in a day. The aircraft was fully serviceable after the flight and, two hours after arriving at Aldergrove, VX185 was back at Warton where, in the company's typically professional manner, a debriefing was held. It was unanimously agreed that 26 August 1952 had been a good day. A considerable amount of valuable test information had been gathered and the enormous publicity gained, although technically a by-product, could do nothing but good for the company, as well as for the British aircraft industry as a whole. Beamont received a telegram of congratulations from the Queen, but she was not buying aeroplanes and English Electric did not receive a production order for the Canberra Mark 5. VX185 comes back into the Canberra story later, as the prototype for the first real configuration change that was made to the aircraft.

Further Records

A month after the Atlantic double crossing, on 25 September, Air Vice Marshal Dermot Boyle piloted a B.2 on an unofficial flight from the UK to Luqa, Malta, and back, accomplished in 6 hours 5 minutes. Three days later, on 28 September 1952, the FAI were again confirming a Canberra record flight, this time between London airport and Eastleigh airport, Nairobi. The aircraft was WD987, a production B.2 of No.12 Squadron at Binbrook and the crew comprised the squadron's OC Flying, Wg Cdr H.P. Connelly, together with Sqn Ldr D. Clare and Air Chief Marshal Sir Hugh P. Lloyd. The 4,239 mile (6,821.8km) route was flown in 9 hours 55 minutes 16.7 seconds, at an average speed of 427.3mph (687.65km/h).

One year on, 1953 was a vintage record-breaking time for the Canberra. Seven point-to-point achievements and the type's first height record were officially recognized by the FAI. They started on 27/28 January, when VX181, the prototype PR.3, commenced a ferry flight to Australia, where it

was scheduled to partake in experimental flying for the Weapons Research Establishment, the range at Woomera, deep into South Australia. With pilot Flt Lt L.M. Wittington and navigator Flt Lt J.A. Brown, the target was a flight between London and Darwin, a distance of 8,608 miles (13,850km), in less than twenty-four hours. This target was handsomely achieved, the total time of 22 hours 21.8 seconds representing an average speed of 391.2mph (629.55km/h). En route, the official record between London and Mauripur airport, Karachi, was also broken, VX181 covering the 3,921 miles (6,310km) in 8 hours 52 minutes 28.2 seconds at an average speed of 441.8mph (710.98km/h).

A standard Canberra B.2, WH699, had first flown early in February 1953 and it was allocated to the Royal Air Force Flying College (RAFFC) at Manby in Lincolnshire, where it was named Aries IV (taking over from Lincoln RE367 Aries III). At the end of 1953, it established new London to Cape Town and Cape Town to London records. On 17 December, Wg Cdr G.G. Petty was the pilot, with Sqn Ldr T.P. McGarry and J. McDonald-Craig as navigators, covering the 6,009.72 miles (9,671.44km) in 12 hours 21 minutes 3.8 seconds, at an average speed of 486.6mph (783.08km/h). Two days later, on 19 December, Wg Cdr A.H. Humphrey (later Air Chief Marshal Sir Andrew Humphrey) piloted Aries IV, with Sqn Ldrs D. Bower and R.F.B. Powell as navigators, when they flew the Cape Town to London leg in 13 hours 16 minutes 25.2 seconds at an average speed of 452.8mph (728.69km/h).

Bristol Engines at Filton in Gloucestershire had used Canberra B.2 WD952 since 13 December 1951, as a flying testbed for their Olympus 99 engine, and the company saw good PR in breaking the world altitude record. At that time, it stood at 59,446ft (18,119.14m), held by de Havilland's Chief Test Pilot John Cunningham in Vampire F.1 TG278. On 4 May 1953, Bristol's Assistant Chief Test Pilot Wg Cdr W.F. 'Wally' Gibb, with engine observer Joe Piper, took off from Filton, and climbed at 3,000ft/min (915m/min) up to 50,000ft (15,200m). He levelled out and burned off fuel, leaving the pre-calculated 90 gallons (410 litres) considered adequate for the record attempt. He climbed WD952 once more until, at 63,000ft (19,200m), the engines flamed out. Making a slow glide down to 40,000ft (12,200m), Gibb relit the engines and returned to Filton. Later confirmation by the

FAI ratified the altitude reached as 63,668ft (19,406m) and set it as a new record.

Only one record was claimed in 1954 – the first British jet-powered aircraft flight over the North Pole, made on 14/15 October. Aries IV flew the Norway to Canada route from Bardufoss, over the Pole and back to Bodo, Norway, in 6 hours 43 minutes. Two of the crew for this new time and distance record were the same as on the aircraft's previous Cape Town to London flight – pilot Wg Cdr Andrew Humphrey and navigator Sqn Ldr D. Bower. The new second navigator was Sqn Ldr F.R. Wood.

During 1955, an improvement in performance figures was again high on the agenda, with no less than five official and two unofficial new point-to-point records being achieved, as well as another altitude record for Wally Gibb in the Olympus Canberra. On 28 February, Air Vice Marshal J.R. Whitley is known to have flown from Scampton to Nicosia, Cyprus, in 4 hours 13 minutes. The aircraft details have not been confirmed. However, official recording was again in action on 28 July, when Sqn Ldr Ivor G. Broom was at the controls of Aries IV. With navigators Sqn Ldrs D. Bowen and R.A. Seymour, the aircraft broke the Ottawa to London record, flying the 3,330.416 miles (5,359.638km) in 6 hours 42 minutes 12 seconds at an average speed of 496.82mph (799.53km/h).

Two months later, on 23 August, PR.7 WT528 broke three records in one day, flying a double Atlantic crossing. A Silver City Airways crew, pilot J.W. Hackett and navigator P.J. Moneypenny, who had been employed by English Electric for some time on Canberra deliveries, handled WT528 for the flight. The outward leg of 3,475.96 miles (5,593.86km) from London to New York was flown in 7 hours 29 minutes 56.7 seconds at a record speed of 461.12mph (742.08km/h). The aircraft took off from Heathrow but had to over-fly Croydon to start the city-centre to city-centre route, as laid down in the rules. After a refuelling stop of thirty-five minutes at New York, the return, to over-fly Croydon again, was made in 6 hours 16 minutes 59.5 seconds, the average speed of 550.35mph (885.67km/h) representing another record. The overall round trip of 6,915.92 miles (11,129.79km) was covered in 14 hours 21 minutes 45.5 seconds, giving an official record speed for the double flight of 481.52mph (774.91km/h). WT528 was later christened Aries V when it went to Manby and joined the RAFFC.

WD952, the twenty-fourth production B.2, fitted with Olympus 99 engines, at the press call after gaining the first new altitude record, on 4 May 1953. *Aeroplane*

In August 1955, WD952 was re-engined with two 12,000lb (5,443kg) thrust Olympus engines and increased the world altitude record to 65,876ft (20,079m). Author's collection

The Scorpion testbed Canberra, B.2, WK163, starts its display at the 1956 Farnborough SBAC Show. The following year, it raised the altitude record to 70,319ft (21,433m) and was later converted by RRE Pershore for infra-red linescan development. Author's collection

Wally Gibb in the Olympus Canberra, WD952, raised the official world altitude record to 65,876ft (20,079m) on 29 August 1955. The earlier Olympus 99 engines had been replaced by two Olympus 102s, each giving 12,000lb (5,443kg) static thrust. The electrical starters, which each weighed nearly 100lb (45.5kg), were removed after the engines had been started and in theory the previous record should have been beaten by the required three per cent, but, until the figures were confirmed, it was uncertain. In fact, the necessary percentage increase was exceeded by only 278ft (84.73m), but it was enough. It had been attained at the expense of one over-temperature Olympus engine; one of the six turbine blades, which had been burnt in half, was mounted for presentation to Gibb, who still holds it with pride.

The year 1955 was rounded off with an unofficial record flown by PR.7 WT504, from Wyton to Khormaksar. Piloted by Sqn Ldr E.J. Holloway, with Fg Off Broom as navigator, the No.58 Squadron aircraft took 7 hours 45 minutes for the flight, on 24 October. The only record set in 1956 was by B(I).8 WT329. On 16 February, with pilot Peter Hillwood and navigator Dennis Watson, the aircraft was flown to Aden for trop-

ical trials. *En route* it broke the London to Cairo point-to-point record, covering the 2,182.6 miles (3,512.45km) in 3 hours 57 minutes 18.9 seconds, at an average speed of 551.8mph (880km/h).

Two new official records were established in 1957, the first when PR.7 WT528, operating from Manby as *Aries V*, flew from Tokyo to London on 25 May. With a crew consisting of Wg Cdr W. Hoy as pilot, and Flt Lts J.S.L. Denis and P.J. Lageson as navigators, *Aries V* took off from Haneda airport, to fly by way of Alaska, and the thousands of lakes in northern Canada, crossing the North Atlantic for a landing at RAF West Malling. The total distance of 5,942.5 miles (9,563.65km) was flown in 17 hours 42 minutes 2.4 seconds at an average speed of 335.7mph (540.24km/h).

Later in the year, Wally Gibb's altitude record was broken. The engine manufacturer D. Napier & Son, at Luton, employed B.2 WK163 as a flying testbed for their Double Scorpion rocket motor. On 28 August, the company's Chief Test Pilot Mike Randrup, with test observer Walter Shirley, both wearing partial pressure suits with RAE/GQ fixed-visor helmets, took off from Luton and climbed to

44,000ft (13,400m) on the Avons. The Double Scorpion was started and the boosted power took WK163 to a new record height of 70,319ft (21,430.48m).

The last official Canberra record was made on 22 February 1958. Flying the T.4 2E-39 on delivery to Venezuela, the American continent leg from Friendship airport, Washington, to Maiguietor airport, Caracas, was flown in a point-to-point record time of 4 hours 10 minutes 59.7 seconds. The crew of John Hackett, Peter Moneypenny and a Venezuelan Air Force officer flew the 2,062.39 miles (3,319km) at an average speed of 492.95mph (793.30km/h). It has been stated that *Aries V* also made the Washington to Caracas flight, but this has not been substantiated.

The twenty official and five unofficial point-to-point records listed are known not to be the end of the story. Because of the Canberra's great ability, several additional high-speed flights have been made by individual crews and units, but their results have been consigned to the classification of 'rumours', which will no doubt never be confirmed. The Canberra was the sort of aeroplane that had 'challenge' written all over it.

CHAPTER SIX

More Squadrons and More Variants

Photographic Reconnaissance – the PR.3

Photographic reconnaissance, backed up by training, has been the operational role in which the Canberra has been used longest. The current variants in RAF service today are five PR.9s, plus a couple of T.4s. All are with No.39 (1PRU) Squadron, based at Marham.

In the late 1940s, Specification PR.31/46 covered the first photographic-reconnaissance variant of the aircraft, the Canberra PR.Mk.3, with one prototype serialled VX181. It was first flown from Samlesbury on 19 March 1950, with Peter Hillwood at the controls. It was basically a B.2 fitted with a 14in (35cm) extension to the front fuselage, which had provision for six cameras. Five fuel tanks were fitted in the upper centre fuselage and an additional ventral tank was installed under the first four of them, giving the PR.3 a 543-gallon (2,465-litre) advantage over the B.2. With a crew of two, the performance in terms of speed and operational altitude was on a par with the bomber, but the additional fuel increased the maximum range by nearly 900 miles (1,440km), to 3,585 miles (5,740km).

WE135, the first production PR.3, on display while serving with No.231 OCU. George Pennick

WE139, the Christchurch Air Race-winning PR.3, this time carrying the snarling cheetah crest of No.231 OCU. George Pennick

Handling trials with VX181 showed up a serious airframe vibration that was not exactly unexpected. The vibration troubles experienced with the first Canberra prototype, VN799, had been greatly reduced, although not completely eliminated, by a series of modifications. Since VX181 had a 14in (35cm) extension, it was anticipated that the problem could recur. It was decided that by introducing a recommended limiting Mach number lower than that of the bombers (M0.75 compared with M0.84), the PR.3 could go for its preliminary acceptance trials at the A&AEE. They, however, gave it a definite thumbs-down and Warton Flight Operations were left to sort out the problem. This was to prove to be something of a blessing in disguise, as they decided to attempt to eliminate the phenomenon from

(600m) with 560mph (900km/h) indicated, a sudden violent vibration was followed by an audible bang and the aircraft was thrown upwards. The pilot throttled back as he climbed to 10,000ft (3,050m) where, on levelling off and finding the aircraft responsive to control, he set a course for Samlesbury. On the approach, elevator control was found to be lethargic and, after making a heavy landing, examination of the elevators revealed that a mass balance weight had departed, damaging the assembly to such an extent that only one side of the elevator was properly connected.

The mass balances were increased, the shroud gaps were attended to, stiffening plates were added to the rear fuselage, and the PR.3 was accepted for service release. WE135, the first production aircraft,

Canberra B.6

The next Canberra bomber variant entered squadron service in 1954, when No.101 Squadron, still at Binbrook, was the first recipient when the Canberra B.6 arrived. The B.6 had two major advantages over the B.2: a 450 gallon (2,045 litre) integral fuel tank fitted in each outer wing ahead of the main spar and 7,500lb (3,410kg) Avon Mk.109/RA.7 engines. With a fuel load totalling 2,788 gallons (12,680 litres), the normal maximum range increased to 3,400 miles (5,440km) and the maximum speed at high altitude improved by 10mph (16km/h) to 580mph (930km/h). The B.6 also benefited from the record-breaking one-off Mk.5, by having a Dunlop

Canberra PR.3, WH774, was used by the RRE for satellite tracking station calibration, from 1970 to 1976, with the tip tank showing signs of conversion for these duties. George Pennick

the Canberra as a whole, rather than make piecemeal modifications mark by mark.

All the flying prototypes were resonance-tested in Warton's No.25 hangar, where it was confirmed that, while the fuselage was rigid, the tail assembly moved under turbulence. The aerodynamic buffeting of the longer fuselage affected the delicate elevator mass balancing and tabs that had been incorporated on production B.2s.

While these intensive investigations were being carried out, test pilot Johnny Squier experienced the first significant result of the vibrations while testing the fourth production PR.3, WE138. When flying at 2,000ft

from a part of Contract No.6/ACFT/3520/CB6(b) covering twenty-seven PR.3s with serials WE135 to WE151 and WE166 to WE175, was attached to No.541 Squadron at Benson for a trials period starting in November 1952. The first unit on the European mainland to be fully equipped with the PR.3 was No.69 Squadron. This had been a former Mosquito operator, disbanded at B119/Wahn, ten miles southeast of Cologne, on 7 November 1947. Seven years later, on 1 October 1954, the squadron was re-formed at another ex-*Luftwaffe* airfield, Y99/Gütersloh, where PR.3s WE137 and WE138 were early arrivals.

'Maxaret' anti-skid braking system. In view of the fact that it was basically similar to the B.2, incorporating B.5 features that had been test-proved on VX185, there was no B.6 prototype.

On 20 September 1950, contracts were issued to English Electric at Preston and Short Bros at Belfast for B.6 production. Preston received Contract No.6/ACFT/5786/CB6(b) for twenty-six aircraft, with serials running from WJ712 to WJ734 and WJ751 to WJ753. Contract No.6/ACFT/5790/CB6(b) went to Belfast, calling for forty B.6s numbered WH945 to WH984. English Electric's first production B.6 had its maiden flight on 11 August 1953, while Short Bros had to get their line working, and their first Canberra did not get airborne until 29 October 1954.

A month after Binbrook received its first B.6, in July 1954, No.192 Squadron at Watton started to add the new mark to the B.2s that they had operated since January 1953. No.109 Squadron at Hemswell went through a similar operation in December, when its first B.6 was delivered.

Photographic Reconnaissance – the PR.7

In parallel with B.6 production at Preston, the PR.3's successor was coming on line. This was the PR.7, which was to the PR.3 what the B.6 was to the B.2, incorporating the wing tanks, Avon RA.7s and Maxaret brakes. English Electric's first production PR.7s formed a part of their original B.6 contract for twenty-three photographic-

reconnaissance aircraft, with serials WH773 to WE780 and WH790 to WH804 being added to the twenty-six bombers.

As with the B.6, there was no prototype and WH773 first flew on 16 August 1953. During 1954, three squadrons started receiving the new aircraft, the first being No.542 Squadron, which re-formed at Wyton on 15 May and received its first PR.7 the same day. The next month, No.540 Squadron, also at Wyton, started getting the photographic-

(Above) No.9 Squadron's CO leads a formation rehearsing Operation African Tour early in 1956. WH977, WH974 and WH969 were all later converted to B.15 standard. Author's collection

(Below) WH773, the first production PR.7, before its first flight on 16 August 1953. Author's collection

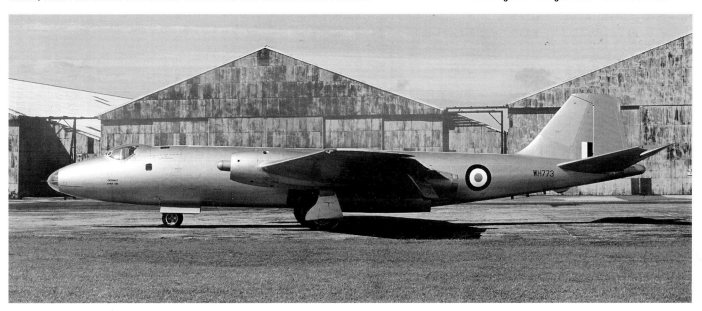

A NATO reconnaissance trio. Canberra PR.7 of No.31 Squadron, based at Laarbruch, leads an RAF Supermarine Swift FR.5 and a Lockheed RT-33 of the Royal Netherlands Air Force. Author's collection

(Below) WH779, the seventh production PR.7, flying with what looks suspiciously like a leak from the starboard wing integral fuel tank. As the aircraft went on to serve with Nos 542, 13, 80 and 31 Squadrons, it is presumed to have landed safely after the photo session. Author's collection

reconnaissance variant and, by September 1954, it had given up all its B.2s and taken on a new PR role. In October, Wyton's other resident, No.82 Squadron, started upgrading its aircraft, with PR.7s replacing the PR.3s that it had flown since October 1953. With the Canberra PR.7, the foundations were laid for the RAF's photographic requirements for more than two decades.

During 1955, six squadrons were re-formed and five more improved their aircraft, starting with No.58 Squadron at Wyton. In January, it received its first PR.7 and by October all the PR.3s that it had flown since December 1953 had gone, leaving it with a full allocation of the later mark. One month later, in February 1955, No.139 Squadron got its first B.6 at Hemswell to replace the B.2, the whole changeover being completed by July. No.617 Squadron at Binbrook also started a similar process in February but all its B.2s had gone by April. Some of them could have gone to Gütersloh where, on 15 March, No.104 Squadron was re-formed and equipped with B.2s as part of the 2nd Tactical Air Force's (2ndTAF) contribution to NATO forces in Europe. Two weeks before this, on 1 March, No.31 Squadron was re-formed at Laarbruch, as another addition to 2ndTAF. This was a big upgrade; up to that date the squadron had been flying Chipmunk T.10s at Hendon, before that sphere of operations was reverted to the Metropolitan Communications Squadron, whereupon the unit was disbanded and re-formed in Germany on the same date. Their new aircraft was the Canberra PR.7, which they retained for the next sixteen years. No.12 Squadron, also a B.2 operator at Binbrook for over

three years, started sending the earlier variants to MUs in May, as Canberra B.6s began replacing them.

Another re-forming took place at Laarbruch on 15 June 1955. No.214 Squadron had flown Lincoln B.2s until being disbanded at Upwood on 30 December 1954 and, on being re-formed, it received Canberra PR.7s as its first turbojet aircraft. The association was short-lived; two months later, on 1 August, No.214 Squadron was renumbered No.80 Squadron. It remained at Laarbruch until moving to Brüggen in June 1957, taking its PR.7s with it, where it stayed for twelve years until being disbanded on 30 September 1969.

The Canberra B.6 and PR.7 were both being produced at a rate of four to five

Canberra Units, December 1955

By the end of 1955, thirty-seven squadrons were operating Canberras, seven of them having re-equipped with later marks after their initially allocated variant.

Squadron	Date First Received	Mark	Representative Aircraft	Squadron	Date First Received	Mark	Representative Aircraft
9	May 52	B.2	WD946, WD997		Jun 54	B.6	WJ758, WJ759
10	Jan 53	B.2	WH665, WH666	102	Oct 54	B.2	WH903, WJ611
12	Mar 52	B.2	WD987, WD988	103	Nov 54	B.2	WD995, WD999
	May 55	B.6	WH945, WH948	104	Mar 55	B.2	WH640, WH644
15	May 53	B.2	WH724, WH725	109	Aug 52	B.2	WD963, WF891
18	Aug 53	B.2	WF908, WH740		Dec 54	B.6	WH954, WH955
21	Sep 53	B.2	WD955, WH668	115	Feb 54	B.2	WF887, WF916
27	Jan 53	B.2	WH728, WH729	139	Nov 52	B.2	WH649, WH650
31	Mar 55	PR.7	WT509, WT510		Feb 55	B.6	WT306, WJ766
35	Apr 54	B.2	WH637, WH904	149	Mar 53	B.2	WH711, WH713
40	Oct 53	B.2	WH643, WH871	192	Jan 53	B.2	WH670, WH698
44	Apr 53	B.2	WD993, WH717		Jul 54	B.6	WJ775, WT301
50	Aug 52	B.2	WD980, WH646	199	Jul 54	B.2	WJ616
57	May 53	B.2	WD996, WH655	207	Mar 54	B.2	WH645, WH876
58	Dec 53	PR.3	WE143, WE148	214	Jun 55	PR.7	No aircraft allocated, renumbered 80 Sqn Aug 55
	Jan 55	PR.7	WJ817, WJ821				
61	Aug 54	B.2	WH741, WH907	527	Dec 54	B.2	WH642, WJ620
69	Oct 54	PR.3	WE168, WE169	540	Dec 52	PR.3	WE136, WE145
76	Dec 53	B.2	WH652, WH873		Jun 53	B.2	WD990, WH726
80	Aug 55	PR.7	WT516, WT517		Jun 54	PR.7	WJ815
82	Nov 53	PR.3	WE144, WE167	542	May 54	PR.7	WH779, WH780
	Oct 54	PR.7	WJ819, WJ820		Nov 55	B.2	WH881, WH884
90	Nov 53	B.2	WH870, WH880		Nov 55	B.6	WH949, WH957
100	Aug 54	B.2	WD986, WD989	617	Jan 52	B.2	WD961, WD965
101	May 51	B.2	WD936, WD944		Feb 55	B.6	WH946, WH947

There are few places colder than an airfield in winter and No.9 Squadron at Binbrook had its share of cold weather on 24 January 1956, as it prepared for ceremonial flights that were to be made during the Queen's tour of West Africa. Author's collection

The clandestine unit at Sculthorpe in 1952, with its RB-45Cs devoid of serial numbers and a mixed group of RAF and USAF personnel. Philip Jarrett

aircraft a month, so it was possible to maintain the impetus of establishing them in squadron service. In September 1955, No.9 Squadron at Binbrook (where it had been since 19 April 1946) began receiving B.6s to add to the B.2s that it had started operating in May 1952. By June 1956, all the earlier variants had departed and the squadron retained the newer aircraft until it was disbanded at Coningsby on 13 July 1961. Canberra B.2s and B.6s also made up the complement of No.1323 Flight when it was renumbered No.542 Squadron on 1 November 1955. A month later, No.76 Squadron, based at Weston Zoyland with Canberra B.2s, started accepting B.6 replacement aircraft, which it flew for the next five years, until being disbanded on 30 December 1960. Detachments from the squadron served in Australia and Christmas Island during the *Grapple* series of nuclear bomb tests in the late 1950s (*see* Chapter 14).

Photographic Reconnaissance – Over the Soviet Union?

One area of RAF Canberra photographic-reconnaissance history that still remains shrouded in uncertainty and conjecture is the aircraft's rumoured operations over the Soviet Union in the mid-1950s.

The USAF's Strategic Air Command (SAC) was placed under the command of the charismatic General Curtis LeMay in October 1948; high on his agenda was the desire to get radar photographic coverage of as much of the USSR as possible, in order for SAC bombardiers to recognize potential target areas. Of course, at this time a significant amount of mutual suspicion existed between the NATO powers and the Soviets, in what was known as the Cold War. Consequently, LeMay's ideas of setting up SAC reconnaissance flights over the USSR were officially flatly vetoed by the White House, so that the Soviet Union should have no excuse to carry out military action against NATO.

However, aircrews did experience 'errors in navigational equipment' and aircraft did 'stray' over Eastern areas of the Soviet Bloc during the Korean War. Also, in April 1950, a US Navy Consolidated PB4Y-2, engaged on an electronic intelligence (Elint) flight over the Baltic Sea, was shot down by Lavochkin La-11s; their pilots said it was a B-29.

In view of Washington's official reluctance, discussions between the Joint Chiefs of Staff, of Britain and the USA, worked out a deal. RAF aircrews would fly American aircraft from bases within the UK, as the Canberra's electronics were, at that time, still being developed. Radar target

plots obtained would be shared between the air forces of the two countries. The aircraft selected for these missions was the four-engined North American RB-45C and, in the autumn of 1951, a small party of RAF aircrew, under the leadership of former No.617 'Dambuster' Squadron member Sqn Ldr 'Micky' Martin DSO, DFC, AFC, was established. Martin failed the preliminary medical for high-altitude flying and his place was taken by Sqn Ldr John Crampton, the Commanding Officer of No.101 Squadron, with its Canberra B.2s.

The party was detached to Barksdale Air Force Base (AFB) in Louisiana for the necessary training programme, which was continued at Langley AFB in Ohio, until December. Then, the party transferred to Sculthorpe in Norfolk, from where the USAF 91st Strategic Reconnaissance Wing operated the 322nd Reconnaissance Squadron, one of three RB-45C squadrons stationed around the world. Four aircraft at Sculthorpe were painted up with RAF roundels and large, non-standard fin flashes, but were not allocated serial numbers.

Three of the RB-45Cs were flown on the first missions, in the early summer of 1952, on courses set over north, central and southern areas of the Soviet Union. After the flights, the aircraft were returned to the USA and the RAF aircrews rejoined their respective units.

Early in 1954, Sqn Ldr Crampton was put in charge of another mission and his navigator was again Sqn Ldr Rex Saunders. This time, their brief was to penetrate further into Soviet airspace than they had in 1952. Crampton and Saunders took radar photographs of over thirty different targets during a flight that covered more than 1,000 miles (1,600km). Again, following the missions, aircraft and aircrews returned to their squadrons and nothing has officially been released about these episodes.

Coupled with these known RB-45C flights, rumours have referred to Canberras taking part in an Operation *Robin*. What is known for fact is that, in 1951, the Soviets set up a missile production plant in the Kapustin Yar area of the USSR, and NATO was extremely anxious to find out just what type of missiles were involved. It is also a known fact that No.13 Squadron, which had moved to Fayid with its Mosquito PR.34s on 5 February 1947, had a detachment deployed to Habbaniya, in Iraq, at the end of 1948, in order to carry out intelligence-gathering flights over southern areas of the USSR.

No.540 Squadron had started receiving Canberra PR.3s in December 1952, while still operating with B.2s. Its records show that, on 27 and 28 August 1953, various crews flew long-range missions connected with Operation *Robin*. B.2 WH726 and PR.3 WH800 were used, with Wg Cdr Ball, Sqn Ldr Kenyon, Flt Lt Gartside, together with Flt Sgts Brown and Wigglesworth listed as taking part. Another of the squadron's PR.3s, WE142, participated in the New Zealand Air Race as 'No.2' and is confirmed as having 'strayed off course a little' on 8 October during the race. This 'straying' went over Communist territory. Furthermore, the aircraft was 'delayed' at Basrah and took third place in the race results. Whether anything can be deduced from these facts depends on an interpretation of semantics.

During 1953, the squadron was loaned an American camera, fitted with a 100in (250cm) focal length lens; it is known that B.2 WH726 was converted to accept this massive piece of optics. When the camera was being tested, locations in London were photographed while the aircraft was flying

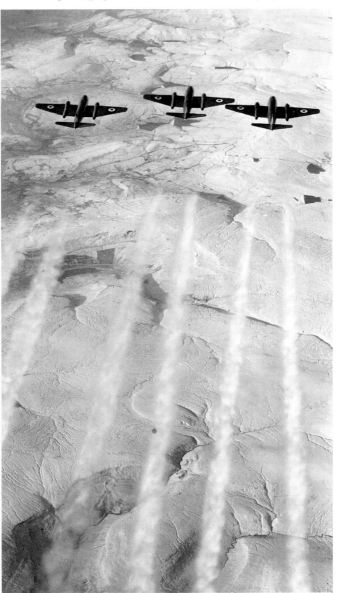

High Flyers. A trio from No.18 Squadron at Upwood stream out con-trails on a January day in 1956. Author's collection

over the English Channel. With a camera having that type of performance on board, it is certainly not beyond the bounds of possibility that WH726 took part in a Kapustin Yar overflight. There was such a flight and this has been confirmed by no less an organization than USSR intelligence.

Soviet records state that Lt Mikhail Shulga, flying an undisclosed type of MiG fighter, was vectored by ground control on to an aircraft in the Kapustin Yar area, recognized as a Canberra. At about 50,000ft (15,200m) and still below the Canberra, the Red Air Force aircraft was at the stall and Shulga's intended interception had to be aborted. Whether the Canberra in this event was WH726 has never been confirmed, but what has is the fact that this aircraft was something of a special B.2, which was also operated from Wyton by No.58 Squadron. A Flt Lt Gingell of that squadron flew WH726 to the USA in March 1954, for a series of joint RAF and USAF trials, quoted as Project *Robin* and American records cite the aircraft as being a 'modified Canberra B.2'. The trials occupied six weeks, after which the aircraft returned to the UK and is confirmed as being on Wyton's strength on 10 April 1954.

Later in the same month, an Operation *Robin* mission was flown, followed by two more on 8 and 11 May. On 26 August and on 30 August, further Operation *Robin* sorties are known to have been carried out, with all being accepted at Wyton – but officially unconfirmed – as reconnaissance missions over the Soviet Union. Perhaps the correlation between the red-breasted bird and the national colour of the USSR reflects a typically British sense of humour.

Predictably, the Ministry of Defence (MoD) refuses, on the grounds of 'international sensitivity', to release files relating to Operation *Robin*, even in the current atmosphere of improved relations between the west and the former USSR. However, surely the simple fact that Whitehall holds these files is some proof that all is not conjecture.

On 1 February 1966, WH726 was sold to the British Aircraft Corporation (BAC) (later British Aerospace), and on 21 September of the same year the aircraft was delivered to the *Fuerza Aérea del Peru*, with serial number 236, to join the Peruvian *Grupo de Bombardeo 21* at Limatombo.

CHAPTER SEVEN

Canberra Gets the Low-Down

In 1956, the Canberra was destined to begin work in an entirely new role, for which it would change to a physical profile that is still in current service.

The Intruder Bomber

In the mid-1940s, the unarmed, high-altitude, turbojet-powered bomber was considered to be the optimum strategic offensive weapon; however, advances in ground-to-air missiles had provoked a change of thought in the Air Staff within a decade. The favourite consideration in these revised plans was a specialized interdictor variant of the Canberra, able to operate at low level with visual ground contact, carrying a variety of bombs and rockets, plus, for the first time on the Canberra, a cannon armament.

Operational Requirement (OR) 302 resulted in the issue of Specification IB.122

('IB' denoting 'intruder bomber'), for the design and construction of a prototype based on the modification of the existing basic airframe. The design department at Warton was full to the gunwales with P1A and P1B work, so it was decided to set up a new design office to handle IB.122. Over the years, English Electric had absorbed just about all the engineering design potential in the area, so the company proposed to tap into the latent abilities known to exist in London and the Home Counties. The new design facility was established at the Napier works in Acton, which English Electric had taken over in December 1942.

Albert Draper, one of Warton's senior designers on the Canberra programme, was given the responsibility of setting up the Acton department and a completely new design team was inaugurated into the Air Staff's requirements. An entirely new cockpit and nose section ahead of Station 12 was proposed, plus the ability to fit an

optional gun armament for a ground-attack role, together with external under-wing stores. A mock-up of the proposed revised front fuselage was constructed at Acton and it was considered that the quickest way to get the new variant air-borne was to convert the existing one-off Mk.5 airframe VX185, retaining the Avon Mk.109(RA.7) engines.

The design of the optional cannon armament was placed with Boulton Paul Aircraft. They came up with a neat ventral pack, holding four 20mm Hispano cannon, which fitted into the rear of the bomb-bay, together with containers holding 525 rounds per gun, which in theory provided the lethal barrage of fifty seconds' firing. Special doors were designed to facilitate the addition of the pack, while retaining the bomb-carrying ability of the front portion of the bomb-bay. Two underwing pylons were fitted, each capable of holding a 1,000lb (455kg) bomb, or a Matra rocket launcher containing thirty-seven SNEB 2in (5cm) missiles. The standard 10,000lb (4,550kg) bomb load of the B.6 could be carried when the gun pack was not fitted and there was also provision to deliver a nuclear weapon.

One aspect of the original Canberra design was its restricted forwards/downwards visibility for the pilot. This was quite satisfactory in the roles for which it was originally designed, but for ground-attack purposes it was definitely inadequate. A neat, fixed, fighter-type windscreen and blown canopy were designed, off-set on the port-side, while the crew reverted to the original two of the B.3/45. The navigator/bomb-aimer's station was sited on the starboard side, ahead of and below the pilot. The pilot sat in a Martin-Baker Mk.2 seat, but this was to be the first time a Canberra navigator did not have an ejector seat. For an emergency evacuation, he jettisoned the crew entry door and a hydraulic-operated windbreak came out ahead of the resultant aperture, to afford him some protection from the slipstream while exiting.

When the prototype B(I).8, VX185, the reconstructed B.5, first flew on 23 July 1954, it had yet to receive the Boulton Paul-designed ventral gun pack. Author's collection

Conversion and Testing

VX185 went into the shops on 28 January 1954 for conversion to the new variant, given the designation Mk.B(I).8. The major refurbishment was completed in seven days short of six months. The new nose was glazed as the B.2 and B.6, with two additional windows on either side of the transparent nose-cone. Although a bomb-aimer's flat window was incorporated and the navigator carried a secondary 'bomb-aimer' title, there was no bombsight, as weapon delivery was actuated by the pilot.

'Bee' Beamont gave the newly configured VX185 its first flight from Samlesbury, on 23 July 1954, in weather that was rather typical of many an English summer day – it was pouring with rain. One advantage of this was that the CTP was able to confirm at a very early stage that visibility through the new canopy was not affected. In fact, compared with all existing Canberras, the view from the new cockpit was excellent; of course, the operational requirements of earlier marks had been different, since there isn't much to concentrate on outside the canopy at 45,000ft (13,700m)!

Testing continued through August and, by the time that the B(I).8 prototype appeared at the SBAC Display, which began at Farnborough on 6 September, a large part of the programme had been successfully completed. Beamont was able to demonstrate the aircraft proven to its new role. His usual low-level display programme was more relevant to the aircraft's operational environment than had been the case in the past. The 1954 Farnborough was quite a Canberra benefit, as no less than five were present; they were matched only by Gloster, which put up five Javelins. The Javelins, however, only operated in one role – all-weather interception – whereas each Canberra present was tailored to individually different requirements: bomber, interdictor, photographic reconnaissance and two separate engine testbeds. In its all-over glossy black paint finish, VX185 was possibly the first Canberra that looked really menacing.

Production and into Service

English Electric had received Contract No.6/ACFT/6445/CB6(b) on 28 February 1951, for the production of thirty Canberra B(I).8s, allocated serial numbers WT326 to WT348 and WT362 to WT368. Of these, WT337, WT340, WT342, WT345, WT347, WT363 and WT366 were all subcontracted to Short Bros for construction. The contract also covered the manufacture of nineteen B.6 conversions, designated B(I).6, as a form of compromise intruder bomber. This was a standard B.6 adapted to take the Boulton Paul gun pack and revised bomb doors. They were given serial numbers WT307 to WT325.

WT307 made its first flight on 31 March 1955, then it went to the A&AEE, to Boulton Paul for modification and back to Boscombe Down, before it was cleared for squadron issue. Three additional B(I).6s were later ordered. XG554, added to the original contract, was first flown on 29 February 1956, while XJ249 and XJ257 were

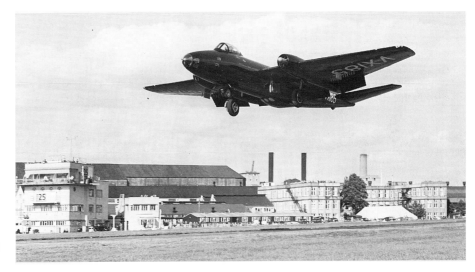

By 6 September 1954, when VX185 flew on the opening day of that year's SBAC Display, the gun pack and underwing weapon pylons had been installed. Shortly after Farnborough, tip-tanks were fitted and a couple of 500lb (225kg) bombs had been found, to attach to the pylons. Author's collection

WT340, the second Short Bros-built B(I).8, on air test before joining No.88 Squadron; here, it shows off its Homing Eye **rear warning radar.** *Aeroplane*

added to Contract No.6/ACFT/5786/CB6(b), as replacement aircraft. They had their first flights on 29 March and 30 April 1956 respectively.

The second and third aircraft on the original order were engaged on RAE testing before both were stored, but from the fourth production aircraft, WT310, all B(I).6s were allocated to the first Night Intruder squadron in Germany. This was No.213 Squadron, specially re-formed at Ahlhorn on 1 September 1955 for the role. Germany was quite a change of venue for the squadron; since disembarking from HMS *Furious* with its Hurricane 1s at Port Said and moving to Abu Sueir on 22 May 1941, it had operated in the Middle East until disbanding at Deversoir on 30 September 1954. No.213 Squadron, the only B(I).6 operator, moved to Brüggen on 22 August 1957, where it remained until being disbanded on 31 December 1969. The squadron took part several times in the Salmond Trophy bombing competition organized by 2ndTAF, first winning it in 1964.

The Canberra B(I).6s had first had an overall silver finish, but this was changed to the RAF Germany grey/green camouflage of the 1960s.

Attrition with the B(I).6 was much higher than average within the 2ndTAF; no less than eight were lost between 1957 and 1968, two of them coming together due to losing sight of each other during formation flying. Another collided with a

WT307, the first production B(I).6, undergoing flight trials in spring 1955, complete with ventral four-cannon pack and underwing pylon-mounted bombs. Author's collection

Victor B(K).1A tanker. The remaining five all unexpectedly came into contact with terra firma during operational sorties.

The beginning of 1956 saw the first Canberra B(I).8 go into service with No.88 Squadron, which re-formed at Wildenrath on 15 January, after having been disbanded as a Sunderland GR.5 operator at Seletar, on 1 October 1954. It retained its B(I).8s at Wildenrath, until again being disbanded on 17 December 1962 and renumbered No.14 Squadron. With its new title, the squadron stayed at

Wildenrath, flying its interdictors until disbanding again, on 30 June 1970. The squadron worked up its dual roles of low-level ground attack and anti-shipping strikes, both at night, proving the aircraft to be more than adequate for the tasks. It was liked by all pilots, who appreciated its versatility and its outstanding, all-round visibility. Navigators were a little less exuberant, mainly due to the absence of an ejector seat, but they too liked the view from the glazed nose section during low-level sorties.

LABS Operations and Training

At Marshall of Cambridge, the eighth production B(I).8, WT333, was used for trial installations of the Mk.10 autopilot, after which it went to the RAE for trials of the new Low-Altitude Bombing System (LABS). The system had initially been tried with the Canberra B.6s of No.9 Squadron, based at Binbrook, which had been modified at No.39 MU Colerne. It was to become a vital component of Canberra operations, which required certain structural modifications, including the strengthening of bomb doors and the installation of detachable perforated plates ahead of the bomb-bay, to decrease buffeting when the doors were open at low altitude. Strengthening of the airframe was incorporated to accept the stresses of high-speed, low-level sorties, while additional equipment for the operational role included an angle-of-release selector, a LABS timer and 'g' meter.

Some of No.9 Squadron's B.6s, suitably modified for LABS operations, went to Castel Benito/Idris in Libya, early in 1959, to act as a trials unit. There, over one thousand 25lb (11.5kg) practice bombs were used during the operations. By April, No.12 Squadron's B.6s had also been modified by No.39 MU and it, too, went to Libya to work up, before joining No.9 Squadron at Coningsby to become the only LABS-equipped unit in the UK. Quick Reaction Alert (QRA) was instigated at the base in October 1960 and, while certain restrictions were placed on LABS operations for a short period, due to bombs not clearing the bomb-bay, the technique was generally regarded as successful. Close monitoring of airframe fatigue during these operations had been directed by Bomber Command, but no serious problems were encountered.

Four Canberra PR.7 operators came on line during 1956. No.13 Squadron at Akrotiri, on the southern tip of Cyprus, started replacing their Meteor PR.10s on 10 February. In April, Watton-based No.527 Squadron added PR.7s to the B.2s that they had held since December 1954. No.17 Squadron, which had flown Beaufighter TT10s when disbanded on 13 March 1951, was re-formed at Wahn on 1 June 1956 with Canberra PR.7s, which they held until finishing as a photographic-reconnaissance squadron on 31 December 1969. In August 1956 at West Raynham in Essex, No.100 Squadron added B.6s, PR.7s and B(I).8s to the B.2s that they had used since April 1954.

Canberra B.2 squadrons were still being formed. No.59 Squadron was re-formed at Gütersloh, by the renumbering of No.102 Squadron, on 1 September 1956 (and was renumbered No.5 Squadron in 1961), when it accepted its first B.2s, but in February 1957, these were replaced by B(I).8s. In January 1957, a detachment of No.32 Squadron took on B.2s at Weston Zoyland, before taking them back to their parent base at Akrotiri. No.73 Squadron went through exactly the same operation in March, while in July a detachment of No.6 Squadron went from Akrotiri to Coningsby to receive its B.2s, as did No.12 Squadron in August. On 15 October, No.249 Squadron, having been disbanded at Eastleigh the same day, was re-formed at Akrotiri to fly Canberra B.2s and in the following month, No.45 Squadron sent a detachment from Tengah on Singapore island to Coningsby, to receive B.2s.

No.16 Squadron, which was flying Venom 1Bs when disbanded at B118/Celle on 1 July 1957, was re-formed at Laarbruch on 1 March 1958, and RAF Germany thus had a low-level LABS strike force that would operate as a constituent of NATO for the next fourteen years. A special LABS ground-trainer caravan commuted between units, in order for crews to become fully proficient with the system, without building up airframe hours. Flying at 320mph (512km/h), 250ft (760m) above the European landscape for over two hours, with the speed increasing to 500mph (800km/h) over the target area, required ultimate concentration. LABS training was still carried out over the Libyan Tarhuna range at Idris with practice bombs, wing pylon-mounted rockets and 20mm cannon, the latter involving strafing canvas targets set out in the desert.

Practice sorties were also flown in connection with the force's ability to deliver the 'special store'. This was the euphemism applied to the American

By the time B.6, WT303, had joined No.6 Squadron at Akrotiri and was photographed at Khormaksar in 1962, it had been converted to B.16 standard. Ray Deacon.

No.213 Squadron was B(I).6, WT323's last unit before the aircraft was broken up at Samlesbury in July 1976. P. Vawt End/George Pennick

'Bluff Shape' nuclear store, a weapon that was 13ft 8in (416cm) long, weighed 2,000lb (910kg) and was quoted as having a yield of one megaton. At the height of its operational capability, RAF Germany had a B(I).8 maintained at fifteen-minutes readiness at all times, to execute a nuclear strike.

During the annual UK air-defence exercise *Mandate*, in July 1959, Canberra B(I).8 low-level sorties were flown without any fighter interceptions, although many sightings were reported. Frequent NATO Tactical Evaluations (TACE-VAL), together with Bomber Command exercises *Cenobite*, *Topweight* and *Whipsaw* were entered, as well as the Supreme Allied Commander Europe (SACEUR) exercise *Checkmate*, kept the strike force in a prime state of readiness, with a good record of results.

On 21 August 1958, No.51 Squadron was re-formed at Watton with the renumbering of No.192 Squadron, to receive a mixed collection of Canberra B.2s and B.6s. Two months later at Upwood, No.21 Squadron absorbed No.542 Squadron on 1 October and, while retaining the old squadron's B.2s, took delivery of Canberra B.6s. The operation's result was rather short-lived. On 15 January 1959, No.21 Squadron was disbanded and its role was changed when four months later, on 1 May, it was once more re-formed, this time at Benson, where it was equipped with the Twin Pioneer CC.1.

Low-Level Strikers

A total of seven Canberra squadrons operated in the interdictor-bomber role in the UK and mainland Europe, over a period of fourteen years.

The weapon diversity of the Canberra B(I).6 is graphically illustrated in this BAC publicity shot. Among the array of stores are the 4 × 20mm Hispano cannon pack; 500, 540 and 1,000lb bombs; 100-gallon underwing fuel tank; SNEB 2in rocket projectiles; GEC Minigun pools; Matra rocket launchers, as well as 25lb and 28lb practice bombs. Author's collection

Squadron	Date First Received	Mark	Representative Aircraft
3	Jan 61	B(I).8	XH208, XM275
14	Dec 62	B(I).8	WT362, WT368
16	Mar 58	B(I).8	XM263, XM265
59	Feb 57	B(I).8	WT363, WT366
88	Jan 56	B(I).8	WT331, WT368
100	Aug 56	B(I).8	WT327, WT347
213	Mar 56	B(I).6	WT316, WT323

No.59 Squadron was renumbered No.3 Squadron in January 1961 and No.88 Squadron became No.14 Squadron in December 1962. The dates shown are when each squadron received its first aircraft, operating under the squadron number shown.

CHAPTER EIGHT

Canberra 'Gets Its Knees Brown'

After the First World War

With the formation of the Air Council, on 2 January 1918, Hugh Trenchard had been appointed Chief of Air Staff (CAS). However, a clash of personalities with Lord Rothermere led to his resignation from the post four months later. On 11 January 1919, as Sir Hugh Trenchard, he resumed the CAS mantle, working under the Secretary of State for the War Office and the Royal Air Force, Winston Churchill.

Churchill requested Trenchard to draw up his proposals for the post-war RAF. Among the many and far-reaching suggestions was the establishment of nineteen overseas units, of which Nos 6 and 19 Squadrons went to Mesopotamia (now Iraq)

and No.14 Squadron served in Palestine. Nos 47, 55, 56, 70, 208 and 216 Squadrons were posted to Egypt, with No.247 Squadron going to Malta, while Nos 1, 3, 20, 31, 48, 97, 99 and 114 Squadrons went to India. The other four units were spread through Ireland and Germany.

Such were the foundations that kept the RAF flying operational sorties non-stop after the Armistice, which had been signed on 11 November 1918, putting on hold the conflict between the United Kingdom and Germany. Uprisings of dissident tribes were rife throughout Asia Minor and the Far East Station, against which the RAF acted as a 'peace-keeping' force in its own right, as well as supplying support to ground forces.

The Middle East

The advent of the Second World War brought about a change of direction and a vast expansion of the RAF units in the areas. However, once victory against the Axis powers had been consolidated, it was 'business as usual', with local unrest rearing its head once more. This time, it was nations instead of tribes, fired by the centuries-old conflicts of religions. It also involved the spread of Communism, together with the build-up to, and result of, the establishment of the State of Israel, on 14 May 1948. In the following year, the United Nations recommended that Palestine should be partitioned into two separate states. The violent Arab reaction,

B.2, WH666, was flown by No.56 Squadron, before it was sold to Zimbabwe in March 1981, with the serial 2250. Author's collection

which was not entirely unexpected, plunged the country into a virtual state of civil war. The British withdrew in May 1948, leaving the participants to sort it out for themselves, and removing any influence that they had been able to administer; of course, this influence had not necessarily always been unbiased.

So much of the world's economy was based on natural minerals, and particularly on the oil of the Middle East, that stability within the area was of paramount importance. To this end, in February 1955, the Baghdad Pact treaty of alliance was drawn up for signature by Iraq and Turkey. Two months later, Britain signed a treaty with Iraq and, with Iran becoming a signatory later in the year, there was an agreement that all the member countries would honour the Baghdad Pact. While the basis of the pact was intended to be economic, it was hoped that such an association would also stem the spread of Communistic influences within the oil states.

Before the Baghdad Pact, Colonel Gamel Adbel Nasser had taken over the Presidency of Egypt and a rising tide of nationalism called for the withdrawal of Britain from her bases within the country, which had been maintained since an Anglo/Egyptian treaty signed in 1936. While Britain was prepared to undertake a withdrawal, its interests in the Suez Canal – indispensable for the transportation of oil and trade to the Far East, and enhanced by a 1946 treaty – could not be ignored. A plan of withdrawal in phases was drawn up, with the proviso that, should the canal be threatened, a British presence would be retained. The Anglo/Egyptian Agreement was signed in October 1954 and Britain's withdrawal from Egypt was completed, without further reason for delay, in June 1956.

Relations between some member states deteriorated to the point that, within four years, following a coup, Iraq rejected the Baghdad Pact. The pact's title was amended to the Central Treaty Organisation (CENTO), and Pakistan was also drawn in. It had been clear from the start, in 1955, that some form of armed assurance would be required, to forestall any potential threats to the various agreements signed and that this would have to be provided, in the main, by Britain. The RAF was the logical contributor of any quick defence requirement. In 1956, it was decided to withdraw the Venom FB.1s of Nos 32 and 73 Squadrons, plus No.6 Squadron's Venom FB.4s, together with those of No.249 Squadron. In their place a medium-range strike wing would be established on Cyprus and the four squadrons would be re-equipped with Canberra B.2s.

Operation *Musketeer*

Events overtook CENTO's plans for, on 26 July 1956, Nasser laid out his government's intentions to nationalize the Universal Suez Canal Company. The plans were actually being enacted while he was addressing the crowds in Alexandria, to prove once again that the only real beneficiary of any treaty within the area was the printer. The British and French governments, formerly prime controllers of the canal, immediately considered putting into practice an outline plan already drawn up for the Middle East Air Force (MEAF). Codenamed *Musketeer*, the plan involved a joint operation against Egypt, in the event of that country posing any threat to the canal, in order to return it to some form of international control. It was thought that any form of military action by superior forces against Egypt would prompt the overthrow of Nasser's government; although the UN Security Council

WJ572, a camouflaged No.27 Squadron B.2, receives its 1,000lb (455kg) bombs at Nicosia.
Author's collection

worked hard to placate the situation, it did not succeed.

General Sir Charles Keightley had been appointed Commander-in-Chief (CinC) of all proposed operations on 11 August 1956, and Air Marshal D.H.F. Barnett, who had previously been AOC in the area, was made Air Task Force Commander.

The first phase of Operation Musketeer would be the destruction of the Egyptian Air Force (EAF); Cyprus, with its three airfields, was to be the main base for these operations, supplemented by the two military airfields on Malta. In 1955, Egypt had purchased a considerable number of modern aircraft from Czechoslovakia, which was estimated to include over a hundred MiG-15s and nearly fifty Il-28s. These, added to a good number of Meteor F.8s and NF.13s, plus

Squadron at Royal Naval Air Station (RNAS) Hal Far, all operating B.6s. On Cyprus, at RAF Nicosia, Nos 10, 15, 18, 27, 44 and 61 Squadrons all operated B.2s, while No.139 Squadron was equipped with B.6s. Of the Nicosia-based units, Nos 18 and 139 Squadrons were dedicated to target-marking. The newly constructed airfield at Akrotiri, on Cyprus, hosted No.13 Squadron, flying Canberra PR.7s. Four of these aircraft, together with seven Republic RF-84Fs of the French Air Force, flew the first official sorties over Egyptian airfields.

The Canberra bombing element was more restricted than they would have wished. The aircraft were fitted with Gee-H-ARI5829 as a blind bombing aid, but no Gee-H cover was available over Egypt. Bombing would therefore have to be carried

gave the navigator screen returns up to 60 miles (95km) away, at maximum altitude. The aircraft had been modified by Boulton Paul to operate Blue Shadow and were redesignated Canberra B.6(BS).

Attacks on the night of 31 October involved Nos 9, 10, 12, 15, 18, 101, 109 and 139 Squadrons, with a total of thirty-eight Canberras being deployed against Egyptian airfields at Abu Sueir, Inchas, Kabrit and Cairo West. (The latter target was the subject of confusion; after briefing, a signal was received that American citizens were in the Cairo area and Almaza was made the alternative target, but this information was not received by the participating aircraft.) The whole raid destroyed only fourteen EAF aircraft and, because of the small number of attackers

During Operation Musketeer, **HMS Falcon at Hal Far, Malta, was host to several participating squadrons. Here, the B.6s of No.101 Squadron are in the foreground, with No.9 Squadron further along the line and No.12 Squadron on the back row.** Author's collection

about fifty Vampire FB.52s, formed quite a formidable force. While Israel agreed to French Air Force fighters operating from its airfields, as it would be closely involved in any land attack against Egypt, the onus was on Britain, as the only partner with a bomber force, to destroy the Egyptian Air Force before it could get airborne.

The Air Task Force's bomber element consisted of ninety-two Canberras, including forty B.2s, thirty-two B.6s, and twenty B.2 and B.6 target-markers, together with twenty-four Valiant B.1s. Prior to Operation Musketeer officially starting, on 31 October 1956, the RAF strength comprised 289 aircraft on Cyprus and ninety-two on Malta. The Malta-based Canberra element was made up by Nos 12, 101 and 109 Squadrons at RAF Luqa, plus No.9

out at night, with the Second World War target-marking procedure being adopted. The two marker squadrons involved had been cleared for 250lb (115kg) target indicators and 4½in (11.25cm) parachute flares. Their Canberras had the standard bomb-aimer's position replaced by a 90-degree, sideways-looking radar, codenamed Blue Shadow. Positioned to look to starboard, it

---

Conversion of B.6 to B.6(BS)

Modifications made by Boulton Paul Aircraft Ltd, to twenty-five aircraft: WJ767, WJ769, WJ770, WJ771, WJ772, WJ773, WJ774, WJ776, WJ777, WJ778, WJ780, WJ781, WJ782, WJ783, WT302, WT303, WT304, WT306, WT369, WT371, WT372, WT373, WT374, XH569, XH570

---

employed, damage to the target airfields was insufficient to put any of them out of commission.

The lesson was learned and 1 November saw twenty-one separate raids by Canberras, spread over the whole period of daylight. These resulted in a significant amount of damage to EAF aircraft and airfields. Very little opposition was put up by Egyptian fighters and anti-aircraft gunfire was ineffective, so that all aircraft returned safely to their bases. Valiants joined further Canberra sorties during the night and, by 2 November, photographic-reconnaissance flights provided proof of the destruction of 158 modern EAF aircraft, while others had obviously taken refuge in neighbouring Arab counties. Canberra targets had included Fayid, Kasfareet and Luxor, where a concentration of Il-28 bombers had been confirmed by PR coverage.

Air attacks against selected key areas, such as Cairo Radio, barracks, communication centres and transportation targets, were begun on 2 November. These attacks increased in intensity the following day; a Venom and its pilot were lost during a low-level sortie, while Canberras inflicted great damage to the important Nfisha rai-lyards, near Port Said. By 5 November, British and French paratroops were in action on the ground, as well as substantial Israeli land forces, all under an umbrella of combined air support.

Meanwhile, in New York, the United Nations established an emergency Security Council meeting, where a ceasefire was ordered, with effect from midnight on 6 November. Operations were terminated and RAF aircraft losses were assessed: the Venom was one lost, while the Royal Navy lost two Sea Hawks, two Wyverns and a pair of Whirlwind helicopters. French aircraft losses were one F4U-7 Corsair and an F-84F Thunderstreak, while Israel was fifteen aircraft down in its inventory, including ten F-51 Mustangs.

The RAF lost its only Canberra in action on 8 November, during a clandestine photographic-reconnaissance mission. WH799, a PR.7 of No.58 Squadron, was attacked by a MiG-15 of the Syrian Air Force in their airspace, and the aircraft crash-landed in Lebanon. The navigator Fg Off Urquart-Pullen, was killed, but pilot Flt Lt Hunter, and the second navigator were treated in Beirut Military Hospital, before being repatriated. One further aircraft, B.6(BS) WT371, sustained damage in action. Following temporary repairs, it was due for return to the UK when it crashed at Nicosia, on 6 November, killing the crew.

One observation: on 6 June 1944, D-Day in the Second World War, over 1,000 aircraft operated on the day. All Allied aircraft, except RAF and USAAF heavy bombers operated in that role, were painted with two black and three white stripes

No.44 Squadron's white rising pheasant crest is much neater than the Musketeer **stripes painted on B.2, WH718, as it gets bombed up.** Author's collection

The crew of WJ815 brought their own sun hat with them, but it is not known whether the crew of the No.3 Squadron B(I).8 in the background were similarly forward-thinking. Ray Deacon

No.32 Squadron took its Canberra B.2s to the Near East in February 1957, and WH652 displays the typical sooty engine start, as its sun shade is packed away. Author's collection

around the rear fuselage, as well as on both outer-wing surfaces, as a means of rapid 'friendly aircraft' identification. During Operation *Musketeer*, a similar identification system was employed on some RAF, FAA and French AF aircraft, using two black and three yellow stripes – although, due to a temporary shortage of yellow paint, some Canberras, including WH640 of No.10 Squadron, had white stripes. In view of the fact that, on the day of the most concentrated attacks, 1 November, fewer than forty aircraft were used at any one time, it seems unnecessary to have adorned the aircraft in such a way, especially as the Valiants, Shackletons or any of the seventy-two transports were not painted. The aircraft of the Israeli Air Force, with whom the British and French were in partnership, were also devoid of any stripes! There is also the fact that the USAF, US Navy, RAAF, North Korean AF and Chinese AF had no difficulty in identifying each other for over three years, without resorting to any special decorations.

Following the ceasefire on 6 November, a United Nations Emergency Force took over from the ground forces and the results of the RAF side of operations were evaluated. The main conclusion was that, in view of the United States taking a non-co-operative stance, the British nuclear weapons programme should be stepped up. Two of the participating types in Operation *Musketeer*, the Valiant and the Canberra, would be involved in the resultant nuclear tests (*see* Chapter 14).

The ASW and NEAF

No.32 Squadron's scheduled return to the UK for re-equipping was delayed by Operation *Musketeer*. While it did not fly against Egypt, it was sent from Malta to Jordan, with its Venom FB.1s, in case Israel mounted any operations against that country, with whom Britain had an alliance. The RAF might well have found itself in partnership with both sides! At the end of 1956, No.32 Squadron left the area for Weston Zoyland in Somerset, to receive Canberra B.2s from No.15 MU Wroughton.

Starting on 15 February 1957, the squadron returned to the Mediterranean theatre, first to Nicosia and then, in the following month, to Akrotiri. By 19 March, the squadron was at full strength on its new base, as the nucleus of the Akrotiri Strike Wing (ASW). No.73 Squadron had moved to Akrotiri from Khormaksar on 21 December 1956, with its Venom FB.4s and, in March 1957, it too sent a detachment to Weston Zoyland. A short course of familiarization with the B.2 was followed by a flight back to Cyprus with four aircraft on 20 March. The remaining four B.2s arrived at Akrotiri on 30 March and, four months later, No.6 Squadron took its Venom FB.4s to Coningsby and swapped them for Canberra B.2s. It arrived back at Akrotiri in July. The Venom FB.4-operating No.249 Squadron left Eastleigh in Kenya in the same month, for temporary detachment at Coningsby, where conversion to the Canberra was completed by October. On the

15th of that month, No.249 re-formed at Akrotiri with its B.2s and the ASW was fully operational.

The island of Cyprus was generally considered a good posting, but it suffered from the on-going friction between the Turks and Greeks. A hardened faction of 'Union with Greece' followers formed the terrorist organization EOKA, led by General Grivas and Archbishop Makarios. For the organization, Akrotiri became a permanent target for sabotage. After the time-bombing of a hangar, which destroyed B.2s WF886 and WP514, as well as PR.7 WT508, a system of dispersing aircraft at night was introduced, with Canberras going as far afield as El Adem, Idris, Gibraltar, Habbaniya, Luqa and Eastleigh.

Operation *Musketeer* had proved that meticulous care in target-marking was essential for good visual bombing results and, in November 1959, No.249 Squadron replaced its B.2s with B.6s to become the AFW's dedicated marker unit with effect from 18 December. Practice bombing took place on the range at El Adam in Libya, which involved a 1,000 mile (1,600km) round trip. Things became easier in 1958, when a live-bombing range was opened at Episkopi Bay, off the southern tip of Cyprus, on 3 February.

On 1 March 1961, the Near East Air Force (NEAF) was formed, with headquarters on Cyprus; four months later, Kuwait was facing hostile threats from Iraq. Britain had an agreement with Kuwait to give assistance, under the codename *Vantage*;

this was revised due to the new threat from Iraq, and given the new codename *Bell-ringer*. The proposal was to move two Canberra strike units, Nos 88 and 213 Squadrons, from 2ndTAF in Germany to Sharjah in the Persian Gulf. Four B(I).8s of No.88 Squadron arrived on 1 July and eight B(I).6s from No.213 Squadron followed two days later. Sharjah was by no means ideal for the interdictors, as the surface was soon cut up badly by the aircraft taking off with a full war-load, and getting airborne from the rutted surface became quite a problem. Fortunately, tension in the area lessened and the 2ndTAF aircraft returned to Germany at the end of the month, with some relief.

B.15 and B.16

Two new Canberra variants came into the Middle East area in 1961/62. A programme of conversions had been undertaken by Marshall of Cambridge, starting with B.6 WH976 being converted to B.15 standard. This involved the trials installation of integral wing tanks, together with additional underwing hard points, to take bombs and Microcell rocket pods. Internally, UHF and HF communications radios were installed, together with a Doppler roller-map with feed-in from a Doppler navigation system. A forward-facing F.95 camera was sited in the nose and a G.45 camera was installed in the starboard-wing leading edge.

Parallel with the B.15 conversion trials, Marshalls had a B.6(BS) for the same programme, this variant being designated B.16. One principal difference from the B.15 was that, because the repositioned *Blue Shadow* required the navigator/plotter to surrender his ejector seat, he had to wear a flying suit with built-in oxygen bottle and chest parachute. This *Blue Shadow* relocation required external trunking to be fitted on the starboard side of the fuselage, above the nose-wheel bay and the bomb-bay.

No.32 Squadron began to receive its new aircraft at Akrotiri in July 1961 but did not have its full complement of eight B.16s until February of the next year. Neighbouring No.249 Squadron followed suit, starting in November 1961, but not getting its eighth B.16 until April 1963. No.6 Squadron received its first B.16 in January 1962 and completed the re-equipping in October 1963. The fourth ASW unit, No.73 Squadron, began getting B.15s in June 1962 and was fully operational by the end of the year.

The new variants had the facility for a 72-rocket projectile pod under each wing, so new attack procedures were introduced.

The 2in (5cm) projectiles were fired, either in a very low-level straight approach on the target, or in a shallow dive. Clearance was given for flying at 50ft (15.25m) for the straight level deliveries on the Larnaca range, while shallow-dive firing usually took place at Episkopi Bay or El Adam. The maintaining of altitude during these sorties was very much the province of the navigator, and it was enough to keep him fully occupied, particularly when formation attacks in pairs was introduced. The LABS weapon delivery procedure, perfected in 2ndTAF, was adopted by the ASW, practices taking place at El Adam and Tarhunna. Simulated low-level napalm weapon deliveries were flown over the ranges, using underwing tanks containing coloured water; no records can be found of live napalm drops.

By January 1966, the ASW was established with eight B.15s or B.16s for each of the four squadrons. Its workload was intensive. The aircraft took part in the large number of exercises set up by CENTO, as well as remaining attached, on a fairly regular basis, to the many far-flung bases within the extensive Near and Middle East Air Force's commands. One major annual event was Exercise *Shabaz*, during which Strike Wing squadrons could be called upon to operate from as far afield as Peshawar, one of the

Despite the problems in the Near East, No.139 (Jamaica) Squadron took its B.16s to Kindley Field, Bermuda, where they lined up prior to a display. Author's collection

Conversion of B.6 and B.6(BS) Aircraft

B.6 to B.15

Trial installations made by Marshall of Cambridge. Production conversion of thirty-nine aircraft undertaken by Bristol Aeroplane Co. Ltd at Filton and English Electric Co. Ltd at Samlesbury: WH947, WH948, WH954, WH955, WH956, WH957, WH958, WH959, WH960, WH961, WH963, WH964, WH965, WH966, WH967, WH968, WH969, WH970, WH971, WH972, WH973, WH974, WH977, WH981, WH983, WH984, WJ756, WJ760, WJ762, WJ764, WJ766, WT205, WT208, WT209, WT210, WT211, WT213, WT370, XK641

B.15, WH959, of the RAF Handling Squadron, stands among a miscellany of contemporaries at A&AEE Boscombe Down. Crown Copyright, DERA Boscombe Down

B.6(BS) to B.16

Trial installations made by Marshall of Cambridge, which then undertook the production conversion of nineteen aircraft: WJ770, WJ771, WJ773, WJ774, WJ776, WJ777, WJ778, WJ780, WJ781, WJ782, WJ783, WT302, WT303, WT306, WT369, WT372, WT373, WT374 , XH570

Three B.16s of the Akrotiri Strike Wing. While WJ771 disintegrated at 5,000ft on 16 July 1964, WT303 and WJ780 were both sold to India in 1970, as B.66s, IF1024 and IF1025 respectively. Author's collection

Containing thirty-seven 2in (5cm) projectiles, a rocket pod is winched into position at Akrotiri. Author's collection

by a dual-thrust solid-propellent rocket motor and had a 510lb (232kg) warhead, which could have a delay or non-delay fuse. It had an accuracy of 30ft (9.14m) at a range of 7 miles (11km). Trials had been conducted on the Sud-Aviation SO-4050 Vautour and it was operational on the G.A.M. Dassault Etendard IVM.

Over 1,000 AS.30s were purchased by the RAF and, in the spring of 1965, several B.15s were modified at Samlesbury to carry the missile on an adapted underwing pylon. WH966 of No.32 Squadron was used as the AS.30 trials installation and crew familiarization aircraft at Samlesbury, while WH967 was used by Boulton Paul for trials, with a ventral camera housing under the forward section of the bombbay. The range at El Adam saw the majority of test firings, first by aircraft with one missile and, by the end of 1966, the Canberra Tactical Evaluation Flight (CANTAC) had cleared the installation for service, with both squadrons' aircraft carrying one under each wing, on the outboard pylons. No.103 MU Akrotiri took responsibility for local modifications and maintenance of AS.30 installations.

Although the missile's manufacturer introduced modifications to increase the weapon's potential, the Canberra's variant remained unchanged, as it proved entirely satisfactory for the operational requirements of the two squadrons. No further units in the ASW were so equipped and, when the two squadrons were disbanded in 1969 – No.32 squadron in February and No.73 squadron in March – that was the finale of the AS.30's service in the Middle East. However, the missile was also used in the Far East Air Force, where No.45 Squadron was adapted to carry it (*see* Chapter 10).

cluster of Pakistan airfields near the Khyber Pass. During one exercise, low-level sorties from Tehran encountered swarms of locusts that were accepted as 'overwhelming odds' and having command of the local airspace.

Coping with the Heat

News of a posting from Europe to the Middle East leads to ideas of being in warmer climes and 'getting your knees brown'. Sometimes, the positive thoughts override reality.

During flight testing with VN799, 'Bee' Beamont had gone on record as saying that the canopy generated a warmth that was sometimes rather oppressive. In the Mediterranean area, this situation was, predictably, exacerbated. Many attempts were made to improve it, but none was completely satisfactory. Various sun shades were constructed, from a plastic sheeting roof mounted on a wheeled framework, which could be positioned over the cockpit canopy, to a perforated frame that bolted on over the crew area. In outside temperatures well over 100 degrees Fahrenheit, the crew soon found out that the inside of a metal tube can become unbearably hot!

A mobile cooler unit, which blew cold air into the cockpit via a flexible hose put through the open entrance door, certainly lowered the internal temperature, but there were not enough coolers to service all aircraft when the squadron was on the ground. Some crews flew in a nylon Air Ventilated Suit (ASV), worn under the standard flying suit. The ASV had numerous air tubes that radiated from a main tube connected to a unit in the crew compartment, which was fed by an engine compressor stage. The system did work, but at the expense of comfort, and personal compromises were set up by individuals. The sweat generated while preparing for take-off became uncomfortably cold when operational altitude was reached.

The AS.30

In 1965, it was decided to equip two of the ASW's units, No.32 and 73 Squadrons, with French air-to-surface (ASM) missiles, the AS.30, designed and produced by Nord Aviation, until the formation of the Société Nationale Industrielle Aérospatiale. Weighing 1,146lb (520kg), the 12¾ft- (3.88m-) long missile was powered

---

Nos 32 and 73 Squadrons in the ASW

Aircraft confirmed as having operated with No.32 Squadron, with aircraft modified to carry AS.30 missiles in italics: *WH947*, WH955, *WH957*, *WH960*, *WH966*, WH970, WH971, *WH972*, WH984, *WJ774*, *WJ776*, *WJ777*, *WJ778*, *WJ781*, *WJ782*, *WJ783*, WT303, WT369, WT373, XH570

Aircraft confirmed as having operated with No.73 Squadron, with aircraft modified to carry AS.30 missiles in italics: WH954, WH956, WH961, *WH964*, WH968, *WH973*, WH974, WH977, WH981, *WH983*, *WJ760*, WJ762

Boulton Paul used B.15, WH967, for the installation trials of the Nord AS.30 ASM, for which a cine camera was fitted in the forward portion of the bomb-bay. Author's collection

Photographic Reconnaissance

The NEAF's photographic-reconnaissance requirements were first handled by No.13 Squadron, which traded in its Meteor PR.10s for Canberra PR.7s, when it moved to Akrotiri in February 1956. On 1 April 1958, No.69 Squadron left 2ndTAF and took its Canberra PR.3s to Luqa in Malta, where, on 1 July, it was renumbered No.39 Squadron. It remained at Luqa until the end of September 1970, having updated to

PR.7, WT535, of Laarbruch's No.17 Squadron, seen in the midday heat of Khormaksar, in 1964.
Ray Deacon

PR.9s in November 1962. Together, Nos 13 and 39 Squadrons operated for CENTO over a vast area, from the Mediterranean Sea to the Seychelles, all over the Arabian peninsula, plus North and Central Africa. Detachments were periodically sent to Sharjah, at the request of units in the Persian Gulf area, and to the island of Masirah, off the Oman east coast, which had been up-dated in the late 1960s, following Britain's evacuation of Aden in 1967. The long-term unrest between Iraq and Kuwait kept the squadrons on readiness for rapid response to local survey requirements. The oil-drilling rights dispute between Saudi Arabia and Abu Dhabi in 1970 called for photographic sorties to be flown on a daily

basis. The camera shutters certainly did not collect any cobwebs.

The two photo-reconnaissance units, Nos 13 and 39 Squadrons, with their PR.9s, were heavily involved in the Persian Gulf area. Khormaksar, on the peninsula jutting out from the mainland into the Gulf of Aden, was interchanged with Al-Muharraq, the base on the northern tip of the island of Bahrain, in the Persian Gulf itself. Early in 1965, three of No.13 Squadron's aircraft were detached to Tengah, on Singapore Island, to assist the resident Canberra PR.7-flying No.81 Squadron, during the troubles with Indonesia. Regular detachments, of three months' duration, to the area were shared between

The Akrotiri Strike Wing's pink flamingo crest is carried on the fin of B.15, **WH983**, of No.73 Squadron, seen at Lyneham on 16 April 1965. R.A. Walker

the two NEAF photo-recce squadrons, until the Bangkok Agreement was signed, on 11 August 1966.

The two-squadron PR partnership was broken on 1 October 1970, when No.39 Squadron was posted as a unit to the UK,

for the first time since it had left Bircham Newton with its DH.9As in April 1921. Its new home was Wyton in Cambridgeshire, where the squadron stayed until being disbanded on 1 June 1982. No.13 Squadron moved from Akrotiri to Luqa on 10

October 1972, and remained there for another six years, until following in No.39 Squadron's steps and joining them at Wyton, on 22 October 1978. Its disbanding took place six months before that of No.39 Squadron, on 5 January 1982.

(Above) **WH947**, a B.15 of No.32 Squadron, Akrotiri Strike Wing, flies over a typical Cyprus landscape. Author's collection

B.16, WJ777, carries the crests of the four Akrotiri Strike Wing squadrons, plus a legend that is self-explanatory. Author's collection

CHAPTER NINE

Altitude and Longevity

HA PR.9

In the Middle East, Nos 13 and 39 Squadrons had carried out photo-reconnaissance operations with the Canberra PR.9. At the design stage, this had been considered a logical extension of the Canberra's already extensive repertoire, but in reality it led to problems.

The ultra-high altitude potential of the Canberra had been recognized since the beginning. In the mid-1950s, being able to operate at 65,000ft (19,800m) was seen as the best defence against existing interceptors or ground-to-air missiles. Existing variants were happily operating around 50,000ft (15,200m). With the 11,250lb (5,110kg) thrust Avon RA.24 engines that English

Electric were installing in production Lightning F.1s, coupled with an increased wingspan, it was considered that a really high-altitude photographic-reconnaissance Canberra could be produced. The designation HA PR.9 was applied to the project, 'HA' denoting 'high altitude'.

When the designers got down to detailed calculations, they realized that simply increasing the span would affect the aircraft's existing Mach trim and buffet limits. Consequently, the answer was considered to be a generous increase in the centre-section chord between the fuselage and engine nacelles, coupled with a slight increase in overall span. A brand-new PR.7, WH793, which had first flown on 23 April 1954, was sent to Napiers at Luton on 25 May, to be modified as the trials airframe for the new wing. Retaining the

standard PR.7 canopy, WH793 could not really be rated as the PR.9 prototype, although it is loosely referred to as such. The new wing had a span increased by 3ft 10in (115cm) to 67ft 10in (20.5m) and the wing area went up by 85sq ft (7.9sq m), to 1,045sq ft (97sq m).

Napier's Chief Test Pilot Mike Randrup gave the reconfigured WH793 its first flight, on 8 July 1955, from Cranfield, with Walter Shirley as the test observer. Beamont also went to Cranfield to fly the aircraft and, having passed its initial flight trials, it flew to Warton for a full test programme. Beamont was heavily engaged in P.1A Lightning testing and Don Knight was given the responsibility as the PR.9 project test pilot.

The first obvious impression when flying the aircraft was the outstanding rate of climb that the Avon RA.24s gave to

PR.7, WH793 was modified by Napiers to be the test aircraft for the PR.9 wing, with the longer span carrying tanks inboard from the tips. Author's collection

WH793, with 30,000ft (9,100m) being attained in 2½ minutes from lift-off. The height of 50,000ft was reached much more quickly than in the Avon RA.7-powered PR.7, but then the rate of climb dropped off alarmingly. The aircraft performed in the flying programme at the 1955 SBAC Display, where the impressive initial rate of climb was readily demonstrated, and belied the high-altitude problems. Testing was resumed after Farnborough and the team began to realize that, when the new centre-section was at the high incidence required for the very high altitudes, induced drag was just about cancelling out the margin of greater engine thrust. Beamont reached 59,800ft (18,227m) on 18 September 1956 and had barely enough fuel left to get back to Warton.

Naturally, everyone was disappointed, but it was decided that the new variant was worthy of development for production. A B(I).8-type nose was adopted, with the offset blown cockpit canopy of the interdictor, but with the nose unglazed, apart from a small window for a forward-facing F.96 camera. Two other fundamental differences from previous marks of Canberra concerned hinges. The cockpit canopy hinged up from the rear, so that the pilot entered via a ladder positioned on the port side and the navigator gained entry through the nose, the front portion of which hinged to starboard. Once aboard, he sat within his own compartment, separated from the pilot and, from the second production aircraft, in a Martin-Baker ejector seat, above which was a large panel that blew out to allow the upwards travel of the seat when activated in an emergency. Incidentally, these hinging facilities proved very popular when the aircraft operated in hot climates.

Production, Evaluation and Redesign

English Electric received Contract No.6/ACFT/11158/CB6(b) on 31 July 1954, for the production of various Canberra marks. It included thirty-two PR.9s and the whole of this element of the order was sub-contracted to Short Bros at Belfast on the transferred MoS Contract No.6/ACFT/14027/CB6(b). Serial numbers XH129 to XH137 and XH164 to XH177 were allocated to the production, which had originally included nine additional airframes, XH178 to XH186, but these were cancelled. A later

At the 1955 SBAC Display, WH793 climbs to exhibit the new wing's increased centre-section chord. Author's collection

contract was issued in 1955, for eleven more aircraft, XK440 to XK443 and XK467 to XK473, but these were also cancelled. The total number of PR.9s built was twenty-three aircraft, excluding WH793.

The first production PR.9, WH129, had its maiden flight on 27 July 1958, from Shorts' airfield at Sydenham. It went to Warton on 11 September, where Don Knight got down to evaluating the aircraft prior to its scheduled flight to the A&AEE at Boscombe Down on 11 October, for service clearance. On the day before, a structural test at 5g, flown at the aircraft's design airspeed, was set up. Knight began in smooth air, off the Lancashire coastal resort of Southport. He built up to 5g in a turn to port and was on the point of rolling out of the turn, when XH129 made an uncontrollable roll to starboard. The aircraft caught fire as it went into a steep

spiral dive and the pilot ejected so low that he was in the water as his parachute deployed. XH129 hit the water while burning fiercely and, sadly, the observer was killed.

Royal Navy divers and a salvage team were brought into Liverpool Bay, to attempt a recovery of the wreckage. Don Knight was able to give a graphic description of what happened but the big question was 'Why?' A large percentage of the remains of XH129 were brought to the surface, together with enough test instruments for a detailed investigation to be made. This showed a failure of the new wing-root skin attachment to the fuselage, induced by flexing under the loads imposed during the 5g turn. The skin had peeled back from the new centre-section's leading edge and the wing had completely failed upwards.

XH134, the sixth production PR.9, was flown at the 1959 SBAC Display, before spending time at Boscombe
Down on various trial installations. It is still in service with No.39 (1 PRU) Squadron. *Aeroplane*

The overall silver finish was worn by No.39 Squadron in 1964, when PR.9, XH134/'A' went to Khormaksar
from Luqa, without underwing tanks. Ray Deacon

XH130 standing on the Khormaksar Station flight pan in 1963. Some PR.9s had an anti-dazzle painted panel ahead of the windscreen, but it was not mandatory. Ray Deacon

XH134/'AA' shows signs of the electronic update that the PR.9 had in the 1970s, with aerials on the fin and rear fuselage tip. In the current hemp finish, the aircraft carries the unit crest of No.1 PRU on its fin.
George Pennick

Don Crowe, the Canberra Chief Production Engineer, assumed responsibility for the required redesign; XH136, the sixth production PR.9, was the first aircraft on the line to incorporate the revised wing attachments. Beamont came off Lightning testing to fly the aircraft and he went on record as finding the Canberra rather heavy compared to the Lightning, even with the more powerful Avons. Being the professional that he was, within a couple of short flights he was, as he put it 'well in tune with the aeroplane again'.

With strain-gauge and wing-deflection instruments fully calibrated, XH136 was ready, on 20 January 1960, for the Chief Test Pilot to undertake the trials. Despite inclement weather, the flight went ahead. The engines were opened to full power as Beamont took the aircraft into a turn, gradually building up the forces, until 5g was attained. The turn was tightened to 5.1g to allow for instrument-reading error, before the pilot rolled back and set a course, through the gloom, to Warton. The fourteen-minute test had proved that Don Crowe's modifications had cured the previous problem.

'Bee' went back to the Lightning and the PR.9 was cleared for service. XH136 was allocated to No.58 Squadron at Wyton in April, where it joined the PR.7s already being flown. By July 1960, the squadron had six PR.9s and although the maximum altitude performance was a little short of the design figure of 60,000ft (18,300m), the new Canberra was able to operate well above the earlier marks.

New Techniques and Equipment

New techniques were tried and tested. These included shipping-reconnaissance sorties flown in conjunction with No.543 Squadron, which was also based at Wyton, with its Valiant B(PR)1s. The Valiant flew as a high-altitude search aircraft and vectored a PR.9 on to the target ship. The Canberra descended to a lower level, to photograph the ship, before returning to its higher operational altitude. The successful trials were the harbingers of later maritime radar reconnaissance operating procedures. In fact, these were brought into play quite early. When the Cuban Missile Crisis developed, in October 1962, No.58 Squadron's high-altitude photo-recce PR.9s became involved in recording the passage of Soviet shipping transporting intercontinental missiles to Cuba.

New operational equipment for PR.9 aircrew also required trials. Partial-pressure helmets and suits had to be worn and a course at the RAF Aeromedical Centre at Upwood was mandatory. The effects of high-altitude flying on the human body were explained and crews were introduced to a simulated high-altitude explosive decompression.

Between 1976 and 1980, significant improvements were incorporated in the standard PR.9 service equipment. As some Vulcans were retired, their Radar Warning Receivers were transferred to the reconnaissance Canberras, as was the Infra Red Line Scan (IRLS) equipment carried in podded installations on the Phantom FGR.2. New Decca Tactical Air Navigation System (TANS) elements and a Sperry Master Reference Gyro were fitted, as was an updated Doppler system, all of which were to prove beneficial in the low-level reconnaissance role.

Squadron Use

No.58 Squadron's retention of the PR.9 lasted just two and a half years. In November 1962, the aircraft were allocated to No.39 Squadron at Luqa, where they replaced the PR.3s that the unit had flown since being re-formed on 1 July 1958. Eight years later, on 1 October 1970, the squadron left Luqa for the United Kingdom and the PR.9s came full circle, as the squadron's new base was Wyton. In June 1982, the squadron was disbanded and acquired the new designation of No.1 Photographic Reconnaissance Unit (1 PRU). Ten years later, the squadron's traditional identity was restored and as No.39 Squadron (1 PRU), controlled by No.18 (Maritime) Group, it is employed on radar reconnaissance, together with survey duties, flown from its base at Marham. It is the sole RAF Canberra operator, a distinction it is likely to hold until at least 2003.

The third Canberra PR.9 user was No.13 Squadron, based at Akrotiri, which received its first aircraft in July 1961. During the fifteen years that the squadron held the PR.9s, it relocated to Luqa on Malta, in September 1965, and returned to Akrotiri seven years later, for nine months, before going back to Malta. There, it gave up its high-altitude Canberras in October 1976.

Today's PR.9

Today's PR.9 is a much more sophisticated photographic-reconnaissance aircraft than when it was first designed. Its role in the shadowy world of gathering information without violating restricted airspace has required new systems and equipment, such as 'System III', which also exists under the codename *Crystal*. This comprises a fixed-focus, 36in (90cm) focal-length conventional camera, fitted with a mirror lens that can be directed in three oblique positions on either side of the centreline or directly vertical. Being fixed-focus, the camera requires its carrier (the PR.9) to operate within a 49,000–51,000ft (14,900–15,500m) margin, in order to ensure pin-sharp images. Large glazed camera ports have been installed on both sides of the rear front fuselage, just aft of the nose-wheel doors.

Additional ports are positioned on the underside centreline behind the former flare-bay doors, one being for a Zeiss RMK camera, which operates on a sliding pallet. This new equipment usually augments, rather than replaces, the three oblique F95 and F49 survey cameras, although different mission roles sometimes decree changes. The navigator has a reconnaissance viewfinder sight at the front of his compartment in the nose and it is believed that an electro-optical long-range camera sensor is installed for certain missions.

Border-surveillance missions have been flown in most of the world's trouble spots, many in Eastern and Far East locations. It has gone on record that No.39 Squadron aircraft could get the results of such operations far more quickly than waiting for a satellite to come into the necessary orbit.

It is not inconceivable that the Falklands campaign may have benefited from PR.9 attention, although this has never been confirmed. Operations would have been conducted from the South American mainland, which would have been a matter of some sensitivity, but Chile did receive three ex-RAF PR.9s after the conflict. The operations over Bosnia were less contentious, and another well-publicized action discovered the human misery of the refugees from the wars in Rwanda. The unrest in Kosovo was another PR.9-reconnoitred event.

Currently, the PR.9s fly in the 'hemp' colour scheme that is in vogue in the late 1990s. They started service in an overall silver finish, which was changed to grey/green camouflage in the 1970s, before the adoption of the latest colour scheme.

High-Flying Cameramen

Canberra HA PR.9 aircraft confirmed as serving with Nos 13, 39 and 58 Squadrons. Aircraft currently serving with No.39 (1 PRU) Squadron at the time of writing are shown in italics.

No.13 Squadron
XH130, *XH131*, XH133, *XH135,* XH136, XH137, XH164, XH165, XH166, XH167, *XH168,* XH171, XH172, XH173, XH174, XH176, XH177*

No.39 Squadron
XH131, XH133, *XH134,* XH135, XH136, XH137, XH165, XH166, XH167, *XH168,* XH169, XH171, XH172, XH173, XH174, XH175, XH176

No.58 Squadron
XH134, XH135, XH136, XH137, XH164, XH165, XH166, XH167, *XH168, XH169,* XH170, XH171, XH172, XH173, XH174, XH175, XH176, XH177*

*Short Bros had the distinction of producing the very last new-build Canberra, XH177. Coming off the line on 30 December 1960, it first served with No.58 Squadron, before going to No.13 Squadron, where it was damaged on 14 December 1965. During repairs by No.103 MU Akrotiri, cracks in the main spar were discovered in April 1966, and the aircraft was struck off charge on 5 July 1967. Only the nose exists and this was held by the Wales Aircraft Museum, Cardiff Airport. At the time of writing, it is with Hanningfield Metals at Stock, near Chelmsford.

The Short Bros Belfast production line manufactured the beautiful shape that is exemplified in this lovely air-to-air shot of No.39 Squadron's XH134/'AA'.
Author's collection and BAe

CHAPTER TEN

Canberra Goes Oriental

Communist Threat

The idea of one-quarter of the world's population being ruled by Mao Tse-tung, Chairman of the Chinese Communist Party, was enough to send shudders through both the northern and southern hemispheres. Australia, Britain, France, New Zealand, Pakistan, the Philippine Republic, Thailand and the USA got together to appraise the considered threat; on 19 February 1955, they signed the South East Asia Collective Defence Treaty, in Manila. Under the terms of the treaty, they agreed 'separately and jointly, by means of continuous and effective help and mutual aid, to maintain and develop the individual and collective capacity to resist armed attack and to prevent any counter-subversive activities directed against members' territorial integrity and political stability'.

As far as Britain was concerned, the effect of communism had been brought sharply into focus shortly after VJ-Day, 15 August 1945. The Malayan peninsula had been witness to fierce fighting by British and Commonwealth forces to recapture the 'rubber state' from Japanese occupation and, to this end, assistance was obtained from local guerrilla outfits, who were readily supplied with arms. Once the Japanese had been driven out, Malaya became one of the many Far East countries whose ambition was to end the centuries-old domination of European governments. The Communist-encouraged anti-Imperialists movement was led by Chin Peng, who had received the OBE for his services against the Japanese. On 16 June 1948, three rubber planters were murdered by Communist terrorists; the official National State of Emergency, declared two days later, was to last twelve years.

Over these ensuing years, hostilities, operated by the Security Forces under the codename Operation *Firedog*, gradually increased in intensity, with RAF and RAAF aerial activity involving wartime Spitfires, Tempests, Beaufighters, Mosquitoes, Dakotas and Sunderlands. In addition to these, Brigands, Hornets and Lincolns were introduced into the conflict in the early 1950s, as well as the first British jet-powered aircraft in the Far East, the de Havilland Vampire. Photographic-reconnaissance Meteor PR.10s took over from No.81 Squadron's Mosquitoes and, at the beginning of 1955, it was decided to add the Canberra to the inventory of aircraft ranged against the Malayan Races Liberation Army (MRLA).

Campaign Against the MRLA

Whether it was planned or just worked out that way has not really been established, but No.101 Squadron, the first unit to receive the Canberra, back in 1951, was the first squadron to use the type operationally

At Butterworth, No.101 Squadron bomb up their B.6s, which have the cockpits protected by sun shades.
Author's collection

against an enemy. Four weeks of special low-level training – flying sorties to search for specific targets within the East Anglian forested areas – were undertaken, before a detachment of four Canberra B.6s, under the command of Sqn Ldr W.D. Robertson, left Binbrook on 7 February 1955, under the codename Operation *Mileage*. The flight deployed through Idris, Habbaniya, Maurpur and Negombo, before landing at Changi, Singapore Island, on 11 February. Two Transport Command Hastings C.2s accompanied the detachment and one NCO

were located either by ground patrols or reconnaissance flights and, before any air raids could be mounted, clearance had to be given by the local police. The specifics of individual raids varied, but the prime objective was to give grief to the terrorists, either by destroying their habitats and depriving them of resources, or by pattern bombing, driving them into areas controlled by the Security Forces.

No.101 Squadron's campaign against the MRLA began on 23 February 1955, when a three-aircraft formation, led by

The 'Datum Point' system technique consisted of the leading aircraft being navigated along a chosen track, at a pre-determined speed and altitude. At a final fix point (the Datum Point), which could be a particular bend in a river or a distinguishing feature in the jungle, a timed run was started and bombs were dropped on the leader's release, which was controlled by his navigator's stopwatch.

The Auster Target-Marking method involved the Canberra flight establishing the optimum run-in to the target at 4,000ft

WH961 leaves Filton, after being converted from B.6 to B.15 standard, prior to being allocated to No.45 Squadron and seeing service in the Malayan peninsula. Author's collection

groundcrew was carried in each Canberra, in addition to the three-man crew. These poor 'spare bods' must surely have suffered badly from the lack of space; even when empty, the Canberra was very cramped, let alone when the pilot and two navigators were aboard.

The Far East Air Force (FEAF) provided much assistance to the newcomers and tropical trials were started within a couple of days of arrival. Just over a week after landing at Changi, the detachment flew up to Butterworth, in the northern Malayan province of Kedah, which was closer to their specific target area. This featured camps in small clearings in the jungle, designated 'pinpoint' targets, or larger communities, known as 'area' targets, which were virtually self-contained, with their own cultivated tracts. These camps

Sqn Ldr Robertson in WH948, attacked a terrorist area, each aircraft dropping six 1,000lb (455kg) bombs. A similar attack was made the following day and, on 25 February, all four of the detachment's aircraft were employed.

Special Techniques

The detachment's aircraft were very much on a learning curve with these attacks and, while some followed techniques proven by Bomber Command and RAAF Lincolns, the Canberra crews perfected some of their own, relating more closely to the abilities of their aircraft. The two procedures that proved most successful were the 'Datum Point' system and Auster Target-Marking (ATM).

(1,200m) and setting up a rendezvous with an Auster Air Observation Post (AOP), airborne at a point four minutes' flying time from the target. R/T contact between the attacking force and the AOP was consolidated, after which, at ten minutes' flying time from the target, the Canberra leader notified the Auster that they were 'bombing in 10'. The message would be repeated, with a decreasing time, at one-minute intervals, until 'bombing in 2', which was followed by 'bombing in 90 seconds'. On this call, the Auster released its marker flare on the target and broke away from the area. With a flight of Canberras approaching at 235mph (375km/h), it was no time to start admiring the finer points of Teddy Petter's design! The lead-aircraft's bomb-aimer took over as soon as the flare was seen and a conventional bombing run was made.

Sorties and Results

No.101 Squadron's detachment lasted nearly four months, during which a total of ninety-eight sorties were flown, of which three were night raids, and 184 tons of bombs were dropped. Forty-seven sorties were flown with Auster Target-Marking and twenty-four were 'Datum Point' attacks. Eighteen sorties were flown as individual raids, determined by the flight leader once the target had been reached, and the squadron's final raid was a three-aircraft, Auster Target-Marking sortie, made on 31 May 1955. Cameras were activated on all sorties and examination of the finished prints by the Joint Air Photographic Interpretation Centre showed a high number of accurate strikes.

In order to supply detachments during the Malayan conflict, a system of rotating the Binbrook-based squadrons was employed, and a four-aircraft flight from No.617 Squadron took over from No.101 Squadron in June. The new arrivals opened their account with the terrorists on 21 June, and flew a total of twenty sorties in the following month. On their first four attacks, 500lb (225kg) bombs were dropped on targets within Butterworth's Kedah province, but from then on, full loads of six 1,000lb (455kg) bombs were used against targets in central and southern Malaya.

When not flying operational sorties against MRLA targets, the aircraft made cross-country navigational practice flights at high level, one of the principal objects being to check radio compasses in tropical conditions. The art of astro-navigation, using the Mk.9 sextant, was brushed up. It was soon found that readings taken through the canopy on the port side were inclined to

(Above) B.15, WH981 of No.73 Squadron, seen at Nairobi before going into action against the MRLA. The aircraft was later converted to E.15 standard, with an updated electronic suite. Ray Deacon

The sun shade over a No.101 Squadron B.6, at Butterworth, was a substantial piece of construction. Author's collection

be inconsistent, due to the navigator having to operate around the pilot's head! Results taken through the starboard side of the canopy were almost always extremely good.

Obviously, the local weather had some bearing on the flying, with early-morning and evening attacks being curtailed by ominous cloud formations. The optimum flying conditions existed within a three-hour margin, either side of midday; unfortunately, this was precisely when the majority of terrorists were away from their camps! Night raids were confined to the moon periods, so that the Auster pilots could read their maps. Despite all these constrictions, results were good.

After the Malayan campaign, No.73 Squadron returned to the UK and WJ618 went into storage at No.33 MU Lyneham. R.A. Walker

At high altitude, the squadron often had to fly through substantial layers of cirrostratus, with the risk of running into well-developed mounds of cumulo-nimbus. One flight is on record in which a Canberra had flown in cirrus cloud for over two hours, when it suddenly entered a cumulo-nimbus mass and was propelled 10,000ft (3,050m) above the 42,000ft (12,800m) course that it was flying. After nearly ten minutes of turbulence, the aircraft popped out at 52,000ft (15,800m) and the pilot found further cumulo-nimbus towering above him for at least another 10,000ft. On an exploratory night flight, another Canberra crew entered a mountain of cu-nim at 45,000ft (13,700m), when a lightning strike shot them up 5,000ft (1,500m) and presented them with a flame-out for good measure! The weather was often less friendly than the ground targets, from which there was no anti-aircraft fire; no doubt the MRLA considered it was on their side.

During its four-month detachment, which ended when it handed over to No.12 Squadron in October 1955, No.617 Squadron had flown sixty-eight sorties, during which over 130 tons of bombs were dropped. In a concentrated three-day, Auster Marker-controlled assault on the central Malayan town of Mentakeb, fifteen sorties each unloaded six 1,000lb (455kg)

bombs on the area. They had encountered outside air temperatures at high altitude of −75°C and, on the ground, cockpit temperatures of 158°F (70°C). Whereas the Godfrey cold-air system provided temperate conditions during low-level sorties, the Canberra's heating was no match for high-altitude temperatures.

No.12 Squadron brought eight Canberra B.6s with it and, after flying three simulated sorties at the beginning of November, six aircraft were deployed for the first live attack against the southern province of Johor, on 22 November. At the end of the month, a nine-day assault was mounted against Seremban, in Selangor province. Fifty-seven sorties dropped a total of 60,000lb (27,210kg) of high explosives on the area, in the most concentrated series of attacks made during the whole eighteen-month Binbrook Wing's association with Operation *Firedog*. Many of the lessons learned and techniques perfected the hard way by No.101 Squadron in the first detachment made succeeding squadrons' operations against the MRLA forces more proficient.

There was a lull in air activity following the Seremban raids and, after one four-aircraft sortie flown on 20 December, it was 9 February 1956 before the next mission was mounted. This was the first of forty-five attacks made in that month, mostly against terrorist targets in Johor province.

On 3 March, the area was the subject of a night raid and that was No.12 Squadron's finale. No.9 Squadron took over in March and its predecessor assessed the results of its detachment.

In the three months of operations, No.12 Squadron had flown 145 sorties, during which 248 tons of bombs had been dropped. This reflects the increase in aircraft that the squadron had at its disposal, compared with the previous two units. On at least eight raids, six aircraft were employed and, on five occasions, seven B.6s were put up. During the concentrated nine-day operation against Seremban, never less than five aircraft took part and, on three days, seven flew.

No.9 Squadron's eight Canberra B.6 operations, from April to June 1956, started on 7 April, but its activities have not been recorded as comprehensively as those of the previous operators. A total of forty-one sorties are believed to have been flown and the dropping of sixty-eight tons of bombs has been confirmed. One recorded event was a flight made by Flt Lt J.F. Stonham, who inadvertently flew into a mass of cumulo-nimbus at 47,000ft (14,300m) over Con Nicobar Island, one of the Nicobar group of islands in the Andaman Sea. Both engines flamed out in quick succession and, during the resultant descent, the pilot tried to contact the radio station on

Con Nicobar, but got no reply. The port Avon was successfully relit at 17,500ft (5,300m), but the starboard one would not follow suit. To add to Flt Lt Stonham's woes, he had no electrics, as the port generator drive had sheared. With only one engine and on primary instruments, he flew over 500 miles (800km) across the Andaman Sea to Butterworth, where he received a green endorsement for his troubles!

delayed-action flares were dropped. In this way, several hours after the last aircraft had landed back at base, the false alarm would bring MRLA forces out of their huts, anticipating a follow-up attack.

In August 1956, No.101 Squadron was recalled to Binbrook in order to stand by for deployment to the Middle East. A month later, it was flying out from Luqa, in preparation for Operation *Musketeer*. In

TF.10, Brigand B.1, Hornet F.3, Vampire FB.9 and Venom FB.1, before a detachment was sent to Coningsby in October 1955, in readiness to acquire Canberra B.2s. The whole squadron moved to Tengah, Singapore Island, on 15 November 1957, where its B.2s were waiting.

After the First World War, No.60 Squadron had disbanded at Bircham Newton on 22 January 1920. Just over

No.101 Squadron's B.6s release a string of 1,000lb (455kg) bombs over MRLA positions in Malaya.
Author's collection

With four squadrons making up the Binbrook Wing, each detachment lasting approximately three months and operations against the Malayan terrorists still being active in June 1956, No.101 Squadron's turn came round again, this time with eight aircraft. The first *Foxfire* mission of its second tour started before No.9 Squadron had left for Binbrook. Furthermore, it resumed the RAF's campaign against the Seremban area on 21 June 1956, dropping over 50 tons of bombs in nineteen sorties flown in the first four days. Several night sorties were flown in loose line-astern formations and, in order to harass terrorist groups even further,

the two months of operations at Butterworth, fifty sorties were flown, during which over 73 tons of bombs were dropped.

Further Squadron Deployment

Both Nos 45 and 60 Squadrons had been in the Far East for many years. The former started to deploy to the region, from the Middle East, on 13 February 1942, taking its Blenheim IVFs with it. Over the years, its equipment ranged from the Vultee Vengeance, Mosquito FB.VI, Beaufighter

three months later, the squadron reformed at Risalpur, near the Khyber Pass, as the renumbered No.97 Squadron. It operated from a multitude of Indian bases until 1 October 1945, when it took its Thunderbolt IIs to Zayatkwin, near Rangoon. By November 1957, it was flying Venom FB.4s alongside No.45 Squadron's Canberras at Tengah. Sharing the Singapore base were No.1(B) Squadron of the Royal Australian Air Force (RAAF), flying Australian Government Aircraft Factory-built Lincoln Mk.30(B)s, and No.14(F) Squadron of the Royal New Zealand Air Force (RNZAF) with its Venoms.

No.2 Squadron RAAF flew its B.20s as a part of the Commonwealth Strategic Reserve, with RAF and RNZAF squadrons. Author's collection

Both squadrons had been an integral part of the Tengah Strike Wing, but, in 1958, No.14(F) Squadron went back to New Zealand and was replaced by No.75 Squadron RNZAF, the only Commonwealth unit to be loaned a whole squadron of fifteen Canberra B.2s. These were former RAF aircraft, fully serviced by MUs before flying out to Tengah, where the RNZAF squadron took delivery of them. As an element of the Commonwealth Strategic Reserve (CSR), the RNZAF squadron worked in close co-operation with the two RAF squadrons, but also flew operations with the RAAF.

No.2 Squadron RAAF had also arrived in the area in 1958, equipped with licence-built Canberra B.20s. These were basically similar to RAF B.2s, although, after the twenty-seventh aircraft, Avon RA.7s were fitted. They also had structural modifications to enable them to operate at an all-up weight (AUW) of 51,000lb (23,180kg), which was over 6,000lb (2,725kg) heavier than the B.2s in service. On 30 September, both Australasian squadrons combined for a mission against the northern area of Perak

province, in the first combined CSR Canberra operation.

The RNZAF squadron remained until the spring of 1962, when it returned the B.2s to their owner and returned to Ohakea, its home base on the lowland near Wanganui, on New Zealand's North Island.

When No.1(B) Squadron of the RAAF gave way to No.2 Squadron in 1958 and returned to its base at Amberley, in New South Wales, the Lincolns were pensioned off so that the squadron could receive Canberra B.20s. Across the Tasman Sea, its former Butterworth colleagues from No.14(F) RNZAF, who had also gone back home in 1958, had swapped their Venoms for Vampire FB.25s; in October 1959, these too were replaced. At Ohakea, the squadron started re-equipping with Canberra B(I).12s, which were modified B(I).8s, with an autopilot, radio altimeter and updated navigation equipment. With its new aircraft, No.14 Squadron's role was changed to that of a light bomber unit, in which it conducted exercises with the Far East Air Force (FEAF). By September 1964, it had returned to Tengah, where it remained until November 1966.

Photographic Reconnaissance

Dedicated Canberra photographic-reconnaissance aircraft did not arrive in the FEAF theatre until February 1960. No.81 Squadron had deployed to Tengah on 1 April 1958, equipped with Meteor PR.10s and Percival Pembroke C(PR).1s. The latter, in particular, had performed sterling tasks far removed from those of its original specification, when it was displayed as the Percival Prince at the 1948 SBAC Display.

In February 1960, the squadron took delivery of its first PR.7, having received a Canberra T.4 for dual-control refresher experience a month earlier. Another PR.7 arrived later in the year, but serviceability was a problem and the squadron had to rely until the next year on its long-standing established aircraft. By March 1961, another four PR.7s had joined the squadron, but not until late autumn were the serviceability bugs ironed out, and No.81 Squadron was able to utilize its Canberras to the full. From then on, although the Malayan emergency had officially ceased, Operation *Firedog* reconnaissance requirements still existed and were able to be met by the PR.7s.

Later in 1961, a very ambitious programme to survey the whole of Borneo was started. The vast areas of featureless jungle presented real problems. To the PR.7's standard complement of six F52 and one F49 cameras, a 12in F95 and a 48in F52 were added for the low-level photographic requirements of this survey. Added to the difficulties of accurate flying over Borneo's terrain was the not inconsiderable problem of the weather. In order to avoid the inevitable build-up of cloud around midday, 'dawn patrol' starts were essential and, to reduce flying time to the survey area, detachments were deployed to the excellent runway facilities on Pulau Labuan (known as Labuan for short), which was off the north-west coast of Borneo. This provided a much-needed increase in actual surveying time, so that, weather permitting, over four hours could be spent producing hundreds of images. Clear skies over Borneo usually indicated storm conditions in the South China Sea and these could progress southwards to the survey area much more quickly than might be expected.

The arrival of the B.15, with its rocket-projectile capacity, provided the Canberra with a new strike ability. No.32 Squadron's WH947 shows the neat packs that each contained thirty-seven 2in (5cm) projectiles.
Author's collection

Canberra B.15, WH976 of No.45 Squadron, lines up ready to depart the Malayan theatre of operations.
Author's collection

The Royal Malaysian Air Force (RMAF) took over the Labuan facilities towards the end of 1968, but No.81 Squadron's detachment was given full access until the survey was, at last, completed, in May 1969. A similar survey of Thailand, started in November 1961, was a much less arduous mission and the squadron had the whole operation completed by March 1962. Around the same time, low-level night photo-flash exercises were instigated and these showed up the fact that infra-red, as opposed to photo-flash, was much better for this type of work. Surprisingly, the request for infra-red was granted, mainly because photo-flashes were in short supply!

In December 1962, No.81 Squadron was back on a 'war footing'. An armed rebellion had erupted in the Sultanate of Brunei, the foundation of which was the desire of President Sukarno of Indonesia to rope in the whole of Borneo as a constituent of an Indonesian 'super-state'. Communist factions had stimulated the rebellion, but there was no lack of support from Indonesia itself and Brunei's neighbouring Sarawak also joined in the conflict. British and Gurkha troops were transported into the area, with air support initially supplied by the B.2s of No.45 Squadron. These were replaced within a couple of weeks by Canberra B.15s operated from the hastily expanded base on Labuan.

In order to respond to photographic-reconnaissance requirements, No.81 Squadron put the Borneo survey operations on hold. The photographs and maps obtained from surveys already made were invaluable to the ground forces. Likely areas where rebel troops could cross the borders were well covered photographically, and No.45 Squadron was supplied with information on areas pin-pointed as potential trouble spots. The arrival of the B.15, with its rocket-projectile capacity, greatly increased the squadron's value in the support of ground operations. A live-firing training range was established at Song Song, between Butterworth and Tengah, while live firing was also carried out on small craft targets anchored off the Malayan coast.

Confrontation with Indonesia

The complicated politics of the area caused an alarming escalation of operations in 1964. A defence agreement between Britain and Malaya had been signed seven years previously, on 16 September 1957 and, while the actual revolt with Brunei had been quickly quelled, a British armed presence within the State was increased. Indonesian rebel units were still crossing the North Borneo frontiers and, in September 1963, the provinces of Malaya elected to join with Sabah, Sarawak and Singapore, to form the State of Malaysia. Under the terms of the treaty, Britain had been given permission to keep bases and forces within the State, so that peace could be maintained in the area.

The formation of the new State was not viewed with enthusiasm by Indonesia, and it heralded an immediate expansion of Indonesian guerrilla activities, together with an increase in Indonesian Air Force B.25 Mitchell flights over the Malayan peninsular. On 23 December 1964, No.45 Squadron began Operation *Birdsong* and a simulated attack was made on guerrilla forces that had infiltrated across the Straits of Johor. Strong Indonesian positions had been established at Kukup, on the mainland of Malaya, and three days after the simulated raid, on 26 December, they received a B.15 rocket-projectile attack as a Boxing Day greeting from No.45 Squadron. The Security Ground Forces followed up this raid and removed the remaining invaders.

The confrontation with Indonesia led to the decision to rotate three-monthly detachments to Tengah from four Akrotiri Strike Wing squadrons. Eight No.73 Squadron B.15s started the detachment cycle in September 1964, with No.32 Squadron taking over in November. In February 1965, an eight-aircraft Canberra B.16 detachment from No.249 Squadron arrived at Tengah; because of increased ground activity at that time, it was moved to a jungle airstrip at Kuantan, on the

A motley group of No.81 Squadron groundcrew stand before their PR.7, prior to the aircraft joining Operation Firedog. Author's collection

Malayan east coast. This had a short runway, surrounded by tall trees. This, combined with the high temperatures, meant that the Canberras had to keep their tip tanks empty in order to get airborne with any useful war load.

Life at Kuantan was a little more primitive than on Singapore and, while Close Air Support (CAS) rocket-projectile missions were flown, some aircrew members were inveigled into making up numbers for ground forces, rounding up bands of Indonesian guerrillas. For some, this was the first time a rifle had been handled since square-bashing days! In July, No.73 Squadron was back again for another

After the treaty, No.45 Squadron became the only FEAF Canberra bomber unit, and No.81 Squadron also remained, to fulfil photographic-reconnaissance requirements. Exercises were flown with Hunter FGA.9s of No.28 Squadron based at Kai Tak, while deployments to Australia, the Cocos Islands, Hong Kong and Gan were welcome breaks. Gan was the most southerly of the Maldives coral islands, over 300 miles (450km) to the south-west of the Indian mainland. Developed as a staging post *en route* to the Far East, it became fully active in 1958 and boasted a radio beacon that emitted an extremely strong signal, on which an aircraft's radio compass could

The AS.30 association with No.45 Squadron became bogged down, and it was the autumn of 1967 before Exercise *Hotshot* was set up. Five B.15s operated from Labuan for the exercise and twenty AS.30s were fired, with very good results. Throughout 1968 and into 1969, various ranges were employed for subsequent *Hotshot* exercises, the farthest being the Australian Weapons Research Establishment range at Woomera.

By the end of 1969, the RAF's withdrawal from the Far East was agreed. Large stocks of armaments – including the AS.30s – had been accumulated through the frugal allocations made to the

Another B.15 of No.73 Squadron destined for Malayan duty. WH983 was later converted to E.15 standard.
Ray Deacon

stretch; its men also had to sample the rigours of Kuantan, while some crews operated under Forward Air Controller (FAC) direction at Labuan until November, when No.32 Squadron's turn came round again. Their stay was of a much shorter duration, due to a marked lessening of guerrilla activity. The ASW's involvement in Malaya ceased in December, so the squadron found itself pulling Christmas crackers back at Akrotiri.

The confrontation finally ended on 11 August 1966, when the Bangkok Agreement was signed. Canberras of the RAF, RAAF and RNZAF contributed in no small measure, in restricting Indonesia to comparatively small, but inconvenient, guerrilla activities, as did the sight of occasional Victor and Vulcan detachments on exercises. They certainly put the abilities of Indonesia's opposition into perspective.

home. Being such a small dot in the Indian Ocean, the odds on finding Gan without a radio compass were very long!

Withdrawal from the Far East

In 1965, the Nord AS.30 air-to-ground guided missile had been introduced to the Akrotiri Strike Wing. In the FEAF, No.45 Squadron had been actively engaged on LABS training during the early part of the same year. Later in the year, representatives from the Société Nationale Industrielle Aérospatiale went to Tengah, to have preliminary discussions about equipping squadron aircraft with the AS.30. It was August 1966 before the first aircraft was fitted out, and the end of the year before a further two were finished, but the absence of a suitable simulator precluded any live firings.

squadrons over the years, and restrictions on their use were lifted. No.45 Squadron flew many happy hours of missile firing before it was disbanded at Tengah on 18 February 1970. No.81 Squadron had disbanded at Tengah on 16 January 1970, and No.20 Squadron, with its Hunter FGA.9s and Scottish Aviation Pioneer CC.1s, followed suit on 18 February.

This was not the end of Canberra operations in the FEAF. Nos 13, 39 and 58 Squadrons supplied the reconnaissance commitments flown between Hong Kong, the Maldives and Singapore, with No.13 Squadron being given the additional responsibility of overseeing the movements of Vietnamese 'boat people' in Hong Kong waters, which was a time-consuming exercise. Today, No.39 (No.1 PRU) Squadron is called upon, when circumstances warrant it.

CHAPTER ELEVEN

Targets, Drones and Nose Jobs

The last new-build Canberra to be produced for the RAF was PR.9 XH177, built to the MoS transferred Contract No.6/ACFT/14027/CB6(b) by Short Bros at Belfast, and completed by 30 December 1960. English Electric themselves had B(I).8 WT368, their final new RAF aircraft, ready for collection by 29 June 1956, while both A.V. Roe and Handley Page had the last of their respective seventy-five B.2s ready in 1955. Avro's WK165 was finished on 28 February and Handley Page had WJ682 awaiting collection on 29 April.

After the PR.9, as if to prove the adaptability of the basic Canberra airframe, the next eleven variants for the service were all produced through the conversion of existing aircraft. Some of this work was undertaken by English Electric and Short Bros, but other contractors were also employed over the years.

Sixteen Additional T.4s

Before looking at the later marks, the production of an additional sixteen T.4s must be mentioned. English Electric manufactured the trainer front-fuselage sections forward of Frame 12A and despatched them to Belfast. There, Short Bros received sixteen B.2s for conversion and, with their front fuselages removed, they grafted on the trainer sections supplied from English Electric. The earliest B.2 received was WD944, which had served only with No.101 Squadron before going to Belfast.

Of the remaining fifteen B.2s, WD954 is of interest, as it came off the production line on 12 December 1951 to be transferred on charge to the Ministry of Supply Controller (Aircraft), who passed it to the Aircraft & Armament Experimental Establishment for tropical trials in Kenya. Following its completion on 14 May 1952, the aircraft was restored to the RAF charge for which it was originally ordered and went to Short Bros for trainer conversion. WJ566 was the third Handley Page-built aircraft, which

served with No.44 Squadron before going to Belfast, while the two newest aircraft, WJ991 and WJ992, were both built by A.V. Roe. They only saw service with No.76 Squadron at Wittering, before being allocated for trainer conversion.

Additional Classrooms

Sixteen Canberra B.2 aircraft confirmed as being converted to T.4 standard by Short Bros, using trainer front fuselage sections manufactured by English Electric: WD944, WD954, WD963, WE111, WE118, WH637, WH651, WH659, WH706, WH854, WH861, WJ566, WJ568, WJ617, WJ991, WJ992

Canberra U.10

Short Bros were also the suppliers of eighteen pilotless target drone variants, designated the Canberra U.10. The company received a contract to design, develop and produce the variant, which was used almost exclusively by the Weapons Research Establishment (WRE) at Woomera. Handley Page-built Canberra B.2 WJ624 arrived at Belfast from No.45 MU Kinloss, on 6 September 1955, to fulfil the requirements for a trials aircraft. The conversion took twenty-one months and WJ624 first flew in its new configuration on 11 June 1957.

Development was a protracted affair, with modifications being incorporated over the years, and the aircraft never went to Woomera. Trials were conducted at RAE Bedford, starting early in 1958 and the following year, on 15 October 1959, the aircraft went to the RAE's drone test facility at Llanbedr in North Wales for evaluation. Initially, the aircraft had a pilot, who flew it via a supervisory panel installed in the cockpit to simulate, through push buttons, the thirteen inputs that would later be transmitted over a radio link when the aircraft was pilotless.

Woomera began U.10 operations, with WD961, on 25 June 1959. All seventeen

aircraft had the supervisory panel, as tested on WJ624, which gave them the ability to be piloted should the sortie require it. When in pilotless condition, an aircraft was operated by a master controller in a control van, who transmitted through a VHF radio link. Landings and take-offs were controlled by two separate operators, one handling horizontal commands, with the other being responsible for pitch control, and a parachute was deployed when landing. Each aircraft also had an explosive charge fitted for detonation, should it get out of control and require destruction. Because firings were done with dummy warheads, the Canberras were fitted with the necessary telemetry to measure 'miss' distances. Seventeen aircraft would not have lasted too long had live firings been made. On the few occasions that they were used, the result was nearly always the demise of the target aircraft.

U.10 delivery to Woomera was spread over three years, the last aircraft, WH705, arriving in July 1962. They were painted an overall white, with a broad coloured band on both surfaces of the outer wings. These bands have been referred to as being both red and black, but neither colour has been confirmed. When Meteor NF.11s operated by the WRE were painted overall white, areas of red were applied, so this could indicate that this was the colour of the U.10's bands, but it is only conjecture.

Canberra U.14

At Llanbedr, WJ624 was converted into a U.14 for the Royal Navy; again, it underwent a trials programme. The principal difference between the two pilotless marks was the RN's requirement for the aircraft to have the hydraulic-operated, servo-assisted controls of the PR.9 and, besides WJ728, which remained a trials aircraft, six B.2s were converted by Short Bros into U.14s. The six were issued to No.728B Squadron, FAA, which operated from its Maltese base at Hal Far, on guided

(Above) Built as a B.2 by Short Bros, WH885 was painted overall white while being converted to U.10 configuration in 1962 and is seen on the Khormaksar Station flight pan, while en route to WRE at Woomera. The black target-drone markings can be seen on the upper central fuselage and the wing, inboard of the tip tank. The aircraft was written off in an accident on 1 April 1964. Ray Deacon

(Below) WH860 was also built at Belfast as a B.2, before being refurbished into a U.10 and is shown at Lyneham in April 1962, before going to the Woomera range, where it was destroyed by a missile on 24 May 1964. R.A. Walker

weapons trials conducted with Short Seacat and Hawker Siddeley Seaslug surface-to-air shipborne missiles.

Delivery of the six U.14s began on 25 May 1961 and the first pilotless flight is recorded as being made in August of that year. No.728B's activities with the U.14 lasted less than a year, but it was a very concentrated period, in which many firings were made with both types of missiles, the majority of them with dummy warheads. Live firings were occasionally made and, on 6 October 1961, U.14 WH921 received a hit by a missile fired from HMS *Girdle Ness*, the debris plunging into the Mediterranean Sea.

At the beginning of December, the squadron disbanded and the remaining five Canberras flew back to the United Kingdom between 5 and 12 December 1961, for storage at the Radar Research Establishment (RRE) at Pershore. Three of them were eventually broken up at the RRE while, coming full circle, WH876 and WH638 were converted by the Establishment, back to B.2 standard. Later, WH876,

while on charge to the A&AEE, was converted back into a U.10, before eventually being broken up in January 1990.

EW/ECM Training Units

On 18 April 1963, No.98 Squadron ended four years as a Thor ICBM unit at Driffield in Yorkshire and, the following day, was reincarnated at Tangmere, taking over a renumbered No.245 Squadron. Canberra B.2s were issued to the new squadron, together with a few Canberra E.15s. One month later, on 24 May, another Thor unit, No.97 Squadron at Hemswell, was disbanded, to be re-formed at Watton a day later, taking over the renumbered No.151 Squadron. Canberra B.2s and a B.6 were on the unit's strength, together with a Hastings C.2 and Varsity T.1s. The Canberras were formed into 'B' Flight, in which a Special Operator was often carried on sorties, for training on the Electronic Warfare (EW) and Electronic Counter-Measures (ECM) equipment carried.

In February 1964, the Ministry of Aviation (MoA) invited the unit's Commanding Officer (CO) to attend a meeting to discuss the forthcoming flight trials of a new Canberra variant, the T.17, a dedicated

WH863, the Canberra T.17 development aircraft, is shown as 'L' of No.360 Squadron, at Cottesmore's Battle of Britain Open Day in 1973. *Aeroplane*

EW/ECM training aircraft for both the RAF and Fleet Air Arm (FAA). One major outcome of the MoA discussions was the decision to form a joint RAF/FAA unit, since training in the increasingly important field of EW/ECM was germane to both services. Twenty-four B.2s were flown to Samlesbury, for conversion to the new T.17 standard, with WH863, built by Short Bros early in 1963, allocated as the type's development aircraft.

Extensive modifications were made to the basic B.2 airframe, including the installation of ECM equipment in the bomb-bay, together with a new power supply. The most visible alteration was an entirely new, very unphotogenic nose forward of Frame 12A. It had a large hemispherical radome, with four small blister housings covering the Druce Moth receive and transmit aerials that were set around it. This necessitated the relocation of the pitot head, from its former position at the front of the glazed bomb-aimer's nose, to the port wing, adjacent to the tip tank.

Flight testing of the reconfigured WH863 started at Warton in September 1964 and the first aircraft converted to full T.17 operational standard, WJ977, had its maiden flight on 3 September 1965. Following manufacturer's preliminary testing flights, it went to Boscombe Down in spring 1966, for service acceptance trials. No.97 Squadron's involvement in T.17 discussions, right up to the acceptance conference in May 1965, naturally encouraged it to anticipate receiving some of the new variants, but it was to be disappointed. In fact, when a new No.360 Squadron was formed at Watton on 23 September 1966 to operate T.17s, the nucleus of its

aircraft fleet were the Canberra B.2, the five B.6s and the T.4 on the strength of No.97 Squadron's 'B' Flight, leaving just the Hastings and Varsities. To rub salt into the wound, No.360 Squadron received its first Canberra T.17, WJ988, in December 1966 and, on 2 January 1967, No.97 Squadron was disbanded.

The 'Joint RAF/RN Trials and Training Squadron', as the new No.360 Squadron was ponderously subtitled, was administratively divided 75 per cent/25 per cent in favour of the RAF; every fourth Commanding Officer belonged to the Royal Navy. The FAA's No.831 Squadron was absorbed into the combined unit and the RAF's No.361

T.17, WH874, banks to port and displays an array of intakes and vents. The aircraft joined No.360 Squadron and was lost while flying from Cottesmore, in an accident with a T.4, on 29 January 1971. Author's collection

Squadron was formed at Watton on 2 January 1967, with the object of becoming another EW/ECM unit, which would eventually operate in the Far East. However, although the first true T.17, WJ977, arrived at Watton on 19 September 1966, it was purely an introduction of the variant to the base; the aircraft had departed within the week and, due to conversions at Samlesbury taking longer than originally estimated, No.360 Squadron had to function with the

mers and false signalling were employed, to make the location of target aircraft more difficult. Observers from the squadron occasionally flew in the spare seat of Lightning T.4s, to appreciate the effects of particular jamming procedures and to suggest improvements, where they were felt necessary, to both the interceptor's reactions, as well as to his squadron's techniques.

A move to Cottesmore was made on 21 April 1969 and detachments were deployed

to Samlesbury in 1985, to act as the trials aircraft for the new electronic fit. The *Green Satin* doppler-fed Ground Position Indicator (GPI) had been replaced by an Omega VLF self-fixing navigation system, while the TACAN and VOR equipments had been retained. Two Sylvania communications jamming aerials had been fitted, one under each wing, outboard of the engine nacelles. Once WD955 had been cleared for service, five additional T.17s

T.17, **WH664/'EH'**, has the red bar/lightning flash of **No.360 Squadron** either side of the fuselage roundel.
George Pennick

ex-No.97 Squadron 'B' Flight aircraft until the end of the year.

By the middle of 1967, fourteen T.17s were on the strength of No.360 Squadron, some of which were being held for No.361 Squadron. However, with British units being withdrawn from the Far East earlier than originally planned, there was no place for the squadron out there and, on 14 July 1967, it was disbanded. It had existed for just six months, during which it had received no aircraft. The defunct unit's Commanding Officer joined No.360 Squadron as Administration Officer, and some senior engineers also stayed at Watton with their CO.

The principal role of No.360 Squadron was to provide training for all branches of the armed services, to teach them how to operate in a hostile electronic counter-measures environment. This was achieved by jamming communications and radar signals between the ground controllers and interceptors. Chaff dropping, active radar jam-

to the Mediterranean area, as well as to NATO bases in Europe. The T.17's appearance also underwent a change, with the dark sea grey/dark green/light aircraft grey underside paint finish being altered to a two-tone hemp scheme. Upgrading of the aircraft's electronics fit was an on-going exercise. Continual improvements in airborne and air-defence radars meant that developments in training were also necessary if they were to be of any operational value. When No.231 OCU closed down, in April 1973, a number of former No.100 Squadron Canberra PR.7s were transferred to No.360 Squadron, where they were fitted with modified tip tanks, which had been adapted as chaff dispensers.

Another relocation took place on 1 September 1975, when No.360 Squadron left Cottesmore for Wyton, where improvements in the T.17's navigation and EW equipment brought the T.17A into existence. T.17 WD955, originally the twenty-seventh production B.2 back in 1951, went

were similarly modified, and all six aircraft were operational at Wyton by May 1987.

No.360 Squadron provided radar jamming for Tornado F.3 intercept sorties, and liaison between the Squadron and the Tornado OCU was instrumental in developing the *Foxhunter* intercept radar that had such a problematic gestation period. The annual utilization of the EW/ECM trainers was bound to take its toll – by spring 1994, nearly 400 hours per aircraft were being flown. The squadron was down to eight EW aircraft, which included all T.17As, plus two T.4s and two PR.7s. A decision was made to stand down the service's only airborne Electronic Warfare unit and, on 31 October 1994, No.360 Squadron was disbanded. The unit's surviving T.4, together with two PR.7s, were transferred to No.39 (1 PRU) Squadron at Marham. At the time of No.360 Squadron's disbanding, its T.17A WD955/'EM', was the oldest Canberra still flying with the RAF, with forty-three years' service behind it.

Electronic Trainers

Twenty-four Canberra B.2 aircraft confirmed as being converted to T.17 standard by English Electric at Samlesbury and issued to No.360 Squadron.

One aircraft converted for type trials. This aircraft went to No.360 Squadron after the trials: WH863

Twenty-three aircraft directly issued to No.360 Squadron after conversion: WD955, WF890, WF916, WH646, WH664, WH665, WH740, WH872, WH874, WH902, WJ565, WJ576, WJ581, WJ607, WJ625, WJ630, WJ633, WJ977, WJ981, WJ986, WJ988, WK102, WK111

Six Canberra T.17s confirmed as being converted to T.17A standard by BAe (formerly English Electric) at Samlesbury and issued to No.360 Squadron.

One aircraft converted for type trials. This aircraft went to No.360 Squadron after the trials: WD955

Five aircraft directly issued to No.360 Squadron after conversion: WH646, WH902, WJ607, WJ633, WJ981

A hemp colour scheme had been introduced by 1989, when T.17A, WD955/'EM' arrived at Brize Norton, with special fin-rudder markings appropriate for the oldest Canberra in RAF service. Author's collection

The 'Rushton' Target and Winch

In the summer of 1957, the first of forty-four Gloster Meteor NF.11s converted to TT.20 standard began service with the Royal Navy. The RAF operated some through No.3 Civilian Anti-Aircraft Co-operation Unit (CAACU) at Exeter, and a few were flown by No.1574 Target Facilities Flight (TFF) on Singapore. Two years later, the American Hayes target came to Flight Refuelling Limited (FRL) for trials, for which Meteor TT.20s WM167 and WM234 were allocated.

FRL came to the conclusion that the significant modifications required to make the target adaptable for service use were uneconomic, and, consequently, considered it better to design their own. This resulted in the 'Rushton' target and winch, named after FRL's location, at Tarrant Rushton in Dorset. It was equipped with hit-and-miss distance recorders and a flare pack. The winch employed a series of winding capstans, together with a stepped-diameter towing cable, to match the progressive change in drag-induced tension throughout the cable length.

The Meteor was capable of carrying only one target, fitted to a launcher sited in a ventral position on the rear fuselage centre-line, while the winch was installed on the top surface of the starboard wing centre-section. It was obvious that, in order to carry

two targets, a larger aircraft was required and the only real choice was the Canberra. In the summer of 1966, after conversion by English Electric, the Handley Page-built B.2 WJ632 went to FRL for Rushton trials. These were undertaken by Johnny Squier, one of Beamont's team of test pilots engaged on Canberra development between 1949 and 1954. The aircraft appeared at the SBAC display and then, a week later, in September 1966, flight testing began with one Rushton winch installed on a pylon under each wing. Ex-A&AEE pilot Paddy O'Brien joined the test team.

The TT.18

The Rushton winch system was cleared for service use at the beginning of 1970 and the new variant was designated Canberra TT.18. Eleven B.2s were delivered to Tarrant Rushton from No.27 MU Shawbury, for winch installations, while other conversions were engineered by English Electric at Samlesbury. FRL's first conversion had its maiden flight on 14 April 1970.

A total of twenty-three B.2s, including WJ632, were converted into TT.18s; fourteen were issued to the RAF and nine went to the FAA. FRL instructors gave several weeks of systems training to members of both services, following which, on 1 May 1970, the RAF re-formed No.7 Squadron, an ex-Valiant B(PR)K.1 unit, which had been disbanded at Wittering on 30 Sep-

tember 1962. The re-formed squadron's home base, at St Mawgan in Cornwall, was not ready immediately, and it therefore began operations from Tarrant Rushton. While there, the squadron employed its targets for Tiger Cat surface-to-air missiles, as well as live Lightning firings, with the targets streamed over 40,000ft behind the tugs; still, seven and a half miles wasn't far where SAMs were concerned! On 1 July, the squadron performed a flypast over Tarrant Rushton with the TT.18s, and then set course for St Mawgan, which was now ready to receive it. This was to be the squadron's home base for the next twelve years.

The Royal Navy's TT.18s were accepted by No.776 Fleet Requirements Unit (FRU) at Hurn, which was run by Airwork Services FRU (Hurn). In 1972, it moved to Yeovilton and was absorbed into the Air Direction Training Unit, to become FRADU, run by FRL.

While No.7 Squadron was the only recorded operator of the Canberra TT.18, No.85 Squadron at Binbrook received three aircraft in 1970, but serviceability problems curtailed their use by the squadron and the TT.18's stay was brief. At St Mawgan, No.7 Squadron flew with either Rushton Mk.2 targets or the conventional sleeve targets, the latter also being used by No.100 Squadron at West Raynham, and TFFs were detached to the Mediterranean area on a regular basis. Whereas the Rushton target was deployed several miles behind its Canberra, 30ft- (9m-) long sleeve targets trailed

Flight Refuelling's Avro-built Canberra B.2, WK143, still with its nose probe from earlier refuelling trials, was converted to TT.18 standard. It releases a target from the starboard Rushton winch.
Flight Refuelling Limited

a mere 900ft (275m) away – not far when 30mm cannon shells are being fired from a pair of Lightnings!

The procedure with sleeve targets was rather antiquated. The light fabric target, which was dyed contrasting colours to make it visible against light or dark backgrounds, was attached to a re-usable radar reflector. The whole assembly was laid out on the runway, hitched up to a length of the 900ft (275m) steel cable hanging from the Canberra and simply towed into the air. The target did not seem to suffer from bouncing along the runway for about a thousand yards before the Canberra tug got airborne. On returning to base, the Canberra pilot flew a pass along a grassed area of the airfield at 500ft (150m), and released the target, before turning into the landing approach. Target flights, referred to as 'flags', usually lasted about an hour

Flight Refuelling showed their Rushton target and winch at the 1966 SBAC Display.
Author's collection

and a half, which meant that two or three sorties could be flown in a day. They were not exactly exciting! The squadron flew many target flights for the benefit of naval warships – surprising, considering that FRADU had its own TT.18s – as well as supplying live-firing practices for the Army's Rapier ground-to-air missile units. It was a busy life at St Mawgan.

At the end of 1981, it was decided to disband No.7 Squadron and, on 5 January 1982, it was formally stood down. The remaining TT.18s were distributed between No.100 Squadron, which had moved to Wyton before receiving six of them, FRADU at Yeovilton and storage at Samlesbury. FRADU operated its TT.18s until at least 1986, after which the aircraft were placed in storage at No.32 MU St Athan.

WK143

On 10 March 1955, FRL received Avro-built B.2 WK143 for flight refuelling trials (*see* Chapter 14). In addition to these trials, the company's engineering facility converted the aircraft to TT.18 standard and flew it on a series of non-military sorties. Flights were made to determine wave spectra, to assist the Department of Energy in its investigations into using wave energy as a power source. At one time, the aircraft was held on stand-by at Coningsby, in readiness to fly a mission to record freak wave conditions, similar to those believed to have been responsible for the loss of two trawlers off

Dogger Bank. The fact that this particular sortie was cancelled did not provoke the usual 'mission-aborted' groans – it would have entailed flying very low over the North Sea, in severe turbulence conditions.

In 1976, FRL flew WK143, towing a special target fitted with radar-reflecting units, along the airways approaching the United Kingdom's west coast, in order for the Civil Aviation Authority's (CAA) Evaluation Unit to calibrate several major airport radar installations.

In 1975, the aircraft was demonstrated by FRL pilots Arthur Chant and Dennis

---

Towing the Line

Fourteen Canberra B.2 aircraft confirmed as being converted to TT.18 standard for the RAF.

One aircraft converted for type trials. This aircraft went to No.7 Squadron after the trials: WJ632

Thirteen Canberra B.2 aircraft confirmed as converted to TT.18 standard for the RAF: WH718, WH856, WJ629, WJ632, WJ639, WJ680, WJ682, WJ715, WJ721, WK118, WK122, WK124, WK127

Nine Canberra B.2 aircraft confirmed as being converted to TT.18 standard for the FAA.

WE122, WH887, WJ574, WJ614, WJ636, WJ717, WK123, WK126, WK142

One Canberra B.2 aircraft confirmed as being converted to TT.18 standard by Flight Refuelling Limited and retained by them for special trials.

WK143

Lewis, together with Sqn Ldr Nelson of No.7 Squadron, to the Indian Air Force (IAF) at Bangalore. This demonstration was instrumental in the IAF's decision to purchase six T.4 aircraft from English Electric and to convert them in India for target towing; for this, they were designated TT.418. Eventually, WK143 was struck off charge at Tarrant Rushton and, in August 1989, the aircraft was transported to the fire dump at RAE Llanbedr.

T.22

The Royal Navy's interest in the Canberra was extended in 1973, when seven PR.7s were converted to T.22 standard at Samlesbury. This variant was to meet the requirement for an aircraft to assist in training future radar operators on the Buccaneer S.2. PR.7 WT510 served with the RAF until 15 February 1971, when it was transferred to the Royal Navy and, a year later, was back at Samlesbury for conversion to the T.22 prototype. This featured a recontoured nose, reminiscent of a mediaeval jousting helmet, to house the complete Buccaneer radar, and the aircraft made its maiden flight as the T.22 prototype, on 28 June 1973, in an unpainted condition. Manufacturer testing was followed by A&AEE service acceptance trials, and the aircraft was released to FRADU at RNAS Yeovilton on 30 August.

Six more PR.7 conversions followed and, over the next twelve years, the T.22's role

WJ717 was converted from B.2 to TT.18, before it flew with a FRADU detachment at the Key West Air Naval Station in Florida, during October 1978. In 1985, it was given the Instructional Airframe number 9052M, for training at St Athan. Author's collection

(Top) WT510, after refurbishment from PR.7 to TT.22.
BAe

(Above) The TT.22 did not often appear at air displays, but here WH803/'856' stands alongside an
EA-3B Skywarrior at a Coltishall Open Day. George Pennick

was extended to cover ECM training, together with target simulation exercises, which greatly increased their use. By 1985, the variant was due for replacement and the Dassault-Breguet Falcon 20DC was chosen. The first of eight, obtained by Flight Refuelling Aviation Ltd from the United States on a leasing arrangement, and flown with US civil registrations, landed at Yeovilton on 5 February 1985. On 31 May 1984, WH803, the first T.22 to be retired, flew to No.32 MU St Athan for storage. The remaining six followed at intervals and on 6 September 1985, St Athan received WH801, the last to leave FRADU.

Canberra T.11

The need for an Airborne Interceptor (AI) training aircraft, to convert navigators on to the radar fitted in the Javelin,

was met by a further B.2 conversion. Designated the Canberra T.11, the conversions were engineered by Boulton Paul at Seighford, although the B.2 selected for trials, WJ734, was converted by Boulton Paul's outstation at RRE Defford. Between 1952 and 1965, Boulton Paul was a major sub-contractor to English Electric on Canberra work, being responsible for many important installations, as well as the development of the T.11.

As Boulton Paul's airfield at Wolverhampton had grass runways, Defford was used for all Canberra-associated flying. The aircraft arrived at Defford on 20 August 1956 and the necessary modifications to fit the AI17, as installed in the Javelin, gave WJ734 an extended nose, with the scanner unit's dielectric cone finishing in a very sharp, symmetrical point. Following its initial flight testing, the aircraft went to Boscombe Down on 21 May

1958 for service clearance and handling trials. Modifications detailed by the A&AEE were undertaken by Boulton Paul, before the aircraft was released to No.228 OCU at Leeming, which already had a number of Meteor NF.14s, as well as a Canberra T.4, a Meteor T.7 and a lot of Valetta C.1s. The T.11 was cleared to fly at up to 530mph (850km/h) at sea level and Mach 0.84 above 25,000ft (7,600m).

Originally, a total of eight B.2s were converted into T.11s by Boulton Paul, which manufactured the front fuselage sections forward of Frame 12A, which RAF MUs joined to stripped B.2 fuselages. (It is believed that a small number of additional front fuselages were built for subsequent conversion, but this has not been substantiated.) No.228 OCU received the full complement of T.11s during 1959 and operated them until 10 August 1961, when the unit was disbanded.

Preparing for Buccaneering

Seven Canberra PR.7 aircraft confirmed as being converted to T.22 standard by English Electric.

One aircraft converted for type trials as the prototype. This aircraft went to FRADU after the trials: WT510

Six aircraft supplied to T.22 standard after completion of type trials: WH780, WH797, WH801, WH803, WT525, WT535

A dramatic ground-to-air shot of FRADU's T.22, WH803.
Author's collection

With airbrakes out, T.11 WJ610 slips alongside the photographic aircraft. Built as a B.2 by Handley Page, before conversion, the aircraft was later further refurbished to T.19 standard. Author's collection

Canberra T.4, WT478, painted to depict VN799, at the 40th anniversary celebrations held at Wyton on 13 May 1989. Author's collection

(Below) Seen on Masira Island, off the east coast of Muscat and Oman, B.2, WH666 was one of the aircraft loaned to New Zealand in 1958 and was probably en route when this shot was taken. Ian Mactaggart

(Right) PR.7, WH791, seen as Cottesmore's gate guard in June 1996, before it went to the Newark Air Museum. George Pennick

(Below) Built as a B.2, WJ992 was converted to T.4 standard before going to the RAE in June 1957. In 'raspberry-ripple' finish, it is shown at RAE Bedford in September 1991. George Pennick

(Left) Also in 'raspberry-ripple', B.2, WH734 carried a Short SD.2 Stiletto supersonic target under the starboard wing, when attending Wyton's anniversary display. Author's collection

(Below) Formerly B.2, WJ713, Argentina's second aircraft, B-102, has the civil registration G-AYHP allocated for the 1970 SBAC Display. It awaits collection, with a twin rocket projectile pod under each wing. BAe

(Above) Avro-built WK142/'848' was converted from B.2 to the TT.18 standard shown in June 1972. A Rushton winch was carried under each wing at Wyton. Author's collection

(Below) Seen at the 1981 Greenham Common Air Tattoo, B.2, WV787 was modified several times in its working life as a trials aircraft. It was converted to B(I).8 standard when fitted with the ventral icing-trials spray bar shown. Author's collection

A84-223 is seen at the Chewing Gum Field Museum at Tallabadgera, Queensland. It has since been bought by David Lowy and is currently being restored to airworthy condition.
Ian Mactaggart

B.2, 204, of No.5 Squadron, Royal Rhodesian Air Force, Salisbury (now Harare), showing the rocket rail installation ahead of the nose-wheel doors, which was unique to the RRAF.
Winston Brent

(Above) The third of the B.2s supplied to the German Federal Republic in 1966, ex-WK138 was first numbered YA+153. This was changed to 00+03 in 1968 and, when the aircraft was transferred to the Military Geographic Service in 1970, with camera mountings in the rear bomb-bay, it became D-9567. In 1976, the aircraft was again renumbered, to 99+35. BAe

(Below) A84-229 went to the United States in August 1990, in exchange for a Lockheed Ventura. It has returned to Australia several times and is seen overflying the New South Wales territory near the Australian capital. BAe

(Above) One of the seven Canberra T.22s used in the target facilities role and operated by the Royal Navy's FRADU from Yeovilton in the 1970s. BAe

(Left) WH664/'EH' of No.360 Squadron, was a B.2 of the Swifter Flight before being converted to T.17 standard in 1967. At Wyton in 1989, it was displayed in the rain, three years before being broken up at the base. Author's collection

(Above) Venezuelan B(I).88, 0923, was first delivered in 1957 as a new-build B(I).8. It twice returned to Warton for overhaul and is seen on the second visit, having been fully refurbished with new armament and revised avionics, in March 1980. BAe

(Below) A historic aircraft. South African Air Force B(I).12, 456, built from major assemblies made before the English Electric production line closed in 1959, was the very last Canberra to be completed. It first flew on 30 February 1964 and was delivered to the SAAF in April of the same year. BAe

(Above) Classic Aviation Projects' restored 'Scorpion Canberra'. WK163/G-BVWC was originally built as a B.2 in 1955 and captured the height record on 28 August 1957. At RRE Pershore in 1968, B.6 wings and engines were fitted and when CAP received the aircraft at Bruntingthorpe, in December 1994, it had an extended nose, fitted for electronics trials. George Pennick

(Right) The last of the sixty-seven Martin RB-57As built, 52-1492 was preserved and photographed at Wright Patterson AFB on 22 January 1972.
R. Burgess/George Pennick

A very rare bird. The Federal Aircraft Administration's B-57, N97, was photographed at Will Rogers Field, Oklahoma, in April 1963. This was one of two RB-57As that the FAA acquired in 1957 for the evaluation of high-altitude airways in preparation for the introduction of jet-powered commercial transports.
H. Buchanan/George Pennick

Standing on the apron at Da Nang Air Base in May 1965, RB-57E, 54245, was one of six of the type converted by General Dynamics for Project Patricia Lynn, a series of classified reconnaissance missions made over Vietnam, Cambodia and Laos. While carrying out these missions, between May 1963 and August 1971, the aircraft, which carried masses of specialized electronic reconnaissance equipment, were assigned to Detachment 1 of the 33rd Tactical Group, before being transferred to the 6250th Combat Support Group.
D. Menard/George Pennick

Seen at MacDill AFB in August 1971, B-57G, 53-3877 was one of sixteen former B-57Bs converted under Project Tropical Moon III. Forward-looking APQ-139 radar, infra-red and low light level television, plus a lasering device, are installed in the nose. The aircraft was operated by the 4424th Combat Crew Training Squadron, which was responsible for replacement aircrew training for the reactivated 13th Tactical Bomb Squadron, during the Vietnam War. H. Buchanan/George Pennick

An anonymous RB-57D, possibly 53-3964, which is thought to have been employed by the Wright Air Development Center, in connection with cloud sampling near Christmas Island, under Project Dominic. George Pennick

Canberra B.2, WH638, was the first to be converted to B.52 standard for Ethiopia and, as 351, was delivered on 24 July 1968. BAe

457, the first of three T.4s delivered to the South African Air Force early in 1964, was built as B.2, WJ991 by Avro, in October 1953. The conversion to T.4 standard was made to meet the SAAF order, received in 1963. BAe

Originally built as a B-57E in 1956, 55-4280 *(top)* was converted into an EB-57E during the 1960s and is depicted serving with the 17th Defence System Evaluation Squadron, the last unit to operate the type. The close-up of the underwing tank *(above)* shows the stylized presentation of the unit's title. George Pennick

(Above) The 134th DSES, Vermont Air National Guard, The Green Mountain Boys as displayed on the underwing tank, had EB-57B, 52-1503 at Plattsburgh AFB in July 1978. The aircraft was built as a B-57B and the ECM conversion was made for the calibration of missile tracking cameras. R. Harrison/George Pennick

(Right) WB-57F, 63-13291, was built as an RB-57F before being redesignated and operated by the 58th Weather Reconnaissance Squadron, between June 1964 and July 1974. It was photographed at Patrick AFB, Florida, in August 1971. H. Buchanan/George Pennick

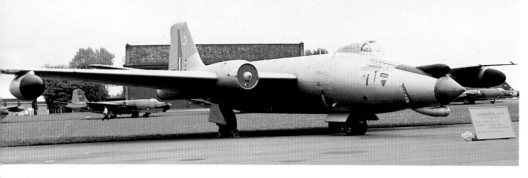

(Above left) XH132 was the fourth production Canberra PR.9, built in July 1959. In March 1960, it was placed on MoS charge and Short Bros were contracted to rebuild it as the one and only SC.9, originally for de Havilland Propeller's *Sky Flash* guided weapon homing head trials, undertaken at RRE Pershore. It went on to serve with the RAE, where it received their 'raspberry-ripple' colour scheme, before going to St Mawgan's Battle Damage Research Flight. It was allocated for disposal, but the front fuselage was saved by a private owner in St Austell, Cornwall, who sold it in 1998 to Albino Panigarri. In Italy, the new owner hopes to refurbish the section as much as possible. BAe

(Below left) Canberra PR.9, XH168, of No.39 Squadron, comes in on the approach to Mildenhall's Air Fete '90, where it took its place in the static aircraft park. Author's collection

(Above) In October 1991, No.100 Squadron, based at Wyton, started to change its aircraft and a photocall was laid on to celebrate the occasion. Sporting the squadron colours, the old and the new flew in formation, the participants being Canberra TT.18, WJ682/'CU' and Hawk T.1A, XX247/'CM'. The Canberra had started life as Handley Page's last B.2 in April 1955 and was converted to TT.18 standard by English Electric, in 1968. BAe

(Below) Fuerza Aérea del Peru B.52, 233, was the first of six ex-RAF aircraft supplied, starting in November 1967. Formerly WJ974, the fourth Canberra built by A.V. Roe in 1952, the aircraft carries the Class 'B' registration G-27-76 in this photograph. BAe

Target Facilities/No.85 Squadron

The aircraft of the disbanded No.228 OCU were transferred to the Central Fighter Establishment (CFE) at West Raynham, to form the Target Facilities Squadron (TFS). Besides flying airborne target sorties for the eleven Bloodhound Mk.1 surface-to-air squadrons dotted around the UK, the TFS provided target sorties for various Lightning operators. They also flew a very concentrated series of sorties during the development trials of the Bloodhound Mk.2, with No.25 Squadron at North Coates in 1963.

On 1 April 1963, the Target Facilities Squadron became the new No.85 Squadron, the original unit having been disbanded the day before, as a Javelin FAW.8 operator. The ceremony took place at West Raynham, with the new squadron holding six T.11s and a T.4 on charge. Just over three weeks later, on 25 April, they all moved to Binbrook and in September, six Meteor F(TT).8s joined the unit, as the squadron's workload had been increased by an additional target-towing role. In July 1965, a re-formed No.228 OCU at Leuchars became the dedicated night-fighter conversion school with Javelins, plus three T.11s with AI sets, which were employed as radar trainers for over a year.

While these OCU operations were getting established, No.85 Squadron's eight T.11s started another conversion. One by one, from 1965, these aircraft had their AI Airpass radar units removed by various MUs and the modified aircraft became another variant, designated Canberra T.19, the last of which returned to the squadron, after conversion, in 1969. Despite looking rather time-worn, the aircraft continued to be used on demanding schedules until, on 19 December 1975, No.85 Squadron was disbanded at West Raynham and became absorbed into No.100 Squadron.

Four T.19s were retained and two were passed on to No.7 Squadron at St Mawgan but, by 1980, all were suffering from fatigue. Those that still remained – only two or three aircraft – were retired. At least three, WH714, WH724 and WH903, had already been consigned to fire dumps and, at the time of writing, two T.19s, WH904 and WJ975, exist in museums.

A rare visitor at Khormaksar was T.11 WT305, which flew in from Watton in 1963. Ray Deacon

T.19, WH904, in the markings of No.85 Squadron, at Binbrook. This aircraft now lives at the Newark Air Museum. Newark Air Museum

Canberra E.15

When the Akrotiri Strike Wing was disbanded in 1969, the majority of its B.15s and B.16s were placed in storage. From there, some aircraft were purchased by the British Aircraft Corporation (BAC), who had a healthy order book for refurbished aircraft to meet overseas orders. However,

as a requirement arose for aircraft to form a new No.98 Squadron, to fulfil special electronic and calibration duties, eight of the B.15s brought from RAF storage were converted to be fitted with the necessary electronic suits and given the designation Canberra E.15.

No.98 Squadron had been another former Thor unit, which had been based at Driffield in Yorkshire, since receiving its missiles on 1 August 1959. It was disbanded at Driffield on 18 April 1963 and promptly re-formed at Tangmere, by re-numbering No.245 Squadron. The newly numbered squadron operated with Canberra B.2s, moving to Watton later in the year and to Cottesmore on 17 April 1969. It was at Cottesmore, in August 1970, that it received the first of the E.15s and it operated with the two Canberra variants until again being disbanded, on 27 February 1976.

One aircraft, WH973, had crashed on 5 October 1971, but the remaining E.15s were passed to No.100 Squadron at Marham, to join that unit's mix of B.2s and T.19s. This squadron lost two E.15s in accidents – WH948, which crashed on 15 August 1977, and WH972, which crashed on 27 June 1990. Two more, WH957 and WH964, were returned to storage early in 1982, with WH981 following suit in January 1992, the same month that another E.15, WH983, was scrapped. It is believed that WJ756 was the last E.15 to be retired, when No.100 Squadron started receiving Hawk

T.1/T.1As, although the actual date cannot be confirmed.

Canberra B.8

Two B.2s were converted to B.8 standard, for various radar development programmes. Handley Page had WJ643 completed on 31 August 1954 and, eight days later, as an MoS-owned aircraft, it was allocated to Ferranti at Turnhouse. The aircraft went to Boulton Paul's outstation at RRE Defford for conversion to B.8 standard – it had the off-set blown canopy, but no provision for armament or weapon delivery, so it did not qualify for the Interdiction (I) prefix. WJ643 was used extensively by the Ferranti Flying Unit (FLU) with a revised nose section for Airpass radar trials (*see* Chapter 14).

Canberra B.2 WV787 was one of two aircraft added, in 1951, to the first contract that English Electric received in March 1949 – Contract No.6/ACFT/3520/CB6(b). It was used by Armstrong Siddeley for Sapphire Sa.7 reheat trials, before also going to Boulton Paul at Defford for conversion to the same B.8 standard as WJ643. It was also employed by Ferranti, for NA.39 (later named Buccaneer) radar trials, as well as by the A&AEE, for photographic coverage of Jaguar de-icing tests. Given the Instructional Airframe number 8799M at the Battle Damage Repair Flight (BDRF) at Abingdon, before that base was closed down, at the time of writing, WV787 is on display at the Newark Air Museum.

Handley Page-built B.2, WJ643, was converted to B.8 configuration by Boulton Paul and used by Ferranti, as shown, for AI.23 Airpass radar trials. Author's collection

CHAPTER TWELVE

Uncle Sam's Canberras

American interest in the Canberra stems from a committee set up in 1950, which itself was born from the surprise that the USAF received, when the Korean War revealed the modernity of Communist air power. In particular, there was a crying need for a light jet-bomber that would be able to undertake the night-intruder role.

In the Second World War, the light-bomber role had been met for the USAAF by the Douglas A-20, North American B-25 and Martin B-26, all of which were superseded in front-line service by the Douglas A-26 Invader. The A-26 had to serve into the mid-1950s because there was no effective replacement. The advent of the gas turbine engine brought about new designs but, with the American conviction

Typical of the USA's early approach to the turbojet-powered medium bomber were the six-engined Martin XB-48 (top), which first flew in June 1947, and the four-engined North American B-45. Author's collection and Philip Jarrett

that 'big is beautiful', they plumped for putting a quartet of engines into nearly everything that came off the drawing board. They appeared to sacrifice wing loading, with its associated manoeuvrability and high-altitude performance, with the result that they were no match, technically, for the Communist fighters encountered over the thirty-eighth parallel. Furthermore, there was nothing effectively to detect and destroy an enemy in the dark.

It was firmly laid down that the committee should only consider existing designs, as the time-scale precluded a new design, with the protracted testing and development that would be necessary before it could be issued to front-line squadrons. Consequently, a shortlist was

(although, in retrospect, one wonders why), and, because it had been favourably viewed at the 1949 SBAC Display, the English Electric A.1 Canberra. In common with so many observers, the American visitors at that Farnborough event had thought that it looked too conventional and unprepossessing, until Beamont lifted it off the runway. From then on, they looked on with amazement at the performance of an aircraft of such size.

Demonstrating the Canberra

While technical evaluations of the listed aircraft were being amassed, the committee decided to send a delegation to Britain to

base was within a short flying distance of Warton. However, Flight Operations were very hard-pressed keeping up with the existing trials schedule, so they made a proposal to the Ministry officials organizing the demonstration. The suggestion was that, as a ground support party could not be spared, Beamont would fly a prototype over to Burtonwood, land, take off and demonstrate, before flying directly back to Warton, all without switching off the Avons.

The proposal was accepted and, on 17 August 1950, the Chief Test Pilot flew the second Canberra prototype VX169, which had only made its maiden flight on 2 August, over to Burtonwood. After landing, he taxied over to a small group hunched against the drizzly conditions. Flight Test Engineer Dave Walker opened the entrance door, for the delegates to view the interior before making an exterior inspection. Luckily, the rain stopped while this was in progress and English Electric's Aircraft Sales Manager, Air Cdr Strang Graham, gave the go-ahead for the flying demonstration. The engines had not been stopped, so the fuel load was down to 3,000lb (1,360kg); under full power, VX169 lifted off in less than 700 yards, and was pulled up into a roll-off. The absence of other air traffic in the vicinity allowed a completely spontaneous demonstration of the aircraft's and pilot's abilities, before the fuel state indicated an urgent need to return to base. The delegation was presented with an ultra-low pass as a signing off, and Beamont headed back to Warton.

The following month, the American mission went to Warton to see flight trials and to examine the aircraft more thoroughly. At the end of their visit, in September, they declared that they considered the Canberra was more than capable of performing in a medium- to high-altitude bomber role – which English Electric knew already! – as well as in tactical reconnaissance and all-weather fighter roles.

Back in the USA, the original shortlist had basically been narrowed down to the Martin XB-51 and the Canberra, but it was considered that a fly-off of all the types would be useful. A 'shoot-out' would be held in November. English Electric informed the committee that February 1951 was the earliest that a Canberra could be made available for such an exercise. Not unnaturally, the USAF considered that the XB-51 was ideal for their requirements and it was tentatively suggested that perhaps enough Canberras

WD932 was painted in USAF markings when it flew over the Chesapeake Bay Bridge, but it never carried its allotted 51-17387 serial. Author's collection

drawn up of existing American, British and Canadian aircraft considered able to fulfil the role. The principal American contenders were the North American B-45 Tornado and AJ-1 Savage, both of which were in service, and the Martin XB-51, two examples of which were in the early stages of test flying. The Avro Canada CF-100 Canuck went on the list

view the Canberra in more detail. English Electric's Warton Flight Operations received a notification that a demonstration was to be arranged for an American VIP party, headed by Brigadier-General Albert Boyd of Air Material Command. It was requested that the vast USAF Maintenance Unit at Burtonwood be used for the demonstration, if that was feasible, as the

Martin XB-51

Dimensions:	Span 52ft 1in (15.87m); length 85ft 1in (25.93m); wing area 548sq ft (50.90sq m)
Powerplants:	Three General Electric J47 turbojets each producing 5,200lb (2,358.2kg) thrust
Weight:	Gross 64,154lb (29,093.8kg)
Performance:	Maximum speed 595mph (957.5km/h) at sea level Service ceiling 47,800ft (14,569.4m) Combat range 990 miles (1,593.2km) with 18,000lb (816.3kg) bomb load

The two Martin XB-51s, showing 6685, the first prototype, on the right, fitted with RATOG canisters on the rear fuselage, while the arc of wing variable incidence is indicated on 6686. Author's collection

Two prototypes were built, with serials 46-685 and 46-686. The first prototype made its maiden flight on 28 October 1949, the second prototype on 17 April 1950. Neither aircraft has survived.

could be purchased to equip a couple of light bombardment groups until the Martin aircraft was in production. English Electric had already made a guarded agreement to supply 300 aircraft off the production line, subject to RAF approval. Alternatively, the company had consented to licensed production of the aircraft in the United States.

On 21 February 1951, Sqn Ldr A.E. Callard and crew, flew the fourth production Canberra B.2, WD932, from Aldergrove to Gander, in an unofficial record time (*see* Chapter 5). The next day, 'Bee' Beamont took over the aircraft at Andrews Air Force Base (AFB), near Washington, and arrangements were made for a comparative display to be held at the base on 26 February, before the Senior Officer's Board of the Pentagon. Beamont was rather concerned to hear that all the participating aircraft were to fly the same set pattern of manoeuvres in a ten-minute time slot. When he enquired whether the pattern could be varied to suit the individual aircraft, he was left in no doubt that this option was a non-starter!

When he got down to timing, 'Bee' came to the conclusion that the Canberra could complete the set pattern in about five minutes. Nothing had been said about what to do in any time left available – this had not been considered a possibility – so he decided to fill in the time to his, and the Canberra's advantage. On the day, the

B-45 was scheduled to start the competition, the Martin XB-51 would be the penultimate performer, and the Canberra would be last. Beamont could see that the unconventional-looking Martin aircraft was fast, but its very high wing loading severely limited its manoeuvrability.

The XB-51 landed and WD932 was lined up for take-off. With its low wing loading, the Canberra flew the whole set pattern within Andrew's boundaries. When the programme was duly completed, he came in to land, then, finding that he had over four minutes to spare, opened up the engines, retracted the undercarriage, pulled into a tight full 360-degree turn over the ranged observers and half-rolled into a 470mph (750km/h) low flypast. He pulled up into a wing-over, then shut down the Avons for an airbrakes-on tight spiral dive, before pulling out for a glide into the landing pattern, with just the odd touch of throttle to adjust the approach speed after lowering flaps and undercarriage.

Andrews AFB flying control had failed to inform Beamont that, because of recent icy conditions, the white concrete runway had recently been sanded – with white sand. While he was braking to a standstill, both the Canberra's main wheels locked and the tyres burst. The USAF evaluation officer, seated in the navigator's station as an observer, was so overawed by the demonstration that he had witnessed at first hand, that the burst-tyre incident

went virtually unnoticed, especially as it had not affected control of the landing.

The XB-51 was about 100mph (160 km/h) faster in a straight line than the Canberra, but that was it. There was no real contest in overall ability to meet all the required criteria and the Canberra was declared the winner.

Production

Having selected the Canberra, the Pentagon was faced with a decision about its manufacture. The Glenn L. Martin Company, which did not have a very full order book at the time, was selected. In retrospect, this looks like a way of lessening the Pentagon's unease at having to arrange the manufacture of a foreign military aircraft for the first time since the de Havilland DH4 in the First World War. The company received Contract AF33(038)22617 to build 250 Canberras – given the USAF type designation B-57A Canberra – between November 1952 and October 1953. A licence agreement between English Electric and the Glenn L. Martin Company was drawn up on 3 April and signed on 8 May 1951; royalties were established at a maximum of five per cent of a fair selling price per aircraft. English Electric insisted that the name 'Canberra' should be used, but somewhere along the line this seems to have been forgotten, and the American numbered designation alone has become accepted. In June 1951, two Douglas DC-4s were filled with Canberra drawings, to be transported to Martins for conversion to United States measurements – no mean task.

WD932 remained in the United States and was handed over to Martins as the first pattern aircraft. It was allocated the American serial 51-17387, but this was never applied on the aircraft itself which disintegrated in flight, while making a tight turn, on 21 December. The pilot ejected safely but the observer/navigator, who also ejected, was killed, as his parachute did not open. A full investigation into the accident reached the conclusion that the aircraft had been flown with its c.g. outside aft limits, because the forward fuel tanks had been incorrectly used first, thereby placing excessive strain on the wings. This had made the aircraft longitudinally unstable, so that it went into a tightening spiral dive from 10,000ft, thus shedding the port wing.

A second pattern aircraft had already been ordered from English Electric and WD940, the twelfth production B.2, was flown from Aldergrove to Gander on 31 August, to claim the first official Canberra record (*see* Chapter 5). Beamont was at the controls of the aircraft and, on delivering it to Martin Aircraft's airfield at Middle River, Baltimore, he put on one of his displays, which were by now famous. He amazed the assembled company workers, who became convinced that they were going to be making a first-class aircraft.

However, the break-up of WD932 backed up those pressure groups within the Wright Air Development Centre (WADC), whose view was that the Canberra required extensive modifications before it could be accepted for USAF service. They were not really alone in their feelings, but the USAF, always conscious of costs, had played them down, insisting that, if the Canberra was in service with the RAF, then it was acceptable to them. WADC would not let the matter drop and its Commanding Officer Maj Gen F.R. Dent put forward a written list of the deficiencies that he saw in the aircraft, some of which had already been demanded by the Air Ministry, relative to RAF aircraft. Maj Gen Dent's case was accepted by the American Air Materials Command (AMC) and, while Martins had the Canberra in full production to meet the order for 250 B-57As, modifications were demanded. If they were not carried out,

The Americanization of Canberra B.2, WD940, as it is transformed into 51-17352. The Health and Safety inspectors were certainly not around at the time! Author's collection

the future of the Canberra as a USAF operational aircraft was non-existent.

The second pattern aircraft, WD940, was allocated the USAF serial 51-17352. It was operated at Middle River with its RAF markings for some months, before eventually going into the paint shop. The RAF mid-grey/black colour scheme was retained, but the aircraft now carried the star-and-bar USAF insignia and serial. It acted as a trials vehicle for many of the modifications adapted on subsequent B-57 variants, such as multiple underwing pylons, fuselage airbrakes and, more significantly, the tandem cockpit layout. These were tried as static elements before the aircraft was taken apart, for sections to be distributed to subcontractors, including the Cleveland Pneumatic Tool Company (undercarriages), Hudson Motors (rear fuselage and tail assemblies) and Kaiser Metals (bomb-bay doors, nacelles and wing panels).

B-57 production was in full swing at Middle River in 1952 and the first production aircraft, 52-1418, had its maiden flight on 20 July 1953, a mere twenty-eight months after the contract had been received. The pilot for this historic flight was Martin's Chief of Flight Test, O.B. 'Pat' Tibbs. Beamont flew this aircraft a little later and declared that it handled exactly the same as the Canberra B.2 produced in the UK.

The B-57A and Variants

In appearance, the B-57A closely resembled the Canberra B.2, but one major difference lay in the engines. Armstrong Siddeley and Curtiss Wright had a licence agreement, whereby the American company would build the Sapphire for USAF aircraft designs, although initial production

Martin's first production B-57A, 52-1418, takes off for its maiden flight on 20 July 1953. Author's collection

of the engine, designated the J-65, was farmed out to Buick Motors. Producing 7,220lb (3,280kg) static thrust, the Buick-built engines carried the title J-65-BW-2 and the Wright-produced J-65-W-5. Buick got behind in delivery schedules as their engines did not come up to specification and, after the first few B-57A production aircraft, Wright took over full control and became the sole engine supplier, until the much later long-wing B-57 variants. With the front casing of the Sapphire having a greater diameter than that of the Avon, the front of B-57 nacelles were visibly more bulged than on British production aircraft.

Production of the B-57A was confined to just eight aircraft, all of them in natural metal finish, which served on a variety of trials programmes and were never issued to the USAF. Provision had been made to carry eight 0.5in (12.5mm) machine guns in the wings, but these were not fitted to all of the first eight aircraft. Some finished their days as NRB-57As, the 'N' prefix denoting special tests. The main production batch of aircraft resembling the RAF B.2 was the reconnaissance/bomber RB-57A, of which

sixty-seven were issued to the USAF. The 363rd Tactical Reconnaissance Wing (TRW) at Shaw AFB in South Carolina became the first operator, in the summer of 1954. The Wing's red and white checkered markings on the tails became very distinctive on the aircraft standard over-all gloss black finish. The 345th Light Bomber Wing at Langley AFB in Virginia also received its first aircraft at around the same time.

The first production RB-57A had made its maiden flight in October 1953 and this variant had a camera installation aft of the bomb-bay, for day or night photographic-reconnaissance sorties. These were carried out at all altitudes, with a two-man crew of pilot and photo-navigator.

Despite problems with control systems and wing/fuselage attachment fittings, as well as troublesome engines, two Wings were established in West Germany as part of the USAF commitment to NATO. The 10th TRW at Spangdahlem Air Base (AB) and the 66th at Sembach AB received RB-57As, but their tenure was comparatively short, as the Douglas RB-66B started to arrive in Europe towards the end of 1957. Attrition was quite high, with at least ten aircraft being lost due to accidents. Following service with the front-line units, RB-57As were passed on to Air National Guard (ANG) squadrons, including the Arkansas 154th Tactical Reconnaissance Squadron (TRS) at Little Rock, the Kansas 117th TRS at Hutchinson, the Michigan 172nd TRS at Battle Creek and the Virginia 149th TRS.

Later, at least ten of the aircraft were converted to RB-57A-1 standard, to meet

RB-57As of the 363rd Tactical Reconnaissance Wing arrived in Europe in 1956.
Author's collection

Martin's first major change to the Canberra was the rotary bomb-bay, shown here being tested on a RB-57A. Author's collection

The B-57B was the principal production variant. It introduced the redesigned front fuselage, with the pilot and navigator seated in tandem, as well as four weapon pylons under each wing, seen carrying 5in (12.5cm) high-velocity RPs. Author's collection

high-altitude reconnaissance missions codenamed Project *Heartthrob*. These conversions involved fitting J-65-W-7 engines, producing slightly higher thrust and the removal of selected equipment associated with the photo-navigator, this crew member being surplus to requirements, as the RB-57A-1 was a single-seater. (Indeed, it was believed to be the only single-seat Canberra/B-57 variant with any air force.) The all-up weight of the RB-57A-1 was reduced by 5,665lb (2,569kg), to 43,182lb (19,583kg), which gave it an additional 5,000ft (1,500m) service ceiling. The aircraft were issued to the 7499th Composite Squadron (CS), USAF Europe and the 6007th CS in the Pacific area.

Several RB-57As were allocated for research purposes. Northrop Aircraft Inc. was loaned one airframe for laminar flow boundary layer control studies, while several more were employed on atmospheric sampling flights, sponsored by the USAF. The Republic of China received two, under Project *Large Charge*, and 52-1435 was brought up to NRB-57A condition for numerous evaluation flights, until it was retired at the end of 1969.

Martins' conversion of more than two dozen RB-57As to EB-57A standard in less than a year was a more extensive programme. This involved the installation of ECM equipment in the bomb-bay and chaff dispensers mounted on underwing pylons. An Electronics Warfare Officer (EWO) replaced the navigator, and the principal role operated by EB-57As became the simulation of enemy aircraft making hostile approaches into North American airspace.

The first EB-57A had its maiden flight in April 1966 and the Defence Systems Evaluation (DSE) aircraft, as the variant was titled, served into the 1970s with the 4713rd, 4758th and 4677th DSE Squadrons. The squadrons ranged all over North America, as well as NATO Europe and trials were made with various surface-to-air missile (SAM) systems in the different theatres of operation.

Fundamental Modifications – The Martin B-57B

A major element of the WADC list of required modifications to the Canberra, as supplied by English Electric, was the crew layout. The location of the navigator in the 'black hole', as operated by the RAF, went against the grain as far as the WADC was concerned and the tandem seating of the B-47 Stratojet was favourably received by all who flew in it. Boeing reiterated the arrangement in its XB-52 prototypes, but the operational requirements of a much larger aircraft decreed a redesign of the crew compartment for the production versions, into the 'Buff' that is known and loved today.

Martins designed an entirely new front fuselage forward of Frame 12A, carrying the pilot and navigator in tandem, under a large one-piece glazed canopy. It hinged at the rear, to be retained in the open position by a hydraulic ram strut positioned between the two crew members. (Opening canopies were a luxury only enjoyed by Canberra PR.9 crews in the RAF.) The fixed three-piece windscreen had a flat window at the front, which enabled a gun-sight to be installed. This had not been possible on the earlier aircraft with their curved one-piece cockpit covering, due to distortion and flexing of the canopy. Besides the obvious advantage of the navigator being able to see out and, consequently, assist the pilot in this respect, ejector-seat evacuation in an emergency was a better deal for him.

Another fundamental change to the original Canberra was the installation of a 17-ft (5-m) rolling bomb door. Designed by Martin Aircraft engineers Werner Buchal and Albert Wollens, it eliminated the buffeting experienced when the conventional bomb doors were opened, and had the advantage of cutting down on rearming time. The revolving door could be pre-loaded with ordnance, so that when an operational aircraft came in for refuelling and rearming, the empty bomb door could be removed from the airframe and a loaded one installed in its place very quickly. This rotating bomb door was to be found particularly advantageous when LABS deliveries were employed.

Four stores pylons were fitted under each outer wing and four 0.5in (12.5mm) machine guns were mounted in each wing, outboard of the engine nacelles. This armament was replaced by two 20mm M39

On 26 October 1955, two B-57Bs of the 12th USAF, based in France, flew to Warton on a goodwill visit. The group, with a B-57B and Canberra B(I).8 behind them, are, from left to right: Lt L.J. Kaford, USAF; Mr F.D. Crowe, chief Canberra designer at English Electric; Lt J. Acton, USAF; Mr W. Bullock, Martin's European representative; Lt Col T.J. Price, USAF; Lt Col J.R. O'Neill, USAF. Author's collection

Canberra B(I).8 and B-57B at Warton present an interesting comparison. Author's collection

cannon in each wing, on the production line, starting with the ninety-first aircraft. Rear fuselage-mounted airbrakes were fitted, to act in unison with the wing spoilers retained from the original RAF Canberra pattern aircraft.

Internally and, therefore, less perceptibly, there were also changes in the navigation and electronic equipment, compared with the British Canberras. The *Orange Putter* tail-warning radar was replaced by the APS-54 Radar Warning System

(RWS), which operated on a wider coverage angle than the British system, as well as providing the additional advantage of presenting Airborne Interception Warning (AIW) from below and either side. The APW-11 Bombing Air Radar Guidance

---

Canberra Becomes Americanized

Martin model 272 B-57A
Eight new-build aircraft produced between July and December 1953: 52-1418 to 52-1425

Martin model 272A RB-57A
Sixty-seven new-build aircraft produced between October 1953 and August 1954: 52-1426 to 52-1492

Martin model 272R EB-57A
Exact number of aircraft involved in this conversion of existing RB-57As cannot be fully substantiated, but the following have been confirmed as being produced between April 1966 and March 1967: 52-1428, 52-1437, 52-1439 to 52-1442, 52-1447, 52-1448, 52-1450, 52-1461, 52-1464, 52-1481, 52-1489

Martin B-57B
202 new build aircraft produced between June 1954 and May 1956: 52-1493 to 52-1594, 53-3859 to 53-3935, 53-3937 to 53-3939, 53-3941 to 53-3943, 53-3945 to 53-3947, 53-3949 to 53-3962

Martin EB-57B
Twenty-two aircraft involved in this conversion of existing EB-57As: 52-1499 to 52-1507, 52-1509, 52-1511, 52-1515, 52-1516, 52-1519 to 52-1521, 52-1526, 52-1545, 52-1548, 52-1551, 52-1564, 52-1571, 53-3859

Martin JB-57B
Four aircraft involved in this conversion of existing EB-57As: 52-1539, 52-1540, 52-1562 52-1594

Martin NB-57B
Six aircraft involved in this conversion of existing EB-57As: 52-1493, 52-1496, 52-1498, 52-1451, 52-1580, 52-1481

Martin RB-57B
Exact number of aircraft involved in this conversion of existing EB-57As cannot be fully substantiated, but the following have been confirmed: 52-1518, 52-1522, 52-1557, 52-1559, 52-1570, 52-1571, 52-1589, 53-3860, 53-3920

RB-57A, 52-1444, with a solid nose-cone, is believed to be one of the ten aircraft converted to RB-57A-1 configuration for Project **Heartthrob**. Author's collection

EB-57B, 52-1519 of the Vermont ANG – The Green Mountain Boys, **as proclaimed on the underwing tank.**
R. Harrison/George Pennick

System (BARGS), which allowed an accurate run on to the target to be made, was augmented by the navigator/bombardier's Shoran bombing system. Another Americanization was the removal of the Sapphire's manually operated cartridge starter system, replaced by an electrically ignited cartridge, which, on starting, produced the B-57's dense trademark cloud of acrid black smoke from each nacelle. This catalogue of modifications to the original Canberra produced the Martin B-57B.

When Martin Aircraft had received its first contract, AF33(038)-22617, the delivery time-scale was to be between November 1952 and October 1953. This had to be radically amended for many reasons, not least because of the modifications engineered to produce the B-57B. In fact, it was 18 June 1954 before the first example of this version, 52-1493, made its maiden flight. Once production did get under way, deliveries were fairly prompt, within the revised dates, and all 202 examples of this model had been supplied to the USAF by May 1956.

B-57C, 53-3850 'Nite Mare' was in Europe with the 38th BGT, during Exercise Counter Punch. Author's collection

Bomb Groups

The 345th Bomb Group (Tactical) (BG), at Langley AFB, was the first to be equipped with the B-57B, in January 1955. It was to act not only as an operational unit, but also had the responsibility of training and converting its own crew members – rather reminiscent of the role of No.101 Squadron at Binbrook, back in 1951. It was quickly realized that, with other units shortly to be similarly equipped, a dedicated Operational Conversion Unit was required. This was established at Randolf AFB in Texas, as the 3510th Combat Crew Training Wing (CCTW). The first course to qualify became the basis of the 461st BG at Hill AFB, Utah, the second B-57B unit. Further B-57B squadrons were set up in rapid succession and the type joined the USAF contribution to NATO in the summer of 1955, when the 38th BG at Laon, in northern France, replaced its obsolete B-26s. Fourth of the B-57B groups to be formed was the 3rd BGT in Japan, which alternated with the South Korean airbase at Kunsan.

Within the four groups, exercises were held to facilitate quick reactions, should overseas deployment be necessary. Exercise *Sagebrush* was held in the USA during 1955 and, in 1956, NATO Exercise

Counter Punch involved the 38th BGT in France. During this time, a remarkable lack of co-operation between English Electric and Martin Aircraft seems to have evolved. There were several instances of B-57Bs diving into the ground, during low-level sorties, and the type was grounded for a while, pending investigations into the accidents. As with the Canberra, when WD991 crashed on 25 March 1952, killing test pilot Tommy Evans, the culprit was found to be the tailplane actuator. In retrospect, English Electric might well have been more forthcoming with their findings three years earlier. Sad to say, they were not, and Martin Aircraft had to engage in a series of trial-and-error modifications before the faulty actuator was discovered. New actuators were fitted and the B-57 was back in business.

The Bomb Groups at Langley, Hill and Laon had all been deactivated by 1959. The 38th BG at Laon had fielded the very good *Black Knights* aerobatic team for a short time in the mid-1950s and laid claim to it being the first time that bombers had been used in such a team. While this is fundamentally true, it should not be forgotten that No.231 OCU at Bassingbourn, formed in December 1951, also flew a four-aircraft aerobatic team. Bassingbourn's team aircraft were T.4s, but these were similar airframes.

Canberras in Vietnam

A winding-down of the B-57B Groups was planned, but a number of minor international incidents, such as the crisis in Lebanon in April 1958, and Communist China's bombardment of the Chinese Nationalist island of Quemoy later in the same year, led to its postponement. By 1959, the anticipated escalation of these incidents had not materialized, tensions had eased, and all but the 3rd BG had traded in their aircraft for the North American F-100 Super Sabre. A new spate of disturbances began in August 1964, when Communist North Vietnamese torpedo boats attacked the American destroyer USS *Maddon* in the Gulf of Tonkin, off the coast of North Vietnam. Two B-57B squadrons from the 3rd BG, the 8th and 13th Bomber Squadrons (BS), were posted from Clark AFB in the Philippines to the airbase at Bien Hao, near Saigon in South Vietnam. Their aim: to dissuade the Communists from invading Nationalist Formosa.

Ever since the French had been evicted from Vietnam, then known as French Indo-China, Communist doctrines in the north of the country had been on the increase. Despite the presence of some 18,000 US 'advisors' in the southern sector of the country, this area, with its more American-influenced population, was viewed as ripe for a takeover. The B-57Bs at Bien Hao carried out unarmed reconnaissance missions, during which two aircraft were lost in landing accidents. On 1 November 1964, North Vietnamese Viet Cong forces made a concerted attack on the airbase with 81mm mortars, destroying a further five aircraft and damaging fifteen more. Restrained by the Geneva Convention, US forces could not retaliate, but, early in the following year, President Lyndon Johnson considered 'enough was enough'. He gave the US Commander-in-Chief in Vietnam, General William C. Westmoreland, permission to act under emergency regulations, which resulted in him issuing orders on 19 February 1965 to the 8th and 13th BS B-57Bs to attack Viet Cong positions at Bien Gia. The Canberra was in action again, in a new theatre of conflict, and the USA had embarked on a disastrous intervention in Vietnam.

On 11 March 1965, the first B-57B to be lost due to groundfire brought the fact home to the two squadrons that they were in a shooting war and not on exercise. Another was brought down in April, but casualties remained comparatively low, considering the number of sorties flown, and further strikes, flown as part of *Rolling Thunder*, had good results against ammunition dumps. The B-57B was liked by its crews, who found it a very stable gun platform and, because of this, the aircraft was heavily engaged in night attacks on the Ho Chi Minh trail, flown in association with Lockheed C-130 'Blind Bat' flareships. B-57Bs usually carried twelve 500lb (225kg) bombs on the rotating bomb-bay door, plus four 750lb (340kg) bombs on underwing pylons and, although these operations were very successful per aircraft, having only two squadrons available meant that the overall effects on Viet Cong troop movements were never really more than a nuisance.

B-57B attrition increased on 16 May, when a fully bombed-up 3rd BG aircraft, piloted by Captain Fox, exploded at Bien Hoa while starting engines. On an operational airfield, with a tarmac full of tightly packed armed aircraft, the result was disastrous. The intense conflagration resulting from the exploded aircraft destroyed another nine B-57Bs, eleven Vietnamese Air Force (VNAF) A-1H Skyraiders, and a visiting US Navy F-8 Crusader, which had just landed. This visit turned out to be something of a godsend; as it was an unusual aircraft at Bien Hoa, many of the

maintenance crews had gone to watch it land and were therefore away from the tarmac at the time of the explosion. Still, casualties amounted to twenty 3rd BG members and eight Vietnamese killed, and over 100 more injured.

The devastation closed Bien Hoa to seven incoming B-57Bs returning from various missions, the aircraft being diverted to Tan So Nhut. Surviving B-57s were also transferred to this base, from where subsequent strike operations were conducted. Back at Bien Hoa, investigations traced the cause of the B-57B's sudden demise to a short-circuit in the aircraft's weapon fusing. It was considered an isolated defect and no modifications were made to the greatly depleted 8th and 13th BS force. Because B-57 production had finished at Middle River, there followed a frantic scouring through ANG squadrons in order to find replacement aircraft for the 3rd BG, as a temporary measure. Drawn from Kentucky and Nevada ANG squadrons, nine aircraft arrived at Da Nang, where the whole Group came under the command of the 6252nd TFW. It was later renumbered the 35th TFW, and new call signs were allocated – the 8th BS took on 'Yellow Bird' and the 13th BS, 'Red Bird'.

Night interdiction raids against North Vietnam and Laos had begun in the middle of 1965, under the codename Operation *Steel Tiger*. The monsoon season brought a halt to proceedings until November, and the two squadrons rotated sixty-day breaks at Clark AFB, in the Philippines. In December, Operation *Tiger Hound* brought a renewal of strikes against the Ho Chi Minh trail, resulting in successful attacks on anti-aircraft (AA) batteries, and the temporary destruction of several bridges – 'temporary', because the forests provided plenty of natural resources for immediate repairs. These raids brought an understandable reaction from the Viet Cong – a stepping up of the number of AA batteries – and, by May 1966, groundfire was becoming a serious deterrent. Of twenty-five USAF aircraft brought down within a few weeks, at least three B-57Bs were victims, and several more sustained battle damage of varying degrees, which kept individual aircraft grounded for several days.

By October 1966, attrition had reduced the 3rd BG to a point where it had to be withdrawn from the front line and take up residence at the newly constructed Phan Rang airbase, on the east coast of South Vietnam. The plan was that No.2 Squadron

of the RAAF, with its Canberra B.20s, would join them there in 1967. 3rd BG aircraft had by now been camouflaged, and daylight operations were continued whenever enough aircraft were available. Four more were lost over the next 15 months and finally, on 15 January 1968, the 13th BS was deactivated, leaving the 8th BS as the only tactical light bomber unit in the whole USAF. A total of nine B-57s were still operating in June 1969 and a few sorties were still being mounted, but, on 15 October, the last aircraft departed from Phan Rang and, routing via Clark AFB, all the ex-8th BS aircraft were placed in storage at Davis-Monthan AFB. Of the ninety-six B-57s employed in all operations in Vietnam, only thirty-two survived. Some were converted to later variants and the balance were stored.

New B-57 Variants

As might be expected, the war in Vietnam quickened the natural development of new B-57 variants. Like the RAF, with the Canberra T.4, the USAF appreciated the need for a dual-control B-57 trainer and, on 30 December 1954, the first B-57C made its maiden flight. A total of thirty-eight B-57Cs were ordered and the final aircraft of this batch was delivered in May 1956. Four were loaned to the South Vietnamese Air Force in 1955 and, three years later, at least six had been converted to photographic-reconnaissance standard. Designated RB-57Cs, they served with various ANG squadrons and three were operating well into 1973. Four more B-57C trainers were converted to fly weather-reconnaissance missions, under the designation WB-57C.

On 4 November 1953, Martin Aircraft received Contract AF33(600)-22208 to produce fifty-three B-57Ds, but changes were introduced to the order in 1955. Twenty B-57Ds were transferred to Contract AF33(600)-25825, and given the new designation RB-57D. The remaining thirty-three B-57Ds on the original contract were cancelled and the net result of this complicated transaction was that no B-57Ds were manufactured; all twenty aircraft that were built were titled RB-57D. The RB-57D was significantly different from earlier aircraft, in having wings spanning 106ft (32m), 42ft (13m) greater than previous variants. There was also a change in powerplants, 10,000lb (4,550kg) thrust Pratt & Whitney J-57-P-27 engines replacing the J-65s. This 3,230lb

B-57C, 53840, carries the markings of the 4424th Combat Crew Training Wing, based at McDill AFB.
K. Buchanan/George Pennick

(1,465kg) increase in thrust and the greater wingspan were the requirements for the high-altitude daylight reconnaissance role at 65,000ft (19,800m) that the aircraft was to fulfil, until the Lockheed U-2 came into service. It resulted from a study made at the WADC in 1952 and the four versions produced, under different model designations, were intended for varying operations.

Group 'A' aircraft, Martin model 294, were designated RB-57Ds and six were produced, with the first having its maiden flight on 3 November 1955. On the strength of the Strategic Air Command (SAC), all six were allocated for operation from Yokota in Japan, the first aircraft arriving in spring 1956, and the sixth in March 1957. Under the codename *Black Knight*, these Group 'A'

aircraft, which operated with a crew of two, were engaged on ELINT missions that are still classified after over fifty years. At Yokota, the 6021st Strategic Reconnaissance Squadron flew several older RB-57As, which had been updated with J-57 engines.

Group 'B' aircraft, Martin model 744, were also designated RB-57Ds, differing from the earlier six aircraft by being

---

US Canberra Classrooms

Martin B-57C
Thirty-eight new-build aircraft produced between December 1954 and May 1956: 53-3825 to 53-3858, 53-3936, 53-3940, 53-3944, 53-3948

Martin RB-57C
Six aircraft involved in this conversion of existing B-57Cs: 53-3831, 53-3832, 53-3841, 53-3842, 53-3851, 53-3944

Martin WB-57C
Four aircraft involved in this conversion of existing B-57Cs: 53-3836, 53-3844, 53-3850, 53-3851

The Vermont ANG's 134th Defense Systems Evaluation Squadron had RB-57C, 53-3831, at Pease AFB in New Hampshire, on 12 July 1980. R. Harrison/George Pennick

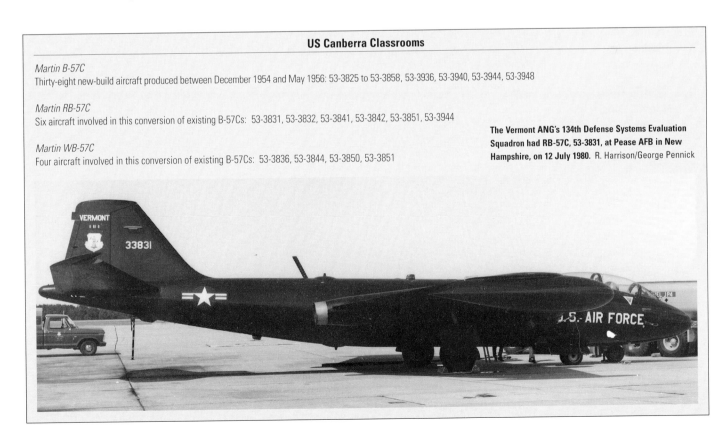

53-3831 was one of the thirty-eight new-build B-57Cs that had been converted to RB-57C before this photograph was taken. Jerry Geer/George Pennick

The notice taped on the front fuselage of 55-4267 proclaims it to be 'NB-57B Canberra, Light Bomber and Test Bed Aircraft, Range 2,365 miles, Speed 520mph, Altitude 45,700feet'. However, records state that the aircraft is in fact one of four B-57Es converted to NB-57E standard. Jay Sherlock/George Pennick

equipped for air-to-air refuelling from Boeing KC-97 tanker aircraft. Seven of this variant were produced and they operated with a pilot-only crew, often flying from Rhine Main AFB in West Germany. Three of them wore Nationalist China markings for a while, operating out of Taiwan between 1959 and 1963, during which time one was shot down. Both Group 'A' and 'B' RB-57Ds were used on Operation *Hardtrack* in association with the nuclear-bomb testing at Eniwetok Atoll.

Group 'C' aircraft, Martin model 797, designated RB-57D-2s, had IFR tail radomes and ferret ECM facilities. Production of this variant was also six aircraft, and a crew of two (pilot and ECM operator) was carried, with this variant also having provision for flight refuelling.

Group 'D' aircraft, Martin model 796, was a singleton. It carried the title RB-57D-1 and was operated by a two-man crew. Extensively equipped, it also carried IFR, plus AN/APG-56 radar, which could

be installed in a lengthened nose or tail radome.

The 106ft (32m) wings, which were constructed with thin lightweight honeycomb sections, skinned and containing fuel tanks, gave rise to many problems, principally concerning structural failures that were usually sustained during landings. Further weight saving was achieved by skinning over the bomb-bay.

Several aircraft were put into storage and a few were converted for other roles.

53-3973 was destroyed when it lost a wing at 50,000ft (15,200m), resulting in all EB-57Ds being grounded and stored for a time. The absence of an alternative aircraft to undertake the high-altitude target role led to the stored aircraft having modifications made to their wings, before being put back into service. Additional ECM equipment was installed and the 4677th DSES at Hill AFB received five aircraft which, in 1962, they flew for the Project *Dominic* nuclear-test programme, being detached to the Christmas Islands as an element of the 1211st Test Squadron (Sampling). By the early 1970s, the EB-57D had outlived its usefulness and all examples, except 53-3982, which went to the Tucson Air Museum, were broken up.

Contract AF33(600)-29645 required Martins to build sixty-eight B-57E aircraft. This was a dual-control variant without provision for delivering weaponry, which was fitted with target-towing winches and reels mounted in the bombbay. The first production aircraft took to the air on 16 May 1956, and the last one of the order was completed in March 1957. Power for the winches was supplied by air drawn off the thirteenth stage of the engine compressor, which came in at about 29,000ft (8,800m), when there was sufficient bleed-off pressure. Two sleeve targets were carried in a pair of tubes, mounted in a ventral position extending from the fuselage airbrakes to the tail

cone. This variant was also equipped with a fully powered rudder and yaw dampers. On target-towing sorties, B-57Es flew with a Lockheed T-33, carrying an observer to score each firing pass. North American F-86D Sabres, with their batteries of twenty-four 2.75in (70mm) *Mighty Mouse* unguided rockets, were among the first fighters to make use of the B-57E's target-towing facilities.

In the autumn of 1965, the need for additional B-57s in Vietnam was met by Martins by the conversion of a dozen B-57Es to bomber and reconnaissance standard. Prior to this, Operation *Patricia Lynn* was initiated by Detachment 1 of the 33rd Tactical Group (TG), on 6 May 1963. The

---

Martin RB-57D

Twenty new-build aircraft produced as four separate Martin models, between November 1955 and March 1957:

Martin RB-57D, model 294, Group 'A' six aircraft: 53-3977 to 53-3982

Martin RB-57D, model 744, Group 'B' seven aircraft: 53-3970 to 53-3976

Martin RB-57D-2, model 797, Group 'C' six aircraft: 53-3964 to 53-3969

Martin RB-57D-1, model 796, Group 'D' one aircraft: 53-3963

53-3972, one of the seven RB-57D, Group 'B' aircraft, showing the single-seat layout, as well as the 106ft (32m) wingspan, to advantage. The colour scheme is black and white.
Author's collection

(Left) **RB-57D, 53-3963, cocooned at the Davis Monthan AFB, on 1 November 1965.** R.A. Walker

As 55-4234, the first of sixty-eight B-57Es lifts off, with the Martin fuselage-mounted airbrake shown to advantage. Author's collection

first two (of five) B-57Es converted to RB-57E standard by General Dynamics (GD) at Fort Worth in Texas, arrived at Tan Son Nhut in South Vietnam. The conversions involved the installation of a significant amount of reconnaissance equipment, which included KA-1 36in (900mm) vertical and oblique cameras mounted in the bomb-bay. Another KA-1 was fitted in a modified nose and a K-477 night/day camera operated from a fuselage mounting.

As soon as the pair of aircraft arrived at Tan Son Nhut, they were put into use. Their first reconnaissance sortie was flown on 7 May, the day after they arrived, using the ferry crews as combat crews – much to their surprise! Detachment 1 had its full quota of five RB-57Es by the end of 1963, and it was deployed to various units under the call sign 'Moonglow'.

The first of the two aircraft to be lost while serving with the detachment was shot down on 6 August 1965 while on a low-level sortie; the crew ejected safely.

The crew members of the second aircraft, lost on 25 October 1968, were not so lucky. However, considering the thousands of hours flown during the eight years that Detachment 1 was active, these losses were relatively light. Nearly all were low-level missions and at least two aircraft each amassed 800 hours of combat flying. One additional RB-57E, 53-4257, was converted as a replacement, and this aircraft had Terrain Following Radar (TFR) fitted as an additional piece of equipment.

During the B-57s' service, many modifications were incorporated, to bring the aircraft up to the requirements of various specialist missions, including *Compass Eagle*, *Compass Hart* and *Compass Light*. These upgradings involved the installation of an infra-red scanner, together with a display screen, which were employed on covert missions flown over Cambodia and Laos, under the codename *Steel Tiger*.

Further conversions of the basic B-57E, to meet a number of operational needs at comparatively short notice, were undertaken in the 1960s. The EB-57E was an example of this, when at least twenty-six aircraft were fitted with existing electronic equipment 'off the shelf', to provide an effective ECM target for airborne and ground radar systems. Defence Systems Evaluation Squadrons (DSES) in the USA and overseas units, such as the 8th TBS at Clark AFB and the 556th RS in Japan, used the EB-57E, and at least one unit, the 17th DSES, is known to have continued until the end of 1979.

A 'one-off' conversion was also made to a B-57E for a temporary testing programme, the resultant aircraft being designated JB-57E, while another four were modified to NB-57E standard, the 'N' prefix denoting 'assigned to special test', which were conducted on a permanent basis. A small, but unknown number of B-57Bs, already converted to B-57Es, plus a few more B-57Es, were reconstructed for the training role and given the designation TB-57E.

55-4244 was one of the few B-57Es that were not converted into a later variant, and is preserved in its original state at the Strategic Air Command Museum. Jerry Geer/George Pennick.

EB-57E, 55-4241, was one of the twenty-six B-57Es that was refurbished for ECM radar target work. R. Harrison/George Pennick

Martin B-57E
Sixty-eight new-build aircraft produced between May 1956 and March 1957: 55-4234 to 55-4301

Martin B-57E
Twelve aircraft involved in conversion to bomber/reconnaissance role of existing B-57Es, without any change to the designation: 55-4238, 55-4248, 55-4251, 55-4259, 55-4265, 55-4268, 55-4269, 55-4270, 55-4274, 55-4282, 55-4284, 55-4285

Martin EB-57E
Twenty-six aircraft confirmed as being involved in this conversion of existing B-57Es: 55-4239 to 55-4242, 55-4247, 55-4253, 55-4254, 55-4260, 55-4263, 55-4266, 55-4275, 55-4276, 55-4278 to 55-4281, 55-4287, 55-4288, 55-4290, 55-4292 to 55-4296, 55-4298, 55-4300

Martin JB-57E
One aircraft involved in this conversion of an existing B-57E: 55-4237

Martin NB-57E
Four aircraft involved in this conversion of existing B-57Es: 55-4257, 55-4258, 55-4262, 55-4267

Martin RB-57E
Six aircraft involved in this conversion by General Dynamics, of existing B-57Es: 55-4237, 55-4243, 55-4245, 55-4249, 55-4257, 55-4264

Close-up of EB-57E's ECM antennas. Author's collection

Martin TB-57E
Exact number of aircraft involved in this conversion cannot be confirmed, but it is known that B-57Bs, already converted to B-57E standard, as well as some original B-57Es, were employed.

RB-57F, 63-13294, of the 58th Weather Reconnaissance Squadron, was originally B-57B, 53-3935.
N. Taylor/George Pennick

The RB-57F

The ultimate in B-57 wings first appeared on the RB-57F, a long-endurance reconnaissance variant produced to operate at altitudes from 80,000ft to 90,000ft (24,400–27,400m). The whole design/manufacturing programme was conducted by GD at Fort Worth, which, while meeting the new aircraft requirements by converting existing B-57B and RB-57D aircraft, created a variant that qualified each airframe to be given a new serial number. Seventeen B-57Bs and four RB-57Ds were involved in the rebuild programme, which occupied Fort Worth from the beginning of 1962 to February 1964.

Assimilating the USAF's experience with the RB-57D, GD designed a new wing, spanning 122ft (37m), with an area of 2,000sq ft (185.8sq m). It was designed as a three-spar unit, with honeycomb sandwich panels that gave strength, but were still lightweight. Having this large span, the wings had a natural tendency to droop when the aircraft was on the ground. Because there was every likelihood of the tips scraping the runway on take-off, provision was made at the design stage for the plastic wing-tips, which contained ELINT equipment, to be easily removed in the field for repair. A correspondingly larger fin and rudder assembly was designed and a pair of Pratt & Whitney TF33-P-11 turbofan engines, each producing 18,000lb

(8,165kg) thrust, were fitted. These were supplemented by two 3,300lb (1,500kg) Pratt & Whitney J-60-P-9 turbojets, slung under the wings outboard of the main engine nacelles, in detachable pods.

The fuselage contained an HTAC high-altitude camera, which weighed nearly 9,000lb (4,090kg) and was capable of taking high-resolution photographs at high altitude, of targets 60 miles (95km) away. A redesigned, lengthened nose housed special ELINT/SIGINT equipment. All in all, the RB-57F was technically well capable of meeting its multifarious specifications: to provide high-altitude photographic and multi-sensor reconnaissance over a prolonged period of flying; to collect air samples in areas of nuclear testing; to monitor upper-air weather conditions, while retaining the ability to deliver an assortment of conventional or nuclear weaponry.

On 23 June 1963, the first of this variant had its maiden flight from Fort Worth, and General Dynamics had sufficient aircraft built for the type to enter service with the USAF at the beginning of 1964. The main user of the RB-57F was the 58th Weather Reconnaissance Squadron (WRS), based at Kirtland AFB in New Mexico. They operated the type for over ten years and deployed individual aircraft to Europe and the Far East. The 7407th Support Squadron (SS) at Rhine Main AB in West Germany had quite regular detachments,

and the 6001st TMS at Yokota AB in Japan housed the aircraft when it was engaged on reconnaissance sorties over the vast Far East theatre covered by the unit.

Three aircraft were lost during its decade of operations, one in December 1965 and another in November 1966. In summer 1972, a third aircraft lost a wing at 50,000ft (15,200m), which raised the question of fatigue. Whereas the RB-57D had suffered from fatigue corrosion, RB-57Fs were showing signs of stress corrosion. Aircraft made numerous visits to Fort Worth for repairs over the years, which enabled them to continue their service.

The aircraft's role in collecting upper-air weather data was emphasized when the designation of the RB-57F was changed to WRB-57F. Its role with the 58th WRS was not fundamentally altered, but the legend 'Weather' was carried on a coloured band across the fin and rudder. By the middle of 1974, excessive wing stress had really passed the regular patch-up exercise and, on 1 July, the 58th WRS was deactivated and its WRB-57Fs went for open storage at Davis-Monthan. Before they were all 'mothballed', a few were retained for operations with the National Aeronautics and Space Administration (NASA), which was embarking on an Earth Resource Technology Programme. The modifications to equip the WRB-57Fs with a battery of very high-resolution cameras, faired

(Top) 63-13288, another one of the 58th WRS RB-57Fs, shows the two lines of vortex generators on the underside of the tailplane, and the strut under the rear fuselage that is required by the variant when it is without crew members. D. Menard/George Pennick

(Above) Former B-57B, 52-1576, was registered N809NA when operated by NASA, at the Ames-Dryden Flight Research Facility. Author's collection

Martin RB-57F

Twenty-one aircraft involved in this conversion by General Dynamics, of seventeen existing B-57Bs and four existing RB-57Ds. The conversions were extensive enough to warrant each aircraft being allocated a new serial number, the old numbers shown here in brackets: 63-13286 (52-1589), 63-13287 (53-3864), 63-13288 (52-1539), 63-13289 (52-1527), 63-13290 (52-1562), 63-13291 (52-1574), 63-13292 (52-1594), 63-13293 (52-1583), 63-13294 (53-3935), 63-13295 (53-3918), 63-13297 (53-3900), 63-13296 (53-3897), 63-13298 (52-1536), 63-13299 (52-1573), 63-13300 (52-1427), 63-13301 (52-1432), 63-13302 (52-1433), 63-13500 (53-3972), 63-13501 (53-3975), 63-13502 (53-3970), 63-13503 (53-3974)

Nearly all these aircraft were later redesignated WRB-57F.

into the bomb-bay, carried a price tag of nearly four million dollars. The USAF was not prepared to share the cost with NASA, so the aircraft were placed on charge to the Administration and flew with NASA insignia. Another NASA aircraft was B-57B 52-1576, registered as N809NA, which flew with the Ames-Dryden Flight Research Facility in 1984, with a substantial nose probe.

A Dedicated Night-Attack Aircraft

During the Vietnam War, the night intruder took on an increasingly important role and, under the codename *Tropic Moon II*, experiments were made with three B-57Bs, carrying a low-light television (LLTV) pod under each wing, operating from Phan Rang AB. The need for a self-contained dedicated night-attack aircraft became apparent and sixteen B-57Bs were sent to Martins' Middle River plant for conversion, in a project originally codenamed *Night Rider*, but later renamed *Tropic Moon III*. The new variant was designated B-57G.

The conversion involved the installation of three sensors, of which the system was handled by Westinghouse. In an ugly fairing under a stretched nose, forward-looking APQ-139 radar was combined with infra-red and low-light television, augmented with a laser targeting system. The system and installation passed USAF acceptance trials in July 1969, which instigated the reactivation of the 13th TBS at

B-57G, 53-3878, seen on the pan at McDill AFB, was one of the sixteen B-57Bs converted under Project Tropic Moon III **and operated by the 4424th CCTW. The bulge under the nose housed the infra-red, low-light television camera and laser-targeting system, which worked in conjunction with the APQ-139 radar housed in the nose-cone.** George Pennick

McDill AFB. By September 1970, eleven B-57Gs had been delivered and, with them, the unit left McDill for UBang AB in Thailand. Four aircraft were delivered and held at McDill with the 4424th CCTW, which carried the responsibility of training replacement crews. The one remaining B-57G from the sixteen-aircraft conversion programme had crashed in December 1969.

Mk.82 smart bombs were deployed, using the laser targeting system for guidance, in operations over Laos. However, although the whole combination proved very effective against Viet Cong supply

The extent to which Martin adapted the basic Canberra is shown well as a B-57A formates with 53-3977, an RB-57D Group 'A' aircraft, built for ELINT operations. Author's collection

routes at night, it was too late to alter the course of the war, which ended in the frantic US withdrawal in January 1973. One B-57G was lost in Laos on 12 December 1973, having been involved in a coming-together with a Cessna O-2A observation aircraft – the Cessna did not survive the encounter either! The Laos operations were terminated in April 1972 and, having first been withdrawn to Clark AFB, the aircraft eventually arrived at Topeka, the home of the Kansas ANG, where they were allocated to the 190th Tactical Bomber Group (TBG).

Due to the complication of its systems, even without the *Tropic Moon* equipment which had been removed at Clark, the B-57G was not easy to maintain. Two years after arriving at Topeka, the aircraft joined the earlier variants, which were cocooned over every orifice and assembly joint, to bask in the sun at Davis-Monthan open-air storage.

Martin B-57G

Sixteen aircraft involved in this conversion of existing B-57Bs: 52-1578, 52-1580, 52-1582, 52-1588, 53-3860, 53-3865, 53-3877, 53-3878, 53-3886, 53-3889, 53-3898, 53-3905, 53-3906, 53-3928, 53-3929, 53-3931

Test Programmes and Non-Military Use

The USA appreciated the stability of the B-57 as a testbed/trials aircraft, just as the UK appreciated the Canberra, and several Martin-built aircraft were chosen as the airborne carriers for various test programmes. However, American utilization was nowhere near as extensive as in the UK. They did not have as many B-57s to start with as the UK had Canberras, and there were also far more different types in America to use as trials aircraft.

NB-57B 52-1497 was flown with a 17-ft (5-m) nose section of the Boeing Bomarc IM-99 missile protruding from its front. The Bomarc's fibreglass radome housed its target-seeking electronics and in the trials, 52-1497 became an extension of the missile, so that the whole airframe simulated a missile defending its airspace, for which T-33s were often flown as the intruder. B-57s also flew electronic trials for the Martin Mace CGM-13 surface-to-surface 'flying bomb' missile.

In Project *APRE* (Aerospace Photographic Reconnaissance Experiment), an RB-57D, specially painted with a series of geometric shapes, and fitted with inset convex mirrors, was flown at high altitude beneath a very large tethered balloon, which carried a series of cameras loaded with infra-red film, to photograph the aircraft. Records show that the American space programme benefited from these tests – but do not explain how! Further trials were flown with B-57Bs carrying Jaguar sounding rockets, to measure radiation in the upper atmosphere. For hurricane hunting, on behalf of the Department of Commerce, eight early B-57s operated out of Miami Airport on Project *Stormfury*, carrying civil registrations. The only confirmed aircraft is one of the eight B-57As, 52-1419, which flew as N1005. Later, this aircraft became the American equivalent of an RAF Instructional Airframe at Miami's George T. Baker Aviation School.

Export Sales

While the Vietnamese Air Force (VNAF) used various B-57 models during the war, the only real export of B-57s by the United States was the sale in 1959 of a mix of twenty-two B-57Bs/RB-57Bs, plus three B-57Cs, to the Pakistan Air Force (PAF). The deal had been agreed by President Eisenhower during a visit to Pakistan earlier in the year, with a guarantee that the PAF would receive bombers equipped to the same standard as USAF aircraft. However, when the ex-345th BG(T) aircraft were taken from storage, the all-weather bombing systems were missing. A later agreement saw spare noses, fitted with the RB-1A *George Peach* bombing system, drawn from stock at the Warner-Robins Logistic Centre and transported to Marsoor airbase outside Karachi, where PAF technicians fitted them as replacements for the existing noses, which were returned to the USA.

PAF engineers made further changes to their B-57s, installing a modified fuel system, which enabled underwing tanks to be carried, in order to extend the aircraft's range enough to reach Calcutta. The unrest that had smouldered along the India-Pakistan border for some time erupted on 6 September 1965, and, for the first time, two Canberra-operating air forces were in conflict with each other.

The PAF B-57s equipped Nos 7 and 8 Squadrons, forming part of No.31 Wing at Mauripur, flew the first sorties against India on the night of 6 September, attacking the Indian Air Force (IAF) airfield at Jamnagor. Further attacks were made during the same night against the Halwara airbase and, on the following night, continuous

The Boeing Bomarc IM-99 nose section was test flown on NB-57B, 52-1497, with the target-seeking electronics housed within the fibre-glass radome and the aircraft acting as the missile's body. Author's collection

B-57B, 53-3885, was one of twenty-five aircraft sold by the United States to the Pakistan Air Force in 1959. The revised nose-cone indicates that the aircraft has been fitted with the RB-1A George Peach **bombing system.** Author's collection

heavy bombing missions were flown against other Indian airfields, forcing the IAF to withdraw its own Canberra force to bases deeper into the country. On 12 September, four PAF B-57s had F-86 escorts when they dropped nearly 30,000lb (13,630kg) of bombs on Amritsar airfield, which housed the radar unit that controlled all IAF operations in the area. The attack was made at low level, as the airfield was defended by SA-2 Guideline surface-to-air (SAM) missiles supplied by the USSR.

Several dawn sorties were carried out against Indian troop concentrations, using 2.75in (69.8mm) rockets carried in batches of fifty-six in underwing pods, as well as 20mm cannon shell salvos and 4,000lb (1,820kg) bomb loads. By the time the first week of hostilities had passed, PAF B-57s had flown over 120 missions. One aircraft had been lost, on 14 September, due to Indian AA fire. Three days later, a second aircraft was destroyed in a bad-weather landing.

The war ended on 29 September 1965, by which time 167 B-57 sorties had been carried out, for the loss of three aircraft. However, because of the war, United States aid to Pakistan was withdrawn and, while airframe maintenance could be handled by local engineering firms, the absence of spares for J-65 engines caused the grounding of several aircraft. In 1970, the US was becoming aware of the imbalance of power

in the area and offered the PAF seven additional B-57s. However, as China was beginning to supply aircraft, Pakistan refused the offer. Their remaining B-57s had been brought up to operational standard and, when the second conflict with India broke out, in December 1971, No.7 Squadron took over No.8 Squadron's aircraft.

This renewal of hostilities lasted fourteen days, during which Indian airfields again sustained heavy attacks, and it is believed that five B-57s were lost. No.7 Squadron held on to its B-57s until being

disbanded at the end of 1986, by which time the aircraft had been fitted with new electronics, giving them a maritime strike capacity. When the squadron did disband, its aircraft were passed on to No.22 Squadron at Faisal. Later, they joined the 32nd Fighter Ground Attack Wing, but, by 1987, the B-57s were too long in the tooth and were withdrawn from PAF service. In the twenty-eight years during which Pakistan flew the B-57, the aircraft performed well and met all its roles to everyone's satisfaction – except perhaps the Indians.

American Canberras

Glenn L. Martin built a total of 403 B-57s, in six variants, broken down as follows:

Model	B-57A	RB-57A	B-57B	B-57C	RB-57D	B-57E
Number built	8	67	202	38	20	68

Martin B-57A, RB-57A, B-57B, B-57C and B-57E

Dimensions:	Span 63ft 11in (19.3m); length 65ft 6in (19.96m); height 15ft 7in (4.50m); wing area 960sq ft (89.18sq m)
Powerplants:	Two Wright J65-W-5 turbojets each producing 7,220lb (3,274.2kg) thrust
Performance:	Maximum speed 590mph (949.4km/h) at altitude Service ceiling 47,000ft (14,325.6m) Maximum range 2,300 miles (3,701.3km)

Martin RB-57D

Dimensions:	Span 106ft (32.3m); length 67ft 10in (20.68m); height 15ft 7in (4.80m); wing area 1,435sq ft (133.3sq m)
Powerplants:	Two Pratt & Whitney J57-P-37A turbojets each producing 11,000lb (4,988.5kg) thrust
Performance:	Maximum speed 590mph (949.4km/h) at altitude Service ceiling 70,000ft (21,336m) Maximum range 3,000 miles (4,827.9km)

All other variants were derivatives of these aircraft and specifications varied according to modifications and roles.

CHAPTER THIRTEEN

A Nice Little Earner

In terms of revenue for English Electric and the British Exchequer, the Canberra was a profitable piece of engineering. The United States paid $1,018,388 for the two pattern aircraft in 1951, while royalties on Martin-built B-57s were about five per cent per aircraft. A breakdown of exported and overseas licence-built Canberras shows that 146 were new-build aircraft, 112 were refurbished and 451 were built under licence. The value of royalties, plus exports of new and refurbished aircraft, to sixteen different countries, was quoted at £164 million, in July 1982. The first two overseas customers were Australia and the United States, who both expressed interest in 1949, while the first direct sale was to Venezuela, in January 1953.

Refurbishment

The refurbishment of existing aircraft to meet overseas and, later, RAF requirements, was handled in No.2 Shed at Samlesbury, as an uninterrupted programme lasting twenty-two years. Each aircraft was individually cleared for just one delivery flight, from wherever it was stored to Samlesbury; if it could not be given clearance, it was transported by road.

Once at Samlesbury, all fluids were drained and flying controls removed, before all existing paint was stripped off, leaving the aircraft in bare metal prior to being disassembled. Engines were removed and sent for new-life overhaul, either to Rolls-Royce's facility at East Kilbride in Scotland, or to engine-specializing RAF Maintenance Units. When the wings had been removed and the airframe broken down to the three fuselage sections, the tail assembly was removed, so that all inside elements could be stripped before being vacuum-blasted, to remove any trace of corrosion.

During the disassembling process, every single item removed was labelled, and each aircraft had its own collection of containers, in which these items were stored. This meant that, as far as it was practical,

an airframe received its own parts back again when it was being reassembled. Those that were too corroded or worn were replaced with new items drawn from stores. If the centre spar needed replacing, a special technique had been perfected by company engineers Ian Warnock and Kevin Woods, whereby the fuselage centre-section was separated horizontally, so that a new main spar forging could be inserted to replace the old. This was serious engineering, but it gave the aircraft a guaranteed new life of ten years, during which a major overhaul was required after six years. Several aircraft went through this spar-replacement process twice, which indicates the mileage that could be extracted from the durable Canberra.

For a straightforward refurbishment, the aircraft was finished in about twelve months, but this could extend to eighteen months if special equipment or modifications were demanded by a foreign customer. At the end of its time in No.2 Shed, the aircraft emerged in pristine condition inside and out, with all electrics replaced. Warton Flight Operations conducted a comprehensive test-flying programme and inspection, before the aircraft was painted for its new customer. During these trials, the aircraft was flown in Class 'B' registration condition; each manufacturer had its own identification number, which was stencilled on the aircraft, followed by the individually allocated airframe number. In the case of English Electric, the Class 'B' number was '27', which was prefixed by a 'G', denoting Britain. Consequently, Canberras flying without British service serials or civil registration letters – those engaged on pre-delivery flying for a foreign air force – carried the marking G27, followed by a dash and the individual aircraft's production number. For example, the first aircraft built for Argentina had the markings G27-111 during its pre-delivery flight testing in the UK, which was carried out before it had been painted.

For details on licence production in the USA, *see* Chapter 12. The remaining

fifteen overseas Canberra customers are presented below, in alphabetical order.

Argentina

The first of two Argentinian contracts placed with English Electric was received in autumn 1967; as it turned out, it was, in fact, the only contract to be fulfilled. Ten Canberra B.2s and two T.4s, all refurbished ex-RAF aircraft, were ordered, to which the designations B.62 and B.64 respectively were allocated, for service in the *Fuerza Aérea Argentina*. Delivery was to commence in 1970, and the company made plans for an aircraft from the order to be flown at that year's September SBAC Display, before going to South America. By September 1970, two B.62s were ready and both were sent to Farnborough on the sixth of the month, and given temporary civil registrations G-AYHO and G-AYHP for the duration of the show.

G-AYHO, the first Argentinian production aircraft, was held as a back-up. It was not required, as G-AYHP, the second production B.62, with Beamont at the controls, gave a faultless exhibition of display flying. It was painted in full FAA dark green and mid-grey camouflage, with a light grey underside, carrying its air force serial B-102. Twin rocket pods were fitted under each wing, which had not been in evidence when it was among aircraft in a special line-up at Warton on 13 May 1970. This had been held to commemorate the twenty-first anniversary of the Canberra's first flight and the Argentinian B.62 had been painted overall in Argentina's national colour of pale blue for the occasion.

On 17 November 1970, this aircraft, plus two more production B.62s, carrying the FAA serials B-101, B-102 and B-103, left Warton with Argentinian crews. They had passed through No.231 OCU at Bassingbourn, so that they could deliver the Canberras to their new home at the General Justo José de Urquiza airbase. The *No.1 Escuadron de Bombardeo* of *Grupo 2*

B.2, WJ616, was refurbished to become the first B.62, B-101, for the Fuerza Aérea Argentina. **It was flown at the 1970 SBAC Display, for which it carried the civil registration G-AYHO.** BAe

Argentina's second B.62, B-102, was also at Farnborough, registered G-AYHP for the occasion and fitted with twin rocket-projectile pods under each wing. BAe

de Bombardeo was formed as part of *No.11 Brigada Aérea* to fly the Canberras, and the unit was fully operational when the last aircraft, B-110, was delivered, on 9 September 1971.

B-103, one of the trio in the first delivery flight, crashed on 22 November 1971. Apart from this incident, the FAA and the Canberra had a comparatively trouble-free 'honeymoon' period. The FAA made even more use of the aircraft in a multi-role capacity than the RAF did. The twin rocket pods

positioned under each wing, as displayed at Farnborough, indicated the COIN role that the aircraft fulfilled, and the additional blade aerials were proof of the additional, if unsophisticated, EW electronics carried.

In the summer of 1981, English Electric received a second order, for the delivery of two further aircraft – one B.92 and one T.94. One was a trainer for the other – as indicated by the different designations – but the difference between the B.92 and earlier B.62s has not been given. Both

were refurbished ex-RAF aircraft and the work was in hand at Samlesbury in April 1982, when Argentinian forces invaded the Falkland Islands. The refurbishing went ahead, but both aircraft were 'frozen' on completion, as was the supply of Canberra spares, and neither aircraft was delivered to the FAA.

The conflict in the South Atlantic created a unique situation, in which British-designed and manufactured aircraft were pitted against the forces of their originator.

The FAA deployed its Canberras to Trelew, near the east coast of Patagonia, and on 1 May, in response to the Vulcan bombing raid on Port Stanley airfield earlier in the day, three B.62s took off to search at low altitude for elements of the British Task Force. Britain had declared a 200-mile (320-km) exclusion zone around the Falklands, and when the formation was intercepted by Sea Harriers, they jettisoned their bomb loads. One Canberra (B-110) was brought down by an AIM-9L Sidewinder missile, fired from Sea Harrier XZ451 of No.801 Squadron, Royal Navy.

Argentinian Canberras did not feature again until near the end of the war, when abortive night raids were mounted against British forces. On 13 June, B-108 was brought down by a surface-to-air missile (SAM) fired from HMS *Exeter*, while attacking ground troops from 36,000ft (11,000m), in the last FAA sortie of the conflict. Both crew members ejected and the pilot, who was picked up by helicopter, was repatriated after the Argentinian surrender, but the navigator is presumed to have been killed. The Canberras had flown thirty-five sorties during the war, ten in daylight. It is believed that about 100,000lb (45,350kg) of bombs was dropped around troop positions, although no casualties have been confirmed from these actions.

After the war, the FAA reverted to its exercise activities, undertaken with Chile once again viewed as the target. However, although a mutual dislike had existed for years, neither country took it as far as war. The FAA's tally of Canberra B.62s was reduced to five in August 1982, when another was involved in an accident. However, by progressively updating the

In 1949, an Australian mission visited Warton before the signing of the Canberra licensed-production contract. Members of the delegation posed with English Electric personnel (left to right): Freddy Page; unknown; Bob Hollock; Dai Ellis; unknown; 'Bee' Beamont; unknown; A.V.M. Sherger, RAAF; W.E.W. Petter; Sir George Nelson; unknown; Arthur Sheffield; unknown; Air Cdr Strang Graham. Via R.P. Beamont

electronics, the FAA has managed to keep the aircraft operational for many more years than was once thought possible.

Australia

Right from the beginning, English Electric saw Australia as a potential customer for its jet bomber. The Royal Australian Air Force (RAAF) was still operating some of the fifty-four Avro 694 Lincoln Mk.30(B) aircraft that had been built under licence at the Australian Government Aircraft Factory (GAF) at Fisherman's Bend, outside Melbourne and, like the RAF, wanted to replace them with a more modern aircraft. Whether the decision to name the A.1 'Canberra' was a ploy to stimulate the Australians into accepting the aircraft is a moot point, but, by the time Australian Prime Minister the Rt Hon R.G. Menzies was breaking a bottle of Dom Perignon over the nose of WD292 at Biggin Hill on 19 January 1951, an agreement had been signed.

The RAAF serial system incorporates a prefix 'A', followed by a number allocated to a particular aircraft name – for example, all Lincolns were A73, followed by a dash, so that an individual Lincoln was A73-53. Australian Canberras were allocated the number A84 and licensed production of their version, based on the RAF's B.2, was designated the Mk.20. Two RAF aircraft were diverted off production contracts, to assist the RAAF in training and type familiarization. WD939 came off English Electric's line, to be registered A84-307, on 1 August 1951; seven months later, on 16 March 1952, WD983 followed suit, to become A84-125. Both aircraft went to No.82 Wing at Amberley, in New South

Argentinian Canberras			
Canberra B.62		*Canberra T.64*	
Ten aircraft derived by the refurbishment/modification		Two aircraft derived by the refurbishment/modification	
of ex-RAF B.2 and delivered between November 1970		of ex-RAF T.4s and delivered in February 1971.	
and September 1971.		B-111 (ex-WT476)	G-27-121
B-101 (ex-WJ616)	G-27-111 (G-AYHO at 1970 SBAC	B-112 (ex-WJ875)	G-27-122
	Display)		
B-102 (ex-WJ713)	G-27-112 (G-AYHP at 1970 SBAC	*Canberra B.92*	
	Display)	One aircraft derived by the refurbishment/modification	
B-103 (ex-WJ714)	G-27-113	of ex-RAF B.2. Not delivered due to Falklands war.	
B-104 (ex-WJ913)	G-27-114	?? (ex-WH914)	G-27-373
B-105 (ex-WH702)	G-27-127		
B-106 (ex-WJ609)	G-27-165	*Canberra T.94*	
B-107 (ex-WH727)	G-27-162	One aircraft derived by the refurbishment/modification	
B-108 (ex-WH886)	G-27-164	of ex-RAF T.4. Not delivered due to Falklands war.	
B-109 (ex-WH875)	G-27-163	?? (ex-XH583)	G-27-374
B-110 (ex-WJ619)	G-27-166		

A84-125, ex-WD983, the second B.2 diverted off the English Electric production line for the RAAF, left Lyneham on 1 May 1952. BAe

Wales, for conversion training, but neither carried their RAAF serials until after being converted to Mk.21 dual-control trainer standard at a later date.

Australia's association with the aircraft did not have an exactly auspicious start. An RAAF technical mission went to Warton to evaluate the first A.1 prototype, VN799, with one of its test pilots among the party. On his first flight in the aircraft, he was presented with a major engine problem, following a simulated single-engine approach. The pilot spooled up the idling engine and ground observers heard the distinctive audible signs of a compressor stall ('surge') as he climbed away. His return over the airfield showed the port Avon to be well alight and radio instructions were transmitted for him

immediately to shut down the blazing engine. The high- and low-pressure cocks being closed, the flames abated and the pilot cautiously brought VN799 in for a single-engine landing, with smoke pouring out of the port nacelle. Examination of the aircraft showed that the fire's intensity had nearly burnt through the main spar; the RAAF pilot, in an unfamiliar aircraft, had not recognized the symptoms of a surging engine. Hard work at Samlesbury had the prototype back in the air within a month and the RAAF mission was not put off purchasing the Canberra. It had certainly proved its single-engine prowess.

The GAF commenced Canberra Mk.20 production in 1951, using the two RAF B.2s as pattern aircraft, and their first production aircraft, A84-201, made its maiden

flight from the factory's airfield at Avalon on 29 May 1953. The Mk.20 was fundamentally similar to the RAF's B.2, except for a few detail changes. The wing leading edge was redesigned, to permit the fitting of integral wing fuel tanks, as introduced on the RAF's PR.7. Trials were conducted on the twenty-first aircraft, A84-221, and the changes were introduced into the production line with A84-224. Structural modifications to the airframe and undercarriage were introduced, to allow the B.20 to operate at an all-up weight (AUW) of 51,000lb (23,130kg), while all navigational aids, together with the radio, were extensively modified to Australian operational requirements. One further difference from the RAF's B.2 was the combining of navigator and bomb-aiming

A84-125 arrives in Darwin on 11 May 1952. In 1959, the aircraft was converted to Mk.21 standard. T. Jones

duties into one crew member, so that the RAAF aircraft only carried a crew of two.

The first twenty-seven of the forty-eight Mk.20s on order were fitted with Rolls-Royce Avon RA.3 engines, manufactured in Australia. The remaining twenty-one had Avon Mk.109/RA.7 engines, as fitted in the Canberra B.6 aircraft for the Royal Air Force. Production of the Mk.20 ended with A84-248 making its first flight on 2 July 1958. Its place at Fisherman's Bend was taken by the Mk.21, a dual-control trainer variant produced to Specification AC100, at the request of the RAAF. Seven Mk.21s were ordered and these were provided by the modification of five existing Mk.20s, together with the two British 'pattern' B.2s supplied in 1951/52.

In 1955, Lincoln Mk.30(B) operators Nos 2 and 6 Squadrons RAAF, at Amberley, were the first two units to receive the Canberra Mk.20, thereby being reclassified as light-bomber squadrons. Three years later, in July 1958, No.1 Squadron also replaced its Lincolns and the three squadrons became the only Canberra Mk.20 units to operate in the RAAF. Of the seven Mk.21s, three went to No.1

Fitting out B.20s at Avalon, with the fifth to ninth aircraft shown in final assembly. **A84-205 and A84-206 both crashed at Amberley during their service.** Author's collection

B.20s of No.82 (Bomber) Wing, at Amberley, Queensland. Author's collection

(Bomber) Operational Conversion Unit as a part of No.82 Wing, also based at Amberley, while three went to East Sale, in New South Wales, where the Air Armament and Central Flying Schools operated. The seventh Mk.21 was retained in reserve at a Maintenance Unit.

Like the United States, Australia had a team of military advisers in Vietnam in 1962 and, as the situation in the country gradually deteriorated, Australian ground forces became involved in actions with US troops. At the end of December 1966, the Australian Government announced its intention to transfer No.2 Squadron from

hours in every twenty-four hour period, every day of the week. Named *Combat Sky Spot*, these high-level operations were directed from a ground radar station and were flown for four months, before, in September, Operation *Neutralize* was opened. This entailed the RAAF Canberras being employed, for the first time, at medium and low level against Viet Cong troop concentrations, with very encouraging results. The following year, the Australian Canberras started to operate a new procedure, of carrying six 750lb (340kg) bombs, which could be dropped in any combination to attain any required stick length.

night attack, made from 22,000ft (6,700m), on a target in the Da Nang area; no trace was found of the crew. On 14 March 1971, a second Mk.20 was brought down by a SAM, near the Demilitarized Zone (DZ) between North and South Vietnam. This time, the crew were able to put out a 'Mayday' before ejecting and both men were rescued by helicopter the following day. Two months later, in May 1971, No.2 Squadron flew the last of over 10,000 sorties in Vietnam, with A84-244 dropping the 76,389th bomb – its status was duly recorded on its body by a squadron lettering artist. In June 1971, the unit was back in Amberley, where it took on a new

A84-204, after modification to dual-control Mk.21 standard, in the markings of No.2 (Bomber) Squadron.
George Pennick

Butterworth in Malaysia, to South Vietnam. With its Mk.20s fitted with TACAN equipment, as well as UHF radios and wingtip bomb carriers, No.2 Squadron arrived at Phan Rang on 19 April 1967, where it was assigned to the 35th Tactical Fighter Wing (TFW) as a part of the United States 7th Air Force. Six months earlier, on 13 October 1966, the 8th and 13th Bomb Squadrons (BS) of the USAF had moved to Phan Rang from Da Nang, with their B-57Bs. With the arrival of the RAAF squadron, Phan Rang, 150 miles (240km) north-east of Saigon, became the principal Canberra operating base in Vietnam.

Canberra Mk.20 operations in Vietnam began four days after their arrival when, on 23 April 1967, No.2 Squadron dispatched an aircraft with 500lb (225kg) bombs, piloted by the CO Wg Cdr V.J. Hill, to attack a Viet Cong position. This was the start of a campaign in which the squadron flew an aircraft on a similar sortie every hour, for eight

With the new 750lb (340kg) bomb-release strategy, No.2 Squadron concentrated on the canal system in the Mekong Delta area of South Vietnam, which was heavily utilized by Viet Cong forces. As in the RAF operations in Malaya, target-markers were used. For these, with No.2 Squadron, the VNAF flew the Cessna O-1 Bird Dog, using smoke rockets to mark targets. Named *Boomer* missions, they were flown as tactical support for Australian ground forces, and the squadron's accuracy received praise from American troops, as well as from the 'Diggers'. The fact that the Mk.20s were still equipped with the old *Green Satin* doppler, with the navigator feeding deviation read-outs manually in a T4 bomb-sight, with bombing accuracy being confirmed by camera, reflects well the standard of RAAF airmanship.

The squadron lost its first Canberra through enemy action on 3 November 1970, when A84-231 failed to return from a

reconnaissance role, as well as becoming the only Canberra unit in the RAAF; Nos 1 and 6 Squadrons had traded in their Mk.20s for F-4E Phantoms. No.2 Squadron also took on the additional task of target towing, often deploying to Williamstown in New South Wales and, further afield, to Butterworth in Malaya.

In June 1982, both RAAF Canberra variants were retired. The Aircraft Research and Development Unit (ARDU), at RAAF Edinburgh in South Australia, had used Mk.20 A84-240 for some time, but this too was withdrawn from service, shortly after No.2 Squadron traded in its aircraft.

Entirely separate from RAAF Canberra activities, three B.2s were allocated RAAF serials A84-1, A84-2 and A84-3 for their period of loan to the Weapons Research Establishment (WRE) at Woomera, for trials on behalf of the UK's Ministry of Defence. As things turned out, A84-1 did not go to Woomera and the serial was not

B.20, A84-238, flew with No.2 (Bomber) Squadron on operations in Vietnam, and was later used for cartographic survey work over Australia. George Pennick

applied. A84-2 went out to Australia on 12 March 1952 and returned to the UK on 3 October 1957. A84-3 arrived in Woomera in June 1953 and returned to the UK in November 1957, a month after A84-2. Years later, A84-3, which had reverted to its original RAF serial, WH710, was converted into a U.10 target drone and transported to the WRE again, where it was destroyed by a missile on 26 May 1965. Another, unrelated action took place in summer 1956, when two Canberra T.4s were purchased from the

---

Aussie Canberras

Canberra Mk.20
Forty-eight aircraft manufactured under licence by the Australian Government Aircraft Factory (GAF) at Fisherman's Bend, between 1951 and 1958: A84-201 to A84-248

Canberra Mk.21
Seven aircraft obtained by refurbishment of five existing Mk.20s, A84-201 and A84-203 to A84-206, plus two B.2 pattern aircraft A84-125 and A84-307. Mk.21 serials not confirmed.

Three Canberra B.2s, previously used on various trials programmes in the UK, loaned to WRE Woomera, for trials and allocated RAAF serials for the period of loan: A84-1 (ex-WD935), A84-2 (ex-WD942), A84-3 (ex-WH710)

Two Canberra B.2s purchased by Australian Government as 'pattern' aircraft in 1951/52: A84-125 (ex-WD983), A84-307 (ex-WD939)

Two Canberra T.4 aircraft purchased by Australian Government for conversion training in 1956: A84-501 (ex-WT491), A84-502 (ex-WT492)

UK for conversion training; they were delivered with RAAF serials.

Chile

Chile's military aviation history began in 1913, with the setting up of a flying school equipped with Blériot monoplanes. The country had acquired D.H.4 bombers from Britain in 1921 and had purchased British turbojet aircraft, such as the Vampire and Hunter, for the *Fuerza Aérea de Chile* (FAC) in the past, so it was perhaps surprising that they should be the last country in the world to start operating the Canberra. Furthermore, their purchase of Canberras is something of an enigma – if, in fact, the aircraft were purchased.

The mystery is purported to stem from the Falklands conflict, when unofficial 'If we are asked, we will deny it' landing facilities are said to have been given to an ailing RN helicopter, which was later burnt. The justification for this seems to be the fact that Chile and Argentina were not exactly on good neighbourly terms. Whatever the truth was, three ex-RAF Canberra PR.9s existed at Wyton, Cambridgeshire, in 1982. The aircraft had been in store at No.19 MU St Athan, since No.39 Squadron had disbanded at Wyton, on 1 June of that year.

After a brief conversion course at Wyton for the three *Fuerza Aérea de Chile* crews, the aircraft flew out of the Cambridgeshire base, in the company of a Chilean Boeing 707, on 15 October 1982. They were destined to join *Grupo 2 Escuadrilla de Reconocimento*, based at Los

Cerrillos near Santiago. In view of Chile's relationship with Argentina, it is likely that border reconnaissance and surveillance ranked high on the Canberras' inventory of activities. One aircraft, FAC serial 342, was lost on 25 May 1983, near the southern border with Argentina, but the cause has not been disclosed.

In December 1998, both remaining PR.9s were with the Aeronautics Museum at Santiago.

Thank you Canberras?

Three Canberra PR.9 aircraft delivered from RAF Wyton, on 15 October 1982: 341 (ex-XH166), 342 (ex-XH167), 343 (ex-XH173)

Ecuador

Originated in 1920 with Italian aid, the *Fuerza Aérea Ecuatoriana* (FAE) significantly upgraded its inventory in the early 1950s; the arrival of British turbojet aircraft made it one of South America's most modern air forces. Twelve Gloster Meteor FR.9s were delivered in 1954 and the FAE's acceptance of six Canberra B.6s in the same year greatly improved its tactical abilities.

English Electric received a contract in May 1954 to supply six new-build B.6 aircraft. As there was no great difference from RAF B.6s going down the line, the Ecuadorian aircraft were incorporated into the existing production schedule and the first two were ready for delivery early in 1955. Flying out in pairs, at three- to four-

The crews and officials concerned with the delivery of Ecuador's B.6s (left to right): R. Hothersall, English Electric; P.D.W. Hackforth, English Electric; P. Moneypenny, Silver City Airways; Major R. Sandoval, FAE; Captain J.W. Hackett, Silver City Airways; Major G. Barreiro, FAE; M. Cole, Silver City Airways. Author's collection

complicated serial changes. Taking the first aircraft as an example, at the time of delivery it was numbered 801, shown on the fin. Later, this number was retained on the fin but was repeated on the nose with a 'BE' prefix: BE-801. Later still, a new numbering system was introduced, in which English Electric's Canberra construction number was used. While the company did not use construction numbers as such, in the case of the Canberra, a numbering system commencing at EEP71000 was used as a reference and, consequently, BE-801 became 71390. This was displayed on the nose in this form and was shown as BE-390 on the fin.

Six-Pack for Ecuador

Six new-build Canberra B.6 aircraft, delivered in 1955:

801:
 first change, BE-801, second change, 71390/BE-390

802:
 first change, BE-802, second change, 71391/BE-391

803:
 first change, BE-803, second change, 71402/BE-402

804:
 first change, BE-804, second change, 71405/BE-405

805:
 first change, BE-805, second change, 71411/BE-411

806:
 first change BE-806, second change, 71409/BE-409

---

monthly intervals, all six had arrived by the end of the year and became the *Escuadron de Bombardeo 2123* at Quito, in the north of the country. Each aircraft returned to Samlesbury at least once for refurbishment in the 1960s. BE-805 had to force-land at Ballykelly in Ireland during its flight, and finish its journey on board an Irish Sea ferry.

In January 1977, the FAE started replacing its veteran Lockheed F-80Gs with twelve SEPECAT Jaguar Internationals.

While the Canberras continued to be the main element of Ecuador's offensive force, they were also used to provide fast-jet conversion training, in the low-level strike role, for future Jaguar crews. By the 1980s, however, the B.6s had been reduced to three operational aircraft, with three placed in storage, and it is believed that all are now out of service.

During their service with the FAE, all the Canberras underwent two rather

Ethiopia

In 1960, the United States started providing military aid to the Imperial Ethiopian Air Force, until, with the overthrow of Emperor Haile Selassie in 1974, future delivery of Northrop F-5E/Fs and assorted Cessna aircraft was embargoed by the White House. Surplus Iranian F-5As were purchased to assist in maintaining the Ethiopian Air Force (EAF), as attrition of its older types was taking its toll.

The Arab-supported Eritrean Liberation Front, in the north of the country, had been a threat to stability for many years

landing put one aircraft out of commission, principally due to the lack of technical support to expedite a repair, and another was lost when its pilot defected to an Arab state, taking his Canberra with him. Since the Ogaden war with Somalia in 1977/78, during which Cuban mercenaries flew Soviet-supplied MiG-21s for the EAF, and two Canberras were reported to have been destroyed, Russia has become Ethiopia's main supplier of military hardware. It has been suggested that the aircraft that landed wheels-up may have been repaired at a later date, but this has not been confirmed.

ing of the resulting aircraft, as they were destined for both the *Centre d'Essais en Vol* (CEV) and the *Centre du Tir et de Bombardement* (CTB). All would eventually carry French civil registrations but, at the time of delivery, they had French military marking with a numbering system of their own.

The order was for six new aircraft to B.6 standard and this was met by diverting three new-build B.6 aircraft from RAF Contract No.6/ACFT/5786/CB6(b) and building three additional new aircraft specifically for the French order, one to RAF B.6 standard, with the remaining two as B(I).6s. The first two, carrying the num-

For unknown reasons, when the first B.2 for Ethiopia, 351, which was formerly WH638, was photographed on test, the manufacturers censored the country's insignia on the negative. (For an uncensored shot, see the colour section.) BAe

and, to support the EAF's F-5As, the Ethiopian Government placed an order with English Electric during the mid-1960s for four refurbished ex-RAF Canberra B.2s. The aircraft, intended for the counter-insurgent role, were designated Canberra B.52s. Refurbishment was completed in the summer of 1968 and all four aircraft were test flown with consecutive class 'B' markings, the first carrying G-27-117 prior to delivery which commenced on 24 July. The second was delivered on 12 September, the third on 10 October and the fourth left Samlesbury on 2 November 1968.

Although English Electric expected a repeat order, this did not materialize, and the attrition rate, operating with only four aircraft, was rather high. A wheels-up

Canberra B.52

Four aircraft obtained by refurbishment of four existing B.2s and delivered in 1968: 351 (ex-WH638) G-27-117, 352 (ex-WK104) G-27-118, 353 (ex-WJ971) G-27-119, 354 (ex-WD990) G-27-120

France

The French had never purchased many British military aircraft, and saw no need to break the habit where the Canberra was concerned. A handful of Canberras and Gloster Meteors were ordered to operate as flying vehicles for trials purposes; an order was placed with English Electric in spring 1954, but the *Armée de l'Air* would see noth-

bers F763 and F779, were delivered in autumn 1954, while the third, F784, arrived at the CEV in January 1955. The remaining three, F304, F316 and F318, crossed the English Channel in the latter half of 1955.

The CEV at Brétigny, the French equivalent to RAE Farnborough, used the Canberras extensively for a great variety of trials, as well as engine testbed programmes. Two, F763 and F779, were employed for a large part of their life by the CTB at Cazaux. As with the RAE, many activities remain undisclosed, but it is known that F316, with an extended nose-cone, was employed as a radar trials aircraft at Brétigny, for the CSF Cyrano II AI system destined for the Mirage III. It later went to Cazaux, to become the carrier for test firings of Matra 530 and Super 530 air-to-air missiles (AAMs) carried on underwing pylons fitted with recording cameras. A second pylon outboard of the AAM carrier was equipped with back-up cameras and the aircraft's nose-cone was reprofiled to a sharp point, under which was another camera housing. F779 was the firing platform for the Nord (Aérospatiale) AS.12, AS.20 and AS.30 missiles on the Algerian ranges, as well as the Matra R.530. Later in its life, it was fitted with a B(I).8 front fuselage, but did not have the ventral gun pack.

The Turbomeca Gazibo turbojet, which produced 2,500lb (1,135kg) with reheat, was test flown in a ventral location on one aircraft, while others carried out experimental trials on the effects of high altitude on various electronic systems. Gradually, the aircraft were phased out of use by the experimental establishments and it is known that two were scrapped by the CEV at Bretigny. The CTB withdrew one at Cazaux but one, F763, was retained for the *Musée de l'Air et l'Espace* at Le Bourget.

The French numbering of the Canberras is a bit of a mystery. The first three delivered were allocated numbers in the 700 range, repeating the number part of the aircraft's original RAF serial, yet the later three received numbers in the 300 range, which are presumed to have been the next available numbers in the range allotted to trials aircraft. Furthermore, when the aircraft had been given civil registrations, at least three of these were changed at later dates.

India

After the RAF and USAF, the Indian Air Force (IAF) was the third-largest Canberra operator. English Electric received no less than six orders between 1957 and 1975, while the IAF also purchased some ex-RNZAF aircraft direct from New Zealand. The first order received at Preston, for sixty-eight aircraft and said to be worth about £20 million, was placed in January 1957. It included an option to purchase another twelve (which was taken up in July 1957), and covered the supply of three different variants. Sixty-five were B(I).58s, similar to the B(I).8, eight were PR.57s, comparable to the PR.7, and seven were T.54s, equivalent to the RAF's T.4.

As all were new-build aircraft – although twenty-four were diverted from RAF contracts – IAF-required modifications were incorporated on the production line. These included upgraded navigation equipment, radio altimeters and autopilots, all of which would have been most welcome in RAF Canberra squadrons. One of the diverted aircraft, B(I).8 WT338, was modified by Boulton Paul Aircraft, to act as the trials installation aircraft for the IAF's additional equipment, before becoming a part of the order, deliveries of which began in April 1957. Five IAF units were scheduled to receive the Canberras. Nos 5, 16 and 35 Squadrons would operate the B(I).58s at Agra, southeast of Delhi, together with the T.54s, which would be formed into a Canberra OCU, while No.106 Squadron was to be a reconnaissance unit with the PR.57s. No.5 Squadron became the IAF's first jet-bomber unit in 1958 and the other two squadrons started in 1959. The fifth IAF Canberra operator was No.6 Squadron, which used some B(I).58s in an anti-shipping role and also had ex-civil airline Lockheed Super Constellations on its charge as transport aircraft.

The attrition from involvement in two areas of unrest, together with two full-blown wars, meant that five further orders were placed between 1960 and 1970, in order to preserve the IAF's front-line degree of readiness. Speed of delivery was of the essence and English Electric paid their full part in meeting these requirements. The second order, placed in 1961, was for six new-build B(I).58 aircraft and the company supplied these from assemblies built as

B(I).58, IF898, which was XK959 before being diverted from an RAF contract, staged through Khormaksar in 1962. The 'ONU' inscription on the fuselage indicates that the aircraft was engaged on the United Nations' sanctioned operations in the Congo. The elephant badge shows that IF898 belonged to No.5 Squadron, IAF.
Ray Deacon

Two more IAF B(I).58s, returning to India from the Congo, through Khormaksar. IF908, in the foreground, was XH238 and its partner is IF907, formerly XH237. Both aircraft were diverted from RAF contracts. Ray Deacon

Seen awaiting collection, IF1020 was the first of ten B(I).66s, ordered by the refurbishment of ex-RAF B.15/B.16 aircraft. IF1020 had been a Belfast-built B.6, converted to B.15 standard, and was test flown before delivery as G-27-168. BAe

stock, before the B(I).8 production line closed down. All six aircraft were delivered in 1963 and before this, in the latter quarter of 1962, India submitted its third order. This was for two PR.57s, plus a T.54, which was met by converting two RAF PR.7s and a T.4. The T.54 was delivered in September 1963 and the two PR.57s followed in the spring of 1964. One of the PR.57s was formerly WT528, the PR7 *Aries V* from the RAF Flying College (RAFFC), which had made the double-Atlantic record flight on 23 August 1955.

The fourth order, received by English Electric in 1965, called for three further T.54s and these were again supplied by the conversion of ex-RAF T.4s. The first was test flown in Class 'B' markings, as G-27-116, before being delivered in July 1968.

However, the British Government placed an embargo on the other two aircraft and they were not delivered to India. Both were purchased by the newly formed British Aircraft Corporation (BAC), which encompassed English Electric, and one of the aircraft was later sold to Peru as a T.74.

India was not deterred by the 1968 embargo and, in October 1969, placed the fifth order, for twelve B(I).66 and two PR.67 aircraft. Before completion, the number of B(I).66s was reduced to ten and this variant was obtained by the refurbishment of ten ex-RAF B.15/B.16 aircraft. All were test flown in Class 'B' condition and delivery commenced in October 1970. The two PR.67s were updated versions of the PR.57 and two former RAF PR.7s were

modified to the new requirement, for delivery in August 1971, after being test flown in Class 'B' markings.

In 1970, possibly because they negotiated a good price, India turned to New Zealand and purchased some fatigue-life expired aircraft from the RNZAF. These were eight B(I).8 standard aircraft, designated B(I).12s in New Zealand and two T.13s, which were modified as T.4s for the RNZAF. Delivery of the ten aircraft was made in November 1970.

The sixth and last order was received from the Indian Government in 1975, for six T.4 aircraft without any conversion to IAF requirements. The order was fulfilled by taking six RAF trainers straight out of store at No.5 MU Kemble, so that delivery could be made in the same year that the order was received. The first left Kemble on 18 June and the sixth on 23 September. After arriving in India, all six were modified to fulfil a target-towing role and were designated Canberra TT.418s.

The IAF and their Canberras first went into action when No.5 Squadron was deployed to Kamina, near Leopoldsville, in October 1961, to join the United Nations (UN) military force assembled to assist the Congolese Central Government. The country had obtained independence from Belgium the year before and the province of Katanga declared a separate independence for itself, taking up arms against the government in a rebellion that degenerated into outright hostility against all European interests. The squadron made attacks on rebel positions in the province, as well as on

their airstrip at Kolwezi, where the B(I).58's ventral 20mm cannon packs caused havoc among parked aircraft and hangar buildings. The six IAF Canberras involved returned to Kamina, where a quick turn-around ensured that they could make another attack on Kolwezi before the previous raid's devastation could be cleared. All external fuel tanks were set alight and the airstrip was rendered unusable for some time. However, continuous small-arms fire from the Katangese ground troops caused damage to several attacking aircraft.

Further air attacks in support of Government troops, together with a concentrated programme of reconnaissance sorties, kept the squadron very busy until the beginning of 1962, by which time the rebellion had been virtually quashed and

the interdiction activities of the UN force were no longer required. By early March, No.5 Squadron was back at Agra, but later in the year, all IAF squadrons were on full alert, when Chinese troops crossed the border from Tibet into the Himalayan province of Ladakh. Throughout October and November, the Indian army was heavily engaged in the type of mountain warfare for which air attacks were of no assistance, so that by the time the border fighting had finished, at the beginning of December, the IAF was not called upon and the emergency had passed.

It is generally accepted that Pakistan was encouraged by the fact that the Indian Army had been unable to defeat the Chinese in Ladakh. It seemed to indicate that Pakistan stood a good chance of winning in

Two refurbished PR.7s were supplied to India as PR.67s. The second was WJ816 when it flew with No.31 Squadron, which became PR.67, P1099, and it was test flown with the Class 'B' registration G-27-184, before being delivered on 27 August 1971. BAe

Q496 was one of two former T.4s, refurbished to T.54s for the IAF, of which the delivery was embargoed. It is shown at No.5 MU Kemble, where it was stored before eventually being sold to Peru, with their serial '246'. Ray Deacon

This photograph is interesting because the B(I).66 is being test flown without its allotted G-27-171 Class 'B' markings and the IAF serial has been painted as F1028, instead of IF1028. The aircraft was formerly B.16, WJ776. BAe

any hostilities that might evolve from the long-standing disputes with India in Kashmir and the Rann of Kutch. Fighting had begun on a limited scale in the spring of 1965, involving only ground forces on both sides. On 1 September, the Pakistan army launched a full-scale war, when its armoured divisions crossed into Kashmir and the IAF's Canberra force was brought into action. On 6 September, night raids were made against the Pakistan airfields at Rawalpindi and Sargodha from 30,000ft (9,100m). Pakistan Air Force (PAF) F-104s from Sargodha attempted to intercept the attacking force, but the Canberras' *Orange Putter* TWR warned the IAF of the fighters' presence and, by taking evasive action, the IAF aircraft returned to Agra without loss.

For a number of reasons, the IAF Canberra attacks made during September 1965 were not very successful. Whereas their aircraft were modern, their ordnance was not, and many of the bombs dropped on the PAF airfields at Rawalpindi, Sargodha and Peshawar did not explode. IAF airmanship (or lack of it) was also to blame in an attack on Peshawar, when markers gave a low-level attack by a B(I).58 an ideal opportunity to destroy a tarmac bulging with parked B-57s and F-86s. The 4,000lb (1,820kg) bomb dropped, but fell on soft soil that nullified the blast; it was far too short of the aiming point, anyway.

The IAF was fortunate in that the PAF had no dedicated night-fighter force, so the interceptions that were scrambled were by

F-104s and F-86s, armed with Sidewinders. The majority of these interceptions were unsuccessful, but there were bound to be some losses and, on the night of 15 September, the first IAF Canberra B(I).58 was brought down by one of two Sidewinders launched from an F-86. Despite the IAF pilots trying to out-manoeuvre the missiles, they were locked on and one struck the Canberra. Six days later, on 21 September, IAF Canberras, escorted by Indian licence-built Folland Gnats, carried out a heavy daylight raid on the Badin radar station. It was destroyed by the sheer volume of a combination of 4,000lb (1,820kg) bombs and 20mm cannon fire. A few hours before this daylight raid, the IAF lost another Canberra in a low-level night attack against Pakistan positions. The pilot had switched off his *Orange Putter*, because he was getting continuous signals from the ground during his attack. On climbing back to altitude, he forgot to switch the TWR back on and the pilot of an F-104 approaching from the rear got lucky. His first Sidewinder struck the Canberra and it crashed inside Pakistan, killing the navigator. The pilot ejected and became a prisoner of war. He was held only for a couple of days, because, on 22 September 1965, a ceasefire was declared.

A total of five IAF Canberras had been lost: the two shot down by Sidewinders and three by PAF attacks on Indian airfields – by B-57 Canberras! An inquest held by the Indian Air Force High

Command came to the conclusion that they had misused their B(I).58s. The aircraft was designed for low-level interdiction, and bombing from 30,000ft, which they had been doing, was a waste of the aircraft's attributes. Furthermore, their high-level bombing results would have been unacceptable, no matter what aircraft they had been flying.

Hostilities between India and Pakistan broke out again on 5 December 1971, when Pakistan troops attacked border positions in the Kashmir and the Punjab. The day before, an IAF Canberra had been intercepted and shot down by one of a small force of Dassault Mirage IIIEs that Pakistan had purchased during 'half time'. Seventeen of these all-weather fighters had joined the PAF and they certainly boosted Pakistan's ability to intercept IAF Canberra sorties. Learning their lessons from the 1965 war, Indian Canberras were employed on a series of low-level strafing attacks on enemy ground forces in Kashmir, but, on 5 December, two were brought down by concentrated anti-aircraft (AA) gunfire. Similar attacks were also mounted against Pakistan airfields, which cost another B(I).58, also hit by AA fire.

The next day, No.106 Squadron's PR.57s were used on pre- and post-strike reconnaissance sorties, covering successful IAF Hunter rocket attacks on oil refineries, while B(I).58s again strafed enemy ground positions. The day's concentrated activities had incurred no losses, but, on 8

On the range at Tilpat, a B(I).58 fires a salvo from its underwing rocket pod. Author's collection

December, a PR.57 was brought down during a night reconnaissance mission, again by Sidewinders from an F-104. A mixed force of Canberras, Hunters, MiG-21s, Mystere IVAs and Sukhoi Su-7s carried out heavy attacks against a Pakistan armoured division at Chamb on 9 December, together with the lines of communication in the same area. Canberras also made a separate low-level attack on port installations at Karachi. There were no losses from the whole day's activities, but, on the following day, a B(I).66 was lost in the Khem Karan area.

Limited interdiction operations were carried out, without loss, over the next five days, but on the night of 15 December, the heaviest raid of the 1971 war was launched against Karachi and a significant amount of damage was caused to the port area. One Canberra was brought down during this attack, but it was to be the final loss for the IAF, as a ceasefire came into effect on the afternoon of 17 December. Again, the IAF held a post-war inquest and the general consensus was that the use of B(I).58s in their interdiction role was far more successful than in 1965. The higher losses compared with the earlier conflict were due to far more sorties being flown, and to the PAF having re-equipped with more up-to-date air defences.

In the early 1980s, IAF Canberra numbers were down to less than fifty aircraft and the Jaguar International began replacing the B(I).58s and B(I).66s. Soviet MiG-25Rs started replacing the PR.57s at about the same time, but Canberra trainers were retained for conversion duties.

Canberras from the Raj

Canberra B(I).58
One new-build aircraft in the first order, diverted from RAF contract and modified by Boulton Paul Aircraft as trials aircraft for IAF-ordered modifications. This aircraft was later delivered to IAF: IF906 (ex-WT338)

Eighteen new-build aircraft in the first order, diverted from RAF contracts, delivery commencing in April 1957: IF895 (ex-XK953), IF896 (ex-XH203), IF897 (ex-XH205), IF898 (ex-XK959), IF899 (ex-XH227), IF900 (ex-XH230), IF901 (ex-XH230), IF902 (ex-XH232), IF903 (ex-XH233), IF904 (ex-XH235), IF905 (ex-XH236), IF907 (ex-XH237), IF908 (ex-XH238), IF909 (ex-XH239), IF910 (ex-XH240), IF911 (ex-XH241), IF912 (ex-XH242), IF913 (ex-XH243)

Thirty-five new-build aircraft in the first order, delivery commencing in April 1957: IF914 to IF934, IF960 to IF973

Eleven new-build aircraft in option taken up in July 1957, delivery in 1958/59: IF974 to IF984

Six new-build aircraft in the second order, delivered in 1963: BF595 to BF600

Eight aircraft purchased from RNZAF in 1970. IAF and RNZAF serials shown but tie-ups cannot be confirmed: F1183 to F1190, NZ6102, NZ6105, NZ6108 to NZ6111, NZ6103, NZ6107

Canberra T.54
Two new-build aircraft in the first order, diverted from RAF T.4 contract, delivered in 1958: IQ994 (ex-XK647), IQ995 (ex-XK650)

Six new-build aircraft in the first order, delivered in 1958: IQ996 to IQ999

One new-build aircraft in option taken up in July 1957, delivered in 1959: IQ985

One aircraft in the third order, obtained by refurbishment of existing T.4, delivered in 1963: BQ744 (ex-WJ859)

One aircraft in the fourth order, obtained by refurbishment of existing T.4, delivered in 1968: Q495 (ex-WH847)

Two aircraft in the fourth order, obtained by refurbishment of existing T.4s, but delivery embargoed: Q496 (ex-WH845) sold to Peru as 246, Q497 (ex-WE191) used for fire practice 1988

Six aircraft in the sixth order, purchased as T.4s and delivered in 1975. These aircraft were modified in India as TT.148s: Q1791 (ex-WE193), Q1792 (ex-WE195), Q1793 (ex-WT485), Q1794 (ex-WT487), Q1795 (ex-WH839), Q1796 (ex-WJ868)

Two aircraft purchased from RNZAF in 1970. IAF and RNZAF serials shown but tie-ups cannot be confirmed: Q1191 and Q1192, NZ6151 and NZ6152

Canberra PR.57
Three new-build aircraft in the first order, diverted from RAF contract, delivery commencing in April 1957: IP986 (ex-WT539), IP987 (ex-WT542), IP988 (ex-WT541)

Five new-build aircraft in the first order, delivery commencing in April 1957: IP989 to IP993

Two aircraft in the third order, obtained by refurbishment of existing PR.7s, delivered in 1963/64: BP745 (ex-WT506), BP746 (ex-WT528)

One aircraft in the third order, obtained by refurbishment of existing T.4, delivered in 1963: BP744 (ex-WJ859)

Canberra B(I).66
Ten aircraft in the fifth order, obtained by refurbishment of existing B.15/B.16s, test flown in Class 'B' markings and delivered in 1970/71: IF1020 (ex-WT210) G-27-168, IF1021 (ex-WH954) G-27-167, IF1022 (ex-WH959) G-27-177, IF1023 (ex-WH961) G-27-178, IF1024 (ex-WT303) G-27-170, IF1025 (ex-WJ780) G-27-174, IF1026 (ex-WT302) G-27-172, IF1027 (ex-WT373) G-27-173, IF1028 (ex-WJ776) G-27-171, IF1029 (ex-WJ778) G-27-169

Canberra PR.67
Two aircraft in the fifth order, obtained by refurbishment of existing PR.7s, test flown in Class 'B' markings and delivered in 1971: P1098 (ex-WH800) G-27-183, P1099 (ex-WJ816) G-27-184

B(I).12, NZ6106, was delivered to New Zealand in October 1959 and served with No.14 Squadron, RNZAF, but it was returned to Samlesbury due to a faulty spar. It was never re-delivered and was broken up in May 1976. R.A. Walker

New Zealand

The growing pains in forming Malaysia, and President Sukarno of Indonesia's ambitions in that area, kept several Royal Air Force squadrons occupied for some years. During this period, named *Confrontation*, Royal New Zealand Air Force (RNZAF) supported the RAF with its No.14(F) Squadron, equipped with de Havilland Venom FB.4s. The squadron was due to be replaced by No.75 Squadron and this unit had the individual distinction of being the only overseas customer to be equipped with a full complement of Canberras, on loan. In July 1958, seventeen B.2s and three T.4s were supplied to No.75 Squadron, and the following month they took their new aircraft to Tengah, on Singapore Island, as an element of the Commonwealth Strategic Reserve, engaged in *Confrontation*.

For over two years, No.75 Squadron flew alongside the RAF's No.45 Squadron, operating day and night sorties against terrorist positions, until the end of the Malayan emergency, in October 1960. In February 1958, five months before No.75 Squadron received its loaned aircraft, the New Zealand Government had placed an order with English Electric for a total of eleven aircraft. Nine were to be B(I).8 standard aircraft, with additional navigation equipment and an autopilot, similar to the Indian Air Force's B(I).58s, and were to be designated B(I).12s in the RNZAF. Two trainer aircraft, based on the T.4, were included in the order and these, designated T.13s, required modifications to meet RNZAF requirements, which

included an autopilot, plus an additional fuel tank in the bomb-bay. All except one B(I).12 and one T.13, which were refurbished ex-RAF aircraft, were to be new-build aircraft, the delivery of which was to commence in September 1959. Whereas the B(I).12s' delivery was fairly prompt, the two T.13s did not arrive until 1961, which signalled the return of the three T.4s on loan. Two of these were later converted to different variants, while one crashed in June 1967, still a T.4. A second order was placed in spring 1960, for a further two B(I).12s, and these were delivered in May 1961.

No.14 Squadron RNZAF took delivery of its first four B(I).12s in October 1959 and, when another three arrived at the end of the year, the unit operated as an OCU until 1 March. In 1961, the RNZAF aircraft were fitted out for rocket-projectile operations, for which a thirty-seven-missile-carrying Microcell pod was mounted on a pylon under each wing. Besides mounting offensive sorties in support of the *Confrontation* ground forces, the aircraft took on an additional anti-shipping role flown in conjunction with ASR-equipped Short Sunderlands. To keep abreast of aircrew requirements, a few of the Canberras on loan from the RAF were used as OCU aircraft until the ordered B(I).12s arrived in the summer of 1962; then, the fifteen surviving B.2s were returned to the UK. In the four years during which the RNZAF had flown the seventeen B.2s, two had been lost. WF915 crashed in Malaya on 26 October 1961, while WJ605 broke up, due to an on-board

fire during a practice bombing run on the China Rock ranges, on 16 April 1962. It was an unfortunate incident, which was to be repeated with one of the B(I).12s, NZ6104, three years later.

Confrontation eventually ceased, with the signing of the Bangkok Agreement on 11 August 1966, and No.14 Squadron returned to its base at Ohakea, on New Zealand's North Island, to resume the exercises that had been postponed during its

---

Kiwi Canberras

Seventeen ex-RAF B.2s loaned to RNZAF in 1958 and returned to UK (less two, which had crashed) in 1962: WD948, WF915, WH645, WH646, WH666, WH739, WH740, WH878, WH922, WJ102, WJ567, WJ605, WJ630, WJ715, WJ981, WJ986, WJ988

Three ex-RAF T.4s loaned to RNZAF in 1958 and returned to the UK in 1962: WD963, WJ859, WJ864

Canberra B(I).12
One ex-RAF B(I).8 in the first order, modified as trial aircraft for RNZAF. This aircraft was delivered to RNZAF in 1960: NZ6101 (ex-WT329)

Eight new-build aircraft delivered in 1959/60: NZ6102, NZ6103, NZ6104, NZ6105, NZ6106, NZ6107, NZ6108, NZ6109

Two new-build aircraft in the second order, delivered in 1961: NZ6110, NZ6111

Canberra T.13
One new-build aircraft delivered in 1961: NZ6151

One aircraft obtained by refurbishment of existing T.4, delivered in 1961: NZ6152 (ex-WE190)

deployment to Butterworth. By July 1970, the Canberra ceased to feature in the RNZAF inventory. Two had been lost in accidents and one, NZ6106, was at Samlesbury having a faulty main spar renewed. It did not return to New Zealand, and was later broken up at Samlesbury. The surviving eight B(I).12s, plus the two T.13s, were sold to India in November 1970.

Peru

Peru first established a military air corps in 1919, using a mixture of British and French aircraft. In 1929, the *Cuerpo de Aeronautica del Peru* (CAP) was formed, its title changing in 1950 to *Fuerza Aérea del Peru* (FAP). Flying North American B-25 Mitchells and Lockheed PV-2 Harpoons, the FAP took the first steps towards upgrading its equipment in November 1955.

English Electric's first order received from the FAP was for eight B(I).8, and was met by diverting four aircraft from RAF contracts, and manufacturing four new-build aircraft. Delivery of all eight was made between May 1956 and March 1957. The FAP serials at the time of delivery were in the range of 474 to 476 and 478 to 482 inclusive, but these were changed in 1960 to 206 to 212. (The reason why there were only seven later serials was the crashing of 479 during its first air display at Lima on 23 August, only seventeen days after it left the UK.) The FAP aircraft formed one squadron in *Grupo de Bombarde 21* at Chiclayo and they were utilized in exercises to perfect the unit's expertise in COIN operations.

Another aircraft, 476, was lost in an accident on 11 June 1959 and in autumn 1959, English Electric received a second order from Peru, for one new-build B(I).8, to replace 476. It was manufactured from stock major assemblies, so that it was ready for delivery in November 1960.

In 1965, the FAP drew up plans to form a second squadron in *Grupo 21* and a third order was placed. By now, the supplier was the British Aircraft Corporation (BAC), of which the former English Electric Company was a constituent, at Preston. The order was for eight refurbished ex-RAF Canberras – six B.2-standard aircraft and two T.4s. The two trainers were delivered in the early summer of 1966, while the six B.2s were all test flown in Class 'B' markings before delivery, which took place between August 1966 and January 1967. It is believed that the BAC later supplied updating kits for

both variants to Peru which, when installed, gave the aircraft new designations. The B.2s became B.72s and the trainers became T.74s. In August 1968, a B.72 was lost in an accident and a second crashed in December 1969. A third aircraft from the batch of six B.72s crashed in February 1981. Deployment of the two squadrons ranged between Chiclayo and Limatomb, while the Jorge Chavez Airport at Lima, the home base of the transport *Grupo 41*, has also been quoted as being host to the Canberra squadrons at some time.

The Peruvian Government dispatched its fourth order in 1968, for the supply of six B(I).56 aircraft. It was met by the refurbishment of three ex-RAF B.2s and three similar B.6s, with used assemblies being mixed with new-builds. All six aircraft were test flown in Class 'B' markings before delivery, which took place between February and June 1969. Due to attrition, a fifth order had to be placed with BAC in 1969, for a single B(I).68, which was supplied by the refurbishing of an ex-RAF B(I).8. It was test flown before being

delivered in July 1971, but the FAP only had it on charge for eleven months, as it crashed in Brazil on 30 June 1972.

In 1971, order number six arrived at Preston. Again, it was for a single aircraft, this time a T.74, for which a refurbished ex-RAF T.4, originally intended for India but embargoed before delivery, was ferried to Peru in February 1973. FAP Canberras were fitted out for operating with a wide range of weaponry, which included Nord air-to-surface missiles mounted on enlarged underwing pylons, as well as Microcell multi-rocket pods, twin 7.62mm gun pods and pylon-mounted 540lb (245kg) or 1,000lb (455kg) bombs, all of which were additional to the varied internal loads carried.

Due to its heavy commitment, as part of Panavia Aircraft GmbH, to Tornado GR.1 production and testing, BAC had to farm out Peru's seventh and last order, placed in June 1973. It was passed to Marshall of Cambridge, although the centre fuselage structures between Frames 12B and 31A were refurbished at Samlesbury, as they were better equipped for this work than

---

Canberras for Peru

Canberra B(I).8
Four aircraft in the first order, obtained by refurbishment of existing B(I).8s, delivered in 1956. FAP serials were changed in 1960: 474 (ex-WT343) later 206, 475 (ex-WT348) later 207, 476 (ex-WT367) crashed before 1960, 478 (ex-XH206) later 209

Four new-build aircraft in the first order, delivered in 1956/57: 479 crashed before 1960, 480 later 210, 481 later 211, 482 later 212

One new-build aircraft in the second order, delivered in 1960: 208

Canberra B.72
Six aircraft in the third order, obtained by refurbishment of existing B.2s, the first two test flown in Class 'B' markings and delivered in 1966/67. Updated to B.72 standard, engineered in Peru, using BAC-supplied kits: 233 (ex-WJ974) G-27-76, 234 (ex-WJ976) G-27-77, 235 (ex-WK112), 236 (ex-WH726), 237 (ex-WH868), 238 (ex-WE120)

Canberra B(I).56
Six aircraft in the fourth order, obtained by refurbishment of three existing B.2s and three existing B.6s, test flown in Class 'B' markings and delivered in 1969: 239 (ex-WT208) G-27-96, 240 (ex-WJ757) G-27-97, 241 (ex-WJ754) G-27-98, 242 (ex-WH880) G-27-99, 243 (ex-WJ712) G-27-100, 244 (ex-WH719) G-27-101

Canberra B(I).68
One aircraft in the fifth order, obtained by refurbishment of existing B(I).8, test flown in Class 'B' markings and delivered in 1971: 245 (ex-WT344) G-27-145

Eleven aircraft in the seventh order, placed with Marshall of Cambridge, obtained by refurbishment of existing B(I).8s (centre fuselages refurbished by BAC), test flown in marshalls Class 'B' markings and delivered between 1975 and 1978: 247 (ex-WT368) G-52-2, 248 (ex-XK951) G-52-3, 249 (ex-WT342) G-52-4, 250 (ex-WT364) G-52-5, 251 (ex-WT340) G-52-6, 252 (ex-XH234) G-52-7, 253 (ex-XM273) G-52-8, 254 (ex-XM936) G-52-9, 255 (ex-XM263) G-52-10, 256 (ex-XM276) G-52-11, 257 (ex-XM278) G-52-12

Canberra T.74
Two aircraft in the third order, obtained by refurbishment of existing T.4s, delivered in 1966. Updated to T.74 standard engineered in Peru, using BAC-supplied kits: 231 (ex-WH659), 232 (ex-WJ860)

One aircraft in the sixth order, obtained by refurbishment of existing T.4 originally prepared for India but embargoed, test flown in Class 'B' markings and delivered in 1973: 246 (ex-WH845) Q496 for India, G-27-224

Five B(I).12 aircraft purchased from SAAF in 1991, FAP serials not confirmed.

One T.4 aircraft purchased from SAAF in 1993, FAP serial not confirmed.

The first of eight B(I).8s for Peru, serial 474, leaves Warton, on the start of its 7,150-mile (11,506-km) delivery flight. 474 was originally WT343, diverted off an RAF contract; later in its life, its Peruvian serial was changed to '206'. Author's collection

Carrying the Class 'B' registration G-27-76 for pre-delivery test flying, '233' was the first B.72 for the FAP. BAe

The fourth aircraft in Peru's B(I).56 order, '242', previously Belfast-built B.2, WH880, is shown on test wearing a Class 'B' registration. Author's collection

Marshall. The order was originally for eight ex-RAF B(I).8s, but this was increased to eleven; the updating to Peruvian requirements provided a redesignation to B(I).68. On completion, each aircraft was test flown with Marshalls allocated Class 'B' registration G-52, and deliveries were spread over three years from March 1975 to May 1978.

Since the arrival of the first aircraft, on 25 May 1956, the Canberra has formed the backbone of the FAP's bombing capacity. Today, the Cessna A-37B has joined the remaining B(I).8s, B(I).56s, B(I).68s and B.72s, of which at least a dozen are still operating at the time of writing. In December 1991, five B(I).12s were purchased from the South African Air Force to boost the FAPs' number of Canberras, and two years later a T.4 was bought from the same source. FAP crews converted to the B(I).12 with the SAAF at Waterkloof Air Force Base (AFB), after which the aircraft left South Africa on 17 December 1991 and arrived at Lima on 3 January 1992, carrying no markings apart from a Peruvian flag painted on the fin, together with the SAAF serials. The T.4 was dismantled and transported by ship to Peru in crates.

Rhodesia

Towards the end of 1957, English Electric received an order from the Rhodesian Government for fifteen Canberra B.2s. These were supplied as refurbished ex-RAF aircraft and, early in 1958, a second order was received, for three T.4s.

The B.2s were taken out of storage at No.15 MU Wroughton to be refurbished to Royal Rhodesian Air Force (RRAF) requirements, allocated serials RRAF159 to RRAF173 inclusive. Delivery was made between 10 March and 2 June 1959. The three T.4s required more engineering than the bombers, as three B.2s were taken out of storage to be transported to Samlesbury, where new-build T.4 front fuselages, from Frame 12A, were fitted to replace the removed bomber sections. Serials RRAF 174 to RRAF176 inclusive were allocated and the three aircraft were ferried to Rhodesia in March 1961. Six spare Avon Mk.1/RA.3 engines, together with a large quantity of spares, were included in the order, which was worth over £2 million.

RRAF aircrews went through Course 160LB at No.231 OCU Bassingbourn, while selected groundcrews were instructed at the Canberra Technical Training Course, run at Warton. In Rhodesia, two Canberra squadrons were formed, No.5 (Bomber) Squadron with seven aircraft and No.6 (Photo-Reconnaissance) Squadron, with eight aircraft, both based at New Sarum, near Salisbury. However, in October, shortly after their formation, No.5 Squadron went on a month's detachment in Cyprus, with some of its Canberras and, a month later, it was at Sargodhar in Pakistan to participate in Exercise *Shabez*, organized by CENTRO.

In July 1960, a second detachment to Akrotiri involved all seven aircraft and a third visit was made in July 1963. Low-level practice bombing sorties were flown on the Middle East ranges, using their unique rocket-projectile system, as well as liaison flights to Hal Far on Malta.

On the grounds of cost, the RRAF could not purchase B.6s or B(I).8s, with their outboard underwing pylons that were able to carry rocket missile pods. However, the CO of No.5 Squadron requested that an investigation be made as to whether a rocket-projectile firing system could be installed on their B.2s. The fitting and harmonizing of a gyro gun-sight was also ruled out as being too expensive, so a centreline fitting, in conjunction with a simple sight, was considered to be the best option. Without making modifications to the bomb doors, the only possible site was the area between the glazed nose-cone and the nose-wheel bay. A trial installation of four zero-length rocket rails was made on RRAF171, in order to assess the aerodynamic effects and, during the twenty-three test flights made, RP firings were made on the Kutanga range outside Gwelo. During these flights, made between March and May 1961, RRAF171 suffered a sequence valve failure in the undercarriage hydraulics and had to make a wheels-up landing. RRAF169 was modified to continue the trials while RRAF171 was being repaired and the installation was cleared for service.

Canberra B.2, RRAF169, of No.5 Squadron, Royal Rhodesian Air Force, touches down at Akrotiri during a joint air exercise in 1960. Author's collection

While the RP system was being retrofitted to various aircraft, a Canberra was tasked, in December 1961, to survey the site of a crashed aircraft deep into the country. This was found to be the remains of the Douglas DC-6B that had been carrying the United Nations Secretary General Dag Hammarskold.

In order to make it difficult for foreign intelligence to assess the true strength of its forces, the Rhodesian Air Ministry brought in a new serial system in 1962, which had the numeral part of a serial start with a '2', instead of the former '1'. In the new scheme, Canberras started at RRAF200 (formerly RRAF159) and ran consecutively to RRAF217. This revised system lasted nearly six years, but in March 1968, a third numbering style was brought into use. This introduced the squadron number into the serial of its aircraft, but it was not as straightforward as it sounds. In the case of No.5 Squadron's Canberras, the numeral '5' was added to the existing serial number, but progressively through each aircraft's serial from right to left, while the lettering prefix was reduced from RRAF to just 'R'. This transformed RRAF200 into R2005, RRAF201 into R2051, RRAF202 into R2502 and so on.

The undercarriage problem on RRAF171, which had had to make a wheels-up landing, was encountered by four more aircraft in the course of a few months. Dirt in the hydraulic system was found to be the culprit and, again, the RRAF engineering section was able to meet the problem. A modification was introduced, in the form of a high-pressure relief valve fitted in the main-wheel door's hydraulic circuit, which completely cured the malfunctions. This modification was cheap and quick to install so, when other Canberra-operating countries got to hear of it, they introduced it into their own aircraft. There had been something like twenty wheel-up landings made by other air forces, so a solution to the problem was most welcome; some time later, the modification's designer was awarded the British Empire Medal (BEM) for this work.

The RhAF (formerly RRAF) engineers proved their expertise again in 1967. Premier Ian Smith's Unilateral Declaration of Independence (UDI), on 11 November 1965, had brought a comprehensive list of United Nations sanctions into force. About two dozen Avon engines were in the UK for overhaul at the time, and therefore unlikely to be returned, so the

RhAF was faced with a problem. Ten engines had been lost due to aircraft accidents and attempts to install Avon Mk.109/RA.7s, which could be obtained from friendly countries, had proved impossible. There were many reasons for this, particularly its size, which required a longer nacelle incorporating anti-icing. There was also the fact that much of the ancillary equipment did not mate up with the feeds within the aircraft's wings and

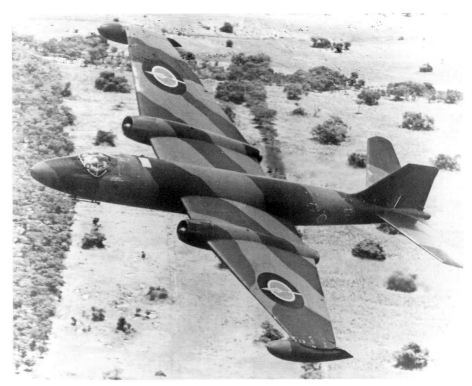

Wearing its second number change, R2175 banks, to show the 'single spear' roundels. The aircraft was first built by Handley Page as B.2, WJ613, which was converted to T.4 configuration before being sold to Rhodesia. Winston Brent

the fuel system was not compatible. The RhAF was stuck with the Avon Mk.1 and was running short of starter cartridges. Attempts to acquire them via sanction-busting sources proved far too costly, but the engineers considered that the matter could be resolved by using high-volume, high-pressure compressed air to spool up the engines. With the aid of quick-release valves fitted to a linked system of four industrial air cylinders, each holding 1,500psi, the cartridge shortage was sorted.

Due to structural failures, several aircraft had to be withdrawn from service – but at least this helped the engine situation!

However, these failures highlighted a problem that came rather close to killing off the Canberra altogether in the mid-1960s. It was of great concern to the Telecommunications Research Establishment at Defford in England. At that time, with twenty-two Canberras of different types on charge, the Establishment was the UK's largest operator of the aircraft; a large proportion of military radar projects were dependent on the aircraft.

Rolls-Royce had extensive metallurgical research facilities in its Research Laboratory at Derby. Early in the Second World War, the laboratory had devised a very strong aluminium alloy for use in forgings, which was registered as Alloy R.R.77, and was adopted by the Government as DTD683. It had a tensile strength of 32 tons per square inch, compared with only 10 tons per square inch for some similar aluminium alloys. W.E.W. Petter had selected DTD683 for the load-bearing strong components in the Canberra, such as the centre-section main spar, engine attachment brackets, undercarriage structure items, fuselage interface attachments, and so on.

Checks on several crashed Canberras had revealed that DTD683 had an unpredictable fatigue characteristic initiated by stress corrosion. Mandatory frequent Non Destructive Testing (NDT) was instigated in all maintenance programmes, until the problem could be resolved. Eventually, the cause was found to be the very high sensitivity of DTD683 to such things as the chatter of the cutting tool during machining operations, insufficient radius at corners and heat-treatment temperatures. Extensive changes were made in processing techniques and these brought about the redesignation of DTD683, which became DTD5024, 5044 or 5114, according to the application. Another, potentially very serious problem had been solved.

The RhAF encountered these effects of stress corrosion and had themselves been forced to use ultrasonic NDT far more extensively than they would have wished. Canberras had to be grounded for lengthy periods while additional plates and brackets were welded in suspected areas. One fitter introduced an inspection access hole in the centre-section forging of Frame 21, which was found to be of great value during detailed maintenance inspections.

In 1967, No.5 Squadron was engaged in countering terrorist operations carried out from Zambia. Its aircrafts' range was increased in 1968, when two bomb-bay fuel tanks were installed, which meant that guerrilla training camps deep inside Zambia could effectively be attacked. Following UDI, the bush wars increased. During Operation *Hurricane* the use of a low-level harmonized bomb-sight was found to lead to better bombing results, and the squadron flew daily sorties throughout the period of unrest. A dedicated photographic-reconnaissance aircraft was constructed in 1971, using assemblies from three different Canberras. It was fitted with a Wild RC8 camera with a 6in lens in the rear fuselage, and could carry a combination of two F.96 cameras with 48in lenses in the bomb-bay, a Wild RC10 in a special bomb-bay fitting, an F.95 with a 3in lens facing to the rear, or a split pair of F96s with 48in lenses in the rear fuselage. The latter could be substituted by a split pair of F.52 cameras with 36in lenses when necessary.

The conflict ended in 1979, and in April 1980 Rhodesia changed its name to Zimbabwe, bringing a third change to aircraft serials – the 'R' prefix was simply removed. The number of operable Canberras had been reduced to eleven with the birth of the new country.

In this 'close finger four' formation, two B.2s are fitted with the under-nose rocket rails unique to the Rhodesian Air Force. Three of the aircraft have the later 'single spear' roundel, while the trailing aircraft without rocket rails has the earlier marking, of three small spears, set within the red of the roundel. Winston Brent

---

Serial Chameleon Canberras

Canberra B.2
Fifteen aircraft in the first order, obtained by refurbishment of existing aircraft, delivered in 1959. Two changes in serials were introduced by the RRAF/RhAF:
RRAF159 (ex-WH867):
    first change RRAF200, second change R2005
RRAF160 (ex-WH653):
    first change RRAF201, second change R2051
RRAF161 (ex-WH662):
    first change RRAF202, second change R2502
RRAF162 (ex-WH672):
    first change RRAF203, second change R5203
RRAF163 (ex-WH707):
    first change RRAF204, second change R250
RRAF164 (ex-WH855):
    first change RRAF205, second change R2055
RRAF165 (ex-WH871):
    first change RRAF206, grounded before second change
RRAF166 (ex-WH883):
    crashed before first change
RRAF167 (ex-WJ571):
    first change RRAF208, second change R2085
RRAF168 (ex-WJ572):
    first change RRAF209, second change R2059
RRAF169 (ex-WJ578):
    first change RRAF210, second change R2510

RRAF170 (ex-WJ606):
    first change RRAF211, crashed before second change
RRAF171 (ex-WK108):
    first change RRAF212, second change R5212
RRAF172 (ex-WK612):
    first change RRAF213, crashed before second change
RRAF173 (ex-WH644):
    first change RRAF2141, second change R2514

Canberra T.4
Three aircraft in the second order, obtained by refurbishment of existing B.2s (RRAF175 had assemblies from two aircraft) with new-build T.4 front fuselages, delivered in 1961:
RRAF174 (ex-WH658):
    first change RRAF215, second change R2155
RRAF175 (ex-WH674/WJ606):
    first change RRAF216, second change R2516
RRAF176 (ex-WJ613):
    first change RRAF217, second change R2175

An additional aircraft, R2519, was obtained by using RRAF207 wings, RRAF213 fuselage nose and centre-section, and R2055 fuselage rear section. This Canberra was used as a dedicated photographic-reconnaissance aircraft. It was grounded in December 1981 and reduced to spares.

South Africa

The evaluation of aircraft for the South African Air Force (SAAF), carried out in 1960, was a rather protracted affair. Their requirement was for a retaliation strike force of light bombers, in case the country was attacked. The potential aggressors were numerous. Of the original types investigated, the English Electric Canberra was considered too old, the Hawker Siddeley

Canberra B(I).12, '454' of the South African Air Force, on air test prior to delivery, in January 1964. South Africa sold the aircraft to Peru in the 1990s. BAe

Buccaneer too new and the Dassault Mirage IVA too expensive. In view of the fact that economics were a consideration, coupled with the declared requirement of a light bomber, it seems rather surprising that both the Avro Vulcan B.1 and Handley Page Victor B.2 were evaluated after the original trio had been rejected!

By April 1962, opinions had changed and recommendations had hardened to the purchase of sixteen Buccaneer Mk.2s, together with six Canberra B(I).8s, the latter being considered as a 'stop gap' pending the arrival of the Buccaneers. The South African Government signed an agreement on 27 September 1962 for six new-build B(I).12s, with Avon 109/RA.7 engines, at a unit price of £312,000. Stringent penalty clauses were included in the order, in the case of late delivery, which was laid down as being between September and November 1963. In fact, this first order for SAAF Canberras ran over the delivery time-scale by five months, but it is not known if the penalty clause was enforced. The first aircraft had its maiden flight at Samlesbury on 31 August 1963, the sixth at the end of February 1964 and delivery was completed in April 1964. Incidentally, this sixth B(I).12 was the last Canberra to be completed at Preston.

In spring 1963, English Electric received the second South African order, for three T.4s, which were obtained by the refurbishment of ex-RAF trainers. Deliveries were made between February and April 1964. While the T.4s were primarily for converting crews to the B(I).12s, it was the view of Combat General B.G. Vilijoen, the Chief of Air Staff in South Africa, that they could also provide adequate dual instruction for potential Buccaneer crews.

All the SAAF Canberras served with No.12 Squadron, based at Waterkloof AFB, by the River Orange. In 1975, Operation *Savannah* was put in motion, in an attempt to overthrow the new MPLA-backed government in Angola. Waterkloof was central in South African territory, well in range for operations over the border with Angola, and No.12 Squadron soon became engaged in high-level bombing of MPLA troops. They quickly returned to their native South-West Africa. In May 1978, further unrest between South Africa and the South-West African People's Organisation (SWAPO) escalated into Operation *Reindeer*. Again, No.12 Squadron's Canberras were called in to attack rebel forces and again the attacks achieved their objectives.

The following year, in Operation *Rekstok*, SWAPO was the instigator of guerrilla

activities in south-western Zambia, which resulted in a series of B(I).12 raids, as a part of Operation *Saffraan*, carried out between March 1979 and February 1980. During Operation *Saffraan*, No.12 Squadron suffered its only fatalities in twenty-eight years of Canberra operations. B(I).12, 452, the second aircraft received by the SAAF, was shot down by groundfire on 14 March 1979, killing the two crew members.

In December 1980, Canberras joined No.24 Squadron's Buccaneers in Operation *Sceptic*. This was a concentrated attack on the SWAPO North-West Frontier HQ, at Oshinehenge, from 19,000ft (5,800m), with 500lb (225kg) and 1,000lb (455kg) bombs. Eight months later, on 23 August 1981, No.12 Squadron was engaged in Operation *Protea*, low-level attacks on Angolan air-defence radar installations at Cahama. During later activities in this campaign, on 6 November, two Mirage F1CZs shot down one of a pair of Angolan MiG-21s. This was the first time the SAAF had shot down an enemy aircraft in aerial combat since the 1952–54 Korean War. A year later, on 5 October 1982, in an action-replay of the August incident, another MiG-21 was destroyed.

The SAAF had a penchant for giving every aerial activity a different codename and the biggest series of all SAAF Canberra raids went under the name Operation *Askari*. Between 24 December 1983 and 8 January 1984, over 180,000lb (81,630kg) of bombs were unloaded on Angolan targets at Cahama, Caiundu and Cuvelai. It was during these raids that T.4, serial 457, was used as a bomber. On these raids, Canberras usually flew in fours and, while many sorties produced good results, there were the occasional glitches of bombs hanging up and targets not being identified.

ship' SSV33 *Kapushka* from 40,000ft (12,200m) off the south-east coast of South African. Photographs were taken of the vessel, which was displaying radar dishes and antennas all over the upper deck, but, hearing the *Kapushka*'s weapons tracking radar switch on, the Canberra brought the mission to a close.

The squadron itself was brought to a close on 22 November 1990, with a parade and flypast at Waterkloof AFB, after which the Canberras were put in store in their old

Sweden

With a policy of armed neutrality, supported by a high-quality, indigenous aircraft design and manufacturing facility in the *Svenska Aeroplan A.B.* (SAAB), Sweden, not surprisingly, does not purchase many foreign aircraft. The only time a major order has been made for foreign aircraft to serve in the *Svenska Flygvapnet* was in 1954, when 120 Hawker Hunters were purchased.

'456' was the last of the B(I).12s which the SAAF received in April 1964. This was the very last new-build Canberra to come out of the Preston plant. The lines had closed at the end of 1959, but '456' was the twelfth aircraft constructed from a stock of a dozen component assemblies that BAC produced before the closure. It was later purchased by Peru. BAe

In September 1987, Operations *Modular*, *Hooper* and *Packer* in Angola involved the use of SAAF Canberras against enemy targets for the last time. However, the hundreds of reconnaissance sorties they had flown supplied the SAAF with first-class information on the vast areas of Angola, Mozambique, Rhodesia, South-West Africa and Zambia. No.12 Squadron's OCU continued using Canberras for Buccaneer conversions, and Rhodesian Air Force aircrews went through the unit as a part of South Africa's assistance to its neighbours. The occasional operational sortie had been flown by the RhAF in conjunction with the SAAF, and, on 3 October 1979, a Canberra was brought down over Mozambique.

No.12 Squadron also flew several EW missions and, on 22 August 1989, it detected the Soviet nuclear-powered 'spy

squadron hangars, pending sale. Peru purchased B(I).12s 451, 453, 454, 455 and 456, which were flown to Peru. T.4 458 was also sold to Peru, but was dismantled and shipped there in crates. Of the two remaining T.4s, 457 went to the SAAF Museum at Swartkop, while 459 is mounted as a gate guard at Waterkloof AFB.

Boer Canberras

Canberra B(I).12
Six new-build aircraft in the first order, delivered in 1963/64: 451, 452, 453, 454, 455, 456

Canberra T.4
Three aircraft in the second order, obtained by refurbishment of existing T.4s, delivered in 1964: 457 (ex-WJ991), 458 (ex-WJ864), 459 (ex-WJ617)

However, in 1959, English Electric received an order for two ex-RAF Canberra B.2s, to be converted for Swedish electronic research programmes. WH711, a B.2 built at Preston in March 1953, and WH905, a Short Bros aircraft built in January 1954, were the chosen airframes. As the type of avionics that were going to be tested had similar properties to the RAF Target Facilities Squadron's Mk.17 AI radar units fitted in the Canberra T.11s, a comparable nose profile was required for the Swedish aircraft, which were to be designated Canberra Tp.52. Boulton Paul undertook the conversions to produce the T.11s for the RAF, so the two *Svenska Flygvapnet* aircraft were treated similarly and both were ready for delivery early in 1960. Given the serials 52001 and 52002, the two Tp.52s were ferried,

The first of Sweden's two Tp.52s, 52001 carries a minute serial and the figure '8', denoting its future operator, Flottiljer 8. BAe

Awaiting delivery in March 1960, the second Tp.52, 52002, is believed always to have been operated without tip tanks. Author's collection

on 1 February and 5 March respectively, to serve with *Flottiljer 8* based at Barkaby, outside Stockholm. The respective serials were only shown in an abridged form, as '01' and '02' carried across the fin and rudder.

Besides acting as trials vehicles, the two Tp.52s performed in an electronic intelligence-gathering ELINT/SIGINT role, and at least one, 52002, is known to have been fitted with a revised nose profile during these activities. The two were employed for nearly thirteen years before being retired on 27 January 1973, and both

have been preserved. 52002 is displayed at the Flygvapenmuseum at Malmen, outside Linkoping, while 52001 is held at the Svedinos Bil Och Flygmuseum, a private museum near the Halmstad AFB set up by Svedino, a former circus performer.

An Electronic Pair

Canberra Tp.52
Two aircraft obtained by refurbishment of existing B.2s jointly by English Electric and Boulton Paul, delivered in 1960: 52001 (ex-WH711), 52002 (ex-WH905)

Venezuela

The first foreign sale of the Canberra, excluding licensed production agreements, was to the *Fuerzas Aérea Venezolana* (FAV), the Venezuelan Air Force. The country had been well-disposed towards the Allies during the Second World War and, after operating with a collection of ex-USAAF aircraft in the late 1940s, it commenced an ambitious modernization programme in 1949. Orders were placed with de Havilland in 1950 for Vampires, and with English Electric in 1953 for Canberra B.2s.

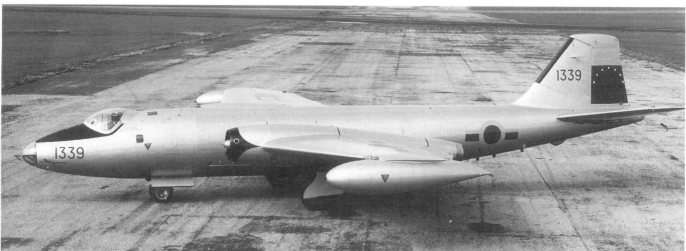

(Top) B.2, 3-A-39, delivered on 9 May 1953, was the first new-build aircraft for Venezuela.
Author's collection

(Above) Refurbished WH649, B.2 '1339', sports an additional paint scheme around the intakes.
Author's collection

2E-39 was the second of two T.4s supplied to the Fuerzas Aérea Venezolana. Author's collection

Negotiations had been held with the Venezuelan Government for several months, and English Electric were confident enough about the outcome to start work on the aircraft in autumn 1952, several months before the order for six new-build B.2s was received, on 27 January 1953. Aircraft under construction to RAF contracts were diverted to meet the order, and the first was ferried, via Gibraltar, by an RAF crew, to arrive at Maracay on 1 April 1953.

FAV serials were rather complicated in those days and the six Canberras were registered 1A-39 to 3A-39 and 1B-39 to 3B-39 inclusive. The second aircraft was also

demonstration had to be handled by Beamont and Wg Cdr Hackforth, and the English Electric technical representatives who were present, together with some Rolls-Royce personnel. These preparations included removing a jacked-up B-25 Mitchell that had been parked in front of the Canberra for no apparent reason – surely not something to do with an American mission that had tried very hard to block the English Electric order?

After 1A-39's pre-flight checks had been completed, it was found that there were only two starter cartridges per Avon; all the rest were in a bonded warehouse in the Port of

forecast indicating that the sun would burn through, the green light was given for the demonstration. First, Beamont was presented to the President, then the Avons were started; now, there were no more cartridges until someone paid a visit to the warehouse. No response was received from a call made to Air Traffic Control, so 'Bee' taxied out from the hardstanding where he had been parked and promptly encountered another surprise. A C-47 came out of the mist on final approach and landed. As the Canberra moved towards the runway threshold, another C-47 appeared across its nose and

Eleven of the fourteen B.2s originally delivered to the FAV were updated to B.82 standard in the late 1970s. '1131', delivered in September 1977, was the second of these conversions. BAe

delivered by an RAF crew, flying the same route, but the remaining four were flown by civilian crews from Silver City Airways, who took a route via Gander. All six were destined to operate with *Escuela 39* at Barcelona.

The handover ceremony for the first aircraft, 1A-39, was handled at Maracay by 'Bee' Beamont, who put on a demonstration flight for the gathered FAV dignitaries. After the display, the British Air Attache Wg Cdr Hackforth asked if 'Bee' would put on a similar demonstration for the Venezuelan President, Perez Jimenez. Arrangements were made for the display to be flown at La Calorta, a small airfield outside Caracas, at 8.30am on the following Monday, 6 April. As the weekend was a religious holiday, preparations for the

Maracay, which was closed for the holiday. This meant that the flight to La Calorta, and a display rehearsal, could be made on Sunday and the demonstration itself could go ahead, provided all four cartridges worked satisfactorily. However, it would not be possible to land and switch off engines after the display. As there was no other alternative, it was decided to go ahead on that basis, with the question of the four cartridges all working first time being left in the lap of the gods. Beamont flew to La Calorta on the Sunday afternoon, noting that it was a small, rough airfield, bounded by the city of Caracas on one side and the mountains of Merida on the other.

Monday surprisingly brought a low cloud base and mist instead of the previous week's sunshine but, with the local

landed, closely followed by yet another. Contact was at last made with the tower, and Beamont was informed that an unspecified number of troop carriers would be landing, although there would be no other traffic during the demonstration. Not wanting to keep a South American President waiting, English Electric's Chief Test Pilot lined up the Canberra and took off.

There has possibly been no other Canberra demonstration like the one at La Calorta. With a light fuel load, 'Bee' got airborne quickly, to make his customary tight turn round the airfield and, in the mist, he passed another C-47 on finals, which set the tone for the whole display. All manoeuvres had to be made between, above or below a continuous stream of landing C-47s, with visibility being something like

'1437' was the third of four FAV B(I).2s that were converted into B(I).82s; it is shown awaiting delivery in February 1979. BAe

B(I).88, '0923', was the last Canberra for the FAV. It had originally been supplied as a B(I).8, but was fully refurbished to B(I).88 configuration and delivered on 12 March 1980. BAe

2 miles (3km) at best. Although he might not admit it, 'Bee' must have seen the lowering fuel load being displayed on his instrument panel with some relief. Fitting a final low pass between another pair of the ubiquitous Douglas transports, he pulled up to disappear into the cloud, and set a course for Boca de Rio.

A second order from Venezuela, received in January 1957, must have offered some consolation for the difficulties at La Calorta. It asked for ten new-build B(I).8s and two T.4s. One B(I).8 was diverted from an RAF contract, but the remaining nine aircraft were all built to the order. The two T.4s were supplied from an MoS-cancelled order and delivery of all twelve was made between June 1957 and January 1958, these aircraft also going to *Escuela* 39 of *Grupo* 13 at Barcelona. They

carried serials 4A-39, 5A-39, 5B-39 and 1C-39 to 4C-39 inclusive. (All FAV aircraft were later renumbered.)

A third Venezuelan order was received in 1965 and this was the first foreign order that English Electric received for refurbished aircraft. Of the fourteen aircraft involved, twelve were B.2s and two were PR.3s. Four of the B.2s were fitted with bomb-bay gun packs, similar to those on the RAF's B(I).6, and these were designated B(I).2s in the FAV. All the aircraft in this third order, delivered between December 1965 and April 1967, served with *Escuela 40* and carried the revised FAV serial system from the start. All the Venezuelan Canberras were very well equipped for high- or low-level roles, as well as for interdiction and close air support. A comprehensive range of weapons was fitted between the variants, including air-to-surface missiles (ASMs). A qualified RAF instructor and navigator were seconded to the FAV in the late 1970s, to assist in training problems; a number of aircraft had been crashing, and subsequent enquiries had attributed these accidents to pilot error.

In common with many foreign purchasers over the years, the FAV returned many of its Canberras to Samlesbury for refurbishing and at least one was refurbished twice. In 1978, the FAV began making modifications in Venezuela, so BAC sent technicians to supervise radio and armament modifications being engineered on site. After they had assisted with work on the first four aircraft, the BAC representatives were satisfied with the standard of engineering and returned to Warton, leaving the FAV fitters to handle all future work on their own. In the course of refurbishments, new designations were applied to some aircraft, with Marks B.82, B(I).82, PR.83, T.84 and B(I).88 appearing on the inventories.

Canberra's Premier Customer

Canberra B.2
Six new-build aircraft in the first order, two diverted from RAF contracts, delivered in 1953. New FAV serial system introduced in 1957/58:
1A-39 (ex-WH708), 2A-39 (ex-WH709) later 6315, 3A-39 later 6409, 1B-39 crashed before change, 2B-39 later 3246, 3B-39 crashed before change,

Eight aircraft in the third order, obtained by refurbishment of existing ex-RAF aircraft, delivered in 1965/67:
0129 (ex-WH877), 1131 (ex-WH647), 1183 (ex-WJ570), 1233 (ex-WF914), 1339 (ex-WH649), 1364 (ex-WD993), 1511 (ex-WH864), 2001 (ex-WJ980)

Canberra B(I).8
Eight new-build aircraft in the second order, one diverted from EAF contract, delivered in 1957/58. New FAV serial system introduced in 1957/58: 4A-39 (ex-XH244) later 3216, 5A-39 crashed before change, 4B-39 later 0923, 5B-39 crashed before change, 1C-39 later 0240, 2C-39 later 0269, 3C-39 later 0426, 4C-39 later 0453

Canberra T.4
Two new-build aircraft in the second order, diverted from cancelled MoS contract, delivered in 1957/58. New FAV serial system introduced in 1957/58: 1E-39 later 0619, 2E-39 later 0621

Canberra B(I).2
Four aircraft in the third order, obtained by refurbishment of existing ex-RAF aircraft, delivered in 1965/67: 1280 (ex-WH881), 1425 (ex-WH712), 1437 (ex-WH730), 1529 (ex-WH732)

Canberra PR.3
Two aircraft in the third order, obtained by refurbishment of ex-RAF aircraft, delivered in 1966: 2314 (ex-WE172), 2444 (ex-WE171)

Canberra B.82
Eleven aircraft obtained by conversion of existing FAV B.2s during refurbishment, re-delivered in 1977/80: 0129, 1131, 1183, 1233, 1339, 1364, 1551, 2001, 3246, 6315, 6409

Canberra B(I).82
Four aircraft obtained by conversion of existing FAV B(I).2s during refurbishment, re-delivered 1978/79: 1280, 1425, 1437, 1529

Canberra PR.83
Two aircraft due to be obtained by conversion of existing FAV PR.3s during refurbishment, but 2444 crashed 9 March 1976, before arriving at Samlesbury. One aircraft re-delivered 1978: 2314

Canberra T.84
Two aircraft obtained by conversion of existing FAV T.4s during refurbishment, re-delivered 1978 and 1980: 0619, 0621

Canberra B(I).88
Five aircraft obtained by conversion of existing FAV B(I).8s during refurbishment, re-delivered 1977/78 and 1980: 0240, 0269, 0426, 0453, 0923

West Germany

The Federal German Government placed an order with BAC in 1965 for three ex-RAF B.2s, to be used as experimental and trials aircraft for *Erprobungstelle 61*, based at Oberpfaffenhofen outside Munich. The aircraft became one of only two all-British types to serve with the *Luftwaffe*; the other was the Percival Pembroke.

All three aircraft were overhauled and modified by Marshall of Cambridge, after which BAC at Warton carried out the pre-delivery inspections, before delivery was made in October 1966. With the German Federal Republic, the three Canberras were used for a number of experimental purposes and changed ownership within Germany a couple of times – and changed serials four times! When the aircraft first arrived in Germany, they carried 'YA' as the type marking. The first change was to this type marking, which became '00'. All three aircraft were transferred to the West German Defence Ministry in 1970, for which they

were placed on the civil register and allotted civil markings. With the Defence Ministry, the aircraft were employed on what was euphemistically referred to as 'special duties'. For these duties, the bomb-bay was fitted out with a battery of cameras, in order to fulfil a photographic-survey role – on courses set conveniently adjacent to the East German borders. One aircraft, D9569, was also transferred to the German Aerospace Research Institute (DFVLR), while the other two were loaned to the Military Geographic Service. D9569 is also known to have carried out high-altitude calibration trials, in addition to infra-red radiometry.

In the late 1970s, the serials of all three were once again changed, this time with the *Luftwaffe* type number '99' being applied. The crews were some of the same personnel who had flown the aircraft when they were with the Defence Ministry, but little has been released about their role. In 1984, 99+36 was mounted on a very unphotogenic tubular structure at Sinsheim, for display purposes, but the other two are

believed to still be 'earning their keep'. They have flown into several IAT shows at Fairford in Gloucestershire, resplendent in their overall dark orange colour scheme.

It has been reported that 99+34 made a wheels-up landing in 1992 and Canberra TT.18 WK123 was donated to the Military Geographic Service as a 'hangar queen'. It is believed that the wings were fitted to the German aircraft as replacements, following the belly landing.

Iron Cross Canberras

Canberra B.2
Three aircraft obtained by refurbishment of existing B.2s by Marshall of Cambridge, delivered in 1966. The German serial numbers of these aircraft have been changed three times:
YA+151 (ex-WK130): first change 00+01, second change D9569, third change 99+36
YA+152 (ex-WK137): first change 00+02, second change D9566, third change 99+34
YA+153 (ex-WK138): first change 00+03, second change D9567, third change 99+35

The last of West Germany's three B.2s, wearing the YA+153 markings, as originally delivered. BAe

YA+153 was later renumbered D-9567, when it was used by the Military Geographic Service, with a camera installation in the bomb-bay. BAe

Zimbabwe

On 18 April 1980, the Rhodesian Air Force (RhAF) ceased to exist and the Air Force of Zimbabwe was formed with the aircraft of the former RhAF. The only change made to the serials was the removal of the 'R' prefix.

Zimbabwe Canberras

Canberra B.2
Eight aircraft ex-RhAF, originally RAF aircraft: 2051 (ex-R2051) originally WH653, 2502 (ex-R2502) originally WH662, 5203 (ex-R5203) originally WH672, 2504 (ex-R2504) originally WH707, 2055 (ex-R2055) originally WH855, 2085 (ex-R2085) originally WJ571, 2059 (ex-R2059) originally WJ572, 2514 (ex-R2514) originally WH644

One ex-RAF aircraft supplied direct from RAF Marham in March 1981: 2250 (ex-WH666)

Canberra T.4
Three aircraft ex-RhAF, originally RAF aircraft: 2155 (ex-R2155) originally WH658, 2516 (ex-R2516) originally WH674, with parts from WJ606, 2175 (ex-R2175) originally WJ613

One ex-RAF aircraft supplied direct from RAF Marham in March 1981: 2215 (ex-WJ869)

CHAPTER FOURTEEN

Specialized Canberras

Several factors combined to make the Canberra the very versatile and effective airborne platform that it was, both for equipment research trials, as well as for flight testing new engines. The principal turbo-jet-powered trials and testbed aircraft for over a decade, from 1945, was the Gloster Meteor; it proved to be an extraordinarily adaptable aeroplane – it was the testbed for two Armstrong Siddeley Sapphire Sa2s, each developing 7,600lb (3,446.6kg) static thrust, although it had originally been designed around a pair of 1,700lb (771kg) thrust Rolls-Royce Welland engines. However, it was basically a 1940 design.

By the mid-1950s, the performance envelope of contemporary military aircraft specifications had enlarged to the point where engine and equipment testing far beyond the Meteor's capabilities were required. The basic prerequisites were very similar: a well-designed airframe, docile to fly, easy to keep serviceable, rugged in construction, with a comparatively low wing loading, plus two engines, was ideal to take over the role of the primary trials and testbed aircraft for the services, as well as for the aviation industry. Furthermore, a conventional design, with engines in separate nacelles and not integral with the wing structure, allowed the engines to be substituted by test engines without any significant alterations or aerodynamic penalties.

The applications given below are divided into three distinct sections and the principal aircraft employed in each are detailed. This does not claim to be the definitive inventory. The RAF made more use of Canberras collectively, for its own requirements, rather than individually, like establishments and industry. It has not, therefore, always been feasible to detail particular aeroplanes used by the service, but they are included where possible. For the establishments and industry, it has been more straightforward to highlight individual airframes, but not always so easy to itemize their usage, particularly in the field of electronics.

The Service

Thermonuclear Tests

The Canberra's association with the British nuclear weapons development programme began in October 1953. Eighteen months before this, Operation *Hurricane* had seen an atomic device detonated on board a time-expired naval frigate, HMS *Plym*, off the Monte Bello Islands in the Indian Ocean, 60 miles (95km) north-west of the Western Australian coastline. This had proved the firing mechanism, but it took the next four years for Dr William Penny, Chief Superintendent of Armament Research at the MoS, battling through a forest of technicalities and politics, to perfect the first British hydrogen bomb.

En route to this goal, another device was tested at the WRE at Woomera, on 14 October 1953. This had far more bearing on the eventual Operation *Blue Danube* atomic bomb, which produced an atomic cloud through which the Canberra opened its account with the thermonuclear test programme. Under the codename Operation *Hot Box*, the Australian Aircraft Research and Development Unit (ARDU) had Canberras B.2 WH710 and B.6 WH962 on temporary loan, the latter from the School of Aviation Medicine (IAM) at Farnborough. Both were based at Edinburgh Field in South Australia and WH962, piloted by Wg Cdr G.H. Dhenin, with Gp Capt D.A. Wilson, the RAF's senior radiology specialist, on board, was adapted to fly through the atomic cloud to gather radiation samples.

Codenamed Operation *Grapple*, with all units collectively known as Task Force 308, the first British hydrogen bomb (H-bomb) drop was scheduled for May 1957. The first American H-bomb test, at Bikini Atoll on 1 March 1954, had revealed such enormous destructive power that Australia insisted *Grapple* must take place well away from its shores. Australia had assisted with the atomic bomb trials Operations *Buffalo* and *Mosaic* in October 1956, with Canberra B.6s of

No.76 Squadron making the air-sampling sorties from Pearce AFB, outside Perth. They flew through the cloud from the first atom bomb, which was dropped over Maralinga, South Australia, but that was as far as the Australian Government was prepared to go. They were having nothing to do with H-bomb testing. Extensive reconnaissance flights by Shackletons of No.240 Squadron led to the selection of a piece of coral named Christmas Island as the operating base for *Grapple*; its highest point was only 25ft (7.5m) above sea level and its only inhabitants were thousands of land crabs. Malden Island, 400 miles (640km) to the south-east, was to be the dropping zone; Air Vice Marshal W.E. Oulton was appointed task force commander and W.R.J. Cook was to be the scientific director.

Preparatory to *Grapple*, in November 1953, a detachment from No.100 Squadron, designated 1323 Flight, was formed to carry out high-level meteorological and photographic flights in the vast Polynesian area of the Pacific. On 1 November 1955, the Flight was renumbered No.542 Squadron at Wyton, taking over the title of the Canberra PR.7 unit disbanded the same day. Four months later, in March 1956, four Canberra B.6s, which had been specially prepared at Weston Zoyland, left for Australia, two to be based at Darwin/Nightcliffe in the north and two at Laverton, outside Melbourne. Seven No.76 Squadron Canberra B.6s also left Weston Zoyland early in 1956, to participate in *Grapple* from Christmas Island, which by April 1957, had two runways, hardstandings, and accommodation for 1,300 people.

The transit route to Christmas Island was via Aldergrove, where tanks were topped up, the Royal Canadian Air Force (RCAF) base at Goose Bay, another RCAF base at Namao, in Alberta, and the American Travis AFB, 60 miles (95km) from San Francisco. From Travis, the route crossed the Pacific to Hickham AFB, which shared the Honolulu International airport, alongside Pearl Harbor, in Hawaii, and then on to Christmas Island. The total flying time was around 23 hours, which

A No.76 Squadron Canberra on Christmas Island, in 1957, during Operation Grapple.
**The wing-tip fuel tanks have been modified into collecting tanks; here, the port one
is cleaned out prior to another sample sortie.** *Aeroplane.*

occupied four to five days. RAF ground-crew were detached at every stopping point along the *Grapple* transit route.

The Canberras had all been modified for their respective roles during the tests. A considerable amount of monitoring and photographic equipment had been installed and each wing-tip tank had been modified to operate as a collecting tank for the samples, taken through a non-return valve set behind an intake cut in the tank's nose. Reconnaissance flights were made over a large area, during which photographs were taken of all the islands, so that they could be recognized on over-flights. These were followed by a comprehensive set of meteorological sorties, to find the winds at various high levels, so that a cross-section of the atmosphere in various areas could be produced. From these, the prevailing wind at any altitude could be worked out and the direction of the nuclear cloud predicted.

The first operation known as *Grapple* involved three H-bomb test drops, the first two on 15 and 31 May, followed by a third on 15 June 1957. All the drops, with the weapon detonating at 10,000ft (3,050m), were made by Vickers Valiants from No.49 Squadron, while Canberra B.6s of Nos 58, 76, 100 and 542 Squadron detachments flew low-level reconnaissance sorties fifteen minutes after each explosion, to determine the condition of Malden Island and the surrounding sea. High-level sampling flights were made through the cloud at various altitudes, after which the Canberras

flew back to Christmas Island for decontamination. The samples from the first drop were packed in special containers and flown back to the UK for analysis, by Canberra PR.7 WT503 of No.58 Squadron. The schedule set for the sample flights allowed seventy-two hours for the whole journey, but this was easily bettered. Another Canberra, PR.7 WT504, accompanied the first carrier to Honolulu, in case it should go unserviceable, while back-up aircraft and crews were stationed along the whole route, to ensure there was no delay in getting the samples to the UK.

Pre-drop dawn flights were made by Canberras to ascertain if the Valiant mission was possible that particular day. Wind velocity, temperature and cloud structure were all determining factors, but no test drop had to be postponed for any natural or mechanical reason. Avro's 'old growler', the Shackleton, operated by Nos 206 and 240 Squadrons, put in sterling support to the whole *Grapple* programme.

Later H-bomb test drops were coded Operation *Grapple* 'Y', in March 1958, and *Grapple* 'Z', at the end of that year. On 8 November, the first operationally configured bomb, containing the equivalent of one million tons of TNT, produced a cloud that mushroomed to over 60,000ft (18,300m), in an awesome demonstration of the power released. Plans had been laid to equip three Canberra B.6s with additional rocket motors, in order to collect samples from higher altitudes than the average 54,000ft (16,500m) that was being

achieved by the Avons on their own. WT206 and WT207 were fitted with Napier Double Scorpion motors, while WT208 had a de Havilland Spectre. WT207 broke up at 56,000ft (17,100m) on 9 April 1958, during its trials, and neither of the other installations was operated during *Grapple*.

Throughout the whole H-bomb test programme, only one Canberra was lost. PR.3 WH790 crashed at Goose Bay, killing both crew members, during a snowstorm, while following up as a reserve aircraft for the first *Grapple* drop sample carrier.

An undertaking such as Operation *Grapple* required vast resources, and it should be recorded that, beside the Valiants that made the actual drops, Shackletons shared the meteorological flights, as well as keeping the areas clear of shipping; No.1325 Flight's Dakotas carried out the inter-island hopping; and Westland Whirlwind helicopters of No.22 Squadron undertook internal-communications duties. A regular schedule of Hastings provided support from the UK, via the United States/Honolulu route, while there was even a vital role for an Auster, which sprayed the camp areas to keep them clear of flies and insects.

Electronic Espionage

No.192 Squadron was disbanded at Foulsham on 22 August 1945, to become the Central Signals Establishment (CSE), which, on 1 August 1952, had an element encompassed into No.527 Squadron, for the calibration of Control and Reporting Units. The number was taken up again on 15 July 1951, when a new No.192 Squadron was formed at Watton, operating Mosquito PR.34s and Lincoln B.2s. Boeing B.29 Washingtons joined them in April 1952, followed in January 1953 by brand-new Canberra B.2s WH670 and WH698, which took over from the Lincolns of 'B' Flight.

A comprehensive fitting of special equipment, including a fourteen-channel tape recorder mounted in the bomb-bay, prepared the two aircraft for intelligence gathering. This began later in the year, with the squadron operating from bases within NATO on the European mainland, as well as from Luqa and Akrotiri. These were the first Canberras to carry AEOs, referred to then as 'Specialist Operators'. Sorties were flown at 35,000ft (10,700m) over the Baltic, in conditions of radio silence, before coming down to 500ft (150m) to monitor signals from new Soviet transmitting stations and pinpointing their locations, before getting back up to their 35,000ft altitude at full bore, to set course back to Watton.

June 1954 was something of a milestone, as No.192 Squadron's Canberras became the first to be fitted with *Green Satin*; this was to become an essential piece of navigation equipment in the Canberra for many years. It sent out radar signals aimed at the surface ahead of the aircraft, to be received back at a slightly different frequency, which could then be displayed to the navigator as groundspeed, as opposed to airspeed. By means of a moveable aerial, which lined up with the return signal, the actual track being flown – the heading – was displayed, compared with the direction in which the aircraft was pointing.

In July 1954, a pair of Canberra B.6s, which had been modified to B(I).6 standard, joined the squadron. Serialled WT301 and WJ775, they operated alongside the B.2s, undertaking similar roles. Three years later, the last of 'C' Flight's Washingtons returned to the United States, to be replaced by three de Havilland Comet C.2(R)s, XK665, XK659 and XK663, which performed in the ELINT role. By the time the unit was renumbered No.51 Squadron, on 21 August 1958, the first B.2 WH670 had left, but the remaining Canberras continued performing the same duties, being joined, or replaced, by B.6s WJ768, WJ775, WT206 and WT305 at various times, until Nimrod R.1s had completely taken over by October 1976.

Swifter Flight

Over the winter months of 1959/60, RAE Farnborough, in conjunction with the Institute of Aviation Medicine (IAM), took on a special flight of six Canberras, for what has sometimes been referred to as Operation *Swifter*. The objects of the exercise were to investigate the effects of turbulence sustained in high-speed, low-altitude flying, on both airframes and aircrews.

Four English Electric-built Canberra B.2s, WD950, WF890, WH648 and WH664, were taken from No.231 OCU Bassingbourn, to be joined by two Handley Page-built aircraft, WJ573, which had been in Upwood's Station Flight, and WJ576, also from Bassingbourn. All were substantially strengthened and fitted out with a comprehensive array of recording instrumentation. A seventh aircraft, Handley Page-built WJ608, was detached from Bassingbourn as a reserve, to be strengthened if necessary, but the requirement did

Personnel of Swifter Flight at El Adam, with Wg Cdr K. Bazarnik of the IAM in the right foreground, with Sqn Ldr Peter Thompson. The Flight's logo can be seen on the fin of the right-hand aircraft, as well as the combination of white/camouflage finish on their aircraft. Author's collection

not arise. The Flight was administered by the Akrotiri Wing, where it was stationed, although all flights were made under the auspices of the RAE. The aircraft were specially painted for the RAE, with a white forward and centre fuselage, plus a Flight logo of a stylized swift, in a triangle set over an arrow, on the fin. As a matter of interest, the logos were all hand-painted and, consequently, considerable variations were to be found between the six aircraft.

A target of 1,000 hours of flying was laid down, although it is not confirmed if this was attained. The flights that took place, in both daylight and at night, were made within an envelope of 410mph (660km/h), between 100 and 600ft (30 to 180m), over a course laid out in Libya. All data readings were forwarded to the RAE and IAM for evaluation, the principal recipient of all findings at that time being seen as the TSR.2 programme, which was beginning to take shape on the drawing boards at Weybridge and Preston. With the cancellation of the TSR.2, the data was placed at

the disposal of the industry and services generally.

None of the aircraft went back to squadron service. WD950 and WH648 went to No.15 MU Wroughton, while WJ573 became Instructional Airframe 7656M at Henlow. WJ576 went to Boulton Paul to be converted for ECM trials, after which it underwent a further conversion, to T.17 standard, as did WF890 and WH664.

Central Fighter Establishment

The CFE's association with the Canberra, at its West Raynham base, was not long-lived. Even the Station Flight aircraft, PR.7, WT529, only lasted two weeks before crashing, killing two senior commanders of Establishment branches. During the annual Exercise *Stronghold*, in September 1956, two AI-equipped trials aircraft from the RRE at Pershore flew with the CFE, B.2, WH660, fitted with AI.Mk.18 telemetry and B.6, WH953, carrying AI.Mk.20.

This No.228 OCU formation includes two of the T.11s that joined the TFS: WJ610/'G' and WJ975/'E'. Author's collection

(Below) Seen in No.85 Squadron markings at Alconbury, on 4 July 1969, WH724/'C' had been converted to T.17 standard. D. Menard/George Pennick

(Bottom) T.4, WT486, of the Wildenrath Station Flight, carries the snake insignia of No.88 Squadron, stationed at the German base. Ray Deacon

The Target Facility Squadron (TFS), formed out of No.228 OCU in 1961, had a fleet of six Canberra T.11s – WH714, WH724, WH903, WH904, WJ610 and WJ975 – at West Raynham. Extensive use was made of these aircraft, for both radar-interception exercises, where they became the targets, or for banner target towing. The TFS also had T.4 WT485 on charge, and all seven aircraft went with the unit when it moved to Binbrook on 25 April 1963. It was renumbered as No.85 Squadron, and the CFE's links with the Canberra were severed.

Miscellanea

Because of its availability, many RAF stations, whether they were Canberra operators or not, had a Canberra allocated to the base for both instrument-flying training and pilot continuation training, as well as Station Flight aircraft. Communications Units, who flew many varied types, found the Canberra to be a useful aircraft for many of their requirements and some MUs employed them for ferry-crew return flights.

Continuation training was an element of the Bomber Command Air Crew Holding Unit (BCHU), formed at Coningsby in January 1958. Operating with a number of B.2s and T.4s, the unit's assignment was to maintain aircrews' flying proficiency, following the disbanding of Canberra squadrons, until they could be posted to another unit. The BCHU's task in this respect was completed early in 1961.

Manby, in Lincolnshire, was home to the RAF Handling Squadron. Its task was to assess the handling of a new type of aircraft about to enter squadron service and to compile the Pilot's Notes. It usually received an early production aircraft, but, in the case of the Canberra, the second B.2 prototype, VX169, was delivered on 3 March 1951. The handling tests were completed within three weeks. Three years later, in November 1954, the fourth production B.6, WH948, went to Manby for its assessment, before joining No.101 Squadron the following month. In January 1958, the Handling Squadron accepted B(I).8 XH209, before it went to No.59 Squadron at Geilenkirchen.

Another Bomber Command division was the Acceptance and Modification Unit (BCAMU), based at Lindholme in Yorkshire. During 1953, the unit began receiving Canberras, to become trials aircraft for various Bomber Command-promoted modifications and installation changes. As with

---

Station Flight Canberras

Canberra T.4s were used extensively in Station Flights, many individual aircraft serving with several Flights over the years. The following aircraft have been confirmed as flying with the Station Flights listed and sometimes a particular aircraft later returned to a Flight where it had previously served, this being shown by the number of times, in brackets.

WE188	Hemswell, Waddington, Upwood, Wyton	WJ872	Akrotiri
WE190	Wyton	WJ873	Wyton
WE193	Upwood	WJ874	Gaydon, Binbrook, Coningsby
WE194	Wyton, Laarbruch	WJ875	Wyton
WE195	Wyton	WJ876	Scampton, Binbrook, Waddington, Akrotiri (x2)
WH841	Geilenkirchen, Brüggen, Wildenrath		
WH842	Brüggen	WJ877	Hemswell, Binbrook (x2), Upwood, Coningsby, Wyton
WH843	Geilenkirchen, Laarbruch		
WH846	Laarbruch	WJ879	Wittering (x2), Hemswell, Finningley, Wyton
WH848	Marham, Binbrook, Gaydon	WJ880	Gütersloh, Laarbruch (x2)
WH849	Marham, Coningsby, Binbrook	WJ881	Akrotiri (x3)
WH850	Honington, Cottesmore, Wildenrath, Laarbruch	WN467	Binbrook, Wittering, Honington, Brüggen
		WT475	Binbrook, Waddington
WJ857	Wittering	WT476	Waddington
WJ859	Scampton, Waddington, Coningsby	WT477	Wyton
WJ860	Binbrook	WT478	Akrotiri
WJ861	Marham, Weston Zoyland, Wyton, Laarbruch	WT479	Upwood, Wildenrath
		WT481	Akrotiri
WJ862	Scampton, Upwood (x2), Binbrook, Brüggen, Laarbruch	WT482	Gütersloh, Wildenrath, Wahn. Brüggen
		WT483	Laarbruch (x2)
WJ863	Cottesmore, Honington, Akrotiri	WT484	Laarbruch
WJ864	Wittering, Gaydon	WT486	Wildenrath (x2)
WJ866	Wyton	WT487	Wahn, Wildenrath
WJ868	Gütersloh, Geilenkirchen, Laarbruch (x2), Brüggen	WT488	Wyton
		WT489	Binbrook
WJ869	Gaydon	WT490	Wyton
WJ870	Laarbruch, Ahlhorn, Brüggen	XH583	Brüggen, Laarbruch (x2)

Instructional Airframes

The following aircraft have been confirmed as serving with the Schools of Technical Training and Radio Schools indicated. Ground instructional airframes have been confirmed at the bases listed, for airframe instruction, fire and rescue training, plus battle-damage repair instruction.

No.1 SoTT, Halton

Canberra B.2
7386M (ex-WF907), 7387M (ex-WD999), 7657M (ex-WH695), 7912M (ex-WK131), 7913M (ex-WK132), 7914M (ex-WK133)

Canberra T.4
7636M (ex-WJ878), 8491M (ex-WJ880), 8492M (ex-WJ872)

Canberra PR.7
8548M (ex-WT507), 8549M (ex-WT534)

No.2 SoTT, Cosford

Canberra B.2
8722M (ex-WJ640), 8762M (ex-WH740), 8763M (ex-WH665), 8780M (ex-WK102), 8871M (ex-WJ565)

Canberra PR.3
7843M (ex-WE145), 8868M (ex-WH775)

Canberra T.4
8102M (ex-WT486)

Canberra B.6
8101M (ex-WH984), 8344M (ex-WH960), 8869M (ex-WH957), 8870M (ex-WH964)

Canberra PR.7
8063M (ex-WT536)

Canberra PR.9
8746M (ex-XH171), 8782M (ex-XH136)

No.4 SoTT, St Athan

Canberra B.2
7659M (ex-WH701), 7590M (ex-WH668), 8440M (ex-WD935)

Canberra B.5
7631M (ex-VX185)

Canberra B.6
9052M (ex-WJ717)

No.9 SoTT, Newton

Canberra T.4
8643m (ex-WJ867)   *(continued overleaf)*

Instructional Airframes *(continued)*

No.10 SoTT, Kirkham	**Fire and Rescue Training**
Canberra B.6	Brawby
7158M (ex-WJ765)	Canberra B.2, 8735M (ex-WJ681)
No.12 SoTT, Melksham	Chivenor
	Canberra B.2, 8747M (ex-WJ629)
Canberra B.2	
7620M (ex-WD959), 7658M (ex-WH884),	Coltishall
7796M (ex-WJ676)	Canberra PR.3, 8740M (ex-WE173)
	Canberra PR.7, 8728M (ex-WT532)
No.1 RS, Locking	
	Coningsby
Canberra B.2	Canberra PR.7, 8726M (ex-WJ815)
7589M (ex-WD936)	
	Manston
No.2 RS, Yatesbury	Canberra B.2, 9093M (ex-WK124)
	Canberra PR.3, 8049M (ex-WE173)
Canberra B.2	
7460M (ex-WD958), 7623M (ex-WH735)	Wyton
	Canberra B.2, 8716M (ex-WJ977)
	Canberra B.2, 8887M (ex-WK162)

Ground Instructional Airframes

Bassingbourn	Canberra PR.7, 8668M (ex-WJ821)
Binbrook	Canberra B.6, 7546M (ex-WJ769)
Brawdy	Canberra B.2, 8735M (ex-WJ681)
Chivenor	Canberra B.2, 8747M (ex-WJ629)
Colerne	Canberra B.2, 7764M (ex-WD990)
Cottesmore	Canberra B(I).8, 8204M (ex-XM271)
Little Rissington	Canberra B.2, 7802M (ex-WD996)
Manby	Canberra PR.7, 8184M (ex-WT520)
Marham	Canberra B.2, 8490M (ex-WH703)
Watton	Canberra B.2, 7637M (ex-WF887)
Wildenrath	Canberra B.2, 8129M (ex-WH779)
Wyton	Canberra B.2, 8761M (ex-WJ977)

Battle-Damage Repair Flight

Abingdon
Canberra B.2, 8864M (ex-WJ678)
Canberra PR.3, 8652M (ex-WH794)
Canberra T.4, 8914M (ex-WH844)

Marham
Canberra B.2, 8693M (ex-WH863)

St Mawgan
Canberra T.4, 8683M (ex-WJ870)

Wattisham
Canberra B.2, 8664M (ex-WJ603)

Wyton
Canberra PR.7, 8695M (ex-WJ817)

RAF College Engineering Flight

Canberra B.2, 8755M (ex-WJ637)
Canberra B(I).8, 8198M (ex-WT339)

---

many trials, some were accepted and incorporated into squadron service, the necessary engineering usually being undertaken by MUs. Those that were just 'good ideas at the time' became unrecorded history. The BCAMU's title was changed to the more manageable Command Modification Centre (CMC) in 1954, and in 1956 it was moved to Hemswell, before the Lincolnshire airfield became a Thor ICBM complex, managed by No.97 Squadron.

Six Schools of Technical Training (SoTT) had Canberras on their syllabuses, with courses spread through airframes, engines and avionics. The schools were No.1 SoTT at Halton, No.2 at Cosford, No.4 at St Athan, No.9 at Newton, No.10 at Kirkham and No.12 at Melksham, while No.1 Radio School (RS) at Locking and No.2RS at Yatesbury were also recipients. Instructional Airframe numbers, suffixed by an 'M', replaced the serial numbers and the majority of production variants were included.

The Industry

The aviation industry's utilization of existing airframes, to perfect the evolution of new products, was met by the Canberra in nearly every aspect of development. In the realms of turbojet and rocket motors, it flew as a testbed for every major British manufacturer, while the fact that well over fifty different airframes served to advance the fields of avionics and radar research illustrates its importance in these spheres. The safe evacuation from a malfunctioning military aeroplane, and the extension of its range of operations, were both enhanced by Canberra trials aircraft.

The world of civil aviation was not ignored either, for both Comet and Boeing 707 engine-silencer trials were conducted on a Canberra in the mid-1950s.

The main participants in this extensive domain of testing and research are listed under the companies involved.

Armstrong Siddeley Motors Limited

Armstrong Siddeley's only big turbojet was the Sapphire, which was developed from the P.9 design, inherited from Metropolitan Vickers when that company withdrew from the field of aircraft engines, combined with Armstrong Siddeley's own experience with the earlier ASX engine. The Sapphire progressed through flight testing of the 7,000lb (3,180kg) thrust ASSa.1 in Lancastrian Mk.2 VM733, to the ASSa.2, rated at 7,600lb (3,455kg) thrust, in Meteor F.8 WA820, together with Hastings TE583. The 8,000lb (3,640kg) thrust ASSa.3 replaced the earlier ASSa.1 in VM733, and the ASSa.7, producing 10,500lb (4,775kg) static thrust, was flown in a ventral nacelle housing on Avro Ashton Mk.2 WB491.

The Canberra came into the programme when the fifth production B.2, WD933, arrived at Bitteswell on 13 April 1951, straight from the line at Preston. Its Avons were replaced by two Sapphire ASSa.3s, developing 7,220lb (3,280kg) thrust and the aircraft made its maiden flight with them on 14 August. Only a couple of months' flying were undertaken with the ASSa.3s, for much of the testing of this version of the Sapphire had been completed on the Lancastrian, and WD933 went back into the shops to be fitted with a pair of 8,300lb (3,765kg) thrust Sapphire ASSa.6 engines. The installation was completed for a first flight from Bitteswell in April 1952, and testing of this version continued for two years.

In April 1954, the aircraft went into the shops once again and, on 13 August, it first flew under the power of two ASSa.7s, each producing 10,300lb (4,680kg) static thrust. Flight testing with these engines, and the use of WD933 as a testbed, came to an abrupt conclusion on 10 November 1954. New Zealander Jim Starky, the company's Superintendent of Flying, with test observer Peter Taylor on board, had the port engine fail at 37,000ft (11,300m). While descending for a return to base, the starboard engine shut down, due to a spot of 'finger trouble', and a dead-stick landing had to be made somewhere. On breaking cloud at 2,000ft (600m), they found Bitteswell below and Starky brought WD933 in for a wheels-up landing on the grass alongside the main runway. While sliding on the grass after a perfect touch-down, the aircraft slewed to starboard, caught the edge of the runway and flipped over on to its back. Fortunately, both crew members survived, but Jim Starky had to be hospitalized and, not long afterwards, he retired from test flying. WD933 was a write-off.

Sapphire trials were continued with B.2 WK141, which arrived at Bitteswell on 14 January 1955 and resumed ASSa.7 testing on 7 May. Another B.2, WK163, also joined the programme on 28 January for re-engining with a pair of ASSa.7s, and a third Canberra, B.2 WV787, which had been at Bitteswell since 10 September 1952, was fitted with reheat-equipped ASSa.7s, for a first flight with the system in March 1954.

The completion of the Sapphire test programme, with variants due to enter service in Hunter F.2s and F.5s, as well as Victor B.1s, saw Canberra WK163 leave Bitteswell on 2 December 1954, later to join Napier's rocket-motor testing at Luton, in May 1956. WV787 was refitted with its standard Avons, before leaving Armstrong Siddeley for Boulton Paul's Defford enclave, on 5 June 1958, where it was modified in preparation for radar trials with Ferranti.

Armstrong Siddeley's work on an expendable turbojet for pilotless aircraft began in the late 1940s. Named the Viper, the ASV.2 weighed only 365lb (165.5kg), but with a simple seven-stage axial compressor, it produced 1,575lb (714.25kg) thrust. First test flown in the rear fuselage of Lancaster Mk.III, SW342, it was developed into a longer-life engine for piloted aircraft and in its ASV.8 version, developing 1,750lb (795kg) static thrust, it was scheduled for testing on a Canberra. WK141, previously used in the Sapphire programme, had an ASV.8 installed on a special pylon under the starboard wing and the combination became airborne for the first time in September 1958. Viper test flying was conducted from both Bitteswell and Filton, in preparation for the merger of Armstrong Siddeley Motors and Bristol Engines, into a new company named Bristol Siddeley, on 18 September 1959. In 1961, the ASV.8 was replaced by a 2,460lb (1,115kg) thrust Viper ASV.11 and, with Bitteswell now closing down, testing of the new engine took place from Filton. Test flying of the Viper finished on 15 January 1963 and two months later, on 8 March, WK141 was struck off charge, to be consigned to the fire dump at Prestwick.

Boulton Paul Aircraft Limited

Having been an aircraft designing and manufacturing company since its incorporation in June 1934, Boulton Paul's substantial involvement with the Canberra is believed to have begun on 24 December 1952. Because its airfield at Sleighford had only grass runways, the company's Canberra work was engineered at a comprehensive outstation sited at Defford, between 1952 and 1965. There was also the added advantage of not having to tow aircraft across a road from the airfield to the workshops, as at Sleighford. Straight off the production line, Canberra B.2 WH671 was delivered on loan to Defford, for Avon de-icing trials, on behalf of the RAE. On 8 August 1953, the aircraft was taken off RAF charge, and the following year it went to Hucknall to work for Rolls-Royce, until 1961.

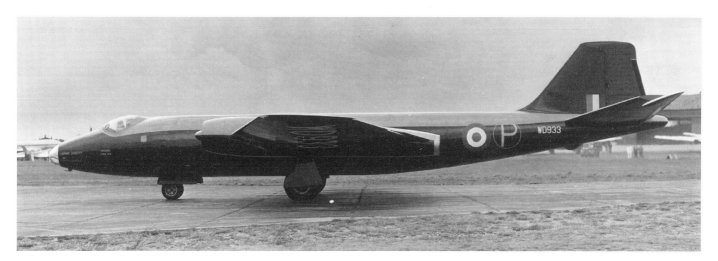

(Above) WD933, powered by a pair of Sapphire ASSa.6 engines, lines up on the threshold at Farnborough's 1952 SBAC Display. Author's collection

The third prototype A.1, VN828, following conversion by Boulton Paul, flies in formation with WJ646. Both aircraft show by their nose profiles that they are serving with the RRE. Author's collection

Boulton Paul's conversion of B(I).8, WT327, to facilitate Ferranti's AI.23 radar trial requirements. Author's collection

From the beginning of 1953, a continual stream of Canberras passed through the company's workshops, for conversions specified by the MoS and the RRE. It was in this respect that Petter's original design concept – of the Canberra as a set of five independent primary structures – came into its own. This 'mix-and-match' arrangement enabled Boulton Paul quite easily to substitute front fuselage sections with replacements configured for specific requirements. When VN828, the third A.1 prototype, arrived on 21 May 1955, having already been with the Telecommunications Research Establishment (TRE) at Defford, for *Green Satin* trials, the whole front fuselage was supplanted by a B(I).8 unit. Further modifications were made to the nose section, which was extended to carry AI.Mk.18 radar within a dielectric nose-cone. The following year, B(I).8 WT327 was engineered for further AI.Mk.23 trials, which were conducted by the Ferranti Flying Unit (FFU) at Turnhouse.

A similar front-fuselage section change was carried out on Handley Page-built B.2 WJ643, for Ferranti. It arrived from Turnhouse on 16 February 1956 and returned a year later, on 18 February 1957. On 20 August 1956, B.2 WJ734 arrived for a trial installation of an extended nose radome, which provided the Canberra T.11. Following acceptance trials at the A&AEE, Boulton Paul manufactured a further seven front fuselages, in order that MUs

could complete the T.11 conversions. Two later, similar modifications, to meet the Swedish Air Force Tp.52 requirements, were also engineered at Defford.

The company carried out the conversions on twenty-one B.6s, to produce B.6(BS) variants, equipped with the *Blue Shadow* radar system that produced the 'wave guide' strake on the starboard side of the fuselage. The use of the French Nord AS.30 air-to-air missile as a Canberra weapon was investigated and WH967, a B.6 that had been modified to B.15 standard, was delivered to Boulton Paul, for an AS.30 to be fitted on a special pylon under each wing for handling trials.

One out-of-the-ordinary piece of research was conducted with Avro-built B.2 WK161, which, having previously been used by the RAE for armament trials, was delivered to Boulton Paul on 14 January 1957. There were several years of testing and assessing various radar absorbant materials applied to WK141, and one of the company's own designs, Balliol T.2 WG125, was used during this programme. The trials were completed at the end of 1963 and the material coating was removed from the Canberra, before it was sold for spares.

In April 1963, a Ministry of Defence project to convert some Canberras into flying classrooms was placed with Boulton Paul. Three B.2s, WH868, WJ645 and WJ647, were supplied, but it is not confirmed

whether any airframe modifications had actually been made before the scheme was abandoned. WH868 was refurbished for sale to Peru, but the other two aircraft were sold for scrap at No.15 MU Wroughton, but modifications may have been in hand before the classroom project was dropped.

Bristol Aero Engines Limited

The earlier gas-turbine engine work of Bristol Aero Engines was centred on propjets. Its first turbojet project, the Phoebus, was in effect a Proteus propjet minus the propeller, reduction gear and turbine; it had less than twenty-four hours flying time when it was abandoned. However, Bristol's Chief Engineer Frank Owen considered that the company was well placed to design a large jet engine, and a projected thrust of 9,000lb (4,090kg) was given to the Project Office for their target.

By 6 May 1950, the engine, named Olympus, was having its initial bench runs and producing 9,140lb (4,145kg) static thrust. A flight engine giving 9,750lb (4,430kg) thrust was ready by December 1951 but, because of the airframes currently available for flight testing, this output had to be de-rated to 8,000lb (3,630kg) thrust. In this state, the engine was designated the Olympus 99. The Canberra was considered a suitable flying testbed and, on 13 December 1951, B.2 WD952 was delivered to Patchway, the company's flight test centre on the opposite side of Filton airfield from the aircraft manufacturing complex.

The conversion of WD952 was completed within eighteen months, so that, on 6 August 1952, Bristol's Assistant Chief Test Pilot, Wg Cdr W.F. 'Wally' Gibb, with engine observer Joe Piper, took the Olympus into the air for the first time. With a lot more thrust than usual, WD952 was a much more lively aeroplane and its critical Mach number of 0.82 was exceeded at 50,000ft (15,200m) on the power of just one Olympus. Early test flights at 60,000ft (18,300m) posed a problem, as the maximum Mach number and minimum flying speed began to converge. An anonymous joker recorded the fact that flying at extreme altitude was analogous 'to riding a unicycle backwards, while blindfolded'.

Test flying at those altitudes became quite routine and it was pointed out that the world altitude record of 59,446ft (18,119m), set by John Cunningham in the modified third production Vampire F.1 TG278 on 23 March 1948, was regularly being exceeded.

Everyone connected with WD952 at Filton, Bristols, English Electric and Lucas saw good public relations in breaking Cunningham's record and the slide rules were produced, to work out the figures for the attempt. Precise fuel weights were calculated for a triangular flight course.

Everyone had great faith in the Olympus and the Canberra. On 4 May 1953, Gibb took off from Filton and climbed at 3,000ft/min (915m/min) to 50,000ft (15,200m). He levelled out and burned off fuel, until the pre-calculated 90 gallons (410litres) was left, this being considered adequate for the actual record attempt. WD952 started climbing again, until, at an indicated altitude of 63,000ft (19,200m), both engines flamed out. Gibb inflated his pressure suit and switched off all electrics, to conserve the batteries. A slow glide down to 50,000ft was followed by an acceleration to 40,000ft (12,200m), when the engines were relit – first time, as usual – and the aircraft returned to Filton. Later, the FAI ratified the altitude reached as being 63,668ft (19,406m) – twice the height of Mount Everest, plus more than another 5,000ft (1,500m)!

In 1954, the Olympus 99s were replaced by two Olympus 101s, each giving 11,000lb

B.2, WD952, powered by two Olympus 99 engines, flies at the 1953 SBAC Display, with its altitude record duly noted on the nose. Author's collection

(5,000kg) thrust and, following over a year's test flying, these engines were replaced by a pair of 12,000lb- (5,445kg-) thrust Olympus 102s. The PR staff felt that, with these engines, the previous altitude record could be bettered and, although Wally Gibb was not too enthusiastic, he agreed to make the fresh attempt. On 29 August 1955, a similar triangular course was flown, but, when he had landed, Gibb was not sure if the required 3 per cent increase over the previous record had been achieved. Later, ratification was given to a new record of 65,876ft

(20,079m) and the pilot was presented with half a burnt-out turbine blade from one of the engines, which had been mounted for him as a memento – the blade was one of six that had been burnt in half during the flight. The aircraft's record achievements were emblazoned in neat sign writing on the port side of the nose.

Seven months later, on 12 March 1956, test pilot Paul Falconer and observer Peter Little lifted WD952 off Runway 28 at Filton. At about 50ft (15m) above the threshold, the port engine failed, and Falconer

Bristol's replacement Canberra, following the accident to WD952, was B.2, WH713. It was fitted with a pair of Olympus 104 engines and was photographed en route to the 1957 Farnborough Display. Author's collection

(Top) VN813, the second A.1 prototype, powered by Rolls-Royce Nene engines and still with the dorsal fin strake, lands at Farnborough, after demonstrating its de Havilland Spectre rocket motor. Author's collection

(Middle) B.6, WJ755, carried a cine camera under the port wing to record Spectre test firings.
Author's collection

(Bottom) De Havilland used B.2, WF909, as a testbed for their Gyron Junior turbojet. Here, the combination lifts off Farnborough's operational runway at the 1957 display. Author's collection

was just able to clear a cottage on the other side of the boundary road, before crash-landing in an adjacent field. The aircraft bounced over a hedge, but had a coming-together with several hundred years' growth of English oak, which removed the port wing, together with its Olympus. Both crewmen were speedily recovered by helicopter, but the aircraft's damage was such that it was despatched to No.39 MU Colerne, where it was scrapped in September.

Bristol Aero Engines looked for a replacement aircraft and the ex-No.15 Squadron B.2, WH713, was delivered to Filton on 2 January 1957. Two Olympus 104s, each producing 13,000lb (5,910kg) static thrust, were installed and the aircraft, with silencers fitted on its jet pipe nozzles, was one of four Canberra engine testbeds at the 1957 SBAC Display. The aircraft continued on Olympus development for another two years, before being struck off charge on 7 September 1959 and sold as scrap on 26 May 1960. Further Olympus test flying was carried out on Avro Ashton Mk.3 WB493.

The merger of Armstrong Siddeley and Bristol Aero Engines, to form Bristol Siddeley Engines, brought Viper development to Patchway and, in 1958, Canberra B.2 WK163, a former Sapphire testbed, spent time at Filton on Viper nacelle testing. It is presumed that the starboard underwing pylon fitting, as on WK141, was utilized, but the programme was quite short-lived, as the aircraft is recorded as being engaged on trials at RRE Defford in 1959. As far as the Canberra and Patchway are concerned, that was the end of the association.

De Havilland

The scope of the de Havilland Group was quite varied. While the aircraft-manufacturing company had no interest in using the Canberra, both D.H. Propellers Limited and the D.H. Engine Company used several examples.

The earliest Canberra to arrive at Hatfield was VN813, the Nene-powered second A.1 prototype, which had been modified for the engine company by Folland Aircraft, at their Chilbolton works in Hampshire, during 1953/54. They were well able to handle Canberra work – after all, it was their Managing Director who had designed it! The aircraft was delivered to Hatfield on 9 July 1954, to be used as a test platform for the D.H. Spectre HTP-fuelled, variable-thrust rocket motor, which was being developed for Saunders Roe's SR.53 mixed-powerplant research prototype. On VN813, the test motor was fitted in a bulged ventral installation at the rear of the bomb-bay, with a stainless-steel protection covering over the underside of the rear fuselage. Following extensive ground running, the flight programme began on 18 December 1956.

Development of several Spectre variants continued until the end of 1959, when, due to a lack of funding, the programme finished, but not before VN813 had been joined on 23 April 1959 by Canberra B.6 WJ755, which had also been modified by Folland. On 8 December 1955, B.2 WF909 arrived at Hatfield, to become a flying testbed for the 7,000lb (3,180kg) thrust D.H. Gyron Junior engine. One engine was installed in the port nacelle and the first flight was made on 28 May 1957. Later in the year, a Gyron Junior was fitted in the starboard nacelle and full flight testing was carried out until the aircraft was broken up at Hatfield in 1962. During the trials, with the engine destined for the Buccaneer S.1, a complete Buccaneer intake was tested on WF909's port nacelle.

Two years before D.H. Engines received VN813, on 25 April 1952, D.H. Propellers took delivery of B.2 WD992. Besides propellers, the company's sphere of operations included guided weapons and the Canberra's role was to assist in the development of

an air-to-air missile (AAM), codenamed *Blue Jay*. WD992 was to be the flying platform for the missile's guidance system, before it went into production as the D.H. Firestreak, which became the principal armament of the Sea Vixen and later Gloster Javelin variants, as well as early marks of the Lightning. The missile's evolution was a quite protracted affair. Canberra B.2 WH735, a brand-new aircraft, joined the programme on 15 July 1953, to be fitted with an AI.Mk.18 scanner in a revised nose-cone. A year later, on 25 August 1954, B.2 WK135 arrived to become another member of the team. On 9 September 1955, yet another Canberra, B.2 WH700, arrived at Hatfield to become a *Blue Jay* trials aircraft, and when B.2 WJ978 was delivered on 29 March 1956, Hatfield was awash with Canberras.

No.12 Joint Service Trials Unit (JSTU) at the WRE at Woomera had originally been set up at Hatfield, to conduct *Blue Jay* air firing trials. On 4 February 1957, WH700 left Hatfield for Australia, never to return to the UK. It was retained at Woomera after the completion of de Havilland's programme and eventually was allocated to the Parafield Museum in 1987. Canberra B.2 WJ644 went to D.H. Propellers at the end of 1954, after having a modified nose-cone fitted by Boulton Paul at Defford and this aircraft also went to Woomera, where it became a member of 12JSTU for *Blue Jay* acceptance trial launchings. Later in the decade, WJ644 became a test firing aircraft for *Blue Jay's* successor, the D.H. Red Top AAM.

In Australia, *Blue Jay* programme Canberras were based at Edinburgh Field, a short flying distance from the WRE range. The trial firing aircraft had the infra-red homing missiles mounted on underwing pylons, and Meteor U15/U16 or Jindivik drones were used as targets. The guidance scanner was mounted in the Canberra's nose behind a dielectric cone, while the

A grainy frame from a cine film shows B.2, WJ644 firing a Blue Jay **test round, during acceptance trials on the WRE range.** Ian Mactaggart

The Short SC.9 shortly after being built at Belfast. Author's collection

launch system's electronics were accommodated in the bomb-bay. Acceptance trials began in September 1957, but several frustrating problems arose, necessitating modifications to the control system actuators, and it was towards the end of 1959 before the trials came to a satisfactory conclusion. Out of twenty high-altitude firings, only three failed and five direct hits were scored on the target aircraft.

Short Bros had PR.9 XH132 ready for collection on 9 June 1959, but it was not allocated for squadron service. The aircraft was passed to MoS charge on 31 March 1960 and was put back into the Belfast works for modifications to be incorporated in order that it could become a test aircraft for D.H. Propellers. While the *Blue Jay* acceptance trials were progressing, the company was engaged on *Sky Flash*, a Mach 3 AAM that had originally been designated Firestreak Mk.4. When *Sky Flash* went into production as the standard weapon for later Lightning variants, it was called Red Top. A completely new nose was engineered for XH132 by Short Bros, with a collection of radomes different from those on any other Canberra, and it acquired a new designation, the Short SC.9. Electronics were also incorporated in special wing-tip tanks for the *Sky Flash* guidance system. These housings were not exactly on the tips as on standard Bomber Command aircraft, but fitted under the wing about three feet from the tip. The guidance system had been developed by RRE Pershore for the aircraft and, starting in January 1972, the flying trials were shared between Pershore and Hatfield.

On 1 December 1976, XH132 went to the RAE and that heralded the end of the de Havilland Group's employment of Canberras.

English Electric Company

The building of seventy-five Canberra B.2s each was subcontracted by English Electric to A.V. Roe & Co. Ltd and Handley Page Ltd; this represented the two companies' total involvement with the aircraft. However, English Electric, the designer and manufacturer of all new-build prototypes, and the major constructor of nearly all variants, was much more concerned with the aircraft's development. Consequently, many examples of the aircraft were engaged in the numerous phases that go to make a successful operational aeroplane.

All four A.1 prototypes were significantly involved in perfecting the Canberra, although the Nene-powered second prototype, VN813, was only used for a year, before going to Rolls-Royce at Hucknall for engine development and finishing up with de Havilland Engines. Tip-tank trials were flown on VN850, the fourth prototype, before it too went to Hucknall for general Avon testing. Two B.2 prototypes had been constructed at Preston. Of these, VX165, the first, shared its time between the manufacturers and the A&AEE, before crashing at the Establishment on 15 August 1951, just over a year after its maiden flight. The second, VX169, flew for ten years, some of which were spent at the RAE, at the A&AEE, where the main armament trials were conducted, and at Manby's Handling Squadron. The aircraft finished at Shoeburyness's Proof and Experimental Establishment (PEE) on 4 May 1960. Three production B.2s, WD958, WD959 and WD960, were also operated by English Electric for varying periods, in conjunction with the RAE and A&AEE.

The prototype PR.3, VX181, was retained by the manufacturer for nearly a year, before it spread its wings and served with all the UK Establishments, as well as spending some time at Woomera. Camera installations, Sperry's vertical gyro, Ferranti and Litton inertial platforms were all evaluated on the aircraft, which was scrapped at Pershore in September 1969, nearly twenty years after its maiden flight. The ninth production B.2, WD937, was transferred to English Electric straight off the line and was used as a general trials aircraft, before being registered G-ATZW for use as the company's support aircraft, in a striking overall glossy black colour scheme. After seventeen years' service, the aircraft made its last flight on 10 November 1967 before being broken up at Samlesbury.

Handley Page's second production B.2, WJ595, was flown to Warton from Radlett, for flight testing of the ventral gun pack that was proposed for the B(I).6 and B(I).8 variants. XH133, the fifth production PR.9 built at Belfast, also went to Warton, for camera installation trials involving the gyro-stabilized F.49. WT328, the third production B(I).8 was also transferred to English Electric straight off the line, on 31 October 1955, and was engaged on type acceptance trials in association with Boscombe Down, when it crashed into the English Channel on 7 May 1956, due to tailplane actuator failure.

English Electric became a part of the British Aircraft Corporation (BAC) in 1960 and, in testing programmes with later BAC products, Canberras were used as chase aircraft during test flights. Flight trials of Concorde, Lightning, Strikemaster, Jaguar, Tornado and the TSR.2 were all accompanied by Canberras. Four B.2s,

WD937, WE121, WG789 and WJ627, are known to have been used, as were PR.3s WH793 and WH774, and B.6 WH952.

Ferranti Limited

The Ferranti Flying Unit (FFU) was formed around 8 August 1952, with a Dakota, TS423, and Sea Fury T.20, VX301. In October, its first jet aircraft, Vampire FB.5 WG801, joined the unit at Turnhouse and two years later, on 7 September 1954, the first Canberra arrived, a Handley Page-built B.2, WJ643. This aircraft remained with Ferranti for fifteen years, being used for, among other things, AI.Mk.23 Airpass testing, where it was the airborne target for the radar installation in the nose of the Dakota. On 16 February 1956, it went to Boulton Paul at Defford, for a B(I).8 front fuselage to be installed and the FFU had it back on 18 February 1957. While it was away, the AI.Mk.23 airborne trials were put on hold, although VX185 came to the unit in April 1956 and stayed for eighteen months. This was the one and only Canberra B.5, which had been converted to B(I).8 standard at Warton, in 1954. (As a point of interest, Rolls-Royce had no record about one of VX185's engines and very little about the other!)

Because of these engines, a senior RAE pilot was asked to go up to Turnhouse, to try out the aircraft. On 18 October 1956, he took the aircraft for a test flight and decided that its performance was not suitable for a particular programme that the FFU was considering. However, the aircraft continued with the unit for another year and some flights were not without

During the test schedule with B.2 prototype, VX165, time was made for a photocall. 'Bee' recalls bringing the aircraft up to the Lancaster carrying Charles Sims, doyen of photographers, in the rear turret. Sims was changing plates and did not see the approach. Some of the glazing had been removed from the turret in which the photographer was working. When Sims at last looked up, he almost fell out of the turret with surprise seeing how close the Canberra was. The Lancaster pilot later commented on getting a strong nose-down trim change during the flight! Author's collection
(Right) One of the test programmes involved WD956 being flown without the canopy. This was to determine the size and shape of the deflector shield, which was the only protection a pilot had, should the canopy be lost, or released prior to an ejection. Three flights were made; in Beamont's opinion, the last, flown at 523mph (841.6km/h), was enough! Beamont's face was taped for protection, as was the ejector seat, to protect the mechanisms. Author's collection

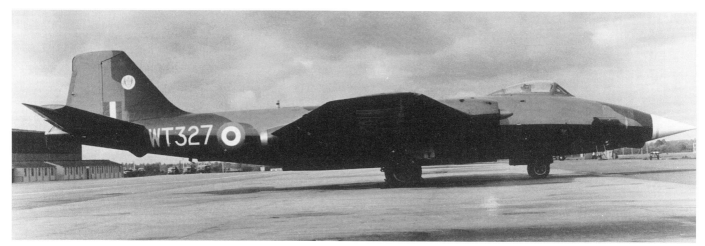

B(I).8, WT327, seen here carrying the badge of the RRE, was used at Turnhouse for several radar trials programmes. The test equipment was housed in a recontoured nose specific to the shape of the radar unit. Author's collection

incident. A new FFU pilot, flying VX185 for the first time, had previous B.2 experience. Due to problems with the flap-selection mechanism, the B.2's selection lever in the cockpit had only two positions – UP or DOWN. With VX185 having a B(I).8 cockpit, it had a variable-position flap selector. The pilot initiated a practice overshoot and selected flap UP, and the flap retracted on one side only. Recovery was achieved by a smart application of full aileron. The FFU finished with VX185 in October 1957, when it went from Turnhouse to No.15 MU at Wroughton. This left the unit with WJ643, and WT327, to carry out the Laser Ranger and Marked Target Seeker (LRMTS) programme.

WT327, a fresh B(I).8, had been delivered to Turnhouse on 2 August 1956, to have AI.Mk.23 installed in its nose, ready for a fresh phase of its development. Much of the engineering was done by Boulton Paul and, when the aircraft was operating in the spring of 1957, a pattern developed with WT327 intercepting VX185, which was flown as the target. WJ643 had spent some time at Defford, but its return to Turnhouse meant that, for the first time, the unit had another AI.Mk.23-equipped aircraft, should WT327 become unserviceable; in fact, many sorties were flown in which both aircraft intercepted each other. In May 1958, W.E.W. Petter had a flight in WT327 and was vociferous about the ghastly seating arrangement. When tactfully reminded that he had designed it,

The AI.23 operator's seat in WT327, about which Petter made some succinct comments. Author's collection

he retorted that he had not designed 'that one – it was designed by a committee!'

This aircraft had a Marconi doppler unit installed and an observer from the company attempted to carry out trials. On returning to his headquarters, he gave a good report on the unit's operations at all altitudes. This surprised the FFU, because only two flights had been made, during which the observer had been violently airsick and the equipment had gone unserviceable on both occasions.

In August 1959, Canberra B.2 WJ627, which had previously served with No.149 Squadron at Gütersloh, joined the unit. It needed a considerable amount of work before it would come up to the required standard, which meant that it could not be finally air-tested and signed off as airworthy until 15 December. Short's Canberra SC.9 XH132 had a spell with the FFU in May 1960 and a further ancient B.2, WD953, was allocated from RAE stock on 30 October, to assist in AI.Mk.23B trials. Samlesbury had to go over this aircraft before it could be cleared, on 11 February 1961.

Canberra B.2 WV787 had been modified by Boulton Paul, to take Ferranti's *Blue Parrot* weapon-aiming radar, for the Blackburn NA.39 (which became the Buccaneer when it went into production). It joined the FFU on 28 October 1959 and worked from Turnhouse until 2 December 1963, when it went to Flight Refuelling Limited at Tarrant Rushton, to become the T.22 aerodynamic trials aircraft.

Other Canberras gradually left Turnhouse in the course of a few years, as work was run down. In September 1972, the last one, WJ643, which had been with the unit for nearly twenty years, left for the RAE at Farnborough.

Flight Refuelling Limited

Canberra B.2 WH734, the first of the type to arrive at FRL's Tarrant Rushton operating base, landed on 2 July 1953. Its task was to be the trials aircraft for the company's Mk.16 Hose Drum Unit (HDU), which was being evolved for the Valiant BK.1, the RAF's first jet-powered flight-refuelling tanker. Its arrival heralded a thirty-year stay with the Flight Refuelling Limited.

The first British all-jet aerial refuelling took place in 1955. WH734, with the HDU installed in the rear section of the bomb-bay, transferred fuel to Meteor F.8 WE934, one of the former No.245 Squadron aircraft that had been fitted with

The last series of trials made with Ferranti's WJ643 was for the Laser Ranger and Marked Target Seeker, destined to be installed in production Harrier, Jaguar and Tornado aircraft. Pilot Len Houston, on the right, and Observer Bill Roberts receive final instructions prior to beginning another flight. Author's collection

a nose probe and its associated plumbing. For airborne-refuelling trials with a Gloster Javelin, also flown in 1955, WH734 had a revised HDU installed in the forward portion of the bomb-bay. Avro-built Canberra B.2, WK143, which arrived at FRL on 10 March 1955 to take part in the busy trials schedule, was fitted with a ventral Mk.20 pod, christened the 'buddy-buddy' system by both the US Navy and Marines. Both Canberras were fitted with nose probes and fuel lines, so that they could each become receiver or tanker, according to requirements. As all HDUs were plumbed into an aircraft's existing fuel, hydraulic and electrical systems, no additional instrumentation was required, apart from one small control panel in the cockpit.

Since the system was comparatively so simple to install, it does seem surprising that the Canberra was never used in the tanker/receiver role in the RAF. The Royal Navy employed the Mk.20 pod on the Sea Vixen, Scimitar and Buccaneer, while a system was designed for the Armstrong Whitworth Argosy but, despite being tested, it did not see squadron service.

FRL's other employment for the Canberra was in the development of its Rushton target winch. Handley Page-built B.2

WJ632, which had been converted to TT.18 standard by Marshall, arrived at Tarrant Rushton on 7 July 1966, and flight trials, with a winch under each wing, commenced in September. Nearly two years later, on 11 April 1968, WJ632 went to Boscombe Down with the Rushton system for service clearance, which was attained early in 1970. WK143 was converted by FRL to TT.18 standard, as was another B.2, WK118, and B.2 WH718, which had been converted into a TT.18 at Samlesbury, joined FRL on 1 March 1972 for testing before going on the strength of No.7 Squadron at St Mawgan. Another Avro-built B.2, WK126, already refurbished to TT.18 standard, was with FRL for a short time. Arriving on 19 June 1970, it was engaged on trials programmes, until going to Airwork Limited at Hurn on 2 November of the same year. It is believed to have been on charge to the Royal Navy during its stay at Tarrant Rushton.

Further to the Rushton system, FRL employed Canberra B.2, WE121, for trials of the Short Stiletto. This was a British version of the supersonic Beech AQM-37A air-launched target drone and the Canberra, which arrived at Tarrant Rushton on 6 May 1974, was fitted with a

WJ632 had been converted to TT.18 standard when Flight Refuelling Limited received it for flight trials of their Rushton winch and target system. BAe

The RAE's B.2, WH734, at Wyton's 40th Anniversary Meeting in 1989, carrying a Short Stiletto under the starboard wing. Author's collection

Stiletto mounting under one wing, while carrying a Rushton winch under the other. With this combination, it went to the RAE range at Llanbedr in North Wales, on 30 December 1974, but was flight-time expired by December 1979. In February 1977, FRL also received another Avro-built B.2, WK128, by road transport from RRE Pershore, where it had been employed since 1954. This was modified at Tarrant Rushton to take the Stiletto and it too went to Llanbedr, in October 1978. It is believed that Short Bros modified PR.3 WE146 for the Stiletto programme, while the long-standing B.2, WH734, also got in on the act. It was converted and flew during 1975 and 1976, with a Stiletto under

the starboard wing and a Rushton winch on the port side.

Folland Aircraft Limited

The common denominator between the Canberra and Folland Aircraft was W.E.W. Petter, who had been the aircraft's designer before taking on the mantle of Folland's Managing Director, as well as Chief Engineer.

The only use of the Canberra as a trials aircraft for the company was B.2 WJ725. Petter's design for a lightweight turbojet-powered fighter, evaluated by the Folland Midge G-39-1, was too small to take any existing Martin-Baker ejector seat, so the

company set about designing its own. When the RAF ordered the Midge's two-seat trainer derivative, the Gnat T.1, WJ725 was loaned to the company so that they could test fly their Type 4 fully automatic ejector seat. Two of these were fitted in the Gnat.

After the tests with WJ725, all further association between Folland and the Canberra involved the modifications required for various trials and testbed programmes, the majority of which were made at the company's Chilbolton Works. Two that can be confirmed are the second prototype A.1, VN813, which was converted in 1964 to take the D.H. Spectre in the lower fuselage, and B.6, WJ755, which was similarly modified in 1956.

Marshall of Cambridge

A large number of Canberra modifications and overhauls were undertaken by Marshalls, over a period of more than twenty years. The company was unwilling to give any details of this work, but it is known that the trial installations of the B.6 to B.15 conversion programme was handled on WH967 and similar action was taken when nineteen B.6(BS)s were converted to B.16s. B(I).8 WT333 is known to have been fitted with various RAE-required avionics in 1956.

The overseas sales of Canberras were assisted by conversions and refurbishments made to provide Peru with B(I).68s, from original B(I).8s.

Martin-Baker Aircraft Co. Ltd

The pioneers of ejector seats, the Martin-Baker Aircraft company spent many years developing its seats, with a succession of Meteors as the trials aircraft. The first dummy ejections were made from Boulton Paul Defiant, DR944, on 11 May 1945. Gloster Meteor Mk.III, EE416, joined the company on 6 November 1945 and on 24 July 1946, Bernard 'Benny' Lynch carried out the first British live ejection. The increasing speeds and altitudes of operational military aircraft overtook the abilities of later Meteor variants. Consequently, on 2 January 1952, Canberra B.2, WD962, was placed on loan to the RAE, to become an airborne ejector-seat launching platform, in conjunction with Martin-Baker, the seat designers and manufacturers. Due to weather and geographical limitations in the UK, a series of test firings, using dummies, was arranged to be conducted from Castel Benito airport in Tripoli, starting on 18 February 1954. The whole programme involved low-level ejections and was deemed very successful.

Emergency evacuations from three-man crewed Canberras was always problematic, due to the metal hatch above the two navigators having to be jettisoned before they were able to activate their seats. Martin-Baker came up with the custom-designed Mk.2C seat for the aircraft, together with a glass-fibre hatch cover to replace the metal one. No.9 Squadron at Binbrook provided B.2 WK126 to serve as the trials aircraft at the company's Chalgrove airfield in the winter of 1955. After ground-based test firings, the first airborne test, with a dummy, was successfully conducted on 19 January 1956. The pilot for the trial

U.10, WH876, being used to test the Type 12H rocket-fired ejector seat for the Harrier GR.5. Author's collection

was ex-Imperial Airways Captain John 'Scotty' Scott, who was at the controls of the Meteor when Benny Lynch made his historic ejection in 1946. The Canberra's glass-fibre hatch was broken by the seat as it shot up its rail, without any damage to the dummy. Further test firings were made with the A&AEE's B.2, WJ638, and two Mk.2C seats were successfully operated.

In the late 1960s, a much-abused Short Bros-built Canberra B.2, WH876, joined the A&AEE, to become a trials aircraft for later Martin-Baker seats. Having been built in October 1953, the aircraft was first converted to U.14 standard at Belfast and flown by the Fleet Air Arm's No.728B Squadron in October 1961. From there it went to Pershore, in 1962, to be converted back into a B.2, after which the A&AEE had it to refurbish into a U.10. In this condition it took on the Martin-Baker work and the company's records show that a total of fourteen ejection tests were carried out with WH876, either over Larkhill in Wiltshire, or Chalgrove airfield, between 1971 and 1985. Two seats were mainly tested – the Type 9B for the SEPECAT Jaguar and the Type 12H for the Harrier GR.5. Test speeds ranged from zero to 530mph (850km/h).

In July 1988, the aircraft was placed in store at Boscombe Down and in January 1990, it was dismantled. Martin-Baker still

use a Meteor hybrid, WL419, for test firings and expect to continue with the aircraft for the foreseeable future.

D. Napier and Son Limited

English Electric purchased all the ordinary share capital of the Napier company on 23 December 1942, but it turned out that Napier was not as closely associated with the Canberra as might have been expected.

WH793 had been built as a production PR.7 in April 1954. A month later, on 26 May, it was flown to Napier for conversion into the prototype Canberra PR.9, although it would not have the same profile as production aircraft. English Electric had drawn up the variant's basic design, so that Napier could undertake the detail design and modifications. Principal among these was a revised wing planform, with an increased centre-section chord and the installation of Avon RA.24 engines. Napier test pilot Mike Randrup, with flight engineer Walter Shirley as test observer, took the modified aircraft for its maiden flight on 8 July 1955, after which Beamont gave it an initial assessment at Cranfield before it went to Warton for its flight-test programme.

Towards the end of 1955, Avro-built B.2 WK163 arrived at Luton, having previously

PR.7, WH793, converted by Napier to be used as the trials prototype for the new PR.9 wing and engines, shown on its way to the 1955 SBAC Display. Author's collection

Napier's Double Scorpion rocket motor first appeared at Farnborough's 1956 SBAC Display; its carrier, B.2, WK163, touches down after its scheduled flying demonstration. Author's collection

served as a Sapphire ASSa.7 testbed at Bitteswell. Napier had been working for several years on rocket-motor designs for both aircraft and missile applications. By 1956, they had produced the H.T.P./ kerosene pump-fed Double Scorpion rocket engine and the Canberra was the natural choice for a flying testbed. The installation of the rocket motor in the rear section of WK163's bomb-bay was completed early in May 1956 and, on 20 May, it made its first flight. A scintillating performance was put up at the 1956 SBAC Display and on 28 August 1957, Mike Randrup, again with Walter Shirley as observer, took the aircraft to a new world altitude record of 70,310ft (21,430.48m). With Wally Gibb's two pre-

vious records, three altitude records had now been achieved by Canberras.

Following another SBAC Display the month after the record flight, WK163 carried out test flying of various Viper nacelle profiles at Filton, before going to the RRE at Pershore. In 1958, Short Bros-built B.6 WT207 was also fitted with a Double Scorpion at Luton, in a similar installation to WK163. However, this aircraft disintegrated when the rocket motor exploded at 56,000ft (17,100m), during a training flight over the Peak District, on 9 April 1958. The crew ejected safely, establishing an unsolicited altitude record at the time; the ruggedness of the Canberra was exemplified by the fact that the whole rear fuse-

lage, complete with empennage, landed intact at Mollyash in Derbyshire. The Double Scorpion was recovered and the whole disaster was found to have been caused by two 'O-ring' seals having been damaged during assembly, allowing the H.T.P and kerosene to unite.

An ambitious re-creation of WK163 as the Double Scorpion Canberra was started in 1996 by the aircraft's owner, Classic Aviation Projects (CAP), in conjunction with the Napier Power Heritage Trust. On the civil register as G-BVWC, the aircraft was by then an amalgamation of parts. At RRE Pershore in 1968, the original WK163 was upgraded to B.6 standard, for which it was fitted with new mainplanes and Avon

Mk.109/RA.7 engines. Then, in 1972, the aircraft's front fuselage was removed and donated to another RRE aircraft, B(I).8 WT327, in order for that aircraft to engage in the Synthetic Aperture Radar programme. WK163, in turn, was fitted with an internally refurbished and modernized front fuselage from the RRE's retired B.2

WG788. This meant that CAP only had the centre and rear fuselage assemblies of the actual record-breaking aircraft.

This situation did nothing to dampen the enthusiasm of those involved with the project at Luton and, as a result of much hard work, together with financial assistance from the volunteer workers themselves, the rejuvenated aircraft was taken into the air for the first time at lunchtime on 28 August 1997. It was not considered practical to reinstall the Double Scorpion, but an appropriate logo was painted on the nose.

Rolls-Royce Limited

The second A.1 prototype, VN813, was powered by two Nenes, as an insurance against the Avon engine problems prevailing in the spring of 1949, which were affecting the prototype flight schedules. Following the aircraft's type trials at Warton, it went to the Rolls-Royce test facility at Hucknall in Nottinghamshire on 30 November 1950, to become a constituent in the Nene development programme. On 8 June 1953, it went to Folland Aircraft at Chilbolton for modifications, to enable it to become a flying testbed for the de Havilland Spectre rocket motor.

The fourth A.1 prototype, VN850, left Warton for Hucknall on 6 October 1950 and became an Avon RA.2 test aircraft until it crashed on the approach, on 13 May 1951, following a complete engine failure. The second production B.2, WD930, went to Rolls-Royce on 22 August 1951, to spend the next nine years on Avon development. Its production Avon Mk.1/RA.3 engines were replaced by RA.7s, followed by

B.2, WK163, climbs after take-off, its Double Scorpion unit having just been shut down. The stainless-steel ventral shield is very evident. Author's collection

The second A.1 prototype, VN813, was used extensively for Nene development. Philip Jarrett

Having completed its flying slot at the 1956 Farnborough Display, B.2, WD930, touches down under the power of its two Avon RA.29s. Author's collection

B.2, WD943, engaged on Avon reheat testing, shows the enlarged rear end of the nacelles required to house the units. Author's collection

RA.14s in July 1953. About a year later, the RA.14s were removed and two Avon RA.26 engines, each producing 10,000lb (4,550kg) thrust, were installed. In 1956, another engine change was made, when the RA.26s were substituted by 10,500lb (4,770kg) RA.29 engines being developed for the civil aircraft market. These were VN850's last test engines and the aircraft was scrapped at Hucknall in August 1960. Avon RA.14, RA.28 and RA.29 test flying was also carried out with a later production B.2, WH671, which joined Rolls-Royce from Boulton Paul in June 1954. This aircraft was released by Hucknall in March 1961 and was broken up in November.

The fifteenth production B.2, WD943, first flew early in October 1951; on 17 October it went to Hucknall to continue Rolls-Royce's Avon reheat programme with the RA.7R, which was developing 9,500lb (4,320kg) thrust. These were later replaced

by RA.14R engines and flight trials continued, until the aircraft went to No.23 MU Aldergrove, on 7 July 1960, to be sold as scrap two years later. From December 1953, B.2 WD959 shared the Avon reheat trials with WD943 and in the mid-1950s, it was used as the flying testbed for RA.24R engines being developed for the Lightning. These produced 11,250lb (5,110kg) thrust dry and 14,430lb (6,560kg) with reheat, which was housed in long nacelle extensions on WD959. On 20 October 1959, the aircraft was allocated the Instruction Airframe number 7620M when it went to the RAE. It ended its days at No.12 SoTT at Melksham, where it was struck off charge on 7 October 1964.

Avon RA.3 and RA.7 surge testing was conducted on B.2 WF909, which arrived at Hucknall on 18 July 1952. The two programmes lasted until 8 December 1955, when the aircraft went to de Havilland

Engines for Gyron Junior development. Avon-relighting trials were carried out with B.2 WH854, in the spring of 1958, before the aircraft was converted to T.4 standard. It first went to RRE at Defford, then to the Empire Test Pilot's School (ETPS) and, prior to the aircraft being sold for scrap in June 1970, the front fuselage went to Martin-Baker Aircraft at Chalgrove.

Short Bros and Harland Limited

Short Bros was a subcontractor for Canberra production, together with A.V. Roe and Handley Page, but the Belfast company became much more involved in the aircraft's subsequent history. A breakdown of the figures shows that it produced almost as many new-build Canberras as Avro and Handley Page put together, as well as being very much involved in the conversion and refurbishment programmes.

Pilots made sure the spectators saw what they were displaying in those days! The Avon-reheat WD943 at Farnborough in 1952. Author's collection

PR.9s under construction at Belfast, with XH133, the fifth production aircraft, in the foreground. Author's collection

The ultimate high-altitude photographic-reconnaissance variant, the Canberra PR.9, was built entirely by Short Bros. (The prototype, not really representative of the production aircraft, but fitted with the new wing, had been produced by modifications made to a PR.7 by Napier.) The first production PR.9, XH129, first flew on 27 July 1958, but it was lost during early type evaluations, due to wing flexing causing the centre-section skin to peel back. A redesign by English Electric cured the problem, so that the subsequent twenty-two aircraft that were built served for many years. Together with a couple of T.4s, five PR.9s are still in service with No.39(1 PRU) Squadron at Marham and are likely to continue doing so into the twenty-first century.

The requirement for pilotless target variants of the Canberra was handed to Short Bros, and Handley Page-built B.2 WJ624 was delivered to Belfast on 6 September 1955 for conversion. Designated the Canberra U.10, the converted WJ624 first flew on 11 June 1957 and another seventeen B.2s were similarly modified. A further six B.2s were converted to a Royal Navy specification for a target drone, which was designated the Canberra U.14.

A further programme involved the conversion of sixteen B.2s into T.4s for the RAF. English Electric built the front fuselages forward of Frame 12A and shipped them to Belfast, where Short Bros, which had separated the B.2s from their original front fuselages, completed the T.4 conversions. Three additional aircraft were similarly converted for the Rhodesian Air Force.

A special 'one-off' Canberra was XH132, the SC.9 that served as an avionics trials aircraft for over thirty years. Produced from the fourth production PR.9, the aircraft was rebuilt with a unique nose profile, originally for trials of the de Havilland Red Top AAM. From Hatfield, it went to RRE Pershore, where it served, between 1972 and 1976, on *Sky Flash* development. This was an air-to-air Micro semi-active homing head produced in conjunction with the Marconi Space Defence Systems (MSDS) at Pershore. The SC.9 went to the RAE for many years after leaving Pershore and then to St Mawgan in Cornwall. It was held in private hands at St Austell in Cornwall for many years, but in 1998 it was sold to Albino Panigarri, who had it shipped to his home in Italy.

Short Bros was also involved in production of a British version of the Beech AQM-37A air-launched target drone, designated

According to service personnel who worked on Short Bros-built Canberra B.2s, their aircraft had a subframe missing in the cockpit area. During squadron modification work, a piece of additional equipment was routinely fitted in Canberras from other production lines by attachment to a certain subframe. It was found that this could not be done in aircraft from Belfast, because the subframe assembly was not there; no explanation for its omission has ever been given.

The Short SC.9, XH132, during its service with the RRE, where the wing-tip tanks were adapted to contain equipment for the aircraft's AI trials. One tank accommodated the 'illuminator' and the other, the 'homing head' that was being developed. Author's collection

B.2, WD956, was engaged on Red Dean development, until the weapon was cancelled. Author's collection

the Short SD.2 Stiletto. Canberra PR.3 WE146 was employed as the trial installation aircraft by Shorts, on behalf of RAE Llanbedr, who took over the aircraft's operations some time in 1967/68, after which the target drone was used in squadron service by No.100 Squadron.

Vickers Armstrong (Aircraft) Limited

In the early 1950s, Vickers Armstrong's Guided Weapons Division at Weybridge had a very healthy development programme in hand, much of it centred around its Type 888 Red Dean. This was a very large, active-homing, all-weather missile weighing 1,300lb (590kg), designed to

Specification 1105. At the time of its conception, it was proposed as the main weapon for the Gloster P.371, a thin-wing variant of the Javelin being projected to meet Specification F.153D.

The Canberra was selected as the missile's launch platform and the seventh production B.2, WD935, was delivered to Vickers' test section on the airfield at Wisley, three or four miles from the works at Weybridge, on 8 August 1951. The company also had production facilities at Hurn and WD935 went there for the necessary engineering. As a missile was to be carried under each wing, local strengthening of the mainplanes was included in the schedule of work on the aircraft. The conversion was

completed in October 1953 and a first flight, with an aerodynamic test missile, was made in January 1954. Wisley airfield was on a plateau and on 21 September 1955 WD935 suffered brake failure while rolling after touchdown and finished up in a field far too close for comfort to the main Portsmouth road. Its use on the Red Dean programme was rather curtailed after the accident; another B.2, WD942, which was in Australia at the time, and had been delivered to Wisley on 28 September 1951 to undertake specific tasks, took over the damaged Canberra's part of the programme.

In 1952, preparations were made for the Red Dean to be test fired on the WRE range at Woomera. This was one of the areas in the programme for which WD942 was scheduled and it was allocated the RAAF serial A84-2 for the duration of the test firings. It flew out from Wisley on 12 March 1952 and the live-firing trials kept the aircraft in Australia until after the accident to WD935. Having completed the Red Dean schedule, the aircraft reverted to its WD942 serial while flying with de Havilland's No.12 JSTU at Woomera, until it returned to the UK in October 1957. It went to the MoS Air Weapons Research Establishment (AWRE) at Shoeburyness and, as its history seems to end then, it is presumed to have been destroyed on the range.

Two further Canberras, both B.2s, were delivered to Vickers Armstrong for the Red Dean programme. WH660 went to Wisley in May 1953 and WD956 joined it in January 1954. Work on Red Dean ended when the Gloster P.371 project was cancelled in July 1956. Although the aircraft got no further than the mock-up stage, Vickers Armstrong's missile was a proven weapon at the time of the cancellation. The trouble was its size – no existing interceptor was capable of carrying a pair of 1,300-lb (590-kg) missiles. Canberra WD956 went to No.15 MU Wroughton, to be sold as scrap in December 1964. WH660 went from Wisley to the RRE at Pershore for AI.Mk.18 development, and continued on various weapon trials until being consigned to Pershore's fire dump in 1971. The wayward WD935 was repaired after its excursion over the Wisley countryside and went to the Bomber Command Development Unit (BCDU) at Finningley before going into store at St Athan on 23 November 1971. It was allotted Instructional Airframe number 8440M in 1976 and, after being sold at auction in 1989, was scrapped, although the front fuselage existed for some time.

The Establishments

In 1948, the British National Health Service was created, promising to provide everyone with health care 'from the cradle to the grave'. In the lifetime of the Canberra, the Ministry of Supply (MoS) was superseded by the Ministry of Defence (MoD) as the governing body of the Establishments that saw the aircraft through all its stages of development and improvement, as well as its adaptability for employment for specific purposes. Furthermore, taking the analogy even further, the Proof and Experimental Establishment (PEE) at Shoeburyness, being the location where new weapons were tried out against existing airframes, often provided the graveyard. The principal bodies concerned are listed here, together with the Canberras confirmed as having been involved.

prototype B.2, VX165, arrived for performance and handling trials on 8 November 1950. Following recommendations by A&AEE test pilots for slight alterations, which were attended to at Warton, it was back again on 12 December. The aircraft was damaged in a landing accident on 15 August 1951, which put an end to its flying.

The second B.2 prototype, VX169, was used for type armament trials in March 1951 and the prototype PR.3, VX181, was cleared for service in November of the same year. The sole B.5, VX185, made the transatlantic record flight and was converted to B(I).8 configuration before it went to the A&AEE, in May 1955.

Production B.2s WD945 and WD958 took part in the flight clearance trials between December 1951 and August 1952, while the second production T.4, WE189, was cleared for use of the Type D

WK122 was used for radio-proving trials in 1968, after having been converted to TT.18 standard.

WH876 was completed by Short Bros in October 1953 and, following RAF squadron service together with a conversion into a U.14 at Belfast, it served with the Fleet Air Arm as a drone. Having safely endured a session of being a target for the missile test ship HMS *Girdleness* operating off Malta, the aircraft returned to the UK to be converted back to B.2 standard and stored. This storage was of a short duration and WH876 was transferred to the A&AEE, to be transformed into a U.10 in the late 1960s. In this condition, it became the Establishment's trials aircraft for Martin-Baker ejector seats. The navigator's hatch was removed and the aircraft was flown unmanned for some of the test firings; the introduction of aileron

Belfast-built B.2, WH876, was flying with the A&AEE's Bomber and Maritime Flight Test Squadron when it was seen at Abingdon on 18 September 1965. W. Hyde/George Pennick

Aircraft and Armament Experimental Establishment

On 1 September 1939, the A&AEE, with the task of evaluating new aircraft and weapons for operational service, moved from Martlesham Heath in Suffolk to Boscombe Down in Wiltshire. Consequently, it was well established when the first prototype A.1, VN799, paid its first visit for initial assessment, on 27 October 1949. The other three A.1s also went to the Establishment at various times, while the

autopilot at the end of 1953. The eighth production B.6, WH952, arrived at Boscombe Down in February 1955 and spent several years with the Establishment before an investigation into airframe fatigue was passed over to Marshalls. There, it was repaired and wing pylons were fitted prior to it returning to the A&AEE, in September 1970, for weapon-release trials. Handley Page's second production B.2, WJ565, flew a bombing trials programme from Boscombe Down in April 1953 and Avro-built

hydro-boosters greatly assisted the ground controllers for these flights. Engineers at the A&AEE fitted a flight-refuelling probe to the nose of WH876, so that it could assist in the trials taking place with the stop-gap tanker conversion of Vulcan K.2 XM571, although the Canberra was not fitted out for in-flight refuelling.

Avro-built B.2 WK121 spent time with the Bomber and Maritime Test Squadron of the A&AEE, painted in a glossy black paint scheme, with cream-coloured elevators and rudder. Torpedo and parachute

A rather poor, but rare, photograph of B(I).8, WT333, at Boscombe Down during the Microcell firing trials programme. The RRE crest on its fin was applied during its time at Pershore. Author's collection

mine-dropping trials were conducted before the aircraft became a target for the Establishment's evaluation of avionics being tested for the Jaguar, Lightning, NA.39 and Sea Vixen, which had been started with WJ723 in December 1959, before WH121 took over.

WV787 was another interesting Canberra used at Boscombe Down. Built as a B.2 in 1952, and used by Armstrong Whitworth for Sapphire ASSa.7 reheat testing, it became the aerodynamic trials aircraft for the T.22, before being converted for Ferranti by Boulton Paul to B(I).8 standard (but without the ventral gun pack). Ferranti employed it on the *Blue Parrot* radar trials for the NA.39, for which a Buccaneer nose-cone was installed. The A&AEE received the aircraft from Turnhouse for use in icing trials; water tanks were installed in the bomb-bay and a ventral spray-bar assembly was fitted, running from the bomb-bay to the rear fuselage extremity, in order to simulate icing conditions. The aircraft was fitted with a rear-facing close-circuit television (CCTV), so that the observer could record results of the spraying on to the test aircraft, one of which was Concorde 002.

WV787 was also used for air-to-air photography during Jaguar testing, before it departed from Boscombe Down to go to the Battle Damage School at Abingdon. There, it had Instructional Airframe number 8799M and narrowly missed being destroyed, before it was acquired by the Newark Air Museum.

On 27 November 1959, the penultimate Avro-built B.2, WK164, which had spent time at Defford, Tarrant Rushton and Cambridge, went to Boscombe Down for a variety of trials programmes. These lasted until December 1977, when it joined No.100 Squadron. In July 1982, it

went to the PEE at Foulness, where it was dismantled and the rear fuselage was delivered to Abingdon. The nose was retained by PEE, while the rest was sold for scrap. Another tenant at Boscombe Down in 1959 was B(I).8 WT333, which arrived on 19 March for firing trials with the Microcell rocket pod, after which it went to Marshall of Cambridge and then back to Warton in July 1965.

Empire Test Pilot's School

At the end of 1942, due to a shortage of pilots to handle the new types of aircraft coming from British factories, and American aircraft arriving under Lend Lease, the Commandant of the A&AEE, Air Commodore D'Arcy Grieg, was asked by the Ministry of Aircraft Production (MAP) to set up a test pilot's school at Boscombe Down. The first three ETPS courses were held at Boscombe Down and the next three at Cranfield, after which the school moved to the Royal Aircraft Establishment (RAE) at Farnborough. This allowed the College of Aeronautics to get established at Cranfield and the school remained at the RAE until 1968. In that year, it returned to Boscombe Down, where it is today.

The first Canberras to go to the ETPS were T.4s WJ865 and WJ867, both arriving at Farnborough in September 1954, to remain with the school for nearly thirty years. They were joined by an ex-RRE B.2, WH854, on 14 December 1967 and another, WJ730, on 18 March 1959. The latter crashed on 25 October 1962 while practising engine failure and asymetric landing. Avro-built B.2 WJ994 became an ETPS aircraft on 11 July 1961, but nearly two years later, on 1 April 1963, the undercarriage collapsed on landing at base and the aircraft was written off.

The last B.2 to go on the school's inventory was WH715, which transferred in March 1962 from RAE Farnborough to the ETPS at Farnborough – not a journey that required any flying! Six years later, it too was lost, in an accident in Somerset. The first two Canberras received by the school back in September 1954 were the last to leave. WJ867 came to the end of its fatigue life in February 1979 and was given the Instructional Airframe number 8643M when it went to RAF Newton in the December. WJ865's fatigue life ended in 1981 and it left Boscombe Down for RAE Farnborough on 5 November 1981, where it is believed to have gone into store.

Royal Aircraft Establishment

Farnborough and British aviation have an association going back to 1905, when the Balloon Factory moved there from Chatham. Renamed the Royal Aircraft Factory, during the First World War it expanded rapidly and, following the formation of the Royal Air Force on 1 April 1918, the complex acquired the title Royal Aircraft Establishment in July of the same year. The production of aircraft ceased after the Armistice and the Establishment's roots as a research facility were put down.

Since then, no single element of British aviation has advanced or been produced without being referred to the RAE, and many schemes have been tested that did not go into production. Within the Establishment's parameters, separate units, such as No.1 School of Photography, the Institute of Aviation Medicine (IAM), the Meteorological Research Flight, the Aero Flight, the Experimental Flying Squadron (EFS), the National Gas Turbine Establishment (NGTE), the Radar Research Squadron (RRS) and the Blind Landing

PR.3, WE173, while on the inventory of the RAE's Meteorological Research Flight. Crown Copyright, DERA
Boscombe Down

Experimental Unit (BLEU), have all had associations with the Canberra. The Meteorological Research Flight (MRF) also used RAE Farnborough and, later, Bedford as its base, although strictly speaking, as a unit of the Meteorological Office, it constituted a part of the Directorate of Research. Gradually, after 1946, the further expansion of the RAE saw the wartime base of the 306th Bomb Group USAAF, at Thurleigh in Bedfordshire, engulfed by a vast new airfield and buildings, entitled RAE Bedford.

VN799, the first A.1, went to Farnborough to test the Mk.IX autopilot. While operating with the Establishment's BLEU, based at Martlesham Heath in Suffolk, the aircraft crashed, on 18 August 1953. The Avon engine trials at Hucknall, involving

several early B.2s, were made in conjunction with the RAE and the third production aircraft, WD931, was flown in March 1951 by RAE pilots, to clear bomb delivery, prior to Binbrook receiving its first aircraft. VX181, the PR.3 prototype, went to the RAE on 8 December 1951, to start radio-compass trials that lasted nearly three weeks. In June 1952, B.2 WD945 was modified by Boulton Paul, prior to its going to the RAE for *Blue Devil* and *Red Cat* avionic trials. The aircraft was involved in target-marker testing in November 1956, followed in July 1957 by the testing of another enigmatically named piece of avionics, *Green Flax*. Many of these codenames referred to electronic projects. In the case of experimental items that were not taken beyond the testing stage, no records were

kept; as WD945 is on record as being a testing airframe for *Green Satin*, there is therefore every reason to assume that *Green Flax* was associated with this navigational aid.

Canberra B.2 WH657 went to No.231 OCU, before being loaned to the NGTE at Pyestock, Farnborough, on 4 June 1953, for use as its high-altitude research aircraft in the development of fuel systems. On 31 May 1960, it was released to RFD Godalming, for parachute-stabilizing development trials. Then, in 1962, WH657 became a satellite tracker, for which the nose was adorned with the caption 'UK-USA Co-operation Space Project NASA'. This programme was finished in the spring of 1966 and the aircraft was used for runway slush-on-take-off experiments at Cranfield later in that year. On 19 July 1969, WH657 was

Mk.IX autopilot trials were conducted with VN799, the first A.1 prototype, at Martlesham Heath. Author's collection

(Top) B.2, WH657, engaged in the runway slush programme at Cranfield in 1966; the original duly signed by the pilot, Ron Wingrove. Brenzett Aeronautical Museum Trust

(Middle) With the RAE crest on the nose, and 'Flook' and kangaroo badges on the fin, B.6, XH568, stands on the tarmac at Buckley, Colorado, engaged on Clear Air Turbulence trials. Author's collection

(Bottom) Seen flying with the RAE's Aero Flight, B.6, WH793, was engaged in Monsoon trials at Bangalore in 1972. R. Brown

sold to RFD in a dismantled condition and in 1986 it went to Booker Air, which had ambitions that did not come to fruition. Booker passed the aircraft on to the Brenzett Aeronautical Museum Trust in Kent, where it resides today.

Three Canberras engaged on Meteorological Flight research were PR.3 WE173, B.6 XH568 and WH793, the PR.3 that was converted into the prototype PR.9 in summer 1955. Each was fitted with a 15-ft (4.5-m) pointed instrumental boom containing a static pressure system, neatly faired into the nose contour, to assist in low- and high-level gust research, as well as the testing of advanced data-collection instrumentation. The aircraft flew with a crew of two, plus a civilian scientist seated beside the navigator; the scientist was the one to decide, in association with the crew, which area of sky looked most likely to provide the

conditions required by a particular piece of research. During the 1960s, XH568 was also used by the IAM, while WH793 spent time on monsoon trials for the Indian National Aeronautical Laboratory at Bangalore in 1972. The following year, it was engaged as a chase aircraft during Concorde prototype trials at Fairford, then was put in store at Farnborough in 1975, prior to going to RAE Bedford.

Before its Meteorological Flight work, XH568 was employed on trials of the homing head for the Sea Skua helicopter-launched anti-shipping guided weapon, and it went to RAE Bedford on 18 November 1976. The PR.3, WE173, joined the Flight in the 1960s and then went to No.231 OCU before returning to RAE charge in the early 1970s. In spring 1973, the aircraft carried out Clear Air Turbulence trials, flying from the Buckley ANG

base outside Denver, Colorado. It continued with the Meteorological Flight until 31 March 1981, when it was withdrawn from service. The next year, WE173 was given the Instructional Airframe number 8740M and delivered to the Battle Damage Repair Flight at Coltishall for fire practice.

Another association with things nautical was the Air Torpedo Development Unit (ATDU). This unit had been based at Gosport for close on thirty-five years, during which it is known that a small number of Canberras operated with the unit on a series of parachute mine-dropping trials for the RAE. The only aircraft actually confirmed as being engaged on this programme was B.2 WH661, which was logged as flying there at various intervals between July 1953 and 17 March 1955.

In 1956, the Blind Landing Experimental Unit (BLEU) moved to RAE Bedford,

B.6, WH952, was used on bomb-bay door-buffeting trials with the RAE in 1964. BAe

Besides the Cranfield trials, RAE Bedford conducted further runway slush tests with B.2, WK135.
Author's collection

In 1962, an arrester gear, using a piston in a cylinder of water, for use on aircraft carriers, was devised by RAE Bedford. During trials with a Canberra travelling at 150mph (240km/h), it was stopped within 200 yards. The aircraft involved, from which the outer wings had been removed, is believed to have been B.2, WJ995. It was devoid of markings, apart from an anchor painted on the fin. Author's collection

having operated from Martlesham Heath since shortly after the end of the Second World War in 1945. The second production T.4, WE189, went to the unit in November 1953 on Type D autopilot trials and, after being fitted with a PR.7 front fuselage by Marshall in September 1955, it returned to Martlesham Heath. New blind-landing equipment was incorporated in the revised front fuselage and the aircraft flew a busy schedule until the 28 September of the following year, when it crashed, killing both crew members.

By 1955, the Flight Division of the RAE had moved from Farnborough to Bedford with a formidable fleet of aircraft, including eleven Canberras. Also, a uniform, high-visibility colour scheme was gradually being applied to RAE aircraft. The areas of red, white and dark blue were referred to colloquially as 'Raspberry Ripple'. In addition, the RAE's Canberra B.2 WK128, engaged on Stiletto target trials at Llanbedr, was adorned with the standard black/yellow striped underside of target-towing aircraft. The visibility of that aircraft was certainly high!

WT333, built as a B(I).8 in 1956, had a busy life, split between several Establishments. On loan to the RAE's Armament Department in July 1956, it was used to evaluate various LABS systems and had modifications handled by Marshall in connection with these trials. Following test rocket firing with the A&AEE and WRE, and a period in store at No.27 MU, the aircraft was converted to take a different front fuselage at Pershore, in 1975.

This operation is quite complicated to record, as the front fuselage was originally built as the B.2 WK135. In 1969, the RRE at Pershore recovered the front fuselage from WK135, which had been consigned to its fire dump after being struck off charge in January 1967. This was married with the fuselage of B(I).8 WT327, and this aircraft now became a B.6 after conversion. The front-fuselage assembly was removed from WT327 in 1972 and, in 1975, it was installed on B(I).8 WT333. After further alterations to the nose-extremity profile, the aircraft was flown to Bedford, on 18 May 1977, for use by the RAE Aerospace Research Squadron.

Today, it resides with Classic Aviation Projects at Bruntingthorpe.

In 1977, RAE Bedford received those Canberras that were still on charge to Pershore, when that Establishment closed down. These included B.2/6 WK163 and T.4 WJ992, the last Canberra to fly out of Pershore. B.6s XH567 and XH568 were still going strong, together with the modified B.8/6s WT327 and WT333. Fifteen years later, Ministry of Defence financial constrictions brought about the closure of Bedford and the surviving Canberras were transferred to the A&AEE at Boscombe Down, one of the centres of British radar research.

As shown, WT333, was referred to as a B.6 hybrid, which had been converted at Pershore to take the 'long-nose' front fuselage monocoque structure, with a semi-spherical front fairing in place of the radome. Through this, the head of a McDonnell Douglas Harpoon anti-shipping missile protrudes, for flight evaluation and approval. Author's collection

T.4, WJ992, converted from B.2 standard and seen in 'raspberry ripple' finish, was the last Canberra to leave RRE Pershore, when it transferred to RAE Bedford on 1 November 1977. Author's collection

Royal Radar Establishment

The development and titling of this Establishment are almost as complex as the engineering tasks that it undertook. It originated as the Air Ministry Research Establishment at Bawdsey in 1936, when the flying was covered by two Avro Ansons detached from No.220 Squadron at Bircham Newton to the A&AEE at Martlesham Heath and allocated to Bawdsey. It progressed, via Dundee University in 1939, to Swanage in 1940, when it was retitled the Telecommunications Research Establishment (TRE). In August 1941, the Telecommunications Flying Unit (TFU) was formed by the amalgamation of the RAF Special Duties Flight (SDF), with other units at Hurn in Hampshire.

May 1942 was an eventful month, when the TRE moved from Swanage to Malvern in Worcestershire, and the TFU was relocated at Defford in the same county. RAF pilots had formed the backbone of TFU aircrew, but in 1945 it became mainly a civilian unit (although there was still a small RAF element), and was renamed the TRE Aircraft Department. Further retitling took

place in 1953, when the TRE became the Radar Research Establishment (RRE) – this was the first time the word 'radar' was associated with the Establishment. In October 1955, the Aircraft Department was renamed the Radar Research Flying Unit (RRFU). Two years later, in 1957, the word 'Royal' was incorporated into the title. RRE now stood for the Royal Research Establishment and the RRFU became an all-RAF unit, while the aviation side was called the RRE Aircraft Department when it was transferred from Defford to Pershore.

In December 1976, the RRE amalgamated with the Signals Research and Development Establishment (SRDE) to form the Royal Signals and Radar Research Establishment (RSRE), and the RRE Aircraft Department at Pershore closed down. The following month, the RSRE severed its involvement with aircraft and the surviving RRE Aircraft Department fleet went to RAE Bedford. It remained there until 1992, when the few remaining aircraft were transferred to the A&AEE, and the circle that had begun in 1936 was completed.

The Canberra was first connected with the Establishment in February 1951. There were very many facets to this particular association over many years; *see* boxes, pages 176–80.

There is no doubt that other Canberras were at both Defford and Pershore over the years, but it is believed that many visits were of a transient nature and, consequently, cannot be considered as Establishment aircraft movements. At one time, the Establishment had more Canberras on charge than any other unit, including individual RAF squadrons. In the mid-1960s, there were no less than twenty-two Canberras on live projects at any one time.

The driving force behind the prodigious amount of work undertaken was the Establishment's Chief Engineer David K. Henderson, ably assisted by his deputy William H. Sleigh, who took over the post on Henderson's retirement and held it until the Establishment was closed. The workshop team of experienced engineers and craftsmen was led by Derek H. Moseley, who, during the Canberra era, became Works Manager. It is surely fair to say that the skills in those Worcestershire hives of secrecy were second to none in the aviation field. They first utilized the Meteor to take their avionics into the jet age, and then turned the Canberra into the ultimate trials platform for the logical development of their expertise.

This 'head-to-head' grouping of B.6, WG789, on the left, and the Short SC.9, XH132, typifies the electronic enterprises of the TRE/RRE. RRE Archives

Worcestershire's Trials Canberras

Serial	Base	Dates	Task	Remarks
CANBERRA PROTOTYPES				
VN813	Defford	1951–52	ARI5844 trials	2nd prototype. Damaged, landing without nose-wheel 24.10.51
VN828	Defford	1951–57	1. *Green Satin* trials	3rd prototype. Damaged, after single-engine failure during
	Pershore	1957–61	2. AI18 trials (Sea Vixen)	o/weight landing 10.6.53. Repaired 5-54, nose conv. start. Dismantled after last flight 14.12.61
VX181	Pershore	1969–75	Training a/c for airfield emerg. services	Flown in 11.6.69, retired from A&AEE. Burned 1975
CANBERRA B.2				
WD929	Defford	1951	1. Radio tests	1st prod. a/c to TFU arrived 9.2.51
			2.Gee H trials	
WD931	Pershore	1958–65	1. Co-op. target	Apprentice training aid after last flight 24.2.65
			2. Seaslug GW fuse trials	Fire practice 1969 onwards
WD945	Defford	1953	Installation and trials *Green Satin*	
WD953	Pershore	1969–70	Storage	Arrived 13.2.69 (last flight) after closure FFU. Dismantled, sent to RAE Bedford, where burned
WD963	Defford	1952	*Blue Shadow* trials	Handed to No.109 Squadron
WE121	Pershore	1972–74	Overhaul and converted for target towing	Not flown on RRE trials
WF892	Defford	1952–53	Installation and *Blue Shadow* sideways look recce. radar	RAF a/c on loan. Crashed on take-off Exeter 23.10.53, birdstrike. Crew killed
WF917	Defford	1952–57	1. RRDE trials.	Nose-wheel collapse on landing 18.2.55. Loan to ETPS 1.4.62. Sold to BAC.
	Pershore	1957–68	2. RRE twin-dish Doppler trials	Flown out from Pershore 22.11.68. Refurbished for Argentina
			3. *Violet Banner* GW IR homing system	
			4. Jamming a/c for GW trials	

B.2, WD953, had lamps fitted under the wing tips when flying with the FFU; these were used to determine range in post-trial film analyses. Author's collection

Worcestershire's Trials Canberras (continued)

WG789 was built as a replacement B.2, for WD940, the second pattern Canberra flown to the USA. It was modified many times for various RRE trials programmes, including the homing systems for the Sea Dart, Sea Skua and Sea Eagle guided weapons, for which a bore-sight camera was mounted above the radome. RRE Archives

Serial	Base	Dates	Tasks	Remarks

WG788	Defford
	Pershore
		1952–57
		1957–76
			1. *Blue Sugar, Blue Study* &
			    Green Garland (IR fuse for
			    Firestreak) trials
			2. IR line scan recce system trials
			3. Sea Dart GW trials
				Nose-wheel collapse on landing 14.9.53. Final flight 23.12.68.
				Nose removed and converted to long-nose, fitted on XH568, 1970.
				Rest of airframe used for fire practice

WG789	Pershore	1959–76	1. Sea Dart GW guidance trials 2. Sea Dart GW homing head trials (flown with WH660) 3. Temp. loan to BAC for Concorde chase a/c 4. Sea Eagle GW homing head trials	First on charge to Boulton Paul, flown & maintained by them. Handed to RRFU 9.6.59. Flown to RAE Bedford 1.11.76. Used by RRS
WH638	Defford	1952–54	*Green Satin* evaluation trials	RAF a/c on loan. To BP at Defford for *Green Satin*. To No.100 Squadron 27.10.54
WH660	Defford Pershore	1953–57 1957–71	1. AI18 fit & flight trials 2. AI research 3. GW trials and stand-in for WG789 4. Sea Dart trials	Retired after last flight 31.10.70. Reduced to spares at Pershore in 1971
WH702	Defford Pershore	1953–57 1957–68	1. *Red Setter* sideways look radar trials 2. *Green Satin* trials 3. G-band recce. radar trials	Retired 1968. Sold to BAC. Flown out Pershore 5.11.68. Refurbished for Argentina
WH857	Pershore	1961	Target for *Orange Yeoman* ground radar	From and to storage at No.15 MU Wroughton 23.2/22.6.61
WJ627	Pershore	1963–72	1. Jamming a/c for GW trials 2. Concorde chase a/c	From FFU to Pershore. Maintenance by Pershore during Concorde tasks
WJ646	Defford Pershore	1954–57 1957–70	1. AI18 trials. 2. Hughes UK-71N IR homer 3. RRE moving target system with AI18	B(I).8 conversion by Boulton Paul at Defford 55–56. Last flight 17.12.68. Dismantled, most of airframe to Boscombe Down for fire practice
WJ679	Defford Pershore	1955–57 1957–68	1. Co-operative target 2. Special target with tip-tank mounted searchlight 3. Cloud IR back-scatter trials	Retired after last flight 13.10.67. Dismantled, most of airframe to Foulness ranges 1969

Worcestershire's Trials Canberras *(continued)*

Serial	Base	Dates	Tasks	Remarks
WJ990	Pershore	1963–68	Jamming a/c for GW trials	Flown to No.15 MU Wroughton 30.5.68
WK119	Pershore	1963–68	Jamming a/c for GW trials	Flown to No.15 MU Wroughton 29.1.68
WK120	Defford Pershore	1955–57 1957–68	1. *Blue Label* & *Blue Streak* trials 2. Tip-tank transponders for GW trials	Last RRFU Canberra to depart Defford 9.10.57. Retired after last flight 2.1.68 and reduced to spares
WK121	Defford	1955–57	Co-operative target fitted with Window launcher	Allotted to Boulton Paul at Defford 54–55. Passed to RRE charge 13.12.55
WK123	Defford	1955–56	*Blue Study* trials	RAF a/c on loan
WK128	Pershore	1958–75	1. Jamming a/c for Window launcher 2. GW fuse research 3. Sea state and cloud reflection measurements with low power laser	Allotted to Boulton Paul at Defford 54–56. Flown to Flight Refuelling 3.75 for TT.18 conversion. Flown to Llanbedr
WK129	Defford Pershore	1955–57 1957	GW trials	Port u/c retraction on landing 23.9.55. Repaired. Flew into high ground in N. Wales 9.12.57, due to engine icing. Crew killed
WK163	Pershore	1959–76	Infra-red	Fitted with B.6 mainplanes and engines at Pershore in 1968. Original nose of XH568 fitted 1972. 1st RRFU Canberra handed over to RAE Bedford 1.7.76

CANBERRA PR.3

Serial	Base	Dates	Tasks	Remarks
WE147	Defford	1953–57	1. *Green Satin* & *Blue Study* trials 2. Doppler radar trials for TSR.2 3. Experimental Doppler radar trials	Final flight 23.2.68. Dismantled and transported to Foulness ranges 1970.
WF922	Pershore	1970–71	Major overhaul for A&AEE	Not flown by RRFU

CANBERRA T.4

Serial	Base	Dates	Tasks	Remarks
WH854	Pershore	1958–61 1969–70	Continuous training and target	Retired at Pershore after final flight 3.3.69. Broken up Pershore 1969, remains sold as scrap, except nose, which went to Martin-Baker
WJ992	Pershore	1962–77	Continuous training	Last RRFU Canberra to depart from Pershore. Flown to RAE Bedford and handed over 1.11.77

CANBERRA B.6

Serial	Base	Dates	Tasks	Remarks
WH945	Defford Pershore	1957 1957–59	1. Installation of extra-long nose with bomb-aimer site on stbd side 2. Installation of ASV21 anti-ship radar, *Blue Silk* & Gee 3 3. Bombing role installation trials.	RAF a/c modified for joint RRE/Bomber Command trials. A/c arrived Defford with Operation *Musketeer* stripes 29.4.57. Returned RAF Wittering 30.4.59
WH953	Defford Pershore	1955–57 1957–76	1. AI20 installation trials 2. RRE exp. single dish CW AI radar. 3. Experimental FMICW radar conversion of item above. 4. Research for JP236 AEW using item 3 5. Marconi exp. AI for Tornado F.3	Delivered to Defford as new a/c 28.1.55. Flown to RAE Bedford and handed over 16.12.76
WJ770	Defford	1955–56	*Yellow Aster* installation and trials	RAF a/c on loan
XH567	Pershore	1961–76	Sideways looking recce. radar for TSR.2, then Phantom recce. pod	Flown to RAE Bedford and handed over 16.12.76
XH568	Pershore	1967–76	Sea Skua GW homing head trials	Converted to B.6 long-nose by fitting ex-WG788 nose modified. Flown to RAE Bedford and handed over 18.11.76.

CANBERRA B.6 (MOD)

Serial	Base	Dates	Tasks	Remarks
WT305	Pershore	1973–74	IR sensor installation	RAF a/c delivered for specialized installation of equipment using Pershore engineering resources. Returned RAF 18.12.74

Worcestershire's Trials Canberras (continued)

B.6, XH567, carried a pair of modified Hunter external fuel tanks, for a ground radar high-reflection airborne target. They were coated with a high silver finish and mounted on two 'stacked' weapon pylons, in order to give enhanced under-fuselage viewing. RRE Archives

(Right) Close-up of the 'stacked' pylons under the wing of XH567. RRE Archives

(Above) The mock-up of a hatch-mounted device, developed by the RRE and BAe, Warton. Fitted on B.6, WT305, the device was to evaluate an American radiometer, as a short-term project at Pershore. RRE Archives

(Left) A fine photograph of the long-nose installation on XH568, showing the Sea Skua guided-weapon homing-head radome. Brandon J. White

Worcestershire's Trials Canberras *(continued)*

Serial	Base	Dates	Tasks	Remarks
CANBERRA PR.7				
WH774	Pershore	1960–76	1. IR radiometer trials 2. Satellite tracking station calibration	Dorsal observer's position. Flown to RAE Bedford and handed over 16.8.76. Used there by RRS
WH776	Pershore	1969–70	Satellite tracking station calibration. Task transferred to WH774	Three cameras each side of rear fuselage in bulges. Used as spares source at Pershore after last flight 30.4.70. Remains burned 1977
WH777	Defford	1954–56	*Blue Study* installation and trials.	
CANBERRA B(I).8				
WT327	Pershore	1966–77	Synthetic aperture radar research	Delivered to Pershore from FFU 12.1.67. Converted to B.6 1969 by fitting nose ex-WK135 replaced 1972 by nose ex-WK163. Flown to RAE Bedford and handed over 25.4.77.

B(I).8, WT327, fitted with the front fuselage of B.6, WK135, and used as a reconnaissance radar airborne laboratory. The lateral radome carried an SAR reconnaissance installation in the front portion of the bomb-bay, which had an internal camera sited behind it. RRE Archives

Serial	Base	Dates	Tasks	Remarks
WT333	Pershore	1969–77		Used at WRE prior to delivery Pershore. Stored No.27 MU 1970–72. Converted to B.6 by fitting nose ex-WT327 modified to long-nose spec. 1975. Flown to RAE Bedford and handed over 18.5.77
CANBERRA T.11				
XA536	Pershore	1965–66	Clutter measurements with standard AI17	RAF a/c on loan. Flown out to Binbrook 10.5.65
CANBERRA D.14				
WH704	Pershore	1961–66	Storage	Flown into Pershore 5.12.61 after drone work with Royal Navy at Malta. Used 1963–66 for apprentice training, then for fire practice
WH720	Pershore	1961–63	Storage	Flown into Pershore 5.12.61 after drone work with Royal Navy at Malta. Broken up and sold as scrap at Pershore 10.63
WH876	Pershore	1961–63	Storage	Flown into Pershore 5.12.61 after drone work with Royal Navy at Malta. Flown out to A&AEE 25.9.63
WJ638	Pershore	1961–62	Storage	Flown into Pershore 12.12.61 after drone work with Royal Navy at Malta. Flown out to A&AEE 27.6.62
SHORT SC.9				
XH132	Pershore	1972–76	Sky Flash GW homing-head trials	Flown to RAE Bedford and handed over 1.12.76. Used there by RRS

CHAPTER FIFTEEN

Canberra Conclusions

Genesis ...

Certain aeroplanes inspire affection from those who have, or have had, affiliation with them. Aircrew, groundcrew or just enthusiast, all express pleasure at the mention of the aircraft's name, and many will come up with an anecdote that becomes more expansive with the passage of time.

The Canberra is such an aeroplane. There were many reasons to be averse to it: the temperature inside every variant (except the PR.9) that had been standing under Sharjah's sun for a couple of hours; the lack of room for two pilots in the T.4; the navigator's claustrophobic, instrument-packed 'black hole', without any temperature control; the awkwardness of having to hump the tip tanks up on their cradles while the explosive release bolts

were screwed in; the difficulties of doing an engine change in the winter, when the hangars were already full; or the inaccessibility of the ventral gun pack under the B(I).6. However, all these problems seem to be forgotten in the rosy tint of nostalgia.

Despite its shortcomings, and every aircraft has some, the Canberra was a fine example of the designer using contemporary knowledge and experience to meet in full the operational requirements laid before him. Pilots found it a good aeroplane to fly. It responded well in its handling and was always capable of meeting the many and varied roles that were demanded of it. At the beginning it was viewed as being too conventional, but, being in continuous service from May 1951 into the twenty-first

century, it has seen off nearly every contemporary, more unconventional successor. The Buccaneer, Hunter, Javelin, Lightning, Sea Vixen, Scimitar, Swift, Valiant, Victor, and Vulcan all originated in the 1950/60 era and only the Harrier/Sea Harrier still ranks today beside the creation of Teddy Petter's teams.

Like every type of aircraft that has ever been designed, the Canberra had its foibles. The fact that the radar bombing system, around which it was designed, was far behind in development when the A.1 was already flying, was not the best of starts. In addition, many doubted the viability of visual bomb aiming from 50,000ft (15,200m), but that was not the fault of the aircraft. The one-piece canopy was often a source of

... Revelation.

problems in various atmospheric conditions, with vision being impaired when facing the sun or haze, and a 'greenhouse effect' that could make things very uncomfortable in the summer. Early on, there were tailplane runway incidents, undercarriage sequence-valve defects and stress-corrosion problems (with DTD683), but all were promptly and successfully rectified. The difficulties had all, at one time, put the whole Canberra programme in jeopardy.

Even the greatest optimist in Petter's team could not have predicted that contracts for the production of the aeroplane in the USA, as the B-57, would be signed seventeen days before the first Canberra was delivered to the RAF. Furthermore, the aircraft would prove to be as well liked by the USAF as by the RAF, and the US even managed to export twenty-four B-57Bs and two B-57Cs to the Pakistan Air Force – which used them against Canberras in the Indian Air Force.

Australian-built Canberras gained a reputation for accurate bombing during the Vietnam War that was greatly envied by the US ground forces. Their record was as much a credit to the aircraft as it was to the aircrew of No.2 Squadron, RAAF.

Argentina, India, New Zealand, Pakistan, Rhodesia and South Africa were all export customers who had occasion to use Canberras on active service. None of them found the aircraft wanting (although Argentina's limited operations during the Falklands episode pitted them against a determined opposition that placed the *Fuerza Aérea Argentina* at a disadvantage).

The Canberra consistently proved itself as a successful military aeroplane. In 1959, a proposed private-venture P.28 variant, incorporating much of the B(I).8 and PR.9, and a reduced wingspan with larger tip tanks, was shelved because the Buccaneer was getting into production. There also still existed an alliance between Britain and France to co-produce a variable-geometry strike aircraft. After France pulled out of the project, the beginnings of what is now Panavia produced the MRCA; they

believed that the acronym stood for Multi-Role Combat Aircraft, but the British aviation fraternity knew better – to them it stood for 'Must Re-spar Canberra Again'!

No greater proof of the Canberra as a stable, robust and adaptable airframe need be presented than the metamorphoses engineered at Defford and Pershore over the years. Petter's original concept of interchangeable primary structures, able to be manufactured at separate factory sites and married at the assembly location, was taken far beyond that which he first envisaged, with remarkable results. The design's contribution to the development of airborne radar in the UK cannot be over-emphasized.

In RAF service at Marham today, No.39 (1 PRU) Squadron's PR.9, XH169, which left Short Bros' line at Belfast on 4 August 1960, is thirty-nine years old. Surely it is safe to bet that the crew members are some years younger, but that they do not consider themselves to be flying a vintage aeroplane.

Canberra Production and Serial Blocks

New-build aircraft to Ministry contracts, including new-build aircraft diverted for export.

The following were manufactured in the UK by English Electric Co. at Preston, A.V. Roe & Co. Ltd at Woodford, Handley Page Aircraft Ltd at Radlett and Short Bros & Harland Ltd at Belfast.

English Electric A.1 Prototypes
Contract No.6/ACFT/5841/CB6(b)
Preston-built: VN799, VN813, VN828, VN850 (4 aircraft)

Canberra B.2 Prototypes
Contract No.6/ACFT/2000/CB6(b)
Preston-built: VX165, VX169 (2 aircraft)

Canberra B.2
Contract No.6/ACFT/3520/CB6(b)
Preston-built: WD929 to WD966; WD980 to WD999; WE111 to WE122 (70 aircraft); WF886 to WF892; WF907 to WF917 (18 aircraft); WG788; WG789 (2 aircraft); WP514; WP515 (2 aircraft); WV787 (1 aircraft); XA536 (1 aircraft)

Contract No.6/ACFT/5786/CB6(b)
Preston-built: WH637 to WH674; WH695 to WH742 (86 aircraft); WJ712 to WJ734; WJ751 to WJ753 (26 aircraft)

Contract No.6/ACFT/5790/CB6(b)
Belfast-built: WH853 to WH887; WH902 to WH925; WH944 (60 aircraft)

Contract No.6/ACFT/5943/CB6(b)
Radlett-built: WJ564 to WJ582; WJ603 to WJ649; WJ674 to WJ682 (75 aircraft); WJ683 to WJ707 (25 aircraft) cancelled

Contract No.6/ACFT/5990/CB6(b)
Woodford-built: WJ971 to WJ995; WK102 to WK146; WK161 to WK165 (75 aircraft); WK166 to WK190 (25 aircraft) cancelled

Contract No.6/ACFT/6446/CB6(b)
Intended Radlett-built: WS960 to WS999; WT113 to WT122 (50 aircraft) cancelled

Contract No.6/ACFT/6447/CB6(b)
Intended Woodford-built: WT140 to WT189 (50 aircraft), cancelled

Canberra PR.3 Prototype
Contract No.6/ACFT/2000/CB6(b)
Preston-built: VX181 (1 aircraft)

Canberra PR.3
Contract No.6/ACFT/3520/CB6(b)
Preston-built: WE135 to WE151; WE166 to WE175 (27 aircraft); WF922 to WF928 (7 aircraft)

Contract No.6/ACFT/5786/CB6(b)
Preston-built: WH772 (1 aircraft)

Canberra T.4 Prototype
Contract No.6/ACFT/6265/CB6(b)
Preston-built: WN467 (1 aircraft)

Canberra T.4

Contract No.6/ACFT/3520/CB6(b)
Preston-built: WE188 to WE195 (8 aircraft)
Contract No.6/ACFT/5786/CB6(b)
Preston-built: WH839 to WH850 (12 aircraft); WJ857 to WJ881 (25 aircraft)

Contract No.6/ACFT/6445/CB6(b)
Preston-built: WT475 to WT492 (18 aircraft); WT493; WT494 (2 aircraft), cancelled

Contract No.6/ACFT/11313/CB6(b)
Preston-built: XH583; XH584 (2 aircraft)

Contract No.6/ACFT/12265/CB6(b)
Preston-built: XK647; XK650 (2 aircraft) diverted to India
Preston-built: XM228; XM229 (2 aircraft) diverted to Venezuela

Canberra B.5 prototype

Contract No.6/ACFT/4689/CB6(b)
Preston-built: VX185 (1 aircraft)

Canberra B.6

Contract No.6/ACFT/5786/CB6(b)
Preston-built: WJ754 to WJ784 (31 aircraft); WT304 to WT306 (3 aircraft)

Contract No.6/ACFT/5790/CB6(b)
Belfast-built: WH945 to WH984 (40 aircraft)

Contract No.6/ACFT/6445/CB6(b)
Preston-built: WT301 to WT303 (3 aircraft); WT369 to WT374 (6 aircraft); WT375 to WT389; WT397 to WT422; WT440 to WT469 (69 aircraft), cancelled

Contract No.6/ACFT/6448/CB6(b)
Belfast-built: WT205 to WT213 (9 aircraft); WT214 to WT224; WT250 to WT279 (41 aircraft), cancelled

Contract No.6/ACFT/11158/CB6(b)
Intended Preston-built: XH138 to XH151; XH158 to XH163 (20 aircraft), cancelled

Contract No.6/ACFT/11313/CB6(b)
Preston-built: XH567 to XH570 (4 aircraft)

Contract No.6/ACFT/12265/CB6(b)
Preston-built: XK641 (1 aircraft)

Canberra B(I).6

Contract No.6/ACFT/5786/CB6(b)
Preston-built: XJ249; XJ257 (2 aircraft)

Contract No.6/ACFT/6445/CB6(b)
Preston-built: WT307 to WT325 (19 aircraft); XG554 (1 aircraft)

Canberra B(I).8

Contract No.6/ACFT/6445/CB6(b)
Preston-built: WT326 to WT336; WT338; WT339; WT341; WT343; WT344; WT346; WT348 (18 aircraft); WT362; WT364; WT365; WT367; WT368 (5 aircraft); WT369 to WT374 (6 aircraft); XK951 to XK953 (3 aircraft); XM224; XM245 (2 aircraft)
Belfast-built: WT337; WT340; WT342; WT345; WT347 (5 aircraft); WT363; WT366 (2 aircraft)

Contract No.6/ACFT/11158/CB6(b)
Preston-built: XH207; XH209 (2 aircraft); XM262 to XM279 (18 aircraft); XH203; XH205; XH227; XH229; XH230; XH232; XH233; XH235 to XH244; XK959 (16 aircraft) diverted to India
XH206 (1 aircraft) diverted to Peru

Contract No.KD/E/01/CB6(b)
Preston-built: XM936 (1 aircraft); XP289; XP290 (2 aircraft) diverted to New Zealand

Canberra PR.9 prototype

Preston-built: WH793 (1 aircraft) converted PR.7

Canberra PR.9

Contract No.6/ACFT/11158/CB6(b)
Preston-built: XH129 to XH137 (9 aircraft); XH164 to XH177 (14 aircraft); XH178 to XH186 (9 aircraft), cancelled

Contract No.6/ACFT/12164/CB6(b)
Intended Belfast-built: XK440 to XK443; XK467 to XK473 (11 aircraft), cancelled

CANBERRA NEW-BUILD PRODUCTION IN UK, INCLUDING PROTOTYPES AND PATTERN AIRCRAFT FOR AUSTRALIA AND UNITED STATES

English Electric Co. at Preston	631
A.V. Roe & Co. Ltd at Woodford	75
Handley Page Aircraft at Radlett	75
Short Bros & Harland at Belfast	144
Total	*925*

LICENSED NEW-BUILD PRODUCTION OVERSEAS, EXCLUDING PATTERN AIRCRAFT

Government Aircraft Factory, Australia	48
Glenn L. Martin Aircraft Co. United States	403
Total	*451*
GRAND TOTAL OF NEW-BUILD CANBERRA AIRCRAFT	**1376**

Canberra Squadrons

Royal Air Force squadrons and Royal Navy FRADU confirmed as having operated Canberras:

Canberra B.2
Nos 6, 9, 10, 12, 15, 18, 21, 27, 32, 35, 40, 44, 45, 50, 51, 56, 57, 59, 61, 73, 76, 85, 90, 97, 98, 100, 101, 102, 103, 104, 115, 139, 149, 151, 192, 199, 207, 245, 249, 360, 527, 542, 617, 231OCU, 232OCU and Royal Navy FRADU

Canberra PR.3
Nos 39, 58, 69, 82, 85, 540 and 231OCU

Canberra T.4
Nearly every Canberra-operating squadron had a T.4 or two for pilot checks, continuation training and/or Station Flights. The prevalent habit of inter-squadron exchange of aircraft has made it impractical to locate precisely every squadron using this variant. Five T.4s were on the strength of the Royal Navy's FRADU.

Canberra B.6
Nos 6, 9, 12, 51, 76, 101, 109, 139, 192, 249, 542 and 617

Canberra B(I).6
No.213

Canberra B.6 (BS)
Nos 6, 9, 12, 109, 139 and 249

Canberra B.6 (mod)
Nos 51 and 97

Canberra PR.7
Nos 13, 17, 31, 39, 58, 80, 81, 82, 100, 540 and 542

Canberra B(I).8
Nos 3, 14, 16, 59 and 88

Canberra PR.9
Nos 13, 39, and 58

Canberra T.11
No.85 and 228OCU

Canberra B.15/B.16
Nos 6, 32, 45, 73 and 249

Canberra E.15
Nos 98 and 100

Canberra T.17/T.17A
No.360

Canberra TT.18
Nos 7, 100 and Royal Navy FRADU

Canberra T.19
Nos 7, 85 and 100

Canberra T.22
Royal Navy FRADU

Canberra Conservation

Over one hundred Canberras of various marks and condition still exist in the UK. A large number are whole airframes, held in museums or storage, while some whole airframes, as well as parts of aircraft, mostly front-fuselage sections, are held in private hands. The following aircraft have been confirmed at the time of writing (listed as originally built, with modifications in brackets where applicable).

SERIAL	PRESENT LOCATION
Canberra B.2	
WD931	Aerospace Museum, RAF Cosford, Shropshire. (*Front fuselage only*)
WD935	Derek Lee, Bridgenorth, Shropshire. (*Front fuselage only*)
WD954	The Cockpit Collection, Rayleigh, Essex. (*Front fuselage only*)
WE113	Private owner, Woodhurst, Cambridge
WF911	Griffin Trust, Hooton Park, Cheshire. (*Front fuselage only*)
WG789	Steve Pickup, Mendlesham, Suffolk. (*Modified front fuselage only*)
WH657	Brenzett Aeronautical Museum Trust, Brenzett, Kent
WH673	PEE Foulness, Essex. (*Fuselage section only*)
WH703	Last heard of at Abingdon, Oxfordshire
WH725	Imperial War Museum, Duxford, Cambridgeshire
WH734	Last heard of at Llanbedr, N. Wales
WH854	Martin-Baker Ltd, Chalgrove, Buckinghamshire. (*Cockpit section T.4 mod*)
WH872	DTEO Aberporth, Dyfed, Mid. Wales
WH876	Last heard of on dump at RAE Bedford, Bedfordshire
WH903	Yorkshire Air Museum, Elvington, N. Yorks. (*Front fuselage only, first fitment*)
WH903	Vallance By-ways, Charlwood, Surrey. (*Front fuselage only, second fitment*)
WH911	Park Aviation, Faygate, W. Sussex. (*Front fuselage only*)
WJ567	Jon Wilson, Houghton, Cambridgeshire. (*Front fuselage only*)
WJ573	RAF Henlow Museum, Bedfordshire. (*Stored*)
WJ603	Private owner, Stock, Essex
WJ637	RAF Cranwell, Lincolnshire. (*Displayed as WH699*)
WJ640	Film Studios, Denham, Buckinghamshire. (*Front fuselage only*)
WJ676	Barry Jones, Heswall, Merseyside. (*Front fuselage only*)
WJ677	FAA Museum, Yeovilton, Somerset
WJ678	Last heard of at Abingdon, Oxfordshire
WK127	No.2424 (ATC) Squadron, Bassingbourn, Cambridgeshire
WK128	Last heard of at Llanbedr, N. Wales
WK144	Last heard of on dump RAF St Athan, S. Wales
WK145	Last heard of at Llanbedr, N. Wales
WK146	Last heard of at Abingdon, Oxfordshire. (*Front fuselage only*)
WK163	Classic Aircraft Projects, Bruntingthorpe, Leicestershire. (*B.6 mod. Civil register G-BVWC*)
WK164	Last heard of at PEE Foulness, Essex. (*Front fuselage only*)

SERIAL	PRESENT LOCATION
WP515	Sue & Roy Jerman, Welshpool, Powys, Mid. Wales. (*Front fuselage only*)
WV787	Newark Air Museum, Winthorpe Show Ground, Newark, Nottinghamshire. (*B.2/B.8 hybrid*)
Canberra PR.3	
WE139	RAF Museum, Hendon, N. London
WE142	Flowers Scrapyard, Chippenham, Wiltshire. (*Front fuselage only*)
WE168	Glen Mitchell, Colchester, Essex. (*Front fuselage only*)
WE173	Robertsbridge Aviation Society, E. Sussex. (*Front fuselage only*)
WF922	Midland Air Museum, Baginton, Warwickshire
Canberra T.4	
WE188	Solway Aviation Museum, Carlisle, Cumbria
WE191	Last heard of on dump, Warton, Lancashire
WE192	Blyth Valley Aviation Collection, Walpole, Suffolk. (*Front fuselage only*)
WH840	Norfolk & Suffolk Aviation Museum, Flixton, Suffolk
WH844	PEE Pendine Ranges, Dyfed, S. Wales. (*Front fuselage only*)
WH846	Yorkshire Air Museum, Elvington, N. Yorkshire
WH848	Last heard of on Wyton dump, possibly now destroyed
WH849	RAF Shawbury, Shropshire
WH850	Barton Aerodrome, Manchester. (*Front fuselage only*)
WJ863	Cambridge Airport, Cambridgeshire. (*Front fuselage only*)
WJ865	Private owner, Stamford, Lincolnshire. (*Front fuselage only*)
WJ872	No.327 (ATC) Squadron, Kilmarnock, Scotland. (*Front fuselage only*)
WJ876	Last heard of at Abingdon, Oxfordshire. (*Front fuselage only*)
WJ880	Dumfries & Galloway Aviation. Museum, Dumfries, Scotland. (*Front fuselage only*)
WJ992	Bournemouth Airport dump, Dorset
WT480	RAF Shawbury, Shropshire. (*Stored*)
WT483	Stratford Aircraft Collection, Long Marston, Warwickshire
WT488	Dunsfold Airfield dump, Surrey
XH584	South Yorkshire Air Museum, Firbeck, S. Yorkshire. (*Front fuselage only*)

SERIAL	PRESENT LOCATION

Canberra B.5

| VX185 | Scottish National Museum of Flight, E. Fortune, Scotland. (*Converted B.8 front fuselage only*) |

Canberra B.6

WH953	Blyth Valley Aviation Collection, Walpole, Suffolk. (*Front fuselage only*)
WJ717	No.4 School of Technical Training, RAF St Athan, S. Wales. (*Front fuselage only, converted TT.18*)
WJ775	Stanford Training area, Bodney Camp, Norfolk
WT205	No.2431 (ATC) Squadron, Eastwood, Essex. (*Front fuselage only*)
XH568	Classic Aircraft Projects, Bruntingthorpe. Leicestershire. (*B.6 mod. Civil register G-BVIC*)

Canberra B(I).6

| WT308 | FAA Fire School, Predannack Airfield, Cornwall |
| WT309 | Farnborough Air Sciences Trust, Farnborough Airfield, Hampshire. (*Front fuselage only*) |

Canberra PR.7

WH773	Vallance By-ways, Charlwood, Surrey
WH775	Sue and Roy Jerman, Welshpool, Powys, Mid Wales. (*Front fuselage only*)
WH791	Newark Air Museum, Winthorpe Show Ground, Newark, Nottinghamshire
WH796	Bomber County Aviation Museum, Hemswell, Lincolnshire. (*Front fuselage only*)
WJ581	BB Aviation, Canterbury, Kent. (*Front fuselage only, serial WJ581 not fully confirmed*)
WJ821	No.2484 (ATC) Squadron, Allenbrook Barracks, Bassingbourn, Cambridgeshire
WT507	No.384 (ATC) Squadron, Mansfield, Nottinghamshire. (*Front fuselage only*)
WT519	RAF Wyton dump, Cambridgeshire
WT520	No.946 (ATC) Squadron, Preston, Lancashire. (*Front fuselage only*)
WT534	No.492 (ATC) Squadron, Haslucks Green Barracks, Birmingham. (*Front fuselage only*)
WT537	BAe Samlesbury, Lancashire
WT538	RAF St Athan, S. Wales. (*Front fuselage only*)

Canberra B(I).8

WT333	Classic Aviation Projects, Bruntingthorpe, Leicestershire. (*Civil register G-BVXC*)
WT339	RAF Barkston Heath dump, Grantham, Lincolnshire
XM279	Norfolk & Suffolk Aviation Museum, Flixton, Suffolk. (*Front fuselage only*)

Canberra PR.9

| XH136 | Phoenix Aviation, Bruntingthorpe, Leicestershire. (*Front fuselage only*) |
| XH165 | Blyth Valley Aviation Collection, Walpole, Suffolk. (*Front fuselage only*) |

SERIAL	PRESENT LOCATION
XH170	RAF Wyton, Cambridgeshire
XH171	Aerospace Museum, Cosford, Shropshire
XH175	Private owner, Stock, Essex. (*Front fuselage only*)
XH177	Private owner, Stock, Essex. (*Front fuselage only*)

Canberra B.15

| WH960 | Malcolm and Sarah Brent, Nottingham, Nottinghamshire (*Front fuselage only*) |
| WH984 | RAF Sealand, Clwyd, N. Wales. (*Front fuselage only*) |

Canberra T.17/T.17A

WH646	Midland Air Museum, Baginton, Warwickshire
WH665	BAe Filton dump, Bristol, Gloucestershire. (*Fuselage section only*)
WH740	Aeropark, East Midlands Airport, Castle Donington, Leicestershire
WH863	Newark Air Museum, Winthorpe Show Ground, Newark, Nottinghamshire. (*Front fuselage only*)
WJ565	Private owner, Binbrook Airfield, Lincolnshire. (*Front fuselage only*)
WJ576	Phoenix Aviation, Bruntingthorpe, Leicestershire. (*Front fuselage only*)
WJ633	RAF Wyton, Cambridgeshire. (*Front fuselage only*)
WK102	Sue and Roy Jerman, Welshpool, Powys, Mid Wales. (*Front fuselage only*)

Canberra TT.18

WE122	Blyth Valley Aviation Collection, Walpole, Suffolk. (*Front fuselage only*)
WH887	Last heard of at Llanbedr
WJ639	North East Aircraft Museum, Sunderland, Northumberland
WJ680	Canberra Flight, Kemble Airfield, Gloucestershire
WJ721	Dundonald Aviation Centre, Dundonald, Strathclyde, Scotland. (*Front fuselage only*)
WK118	John Hancock, Worcester, Worcestershire. (*Front fuselage only*)
WK122	Flambards Village Theme Park, Helston, Cornwall
WK124	Defence Fire Services Central Training Establishment, Manston Airfield, Kent
WK126	Jet Age Museum, Staverton Airport, Cheltenham, Gloucestershire
WK127	No.2484 (ATC) Squadron, Allenbrooke Barracks, Bassingbourn, Cambridgeshire. (*Front fuselage only*)

Canberra T.19

| WJ975 | Bomber County Aviation Museum, Hemswell, Lincolnshire |
| WH904 | Newark Air Museum, Winthorpe Show Ground, Newark, Nottinghamshire |

Canberra T.22

| WT525 | Private owner, South Woodham Ferrers, Essex. (*Front fuselage only*) |

A few Canberras of various marks still exist outside the UK. The following aircraft have been confirmed at the time of writing (listed as originally built, with modifications in brackets where applicable).

SERIAL	MARK	PRESENT LOCATION
Australia		
A84-125 (ex-WD983)	B.2	National Aeronautical Collection, Laverton, W. Australia
A84-307 (ex-WD939)	B.2	No.1 Central Ammunition Depot, Kingswood, NSW
A84-201	B.20	Amberley, Queensland
A84-203	B.20	Stored at Amberley, Queensland
A84-207	B.20	W. Australia Museum of Aviation, Jandakot, Geraldton, W. Australia
A84-208	B.20	RAAF Museum, Point Cook, Victoria, NSW
A84-209	B.20	Campden Museum of Aviation, Narellan, NSW. (*Front fuselage only*)
A84-219	B.20	Alex Campbell Park, Brymaroo, Queensland
A84-223	B.20	David Lowy, Performance Maintenance, Bankstown, NSW
A84-225	B.20	Queensland Air Museum, Caloundra, Queensland
A84-229	B.20	United States of America. (*Swapped for Lockheed Ventura. Flown as N229CA*)
A84-234	B.20	RAAF Museum, Point Cook, Victoria, NSW. (*Front fuselage only*)
A84-236	B.20	RAAF Museum, Point Cook, Victoria, NSW
A84-238	B.20	Willowbank Caravan Park, Amberley, Queensland
A84-248	B.20	Last heard of at RAAF East Sale, Victoria, NSW
WH700	B.2	Lincoln Nitshke Aircraft Collection, Greenock
WK165	B.2	Port Adelaide Aircraft Museum, S. Australia
Chile		
341 (ex-XH166)	PR.9	Aeronautics Museum, Santiago
343 (ex-XH173)	PR.9	Aeronautics Museum, Santiago
France		
763 (ex-WJ763)	B.6	Musée de l'Air et de l'Espace, Le Bourget, Paris
Germany		
99+36 (ex-WK130)	B.2	Auto und Technik Museum, Sinsheim

SERIAL	MARK	PRESENT LOCATION
Italy		
XH132	SC.9	Albino Panigarri
New Zealand		
A84-240	B.20	RNZAF Museum, Wigram. (*Ex-RAAF aircraft*)
WT346	B(I).8	RNZAF Museum, Christchurch
Rhodesia/Zimbabwe		
2504(ex-WH707)	B.2	Zimbabwe Military History Museum, Gweru
South Africa		
457 (ex-WJ991)	T.4	SAAF Museum, Swartkop
450 (ex-WJ617)	T.4	Waterkloof Air Force Base
Sweden		
52001 (ex-WH711)	T.11	Svedinos Bil Och Flygmuseum, Sloinge, Halmstad. (*Tp.52*)
52002 (ex-WH805)	T.11	Flygvapenmuseum, Malmen, Linkoping. (*Tp.52*)
WD955	B.2	Luftfart Museum, Stockholm. (*Converted to T.17A*)
United States of America		
21446	RB-57A	GLM Aviation Museum, Baltimore, Maryland
21447	RB-57A	Private owner, Oklahoma City, Oklahoma
21456	RB-57A	Selfridge Military Air Museum, Battle Creek, Michigan
21458	RB-57A	Private owner, Florence, South Carolina
21459	RB-57A	Florence Air & Missile Museum, South Carolina
21467	RB-57A	Maryland State Airport, Baltimore
21475	RB-57A	Robins AFB Museum, Macon, Georgia
21482	RB-57A	USAF History & Traditions Museum, Lackland AFB, Texas
21485	RB-57A	Selfridge Military Air Museum, Battle Creek, Michigan
21488	RB-57A	New England Air Base, Windsor Locks, Connecticut
21492	RB-57A	Hill AFB Museum, Ogden, Utah
33982	EB-57D	Tucson Air Museum, Arizona
54244	B-57E	Strategic Air Command Museum, Belleville, Nebraska
54274	B-57E	Pima Air Museum, Arizona
WT327/G-BXMO	B(I).8	Airpower Inc., Lakeport, California
XH567/G-BXOD	B.6	Airpower Inc., Lakeport, California

Index

Acton 58
Aircraft & Armament Experimental
    Establishment (A&AEE) 29, 35,
    37, 52, 59, 69, 74, 88–90, 92, 94,
    95, 98, 154, 158, 163, 169, 170,
    174
Airwork Services 92, 161
Akrotiri Strike Wing (ASW) 67, 69, 72,
    86, 98, 149
Argentina/*Fuerza Aérea Argentina* (FAA)
    119, 182
Armstrong Siddeley Motors Ltd 13, 98,
    152, 153
    Sapphire 102, 152, 153, 157, 164,
        170
    Viper 153, 164
Auster AOPs 80, 81, 148
A.V. Roe & Co. Ltd (Avro) 6, 30, 88,
    158, 184
    Avro Lincoln 12, 21, 29, 31, 40, 80,
        83, 121, 123, 148
    Avro Shackleton 147
    Avro Vulcan 87, 139, 169

Beamont, Wg Cdr R.P. 6, 11, 16–18,
    22–7, 29, 35, 42–5, 48, 59, 70, 73,
    77, 100–2, 121, 143, 144, 163
Blue Jay missile 157
Blue Shadow radar 65, 68
Boeing B-29 Washington 21, 31
Boulton Paul Aircraft Ltd 26, 58, 59, 71,
    95, 98, 153, 154, 159, 160, 170
Bristol Engines 48, 154, 157
Bristol Olympus 48, 49, 154, 155, 157
Bristol Siddeley Engines 153, 157
British Aircraft Corporation (BAC) 98,
    158
Burtonwood 100

Canberra:
    A.1 prototypes 6, 13, 16, 18–28, 52,
        70, 100, 151, 153, 154, 156–8, 162,
        165, 169, 171, 176, 181, 183
    B.2 21, 29, 30, 32–7, 39, 40–3, 48, 50,
        52, 54, 56, 57, 59, 61–3, 65–7, 84,
        86, 88–90, 92, 93, 95, 98, 119, 120,
        124, 127, 133, 136, 138, 140–2,
        144–6, 148, 149, 151–3, 155–74,
        176, 177, 183, 185, 187, 189
    B(I).2 144, 145

PR.3 21, 35, 37, 40, 46–8, 51, 52, 54,
    57, 71, 144, 145, 148, 151, 158,
    169, 171, 173, 178, 183, 185, 187
T.4 21, 35, 37–9, 50, 84, 88, 90, 91,
    94, 97, 119, 128–30, 133, 134,
    136–40, 142, 144–6, 150, 151, 167,
    169, 170, 174, 175, 178, 181, 183–5,
    187, 189
B.5 43, 44, 45, 48, 52, 58, 151, 158,
    169, 184, 188
B.6 52, 53, 55, 56, 58, 59, 61, 65, 69,
    81, 89, 90, 125–8, 147, 151, 154,
    157, 162, 163, 169, 172–4, 178, 179,
    184, 185, 188, 189
B.6(BS) 65, 66, 68, 69, 82, 83, 149,
    156, 163, 175, 186
B(I).6 60–2, 127, 128, 144, 149, 158,
    181, 184, 185, 188
PR.7 46, 48, 50, 53, 54, 61, 65, 66,
    71, 73, 84–6, 91, 94–6, 122, 128,
    130, 148, 149, 151, 163, 164, 167,
    180, 186, 188
B.8 98
B(I).8 45, 58–62, 105, 128, 129,
    133–6, 144, 145, 154, 158–60, 163,
    169, 170, 174, 180, 184, 186, 188,
    189
PR.9 71, 73–8, 88, 105, 125, 151, 158,
    163, 167, 173, 181, 182, 184, 186,
    188, 189
SC.9 158, 161, 167, 168, 175, 180,
    189
U/D.10 88, 89, 163, 167, 169
T.11 95–8, 140, 150, 154, 180, 186,
    189
B(I).12 129, 133, 134, 136, 139, 140
T.13 129, 133
U/D.14 88, 89, 169
B.15 53, 68, 69, 71, 72, 80, 81, 85–7,
    98, 129, 154, 163, 186, 188
E.15 87, 89, 98
B.16 61, 68, 69, 72, 129, 186
T.17 89–92, 140, 149, 150, 186, 188
T.17A 91, 92, 186, 188
TT.18 92–4, 145, 161, 162, 169, 186,
    188
T.19 96, 97, 186, 188
Mk.20 46, 47, 84, 121, 123–5, 189
Mk.21 122, 124, 125
T.22 94, 95, 161, 170, 186, 188

B.52 127
Tp.52 140, 141, 154
T.54 128, 130, 132
B/B(I).56 134, 136
PR.57 128, 131, 132
B(I).58 128, 129, 131–3
B.62 119–21
T.64 119, 121
B.66 69
B(I).66 129, 131, 132
PR.67 129, 130, 132
B(I).68 134, 136, 163
B.72 134, 138
T.74 129, 134
B/B(I).82 143, 145
PR.83 145
T.84 145
B(I).88 145
B.92 120, 121
T.94 120, 121
Canberra Tactical Evaluation Flight
    (CANTAC) 70
Central Treaty Organization (CENTO)
    64, 68, 71, 136
Chile/*Fuerza Aérea de Chile* 125
Christmas Island 56, 147, 148
Coventry Ordnance Works Ltd (COW)
    7
Crowe, F.D. 10, 13, 77

De Havilland Group 6, 157
    Gyron Junior 156, 157, 166
    Mosquito 32, 40, 57
    Red Top 157, 158, 167
    'Sky Flash' 158, 167
    Spectre 148, 156, 157, 162
    Vampire 6, 11, 48, 154
    Venom 64, 67, 83, 133
Dick, Kerr & Co. Ltd 7

Ecuador/*Fuerza Aérea Ecuatoriana* (FAE)
    125, 126
Empire Test Pilot's School (ETPS) 170
English Electric Company 6, 18, 42, 44,
    52, 100, 119, 126, 133, 134, 139,
    143, 158, 184
    P1/P1A 14, 15, 100, 101
    S.1 Wren 8, 9
Ethiopia/Imperial Ethiopian Air Force
    (EAF) 127

Far East Air Force (FEAF) 70, 80, 84, 87
Ferranti Flying Unit (FFU) 26, 98, 154, 159, 161
Flight Refuelling Limited (FRL) 92, 94, 95, 161
Folland Aircraft Ltd 15, 26, 28, 157, 162
    Gnat 28, 131, 162
France 127, 128

Green Satin Doppler 124, 149, 154, 171

Handley Page Ltd 6, 30, 33, 88, 158, 184
    Halifax 6, 10, 11, 19
    Hampden 6, 10, 11, 19
    Victor 60, 87, 139
Harrison, Harry 13
Hawker Siddeley Buccaneer 139, 157, 170

Indian Air Force (IAF) 117, 118, 128–32, 134, 182
Indonesia 86

Knight, Don 73, 74

Low-Altitude Bombing System (LABS) 61, 105, 174

Malayan Races Liberation Army (MRLA) 79–83
Manning, W.O. 7–9
Martin-Baker Aircraft Ltd 17, 58, 74, 163, 166
Martin Aircraft Company, Glenn L. 42, 100, 101, 107, 108, 184
    XB-48 99
    XB-51 100, 101
    B-57 42, 117, 119, 182
    B-57A 101–3, 117, 118
    EB-57A 104, 106
    RB-57A 103, 104, 106, 116, 118, 189
    B-57B 104–8, 112, 114, 115, 118
    EB-57B 106
    JB-57B 106
    NB-57B 106, 117
    RB-57B 106
    B-57C 107–9, 118
    RB-57C 109, 110
    WB-57C 109
    B-57D 108
    EB-57D 111, 189
    RB-57D 108–12, 114, 116–18
    B-57E 111–13, 118, 189
    EB-57E 112, 113
    JB-57E 113
    NB-57E 110, 113
    RB-57E 113
    TB-57E 112, 113

RB-57F 114, 115
WRB-57F 114
B-57G 116, 117
Marshall of Cambridge 61, 68, 69, 134, 136, 163, 170, 174
Middle East Air Force (MEAF) 64, 68
Ministry of Aircraft Production (MAP) 11

Napier & Son Ltd, D. 11, 73, 153, 163, 164, 167
    Double Scorpion 50, 164, 165
Near East Air Force (NEAF) 67, 68, 71
Nelson, Sir George 10, 11, 28
Newark Air Museum 97, 98
Nord AS.30 70, 71, 87
North American B-45 99, 100
    RB-45C 56, 57
North Atlantic Treaty Organisation (NATO) 60–2, 148

Operations:
    Birdsong 86
    Blue Danube 147
    Firedog 79, 84, 86
    Foxfire 82, 83
    Grapple 56, 147, 148
    Hot Box 147
    Hurricane 147
    Musketeer 64–7, 83
    Patricia Lynn 111
    Robin 57
    Swifter 149
Orange Putter radar 106

Page, F.W. 13, 28
Pakistan Air Force (PAF) 117, 118, 131, 182
Peru/*Fuerza Aérea Del Peru* (FAP) 57, 134, 137, 138
Petter, W.E.W. 6, 11–16, 22, 28, 80, 137, 160, 162, 181, 182
Phoenix Dynamo Company 7
Pratt & Whitney:
    J-57 108, 109, 118
    J-60 114
    TF-33 114
Preston, Strand Road 10, 28, 52, 140
Preston 'TC' 11, 12, 16

Randrup, Mike 73, 163
Rolls-Royce:
    AJ.65 Avon Mk.101 (RA.3) 19, 29, 44, 123
    Avon Mk.109 (RA.7) 52, 74, 84, 123, 137, 164, 165
    Avon RA.14 165, 166
    Avons on test 73, 163, 166, 167
    Hucknall 27, 28, 153, 165, 166
    Nene 19, 26, 156, 157

Royal Aircraft Establishments (RAEs) 16, 60, 61, 88, 94, 158, 161, 162, 167, 170, 171, 173, 174
Royal Air Force (RAF) Bases:
    Abingdon 98, 152, 170
    Ahlhorn 151
    Akrotiri 39, 61, 77, 87, 151
    Aldergrove 44
    Bassingbourn 35, 38, 152
    Benson 40, 52
    Biggin Hill 28
    Binbrook 33, 34, 39, 48, 52–4, 56, 83, 92, 97, 151, 152, 164
    Brawdy 152
    Brüggen 39, 55, 60, 151
    Butterworth 79–81, 86
    Chivenor 152
    Colerne 152
    Coltishall 95, 173
    Coningsby 34, 39, 56, 61, 94, 151
    Cosford 151, 152
    Cottesmore 38, 39, 90, 91, 98, 151, 152
    Finningley 151, 168
    Gaydon 39, 151
    Geilenkirchen 39, 151
    Gütersloh 34, 39, 40, 52, 54, 61, 151, 161
    Halton 151, 152
    Hemswell 36, 39, 40, 53, 54, 89, 151, 152
    Hendon 54
    Honington 39, 151
    Kirkham 152
    Khormaksar 67, 71, 75, 76, 89, 97, 128, 129
    Laarbruch 39, 55, 61, 151
    Leuchars 26
    Little Rissington 15, 39, 152
    Locking 152
    Manby 48, 152
    Manston 152
    Marham 35, 38, 39, 77, 91, 98, 146, 151, 152, 182
    Melsham 152
    Newton 151
    Nicosia 64, 67
    Odiham 35
    St Athan 94, 151, 152, 168
    St Eval 36
    St Mawgan 92, 97, 152, 161, 167
    Scampton 34, 39, 151
    Scunthorpe 56
    Tengah 61, 71, 86
    Upwood 39, 55, 57, 62, 149, 151
    Waddington 39, 40, 151
    Wahn 52, 61, 151
    Wattisham 152
    Watton 40, 53, 61, 62, 89–91, 97, 98, 148, 151, 152

West Raynham 61, 92, 97, 149, 151
Weston Zoyland 39, 56, 61, 67, 147, 151
Wildenrath 39, 60, 150–2
Wittering 39, 40, 151
Wyton 39, 40, 53, 54, 58, 77, 91, 94, 147, 151, 152
Yatesbury 152
RAF Central Fighter Establishment (CFE) 97, 149
RAF Flying College (RAFFC) 48
RAF Handling Squadron 69, 151, 158
RAF Maintenance Units (MUs) 61, 67, 82, 88, 94, 95, 119, 129, 130, 136, 149, 160, 168, 174
RAF Operational Conversion Units (OCUs) 35, 37, 38, 91, 95, 97, 119, 136, 149–51, 185, 186
RAF Squadrons:
  3 Sqn 62, 63, 66, 186
  6 Sqn 61, 63, 64, 68, 185, 186
  7 Sqn 92, 94, 97, 161, 186
  9 Sqn 34, 40, 53, 55, 56, 61, 65, 82, 83, 163, 185, 186
  10 Sqn 34, 39, 55, 67, 185
  12 Sqn 34, 36, 48, 54, 55, 61, 65, 82, 185, 186
  13 Sqn 57, 61, 65, 71, 73, 77, 87, 185, 186
  14 Sqn 60, 62, 63, 186
  15 Sqn 34, 55, 65, 185
  16 Sqn 61, 62, 186
  17 Sqn 61, 71, 185, 186
  18 Sqn 34, 55, 57, 65, 185
  21 Sqn 34, 55, 62, 184
  27 Sqn 34, 55, 64, 65, 185
  31 Sqn 54, 55, 63, 185, 186
  32 Sqn 61, 64, 67, 68, 70, 85, 87, 185, 186
  35 Sqn 34, 55, 185
  39 Sqn 38, 51, 71, 73, 75, 77, 78, 87, 182, 185, 186
  40 Sqn 34, 55, 185
  44 Sqn 34, 36, 55, 65, 66, 88, 185
  45 Sqn 61, 70, 83, 85–7, 185, 186
  50 Sqn 34, 55, 185
  51 Sqn 62, 185, 186
  56 Sqn 18, 62, 63, 185
  57 Sqn 34, 55, 185
  58 Sqn 40, 54, 55, 57, 77, 87, 185, 186
  59 Sqn 61, 62, 185, 186
  60 Sqn 83
  61 Sqn 40, 55, 65, 185
  69 Sqn 52, 55, 71, 185
  73 Sqn 61, 64, 68, 70, 72, 82, 86, 87, 185, 186

  76 Sqn 40, 55, 56, 88, 147, 148, 185
  80 Sqn 55, 186
  81 Sqn 71, 84, 85, 97, 186
  82 Sqn 40, 54, 55, 185, 186
  85 Sqn 92, 97, 150, 185, 186
  88 Sqn 60, 62, 68, 150, 186
  90 Sqn 34, 55, 185
  97 Sqn 63, 89, 90, 91, 185, 186
  98 Sqn 89, 98, 185, 186
  100 Sqn 40, 55, 61, 62, 91, 92, 94, 97, 98, 147, 168, 185, 186
  101 Sqn 29, 33, 52, 55, 56, 65, 79–81, 83, 88, 195
  102 Sqn 40, 55, 61, 185
  103 Sqn 40, 55, 185
  104 Sqn 54, 55, 185
  109 Sqn 38, 40, 53, 55, 185, 186
  115 Sqn 34, 55, 185
  139 Sqn 38, 40, 54, 55, 65, 68, 185, 186
  149 Sqn 34, 55, 161, 185
  151 Sqn 89, 185
  192 Sqn 53, 55, 62, 148, 149, 185
  199 Sqn 40, 55, 185
  207 Sqn 34, 55, 185
  213 Sqn 60–2, 68, 185
  214 Sqn 55
  245 Sqn 40, 89, 98, 185
  249 Sqn 68, 86, 185, 186
  360 Sqn 90, 91, 185, 186
  527 Sqn 40, 55, 61, 148, 185
  540 Sqn 40, 53, 55, 57, 185, 186
  541 Sqn 52
  542 Sqn 53, 55, 62, 147, 185, 186
  617 Sqn 33, 54–6, 81, 82, 185
  1 PRU 76, 182
  1323 Flt 56, 147
Royal Australian Air Force (RAAF) 83, 84, 87, 121–3, 168, 182, 184
Royal Malaysian Air Force (RMAF) 86
Royal Navy:
  Fleet Requirements & Air Direction Unit (FRADU) 38, 92, 94–6, 185, 186
  No.728B Sqn 88, 89
  No.776 Fleet Requirements Unit (FRU) 92
Royal New Zealand Air Force (RNZAF) 83, 84, 87, 129, 133
Royal/Rhodesian Air Force (R/RhAF) 136, 137
RRE Pershore/Defford 26, 52, 89, 95, 137, 149, 153, 154, 157, 158, 160, 162, 164, 166, 168, 170, 174–80
Rushton target winch 92, 93, 161, 162

Samlesbury 10, 12, 35, 51, 59, 61, 90–2, 94, 119, 134, 136
Second Tactical Air Force (2nd TAF) 60, 71
Short Brothers & Harland Ltd 6, 30, 52, 53, 59, 74, 78, 88–90, 140, 166, 182, 184
Short Stiletto 161, 162
Society of British Aircraft Constructors (SBAC) Air Displays 6, 25, 27, 59, 74, 75, 84, 100, 120, 155, 156, 164, 166
South African Air Force (SAAF) 136, 138–40
Soviet Union (USSR) 56, 57
Specifications:
  F.37/35 14
  N.11/44 14
  B.3/45 13, 16, 58
  E.3/45 13, 21
  PR.31/46 21, 51
  B.5/47 21, 29
  T.11/47 21
  B.22/48 21
  T.2/49 22, 35
  F.153D 168
  IB.122 58
Sweden/Svenska Flygvapnet 140

Tarrant Rushton 92, 94, 162
Tropic Moon 115–17

USAF Strategic Air Command (SAC) 56

Venezuela/Fuerzas Aérea Venezolana (FAV) 141–5
Vickers Armstrong (Aircraft) Ltd 168
Vickers Armstrong Red Dean 168
Vickers Armstrong Valiant 65, 67, 77, 148, 161

Warton 16, 19–21, 28, 29, 44, 52, 58, 74, 90, 100, 121, 138, 158, 169, 170
Weapons Research Establishment (WRE) Woomera 48, 88, 89, 124, 147, 157, 158, 168
West Germany/Luftwaffe 145, 146
Westland Aircraft Ltd 12, 14
Wright Air Development Centre (WADC) 102, 104, 105
Wright J-65 103

Zimbabwe Air Force 63, 138, 146